WITNESS TO AMERICA'S PAST

Two Centuries of Collecting by
the Massachusetts Historical Society

WITNESS TO AMERICA'S PAST:

Two Centuries of Collecting by the Massachusetts Historical Society

Compiled by the staff of the
Massachusetts Historical Society

BOSTON · 1991
MASSACHUSETTS HISTORICAL SOCIETY
MUSEUM OF FINE ARTS, BOSTON

This exhibition was organized by the Massachusetts Historical
Society and the Museum of Fine Arts, Boston. It is made possible
by Fidelity Investments through the Fidelity Foundation.

Printed and typeset in the United States of America by
The Stinehour Press, Lunenburg, Vermont

Designed by Janet O'Donoghue

The printing ornament shown on the half-title page and on page 186
is a tail-piece from Theodor de Bry's *America*, 1590–1595 (no. 11).

Cover: *Indian archer weathervane* by Shem Drowne, ca. 1716 (no. 1)
and *History of New England* by John Winthrop, 1630 (no. 12)

Frontispiece: *Old State House* by James Brown Marston, 1801
(no. 105)

Photography Credits

David Bohl: 2, 3, 4, 5, 6, 8, 10, 11, 12, 13, 14, 15, 16, 17, 18, 19, 20, 21, 24,
25, 26, 27, 29, 30, 31, 39, 40, 41, 42, 43, 46, 47, 48, 49, 50, 52, 53, 54, 55,
56, 57, 69, 71, 72, 73, 74, 76, 77, 78, 79, 80, 81, 82, 83, 85, 86, 88, 89, 90,
91, 92, 93, 94, 95, 96, 97, 100, 101, 102, 103, 105, 107, 108, 109, 112, 114,
115, 123, 124, 127, 129, 130, 131, 132, 133, 134, 135, 136, 137, 138, 139, 140, 141,
142, 143, 144, 145, 147, 148, 149, 150, 151, 152, 153, 154, 155, 156, 157, 158, 159,
160, 161; and color plates: frontispiece, I, IV, V, VI, VII, VIII, IX.

Catherine Dumont, Bowers & Merena: 22, 32, 33, 34, 58, 59, 60, 61, 62,
63, 64, 65, 66, 67, 68, 84, 99.

Richard Cheek: 9, 23, 36, 37, 38, 113, 116, 117, 118, 119, 120, 121, 122,
125, 126; and color plates II, X.

George Cushing: 7, 28, 35, 44, 45, 51, 70, 75, 98, 106, 110, 128, 146.

Alan Kidawski: Color plate III.

Stephen J. Kovacik: III.

Museum of Fine Arts, Boston, Department of Photographic Services:
cover, I, 87, 104.

Library of Congress Cataloging-in-Publication Data
Witness to America's past: two centuries of collecting by the
Massachusetts Historical Society / compiled by the staff of the
Massachusetts Historical Society.
  108 p. 30.5 cm.
  Catalog of a bicentennial exhibition held at the Museum of
Fine Arts, Boston from Apr. to Aug. 1991.
  Includes bibliographical references and index.
  ISBN 0–87846–334–8
  1. Massachusetts Historical Society—Exhibitions.
2. Americana—Massachusetts—Boston—Exhibitions. 3. Material
culture—Massachusetts—Boston—Exhibitions. 4. Massachusetts—Civilization—Exhibitions. I. Massachusetts Historical Society. II. Museum of Fine Arts, Boston.
F61.W58 1991
974.4'0074'74461—dc20   91–4445

ISBN: 0–87846–334–8

Table of Contents

Acknowledgments

"Witness to America's Past," the bicentennial exhibition of the Massachusetts Historical Society at the Museum of Fine Arts, Boston, is the result of the work of many individuals, including staff members of both institutions, technical experts in various fields, and friends of both the Historical Society and the Museum. First and foremost, this exhibition was made possible by Fidelity Investments through the Fidelity Foundation, and to them we extend a special appreciation.

The preparation for this exhibition to some extent involved literally every member of the staff of the Historical Society over the course of many months. Peter Drummey, the librarian, coordinated the entire program with the assistance of Anne E. Bentley, the conservator; Susan R. Milstein, the principal researcher and liaison from the Society to the Museum; and Edward W. Hanson, the associate editor. Ross E. Urquhart, curator of graphic arts, was deeply involved in the early planning for the exhibition, and his untimely death left a gap difficult to fill. Director Louis L. Tucker and Editor of Publications Conrad E. Wright assisted in the planning and execution of many aspects of the exhibition. Jane L. Port, a graduate intern from Boston University, assisted Susan Milstein and prepared numerous entries for the catalogue. In addition to her responsibilities in the planning of "Witness to America's Past," Anne Bentley was responsible for preparing many of the individual items for display. Chris Steele coordinated all the photography work necessary for the catalogue and particularly benefited from the skill of David Bohl from the Society for the Preservation of New England Antiquities. Edward Hanson edited the catalogue which is the cooperative effort of all those staff members individually acknowledged below as contributors.

The Museum of Fine Arts and its director, Alan Shestack, were gracious hosts and guides to the staff of the Historical Society in the development of our bicentennial program. The exhibition owes a special debt to Jonathan Fairbanks, Katharine Lane Weems Curator of American Decorative Arts and Sculpture, for his longstanding interest in the collections of the Historical Society and his commitment to this anniversary exhibition. Assistant curator Jeannine Falino was the main liaison between the two organizations throughout every step of the preparations for the catalogue and exhibition, which as a result, owe much to her versatility, patience, and tact. Aiding her were research assistant Rachel Monfredo and department assistant Maria Pulsone, who graciously assumed additional Museum duties for the duration of the project. Assisting in the planning and selection stages and with reviewing catalogue entries were associate curator Edward S. Cooke, Jr., and assistant curator Lauretta Dimmick, also from American Decorative Arts and Sculpture; Shelley Drake Hawks, department assistant and Jennifer Noering, intern, Asiatic Art; Theodore Stebbins, John Moors Cabot Curator of Paintings; Carol Troyen, associate curator, and Erica Hirshler, American Paintings; Sue Welsh Reed, associate curator, Prints, Drawings, and Photographs; and Deborah Kraak, assistant curator of Textiles and Costumes. Conservators Arthur Beale, Jean Woodward, Jane Weber, Deborah Bede, Jane Hutchins, Jean-Louis Lachèvre, Katharine Untch, and Susanne Gänsicke prepared numerous objects for display.

The exhibition was ably assisted at the Museum by the concerted efforts of the administrative, design, support, and educational staffs: Désirée Caldwell and Catherine King of Exhibition Planning worked tirelessly to produce a smoothly functioning work schedule. Judith Downes, with the assistance of Susan Wong of Design, created a visually appealing installation with sensitivity and intelligence. Special thanks go to Janice Sorkow, William Buckley, and Thomas Lang, who cheerfully provided several eleventh-hour photographic services, as well as Jack Morrison, Sally Keeler, and their experienced Facilities staff, who adroitly installed the exhibition. William Burback, Joan Harlowe, Barbara Martin, Gilian Wohlauer, Laurie Thomas, and lecturer Susan Montgomery of the Education department provided assistance with interpretation and programs to augment the exhibition. Director Carl Zahn and designer Janet O'Donoghue of the Publication department are to be commended for producing this elegant catalogue, as is Robin Jacobson of Fulcrum Media Services for additional editorial services.

"Witness to America's Past" has also benefited from the generous assistance of many individuals and institutions. Contributing their technical expertise were: John Weston Adams; Louise Todd Ambler, Fogg Art Museum, Harvard University; Georgia Barnhill, American Antiquarian Society; Sidney E. Berger, former curator of manuscripts, American Antiquarian Society; Philip Bergen, Bostonian Society; David Bohl, Society for the Preservation of New England Antiquities; David Bowers, Michael J. Hodder, and Catherine Dumont, Bowers & Merena, Inc.; Prof. Charles Brownell, University of Virginia; Davida Deutsch; James Fahey, Massachusetts Department of Military Archives; Martha Gandy Fales; Leonard H. Finn; James A. Ganz, N.E.A. curatorial intern, Department of Prints, Drawings and Photographs, Philadelphia Museum of Art; Martha Haven, Harvard Observatory; Sinclair Hitchings, curator of prints, Boston Public Library; Ann Millspaugh Huff; Dale Johnson, research consultant, Department of American Paintings and Sculpture, Metropolitan Museum of Art, New York; Walter J. Karcheski, Jr., curator, Higgins Armory Museum; Harry Katz, Boston Athenaeum; Eric P. Newman, E. P. Newman Numismatic Education Society; Prof. William Oedel, University of Massachusetts at Amherst; David and Mary O'Neal, David L. O'Neal, Antiquarian Booksellers, Inc.; Michael G. Poisson, horologist; Betty Ring; Prof. Richard Saunders, Middlebury College; Meng Chi Tsen, Skinner Galleries and Coldstream House; Shreve, Crump & Low, Boston; Wanda Styka, Chesterwood; Joan Carpenter Troccoli, curator of art, Thomas Gilcrease Museum, Tulsa; Kenneth W. Van Blarcom; and Stephen A. Wilbur, curator, Gore Place, Waltham, Massachusetts.

CONTRIBUTORS

A.E.B.	Anne E. Bentley
B.M.L.	Brenda M. Lawson
B.M.P.	Barbara M. Pugliese
C.W.	Celeste Walker
E.W.H.	Edward W. Hanson
H.J.C.	Humphrey J. Costello
J.L.P.	Jane L. Port
K.H.G.	Katherine H. Griffin
L.C.G.	Linda C. Genovese
M.E.C.	Mary E. Cogswell
P.B.F.	Patrick B. Flynn
P.D.	Peter Drummey
R.A.R.	Richard A. Ryerson
S.R.M.	Susan R. Milstein
S.W.F.	Sheila W. Falcey
V.H.S.	Virginia H. Smith

Some Uses of History in the Early Republic

THOMAS N. BROWN

Americans in the early Republic looked to history to tell them who they were and where they were going. History's response to such inquiries signified that Americans were a favored people, destined to singular leadership in diffusing civil and religious liberty throughout the world. Liberty's torch, once borne aloft by Britain, was now in their hands. In this all important matter, they were, in the language of Thomas Jefferson's first inaugural address, the "world's best hope."[1]

Both the extravagance of this sentiment and its poignancy, the latter arising out of awareness that failure was possible, reflect the hope laced with fear with which Americans contemplated their experiment in republican government. Hope drew support from past experience, wherein forests had been turned into fields of plenty and independence wrung from a mighty empire, and from the newly emergent belief in history as Progress, whose realization evangelical Protestants anticipated would bring about the millennium—the long-awaited Kingdom of God on earth. Fear fed on other more ancient experience and teachings: that history was a melancholy drama in which nations rose from primitive beginnings to higher levels of civilization and power, only to become enfeebled by the luxuries attendant upon riches and thereafter descended to "degeneracy" and ultimate dissolution. Republics, whose basis in popular sovereignty rendered them dependent for survival upon the slender reed of a virtuous citizenry, were particularly vulnerable to the somber cycle wherein misfortune trod on the heels of fortune.[2]

History as Progress in the early nineteenth century would slowly gain control over the American mind. Still, mankind's experience pulled against optimism and gave hesitation to dreamers. Even after the happy outcome of the War of 1812, the second war with Britain, the traditional concerns survived. The *North American Review* for November 1815 praised the recently published *Collections* of the Massachusetts Historical Society for the portrayal offered of "our heroick forefathers," whose example—the reviewer hoped—would "stimulate future generations to avoid degeneracy."

The first generation of post-Revolutionary historians rejected the traditional providential history practiced by their puritan forebears and were by reason of this something of revolutionaries themselves. They constructed their histories around the action or inaction of responsible individuals. History as fortune leading to misfortune suited their purposes, for it imposed moral effort upon those who would delay or deny the operation of the melancholy cycle. The historians of this first generation wrote to educate the nation, particularly its young, in the dangers posed to republics by enervating luxury and in the virtuous behavior necessary to overcome them. For such purposes the drama of virtue embattled was pedagogically attractive. Even Mercy Otis Warren, the incisive and anxious poet and playwright from Plymouth, wife to one famous Massachusetts revolutionary and sister to another, whom one might expect to have been responsive to millenialism, wrote a history of the Revolution that is a drama of dark tones and flickering lights in which avarice wars with virtue and the harrowing consequences of victory for the latter are made manifest.[3]

Nevertheless, the sense of history as progress expressed by Jefferson's inaugural words could not but influence historical studies. Where the Republic stood and whither it tended—ascending in glory or descending in degeneracy—history was called upon to proclaim. Looking backward to see the future was an old American habit, but at no earlier time had it been charged with such heavy responsibilities.

One consequence of the ordeal was to encourage a passion for facts and for accurate documentation. If reliable measurements of the nation's trajectory—presumably up but maybe down—were to be made, the facts had to be authentic, drawn from reliable documents. Jeremy Belknap, the minister of Boston's Church in Long Lane and the prime mover in founding the Massachusetts Historical Society, whose *History of New Hampshire* revealed his faith in compilations of facts, was indefatigable in his search for documents. So too was Jared Sparks. A Unitarian clergyman of humble origins whose numerous historical publications won him fame and fortune, as well as the presidency of Harvard College and the vice presidency of the Massachusetts Historical Society, Sparks was heroic in his pursuit of documents. Labors such as theirs in the collection and preservation of the raw materials of historical study, undertaken at a time when local, state, and national governments were disinterested, were of incalculable importance to the work of later historians.

These scholars of a later day would not, however, place so unique a value upon the "fact" as had the earlier generation, for whom this irreducible historical unit was of and by itself luminous with truth. "Facts are unchangeable in their nature, and, once recorded, their value is never lost," states the introduction to *An Almanac and Repository of Useful Knowledge*, edited by Sparks and published in Boston in 1830. Lest the mind in its biases tamper with the fact as evidence, there was a reluctance on the part of some purists to arrange the facts in any consciously contrived order other than that of time. A collection of documents so ordered, thought Noah Webster, the lexicographer and cultural nationalist, was "really the best and only authentic history of a country."[4]

It was in these years and under these impulses that the term "statistics" took on its current meaning of facts in the form of numbers and that the American reverence for numbers developed.[5] Statistical annals of the United States, thick with numbers herded into charts, were particularly useful in the ongoing verbal war with Britain over the merits of the American republican experiment. Statistics of growth in population and trade and in the diffusion of philanthropic and religious institutions were addressed to a candid world and were intended to testify to the rising glory of America. The candid world, however, did not always draw the right conclusions from the numbers. It was in response to such a bundle of numbers that Sydney Smith, editor of the *Edinburgh Review* and condescending critic of American culture, raised the famous question infuriating to American cultural nationalists: "In the four quarters of the globe, who reads an American book . . . ?"[6]

Documents were collected and published for the general reader, who pursued them with feelings of awe and wonder. Their popularity, however, had the consequence of limiting their factual value. The public wanted the facts to nurture their patriotism and editors felt free to fit them to that popular standard. Sparks, who was entrusted with editing the papers of George Washington, revised the great man's letters by improving his grammar, syntax, and diction and by deleting, without notice, passages thought incompatible with his nobility. Conventional for his day, for Sparks knew his readers, his editorial practices scandalized early twentieth-century historians who wanted to make history a science and so

deplored any tampering with its factual basis.[7]

Like Thucydides, the Greek historian of the Peloponnesian wars and father of critical history, Americans in the early Republic had no doubt that the recovered past could prove useful to the present. While Ralph Waldo Emerson and later generations of Americans thought the past a burden or worse, they considered the past instructive. One could learn from it. John Adams and other constitution makers learned from the republics of history how to make one of their own. Because they believed that human nature was everywhere and always the same and ever subject to the melancholy cycle, they could employ the past as a kind of laboratory in which they—enlightened political scientists—could put various theories of government to the test. Rome and Greece, as recalled in their deliberations, shaped American state and national governments as well as the buildings which housed them.[8] In the heady years following the War of 1812, the American past by and large replaced classical Greek and Rome as the obsessive concern.[9]

The fashioning of a usable past was a "public enterprise," widely undertaken.[10] The professional—that is the academic historian—would not emerge until near the close of the century. Writers put their books together out of the sources, freely making use of paste and scissors. In a culture that placed no great value on originality, plagiarism was a practice, not a problem. The footnote had not yet taken on its present duties as compurgator to the author.[11] The British *Annual Register*, a publication of English Whigs hostile to George III's government, freely copied by William Gordon and David Ramsay, the first historians of the Revolution, became the bedrock of orthodox accounts of that event.[12]

The writing of history, like the ability to appreciate a fine landscape, was one of the graceful accomplishments of gentlemen; and the responsibilities of republican citizenship frequently obliged them to take up the pen in the interest of wise public policy. James Sullivan, son of an Irish-born Maine school teacher, the first president of the Massachusetts Historical Society and governor of Massachusetts in 1807–1808, was a prolific publisher of historical works, though thought by his son and others to be deficient in the niceties of style. His histories of Maine, Massachusetts land titles, and banking served to illuminate the past in ways useful to the political issues of his day.[13]

In no way was the past more useful to early Americans than as a reservoir of civic virtue. Though the constitution makers had installed fail-safe mechanisms to check the effects of human waywardness upon the workings of government, the traditional notion survived that the security of republics ultimately rested not upon the mechanisms of checks and balances but upon the shoulders of men of civic virtue prepared to serve the commonweal. However much history presented a record of human folly and crime, there was nevertheless embedded in the slag of the past vast deposits of moral greatness. History in the form of biography was a particularly productive way of tapping the deposits and many were attracted to it. The most successful of them was Sparks. The *Library of American Biography*, which he edited, ran to twenty-five volumes between 1833 and 1849.

The model for biographers was Plutarch, the Greek moralist of the first and second century A.D., whose

Parallel Lives scrutinized illustrious Greeks and Romans so as to encourage emulation of their virtues. James Sullivan set forth the psychological workings of this exemplary history in a *Sketch* of John Hancock's life. "The celebration of great men's virtues," he wrote, "affords the most powerful incentive to others to imitate them." Expectations of immortality— that is fame or glory—was the engine driving emulation of the virtuous great. "Patriots will emulate the virtues of Hancock, that like him they may rise above mortality."[14]

Not all would have agreed that Hancock was a happy choice for emulation. The historian William Gordon, minister to a Jamaica Plain congregation before returning to England to write a history of the Revolution and a difficult man in his own right, referred to Hancock as "Mr. Puff."[15] When the newly elected President Washington entered Boston, passing through the Victory Arch (no. 89) in the fall of 1789, "Mr. Puff," standing upon his dignity as governor, was only reluctantly persuaded to pay the journeying President deference. But all would have endorsed the psychological processes observed by Sullivan. The "thirst for glory," said Mercy Warren, was one of the "insepcrable companions of exalted minds." (The other companion was magnanimity.)[16]

At the close of the nineteenth century, believers in scientific history were appalled by the uncritical nature of this exemplary history which they believed too readily found virtue in unworthy subjects. They dismissed it contemptuously as a form of ancestor worship: filiopietism, they called it.[17] The criticism is wide of the mark. It is true that early Americans indulged themselves in what William Tudor, founder of the *North American Review* and Boston's chief promoter of culture, referred to as "delicious feelings of filial gratitude";[18] but this sentimentality did not dominate their lives. While they looked to the past for self-understanding and drew from it an energizing vision of the future, they were not bound by the past. They were engaged in building a bustling world very different from that of their fathers. By the conclusion of the second war with Britain, they had come to terms with the wealth and luxuries their commerce was piling up, so much a matter of concern for the earlier generation who feared that it signified "degeneracy."[19] But the divisive politics that overcame the nation after the 1790s was disturbing to Americans. They had come a long way toward accepting Madison's constitutional balancing acts as more important to the Republic's success than the virtue of its citizenry.[20] But they had not yet found a way of assimilating partisan politics into a coherent system of republican political thought.[21] Therefore, they continued to look to history for exemplars of civic virtue, hoping they would be emulated, and that the emulators would bring quiet to the public forum.[22] The past was called upon to redeem the present and secure the future. In that cause, these sentimentalists were hard headed utilitarians. They mined history's deposits with the same lack of scruples with which they cut Maine timber, dammed the Merrimac, and hunted the whale.[23]

The appropriation of history to serve the present was no monopoly of historians. The backward look was habitual with the other arts. In Thomas Jefferson's designs for his home at Monticello (no. 94) and in the towering Doric column bearing aloft an immense statue of Washington, which the Southern architect Robert Mills designed for Baltimore's Mt. Vernon Square, classical Greece was called upon to serve American purposes. History painting was more highly esteemed than portraiture or the painting of landscapes. The foremost painter of historical scenes in the early republic was John Trumbull of the Connecticut tribe of Trumbulls. His *Death of General Warren at the Battle of Bunker's Hill* (Yale University Art Gallery) for nearly half a century after its completion in 1786 was the best known account of the engagement of June 17, 1775, in which raw militiamen proved themselves the equals of British regulars. The exemplary death of Dr. Joseph Warren, Boston patriot and one of the nation's first revolutionary martyrs, in the battle's closing moments was the chief feature of Trumbull's painting and, like Mills's column, the first of the massive monuments to Washington, was concerned to bring the past to bear upon the moral needs of the present.

Ciceronian oratory, the most highly developed of all early American arts, was probably more widely influential in rendering the past into a moral force than were the works of formal history.[24] Between the emotional uplands of its exordium and peroration, the Ciceronian panegyric, or oration of praise, afford orators a long narrative plain for historical exposition. (Particularly painstaking to get the historical narrative right was the fastidious Edward Everett, the Massachusetts orator and statesman whose Gettysburg address (nos. 152, 153), though little noted nor long remembered, testifies to this practice.) Annual Fourth of July orations, heard by thousands and read in pamphlet form by thousands more, fixed for generation after generation the orthodox history of the Revolution. Oratory, however, was in these years no mere voice for the commonplace. Daniel Webster, the orator-laureate of his generation (no. 122), created for enraptured auditors a revisionist history of New England, which fixed its genetic origins in William Bradford's Plymouth settlement rather than in John Winthrop's Boston (no. 12), the latter possessing in its history Quaker persecutions, witchcraft trials, and other oppressive features inappropriate to a nation boastful of its place in the vanguard of liberty.[25]

The age's exemplary figure was, of course, Washington—"the most magnanimous prodigy of the 18th century," as the mourning handkerchief (no. 92) describes him. He had himself in the course of his life consciously emulated the high-mindedness of the austere greats of ancient Rome—Cato the Younger and Cincinnatus chiefly—and, in turn, he became the object of a vast industry of emulation.[26] His career demonstrated that civic virtue in a society appreciative of it could be an instrument of power. At Newburgh he quelled an army mutiny by the authority of his years of service. ("I have grown gray in your service.") Subsequently, he demonstrated that the denial of power could nurture its growth. At Annapolis in 1783 he gave up command of the Continental Army and at Philadelphia in 1796 the presidency, confirming that he was made in the image of Cincinnatus. Both episodes were recorded in paint and print by the icon makers. Stepping down was a way of stepping up in the hearts of his countrymen.

Works such as the heroic equestrian portrait of Washington (no. 85) brought the viewer into direct contact with greatness. What such a sublime experience could mean emotionally was described by the eminently sensible Abigail Adams after viewing Trumbull's *Battle of Bunker's Hill* in London in 1786: "I can only say that in looking at it my whole frame contracted, my blood shivered, and I felt a faintness at my heart."[27] But to a people schooled, as were many early nineteenth-century Americans, in the sensibilities of associational psychology, things quite humble could have similar effects. A glove, a gorget, a lock of hair, a battle map connected by memory with great men or great deeds could trigger in the imagination of those so instructed a chain of associated images, arousing thereby the appropriate emotion of awe and bringing the mind to a condition of moral sensitivity and reflection.[28] Auguste Levasseur, Lafayette's secretary during his American tour in 1824 and 1825, reported that on the occasion of the banquet given that hero on Boston Common in 1824, the festive tables for 1,200 diners were decorated with soldiers' buttons, spent shot, and other relics of the Revolutionary War found on Bunker Hill and elsewhere. Not souvenirs merely, meant to summon up remembrance of things past, the relics were themselves, as the secretary reported, objects of veneration, looked upon with "almost religious fervor."[29] More than a little of Lafayette's immense appeal for Americans lay in the popular view that in the great affairs of the Revolutionary war he had played the role of son to Washington (no. 71). A living relic of the Revolution, a sublime and parading artifact, Lafayette was looked upon with awe and trembling as his carriage was drawn past the young maidens in white assembled in every city and town to greet him.

The need to find redemptive figures in the past grew more urgent in the years of the Jefferson and Madison administrations, when Henry Adams's definition of politics as the organization of hatreds came close to realization. (Among the casualties of Republican- and Federalist-party animosities was James Sullivan (no.7), whose Republican politics probably cost him the presidency of the Massachusetts Historical Society.[30]) Searching for ways to save themselves from themselves, the distressed frequently looked to the arts, hoping that productions such as Mills's Baltimore monument to Washington would exercise a calming influence.[31] It was a vain hope, for the arts, too, were politicized.

Historical studies were particularly rich in quarrels, as rich as politics, and often for the same reason: History—control over the past—was concerned with power. Jefferson, disturbed by news that Supreme Court Chief Justice John Marshall, his political enemy, was hard at work on a biography of Washington, urged Joel Barlow, author of the visionary epic the *Columbiad* and a Jeffersonian, to produce a history that would counteract the presumed influence of Marshall's work upon the next presidential election. Mercy Otis Warren's history, designedly Republican and anti-Federalist skewered not only Timothy Pickering of Salem, Washington's secretary of war and a Federalist of rigor, but also "Mr. Puff," who headed a Republican faction in Boston by no means congenial to the Warren family.[32]

At stake often was the prestige of families. In the jockeying for social position among families, many of them newly risen with the Revolution, social place was influenced by the family's role in the struggle for Independence.[33] John Adams in his old age recalled for a correspondent the names of those who, corrupted by soft living, had turned Tory in the decisive decades before the break with Britain. "I know the grief, the resentment and the rage, that this narration will excite in many families," wrote the old man. Conspicuous among the names was that of Harrison Gray, grandfather of Harrison Gray Otis, Federalist-party leader and no friend to the Adams family.[34]

The quarrel which pitted the Putnam family of Connecticut against the Prescott family of Massachusetts piled up a library of contentious historical literature.[35] General Henry Dearborn, who had served as Secretary of War under Jefferson, initiated the hostility in 1817 with the charge that Putnam had played the coward at the Battle of Bunker Hill, the conflict soon revolved around the question as to which of the two—Colonel William Prescott or General Israel Putnam—should be honored as the chief hero of the battle. In the controversy family pride was a force, activating maledictions of near-Neapolitan ferocity: "the odium attached to this slander will cling to the Dearborn race until they are extinct," was Daniel Putnam's expectation and no doubt desire.[36] Oliver Prescott, nephew of Colonel Prescott, unhappy with the lassitude of the Colonel's son at a time when the Putnams seemed to be "engrossing" all the honors of Bunker Hill, placed him under a conditional curse: "You cannot, you will not permit such injustice to be done . . . if you did I would expect such apathy toward a father's memory would be punished by the daily and nightly visitation of his ghost."[37]

The Putnams' war with the Prescotts outlasted the latter's war with the British, which may be said to have ended in 1820 when the Colonel's grandson—the future historian William Hickling Prescott—married a descendant of one of the British warriors at Bunker Hill. Putnam partisans, on the other hand, were still at it at the century's close.[38] They were, however, fighting a lost cause. The issue had in fact been decided earlier in the Prescotts' favor when in 1841 the Reverend George E. Ellis, a friend of the family and long time member of the Massachusetts Historical Society, gave an oration, later published, which persuasively featured the Colonel as the foremost hero of Bunker Hill, much to the pleasure of the Prescotts.[39]

However unseemly and hard on the families, quarrels, such as this, had salutary consequences for historical studies. They encouraged the critical spirit, counteracting the age's disposition to waive criticism in favor of praise. They also encouraged accuracy. Richard Frothingham's magisterial study of the *Siege of Boston* (1849) was built on the shards of the Putnam-Prescott controversy.[40]

Of all the peoples of the new Republic, New Englanders were foremost in historical studies. They had inherited from the Puritan past a keen sense of themselves as an elect people, and they projected an historic vision of the nation that was little more than an extension of the role which their forebears believed Divine Providence had long ago assigned to New England. Among historians elsewhere in the nation there was initially surprisingly little dissent from this New England-centered interpretation. John Marshall's *Life of Washington* (1804–1807), which devoted a volume to colonial history before taking up Washington, endorsed the New England view of the nation's origins. But as New England's political and moral influence within the Union declined after 1801, challenges to its historical claims and to the dominance of its historians emerged. A biography of Patrick Henry published in 1817 by William Wirt, a Virginia lawyer and essayist, made Henry the prime force in events leading to the Revolution, thus displacing Massachusetts from the position it had traditionally claimed. John Adams led a vigorous counterattack, and under his encouragement and with the financial help of others, William Tudor answered Wirt with a *Life of James Otis* (1823). In this account not only was Otis, brother to Mercy Otis Warren, the first among American revolutionaries, he was also a world force: the mover and shaker of revolutionary events abroad, threatening the overthrow of tyrants and promising the installation of representative government.

Both Wirt and Taylor were imaginative men and resolute, capable of producing plausible narratives out of scarce evidence and in the absence of authentic source material. Neither the speeches of Otis nor of Henry, upon which their rival claims rested, had survived other than in the memories of old men. Thomas Jefferson certified the authenticity of Henry's defiant speech of May 29, 1765, upon which Virginia's claims of "first" were based; John Adams performed a similar service, authenticating an Otis speech defiant of British authority, uttered three years earlier than Henry's. Out of controversies such as these, generated by local or sectional interests, a national history with national heroes was developed. Both Henry and Otis, with their orations whose credibility may be doubted, are firmly placed in the text-books of the Republic.[41]

"Character is power." With that judgment Daniel Webster in 1818 concluded a defense of Israel Putnam against the charges of General Dearborn.[42] However inscrutable it may appear, given as the tendency to denigrate of the illustrious, to Webster's generation the judgment expressed what was only obvious good sense. It was the axiom upon which exemplary history was founded. While producing some odd results and nourishing some dubious historical practices, exemplary history had the great merit of focusing attention on history in human affairs and on the individual in history. (For many republicans, history of the exemplary kind was the last best hope of the Republic.) The patrician historians of the mid-nineteenth century and after inherited the concern for character; their works gave reality to Webster's judgment.[43] Their conviction that virtue mattered in history may be traced to the creative historians of the early Republic who placed man at the center of the historical drama.

1. The phrase "worlds best hope" was perhaps Jefferson's way of reaching out to the citizens of New England, where the sentiment it expresses had its origins. Wesley Frank Craven, *The Legend of the Founding Fathers* (New York, 1956), pp. 60–61.

2. Stow Persons, "The Cyclical Theory of History in Eighteenth Century America," *American Quarterly* 6(1954): 147–163; Arthur H. Shaffer, *The Politics of History: Writing the History of the American Revolution, 1783–1815* (Chicago, 1975), pp. 74–77; Drew R. McCoy, *The Elusive Republic: Political Economy in Jeffersonian America* (Chapel Hill, 1980), pp. 13–47.

3. Mercy Otis Warren, *History of the Rise, Progress and Termination of the American Revolution*, Lester H. Cohen, ed. (Indianapolis, 1988), 1:xliv, where Warren sets forth the dangers should the Republic fail. See also Cohen, *The Revolutionary Histories: Contemporary Narratives of the American Revolution* (Ithaca, 1980), pp. 185ff; Shaffer, *Politics of History*, pp. 74–76.

4. *Massachusetts Magazine* 1(1789): 476; Lester H. Cohen, "Narrating the Revolution: Ideology, Language, Style," *Studies in 18th Century Culture* 9(1979): 455.

5. Patricia Cline Cohen, *A Calculating People: The Spread of Numeracy in Early America* (Chicago, 1982), pp. 150ff.

6. Sydney Smith, *The Works of Sydney Smith*, 3 vols. (London, 1854), 2:122; Mary Frederick Lochemes, *Robert Walsh: His Story* (New York, 1941), p. 96. Walsh was the author of the powerful rejoinder to Smith and other British critics in *An Appeal from the Judgments of Great Britain Respecting the United States of America* (Philadelphia, 1819).

7. Daniel J. Boorstin, *The Americans: The National Experience* (New York, 1965), pp. 345–349. For a defense of Sparks, see George H. Callcott, *History in the United States, 1800–1860* (Baltimore, 1970), pp. 128ff.; Herbert Baxter Adams, *The Life and Writings of Jared Sparks* (1893, Freeport, N.Y., 1970), 1:xxv–xxxv.

8. Douglas C. Adair, "'Experience must Be our Only Guide': History, Democratic Theory, and the United States Constitution," *The Reinterpretation of Early American History*, Ray Allen Billington, ed. (San Marino, 1966), pp. 129–130, 135–136.

9. Craven, *The Legend of the Founding Fathers*, pp. 57–85.

10. Peter J. Gomes, "Pilgrims and Puritans: 'Heroes and Villains' in the Creation of the American Past," MHS *Proceedings* 95(1983): 1–16.

11. Callcott, *History in the United States*, pp. 134–136. Modern use of footnotes emerges with the patrician historians after the mid-nineteenth century.

12. David D. Van Tassel, *Recording America's Past* (Chicago, 1960), p. 39, n. 25, reviews the literature critical of the historians who borrowed from the *Annual Register*. Craven, *Legend of the Founding Fathers*, pp. 51–54, argues that of even greater importance to the development of an orthodoxy of early American history was George Chalmers, *Political Annals of the Present United Colonies* (London, 1780).

13. Louis Leonard Tucker, *Clio's Consort* (Boston, 1990), pp. 90–91.

14. James Sullivan, *Biographical Sketch of the Life and Character of his late Excellency, Governor Hancock* (Boston, 1793), p. 16.

15. See Van Tassel, *Recording America's Past*, p. 39.

16. Warren, *American Revolution*, 1:146; Douglas C. Adair, title essay in *Fame and the Founding Fathers*, Trevor Colburn, ed. (New York, 1974), pp. 1–26.

17. Van Tassel, *Recording America's Past*, pp. 66ff.

18. *Monthly Anthology*, 9(1810): 156–157.

19. See McCoy, *Elusive Republic*, pp. 96–100.

20. See the comments of Jedidiah Morse, *Annals of the American Revolution* (Hartford, 1824), pp. 399–400.

21. Richard Hofstadter, *The Idea of a Party System: The Rise of the Legitimate Opposition in the United States, 1780–1840* (Berkeley, 1969), passim.

22. See, for example, Alexander Everett, *North American Review*, 31(1830): 309; also his *America: A Survey* (Philadelphia, 1827), pp. 325–333, where he proposes that Washington's Mount Vernon be made a shrine to virtue.

23. See Van Tassel, *Recording America's Past*, p. 74 n. 27, for a frank, even cynical statement by William Hickling Prescott about Charles Brockden Brown, on whose biography he was working.

24. Lawrence Buell, *New England Literary Culture* (Cambridge, 1986), pp. 137ff.

25. Craven, *Legend of the Founding Fathers*, pp. 82–85; Gomes, "Pilgrims and Puritans," pp. 2–6; Paul D. Erickson, "Daniel Webster's Myth of the Pilgrims," *New England Quarterly* 57(1984): 44–64; Van Tassel, *Recording America's Past*, p. 57.

26. Garry Wills, *Cincinnatus: George Washington and the Enlightenment* (Garden City, N.Y., 1984).

27. In *John Trumbull's Autobiography*, Theodore Sizer, ed. (New Haven, 1953), p. 85, n. 16.

28. For associational psychology in American culture, see Robert Streeter, "Associational Psychology and Literary Nationalism in the North American Review, 1815–1825," *American Literature* 17(1945): 242–254; Terence Martin, *The Instructed Vision* (Bloomington, Ind., 1961), pp. 13–14; Archibald Alison, *Essays on the Nature and Principles of Taste* (1790. Boston, 1812) was a major influence in developing the sensibility; Henry F. May, *The Enlightenment in America* (New York, 1976), p. 356.

29. Auguste Levasseur, *Lafayette in America in 1824 and 1825*, J. D. Godman, ed., 2 vols. (Philadelphia, 1829), 1:67.

30. Boston *Independent Chronicle*, May 29, 1806. I am indebted to Louis L. Tucker, Director of the Massachusetts Historical Society, for this reference.

31. *Monthly Anthology*, 9(1810): 156–157.

32. James Leslie Woodress, *A Yankee's Odyssey: The Life of Joel Barlow* (Philadelphia, 1958), p. 221; Warren, *History*, 1:103, 116.

33. Boorstin, *The Americans: The National Experience*, p. 389; Craven, *The Legend of the Founding Fathers*, pp. 86, 99–100.

34. One of a series of ten Adams letters printed by Morse in his *Annals of the American Revolution*, p. 206.

35. Bibliographies of the controversy may be found in Justin Winsor, *Reader's Handbook of the American Revolution, 1761–1783* (Boston, 1880), pp. 35–59; James Hunnewell, *Bibliography of Charlestown and Bunker Hill* (Boston, 1880), pp. 13–29; Richard Frothingham, *History of the Siege of Boston* (Boston, 1873), pp. 378ff.

36. Daniel Putnam to George Brinley, Brooklyn, Conn., Sept. 15, 1824. Connecticut State Library Archives, Hartford.

37. Oliver Prescott to William Prescott, Newburyport, Dec. 16, 1824. Prescott Papers, MHS.

38. See Increase N. Tarbox, *The Life of Israel Putnam* (Boston, 1876), especially chap. 11; William Farrand Livingston, *Israel Putnam* (New York, 1901), chap. 17 and appendix 2.

39. George Edward Ellis, "Sketches of the Bunker Hill Battle and Monument" (Charlestown, 1843); William Prescott to George E. Ellis, Nahant, July 19, 1841. Prescott Papers, MHS; William Hickling Prescott to Washington Irving, May 10, 1842, in Roger Wolcott, ed., *The Correspondence of William Hickling Prescott* (Boston, 1925), p. 303.

40. See "The Miscellaneous pamphlets used by Richard Frothingham in preparing his 'History of the Siege of Boston . . . and Bunker Hill,'" MHS; also Van Tassel, *Recording America's Past*, pp. 122–123.

41. Boorstin, *The Americans: The National Experience*, pp. 357–361.

42. *North American Review* 7(1818):258.

43. Richard C. Vitzhum, *The American Compromise* (Norman, Okla., 1974), pp. 110, 163–165, 214.

From Belknap to Riley: Building the Collection of the Massachusetts Historical Society

LOUIS L. TUCKER

Two hundred years of collecting by the Massachusetts Historical Society have created one of the most important repositories ever available for the study of American history. The Society's bicentennial provides the opportunity to celebrate this great achievement and to look back at the individuals responsible for creating and preserving this national treasure. Almost from the founding of the Society, the leading historical families of Massachusetts, from the Adamses to the Lodges, to the Winthrops, to the Saltonstalls, have regarded the Boston institution as the repository of choice for their personal papers. The range of the collections, however, covers the full spectrum of society, as the recent works in social history have discovered. Private soldiers and shopkeepers are represented alongside presidents and generals.

The history of collecting at the Historical Society began with its founder, Jeremy Belknap (1744–98). Born and bred in Boston and educated at Harvard College, Belknap trained for the ministry and, in 1767, settled in the First Congregational Church of Dover, New Hampshire, where he served for nineteen years. In 1787, he returned to Boston and became minister of the Long Lane Congregational Church, now the Arlington Street Church. He also became involved in a wide range of secular activities, one of which was the founding of the Society, the first institution in the world organized primarily for publishing and collecting historical Americana.

That Belknap should establish an historical society was not surprising. He had a lifelong passion for history. As a boy in Boston, he displayed an "inquisitive disposition in historical maters" and "natural curiosity to enquire into the original settlement of the country which gave him birth." The Reverend Thomas Prince, Jeremy's boyhood minister at the Old South Church, further stimulated his interest. Prince was one of early New England's most accomplished historians and an "American pioneer in scientific historical writing." A voracious collector of historical sources, Prince assembled one of the largest private libraries in the American colonies, over 2,000 books and a huge corpus of manuscripts and other primary sources.

During Belknap's stay in Dover, he began research on a history of New Hampshire. Jeremy was constrained to locate source materials, and he became acutely aware of the difficult problems confronting an American historian. Nowhere in New Hampshire, or anywhere else in the United States, was there an organized body of sources available to a researcher.

Belknap scoured the state for documentary materials. He was doggedly persistent, spending many hours "in the garrets and rat-holes of old houses" poring over musty manuscripts. "I am willing even to scrape a dunghill," he once wrote, "if I may find a jewel at the bottom." In an effort to curtail his travel, which was time-consuming, physically punishing, and costly, Belknap prepared a detailed questionnaire on historical information and mailed it to clergymen and "other gentlemen of public character" in New Hampshire. Through gifts and the questionnaire, Belknap accumulated a vast collection of documentary sources.

From the time of the American Revolution, Belknap noted that important documents relating to the history of the new nation were rapidly disappearing through inattention, fire, natural disasters, and the "ravages of unprincipled or mercenary men." The scattering of Prince's magisterial collection from the tower of the historic Old South Church during and after the Revolution particularly pained and angered him.

American historians needed repositories bulging with source materials in order to practice their craft. Belknap envisioned an historical library in every state of the union, each working in concert with the others, and exchanging information and publications. But he was realistic

Jeremy Belknap (1744–1798)

Belknap employed a variety of means to acquire materials. He developed and had printed another questionnaire, a "Circular Letter of the Historical Society," (no. 4) in which he appealed for both information (under fourteen subject headings) and, more importantly, "any books, pamphlets, manuscripts, maps or plans, which may conduce to the accomplishments of the views of the Society; and any natural or artificial productions which may enlarge its museum." Belknap mailed these circulars to "every Gentleman of Science in the Continent and Islands of America" and to a select number of learned men in Great Britain and on the Continent. One commentator has written that he sent them "to persons almost at the ends of the earth." Belknap requested recipients of his "Circular Letter" to distribute them among friends, correspondents, and all other prospective donors, and to have them printed in local newspapers. He cast his net wide and in every direction.

Belknap importuned residents of Boston who had been key participants in the American Revolution for information on their activities and personal papers. John Hancock, Samuel Adams, and John Adams stood high on his list of contacts. In 1798, he persuaded Paul Revere to write a detailed account of his "midnight ride" to Lexington and Concord on April 18–19, 1775 (no. 52). Although Belknap had requested this account for the library, he promptly printed it in the Society's *Collections*, a publication he had instituted in 1792.

Belknap sought public as well as private papers. Assisted by select congressional representatives from Massachusetts and Connecticut who were members of the Society, he petitioned the federal legislature for copies of "printed acts, journals, reports, treatises, letters, proceedings of courts-martial and other papers relative to the public affairs of the United States, civil and military, foreign and domestic." In seeking federal printed works and documents, Belknap was underscoring the Society's commitment to collect sources relating to all thirteen states of the Union. He was not limiting it to Massachusetts or New England.

Belknap rarely failed to insert an appeal for historical materials for the Society when he wrote to learned men in the United States and abroad. He frequently included a "Circular Letter" to reinforce his solicitation. If he thought that the person was in a strong position to assist in his project, either through ownership of such materials or access to a valued collection, he arranged to have him elected a corresponding member of the Historical Society. In this way, he strengthened the obligation of the potential donor to the Society. He employed this technique with consummate skill in dealing with Christoph Daniel Ebeling of Hamburg, Germany, who had amassed one of the largest collections of historical Americana in Europe. Because of Belknap's shrewd solicitation, Ebeling became a frequent contributor to the Society's library.

On occasion, when the prospect of a major gift appeared in a nearby state, Belknap traveled to the donor's home to complete the transaction. In 1794, for example, he made an arduous, two-day coach journey to Lebanon, Connecticut, and spent four days selecting items from the Gov. Jonathan Trumbull Papers for shipment to Boston. This was an enormous collection of British and

enough to know that such a national network would take years to develop. He was equally aware that it was not yet feasible to establish an historical repository in an unlettered state such as New Hampshire, and certainly not in a small town such as Dover.

Bustling, cosmopolitan Boston, the intellectual nerve center of New England, with a population of some 25,000—and rapidly growing—was another matter. Upon returning to the city of his birth, Belknap set in motion a plan to establish what he first designated as an "antiquarian society." He achieved his objective in January 1791.

Belknap knew that the new historical society would require a well-stocked library. To this end, he invited nine men who were collectors of historical materials to join him as cofounders. In effect, he began by collecting collectors. James Winthrop, for example, owned many books and a large corpus of documents, including "bundles" of Gov. John Winthrop manuscripts. Thomas Wallcut, an eccentric bachelor and zealous bibliophile, had amassed a huge body of pamphlets and historical works. Among John Eliot's private holdings was the manuscript of William Hubbard's "History of New England," once owned by Thomas Hutchinson, the last civilian royal governor of Massachusetts.

Belknap exacted a pledge from each cofounder to make a donation to the Society's library. All but one honored his commitment and made a substantial gift. Belknap's contribution was, by far, the largest and most significant. By 1792, the Society had acquired hundreds of seventeenth- and eighteenth-century books and pamphlets, and a large assortment of documentary sources.

After acquiring this nucleus, Belknap embarked on an aggressive campaign to enlarge the Society's holdings. "There is nothing like having a *good repository*, and keeping a *good look-out*," Belknap advised, "not waiting at home for things to fall into the lap, but prowling about like a wolf for the prey."

View of **Faneuil-Hall** *in* Boston *Massachusetts.*

Faneuil Hall, the second home of the Massachusetts Historical Society from 1792 to 1794.

American documents relating to the Revolution, some public, some private, gathered by the wartime governor of Connecticut. In offering the collection to the Boston society, David Trumbull, son of the late governor, wrote Belknap: "Had the Massachusetts Historical Society existed during his life there is no doubt but He would have chosen to give them to an Institution whose Patriotic Views they would so directly subserve in preference to a Collegiate or other Library, where they probably would soon become 'Food for Worms'."

With a view towards publicizing and perpetuating their efforts, Belknap arranged in 1792 to have an historical supplement added to a newly created Boston newspaper, the *American Apollo* (no. 3). The supplement was sponsored and subsidized by the Society. In this segment, Belknap inserted documents from the Society's collection. In addition to providing historical information to the general public, which was one of his principal objectives, Belknap also hoped to preserve the sources of American history for future researchers. As he wrote:

> There is no sure way of preserving historical records and materials, but by *multiplying the copies*. The art of printing affords a mode of preservation more effectual than Corinthian brass or Egyptian marble; for statues and pyramids which have long survived the wreck of time, are unable to tell the names of their sculptors, or the date of their foundations.

Typically, Belknap also used this supplement as a vehicle for his collecting program by listing all donations and the names of the donors.

The original plan of the founders included a museum as well as a library. "Specimens of natural and artificial curiosities" were to be housed in the Cabinet or Museum (these were synonymous terms in the eighteenth century), an adjunct to the library. Since Belknap did not list criteria for such objects, he received many oddities, for example: "one of the largest Spears used by the Savages on the North West Coast of America"; some shells from the islands of the Indian Ocean; a "War Club, from Oronque"; a silver "Denarius" of the Emperor Valentinian "above 1400 years old"; a tarantula; and a "Golden Cock". Such items explained why contemporaries referred to this collection as a "cabinet of curiosities."

At his death in 1798, Belknap left a rich legacy to the Society. His brief era constitutes the first golden age in the history of the Society's library. It would not see his like again until the mid-twentieth century when Stephen T. Riley served as librarian and, later, director.

As long as the Society had no competition for historical treasures, collecting was easy. Beginning with the New-York Historical Society in 1804, however, societies were founded in other states as the nation expanded, and the flow of non-Massachusetts and non-New England materials to Boston slowed to a trickle. Prospective donors outside Massachusetts now had options for their philanthropy.

Partly due to the new competition but also because of an acute lack of space, the Society began to alter its collecting pattern beginning in the 1830s. Now the focus was upon Massachusetts and, to a lesser extent, the other five New England states. Although not articulated in a formal pronouncement or policy statement, this shift in geographical emphasis can be discerned in the list of library acquisitions reported at meetings. It occurred in a subtle, natural manner and seemingly was dictated by expediency, by the realization that, with limitations of space and manpower, the Society could not possibly function as *the* national repository of historical Americana. On three occasions in the nineteenth century, the Society was forced to find new quarters because it lacked room for its holdings. Library reports for this period repeatedly bemoan the space dilemma, a familiar refrain for all repositories, then and since.

Despite the narrowing of its sphere of collecting and a perpetual lack of room, the Society continued to increase its holdings. Items came in at a steady pace throughout the nineteenth and early twentieth centuries. At no time did the librarian, or any other officer, propose a moratorium on collecting, for that would have been defeating the original purpose.

The manuscript collection experienced the greatest growth. Together with a regular flow of single documents or small bodies of manuscripts, there came periodically an infusion of massive collections of prominent historical figures and intellectuals— like the papers of Thomas Jefferson, Edward Everett, George Bancroft, and Francis Parkman. From time to time, someone donated a document of transcendent importance— for example, George Washington's Newburgh Address (no. 88), Daniel Webster's autobiography, and Samuel Sewall's diary (no. 26). The gift of the Washburn autograph collection contained a special bonus: a manuscript copy of the Declaration of Independence in Jefferson's script (no. 81).

While the book collection did not grow as rapidly as the manuscripts, it also experienced a steady increase. The largest and most significant addition to this segment of the library was the Thomas Dowse gift in 1856.

Dowse (1772–1856) was a singular character. A fall from a tree at the age of six, followed by a siege of rheumatic fever, left him lame. The youngster turned to books as a solace, becoming an omnivorous reader. As an adult, Dowse became a leather dresser in Cambridgeport and in time accumulated a modest fortune. The "literary leather dresser," as he was known in Boston, began to purchase books in a most discriminating manner. He placed as high a value on bindings as on content. A bachelor and semi recluse, he spared no expense on his beloved library.

After fifty years of collecting, Dowse amassed more than 5,000 volumes. His library contained the standard works of English history and literature, and the best contemporary translations of the Greek and Latin classics, and German, French, Italian, and Portuguese literature. It was a "noble collection," the quintessential nineteenth-century gentleman's library.

Recognizing the importance of this resource, George Livermore, Dowse's friend and neighbor, and a member of the Society, urged the eighty-four-year-old bibliophile to donate his books to the Boston institution. Although not a member himself, Dowse agreed in 1856 to make the gift. To honor him for his generosity, the Society voted to house his library "forever" in a special chamber to be named the Dowse Room. It also commissioned Moses

Thomas Dowse (1772–1856)

Wight to paint his portrait, which was placed in the room.

The Dowse gift strengthened an already formidable collection of books, but there was more to come. In later years, the Society acquired additional special collections. For example, in 1919 Mrs. Kingsmill Marrs donated her late husband's library of English county, family, and general histories. In 1938, the estate of Francis Russell Hart, a past president of the Society, contributed Hart's collection of printed books relating to the Caribbean and South America, a region he had written about and in which he had had extensive business connections. In 1962, John M. Wells of Southbridge, Massachusetts, donated his father's library of illustrated books on American history and biography, beautifully bound in fine leather. When Michael J. Walsh, one of the leading experts on printed Americana, delivered an address at the Society in 1953 on "Some Treasures of the Massachusetts Historical Society," he began his presentation with these statements: "Housed in this building is a truly great collection of printed Americana. The extent of the collection in numbers, rarity, and importance makes any attempt at describing it a difficult one." Yet, Walsh made the attempt. His "sampling" covered fourteen printed pages of text in the Society's *Proceedings*.

* * *

While no figure of Belknap's stature emerged during the nineteenth and early twentieth centuries, a coterie of dedicated members made noteworthy contributions to the library. For example, Robert C. Winthrop, who served as president of the Society for thirty years, began to collect the papers of his prominent family. His son, Robert Charles Winthrop, Jr., also a member, continued the process during his lifetime, and upon his death in 1905, he bequeathed the priceless Winthrop Papers to the Society.

The Coolidge family of Boston not only contributed their own papers but also the personal papers of Thomas Jefferson. In 1898, Thomas Jefferson Coolidge I, the great-grandson of the immortal Virginian, made the major gift, approximately 9,000 items. Over a span of sixty years, three Coolidges (Thomas Jefferson Coolidge I, II, and III) acquired additional segments of this incomparable collection and donated them to the Society.

Then there was the irascible Dr. Samuel Abbott Green, who not only procured materials but also dominated the administration of the library for much of his fifty-eight years of membership (no. 10). Green's affiliation with the Society began in 1860. An avocational historian, he developed an enthusiastic interest in the institution and served it in various capacities: member of the Council; keeper of the cabinet from 1860 to 1868; vice-president from 1895 to 1914; and librarian from 1868 to 1918.

A native of Groton and graduate of Lawrence Academy, Harvard College, and Harvard Medical School, Green had a remarkably varied career. He began a medical practice in Boston in 1855; served as a surgeon and medical officer during the Civil War; and became superintendent of the Boston Dispensary in 1865 and city physician in 1871. In 1881, he ran for mayor as a reform candi-

date, was elected, and served one term. He maintained an active civic life, serving on various boards and participating in a variety of *pro bono publico* activities. He was a large figure on the Boston scene, both physically and figuratively.

Green became a constant presence, an "absolute fixture," at the Society in his final twenty years. When not tending to the affairs of the library, he spent much of his time researching and writing the history of his beloved Groton, "a town for which his passion was so great, it was said, he never read a novel unless the scene was laid there." A prolific writer, he published nearly 200 books and pamphlets, of which nearly one-fourth dealt with the history of Groton.

As librarian, Green was a formidable figure. He came to regard the library as his private preserve. A "growling Cerberus," he refused to allow nonmembers to enter. He offended one and all, including president Charles Francis Adams II, who referred to him (behind his large back) as "the everlasting and inescapable Big Medicine Man."

Adams did not wish to antagonize Green since he was wealthy and there was the possibility of a bequest to the Society. In 1905, Adams considered a deceitful plan: resigning as president and placing Green in the position. Adams anticipated Green's early demise and his own return to the presidency. As he wrote Ford: "Green is now 75 and leads not at all a good life—very fat and tremulous, he eats enormously and takes no exercise. He is rich and kinless and may go any day. We ought to get a large legacy from him and I need it for the successful

The Dowse Library, meeting room of the Massachusetts Historical Society since 1857 and installed in its current home in 1898.

Samuel Abbott Green (1830–1918)

reorganization of the Society on the new basis I have long had in mind."

The plan did not materialize and Green continued to rule over his domain, where he did yeoman work adding materials, reorganizing and cataloging the collection, and reducing the chaos. In 1912, he was struck by a cart and appeared on the verge of death. "It is apparently only a question of days," Ford wrote Adams, before they would have to appoint a new librarian. Ford's prediction of Green's impending death was premature. Green suddenly improved, which led President Adams to quip: "He will play on the Groton baseball team yet."

Not long after, a startled Ford looked out of his office window and saw Green arriving at his residence, the Fritz Carlton Hotel, adjacent to the Society on Boylston Street, "with Doctor, Nurse, bag, baggage, chauffeur and incidentals. . . . There is something uncanny about it, for we are dealing with a man who died. I shall try to worm out of the Dr. what passed between him and St. Peter." Green recovered fully and resumed his schedule in the library. Warren Wheeler, a library employee for fifty years, recounted Green's daily routine:

> Daily at the appointed time one or two library assistants, together with Green's nurse and the Society's janitor, brought him down from his room, wheeled him to this building, and lugged him up the stairs to his desk in the circular room where members now gather after meetings for tea or madeira. Stationed there, surrounded by masses of pamphlets and proofs of articles about the antiquities of Groton, he was equally well prepared to shout his orders to his subordinates in the office which is now the Oliver Room and to bar intruders (including readers) from access to the Society's books, manuscripts, and catalogues.

Green resigned as vice-president in 1914 but retained his position as librarian. He died in 1918. To the bitter disappointment of both the Society and Harvard, which was also expecting a windfall, Green left the bulk of his estate to Lawrence Academy.

From the outset, the Society's collection was characterized by diversity. It embodied a wide range of materials. This was in keeping with the broad conception of "history" in the eighteenth century. The founders affirmed in the Society's constitution that they would collect books, manuscripts, records, "observations and descriptions in natural history and topography," specimens of "natural and artificial curiosities," and "a selection of every thing which can improve and promote the historic knowledge of our country, either in a physical or political view." While providing themselves with wide latitude in what they would collect, the founders and their successors tended to concentrate on such conventional and staple source materials (by twentieth-century standards) as books, manuscripts, pamphlets, newspapers, maps, and broadsides.

Over the course of years, the Society also acquired a sizable number of three-dimensional items: antique furniture and artifacts; portraits and other paintings; busts and statues; coins and medals; and an astonishing assortment of historical relics typical of a nineteenth-century museum, ranging from the samp bowl belonging to King Philip to locks of hair of Napoleon Bonaparte and George Washington, and from a fragment of Plymouth Rock to the "first ball" fired at Lexington Green on April 19, 1775.

The rapid growth of the Society's cabinet came to represent a serious problem in the early nineteenth century. The constant shortage of storage space was the critical factor. In 1819, the Society authorized the cabinet keeper and librarian to dispose of "any perishable articles." In 1833, it voted to deposit the specimens of "natural and artificial curiosities" in the Boston Society of Natural History. In 1867, it permitted the curator of the Peabody Museum at Harvard University to select whatever "aboriginal relics" he wished. He took 178 specimens, and this "stripped the Society, for the most part, of its collection of articles in natural history and archaeology."

When the Society moved from the Tontine Crescent to a four-story building on Tremont Street in the 1830s, it established a modest museum program which featured specimens drawn from the cabinet. This was not a sophisticated exhibition. Many of the smaller objects were placed in a few display cases, where they remained for years. Portraits, busts, and statues were positioned in a "picture gallery" and main rooms of the Society. Rarely was there a change made of this setting. Ostensibly, the general public was welcome to visit the Historical Society and view the display, but only a handful of Bostonians ventured in, and no one actively encouraged or promoted such visitation.

When the Society moved into its spacious new quarters at 1154 Boylston Street in the Back Bay in 1899, it established similar displays on the first floor and continued to invite the public to view the exhibition free of charge. In time, however, it became evident that the public had no interest in the museum. A Society report

The Tontine Crescent, Franklin Street, Boston, the third home of the Massachusetts Historical Society from 1794 to 1833.

Home of the Massachusetts Historical Society since 1899, 1154 Boylston Street, Boston.

noted that "it is a rare day indeed that sees a visitor." Because of the lack of visitation and the need of space for its ever-expanding holdings, the Society terminated its museum program in 1959.

* * *

From 1791 to World War I, the Society functioned as a private cultural club and the users of its library were almost exclusively members. It was, in effect, a closed institution. On occasion, it permitted an outsider to use its resources but, in most cases, these researchers were friends or associates of members. To this point, almost all nonmember researchers were residents of the Greater Boston area. The era of the peripatetic researcher had not yet begun.

Toward the close of the nineteenth century, however, dramatic changes were taking place in American higher education, which were to have a profound effect upon the Society. Such universities as Harvard, Yale, Johns Hopkins, and Michigan created graduate schools and began to produce professional historians. The age of the gentleman-scholar was at an end. A growing legion of Ph.D.'s was replacing Francis Parkman, William Hickling Prescott, George Bancroft, *et al.*

Trained in the German tradition of scientific history, the new scholars were committed to the use of primary sources. Those who specialized in American history cast covetous eyes upon the Society's massive documentary resources. Scholars were no longer content with the published offerings of the *Collections* or *Proceedings*. They wished to consult the entire collection, and they made their position known.

The Society began to take note of the rumblings of discontent in the 1890s. The Council's report of 1893 called attention to the need for a more generous policy of accessibility to its manuscripts, affirming that it would insure continued donations:

> While it is our duty to see to the careful preservation of our possessions, while we must surround their use with such precautions as may insure their safety, our policy as to the manuscripts in our hands should be thoroughly generous. This only will secure the continued reception by us of valuable manuscripts. The rooms of this Society are not now the only possible place of deposit for family papers and historical material. Testators and donors can find other repositories and will do so, if we do not let our light shine before men.

The arrival of Worthington C. Ford as editor of publications in 1909 accelerated the movement to open the Society. Formerly chief of the Division of Manuscripts of the Library of Congress, Ford brought an enlightened, liberal point of view. He firmly favored an open-door policy. He proclaimed this policy in the Council's report of 1910:

> It is generally admitted that the relations of the Society, not only to the outside public but to scholars, are far from what they should be, and demand a radical improvement. To accumulate and bury was never the intention of the founders of this Society. To collect and to hold rigidly for the use of the Society would be a suicidal act. The book or the manuscript which enters the doors of this Society has been lost to investigators, on the double plea that it was a private society, and that its collections should be held for the use of its members or its own publications. The Society has lost by cultivating such an impression, and, by what is probably an unconscious narrowness of policy, permitting that impression to become general. . . . Your Council believes in perfect freedom in the use of the Society's accumulations and in giving every facility to those who come to consult them. In this way only can . . . the proper functions of the Society be fulfilled.

Worthington C. Ford (1858–1941)

Despite Ford's forceful pronouncement, change did not occur immediately. Dr. Green was the principal barrier. He was still in command of the library and was not prepared to allow entrance to a horde of academic researchers. This would destroy the clublike character of the Historical Society. But Green was mortal, and his death in 1918 marked the end of the old order and the advent of Ford's open institution, the modern Society.

To this changing institution Stephen T. Riley, a twenty-six-year-old native of Worcester, Massachusetts, who had earned A.B. and A.M. degrees in American history from Clark University, came in 1934 as assistant librarian. Except for three years in military service during World War II, Riley remained until his retirement at the end of 1976. He was appointed librarian in 1947; ten years later he succeeded Stewart Mitchell as director.

Riley's years at the Society constituted a distinct era, a period of unparalleled collection growth. As his long-time colleague Malcolm Freiberg has written: "Where institutional collecting has been concerned, Steve Riley wrote the book." Riley was Jeremy Belknap resurrected, following his paradigm to keep a "good look-out" for things to "fall into the lap," and prowl about constantly "like a wolf for the prey."

In his annual report for 1969 Riley noted, with "the greatest personal satisfaction," the acquisition of the papers of Senator Henry Cabot Lodge (1850–1924), a "truly remarkable collection." The Senator's grandson, Ambassador Henry Cabot Lodge, was the donor. Riley added: "I am certain that at times I reminded Ambassador Lodge of Francis Thompson's poem 'The Hounds of Heaven,' for I did indeed pursue him down the years 'with unhurrying chase and unperturbed pace.'"

On occasion, Riley had to wait until an owner left this earth before acquiring the treasure he was pursuing. A case in point is Henry Lee Shattuck's gift by will of John Singleton Copley's striking portrait of John Hancock (no. 70). Riley worked assiduously for years to add this artistic treasure to the Society's holdings.

Trained as an historian, Riley had an insatiable appetite for manuscripts. He was a tenacious acquisitor, a "manuscript hound extraordinary," as a colleague described him. Riley himself candidly conceded that he had "sticky fingers" when it came to acquiring personal papers of history makers. It was an appropriate admission. When he laid his hands on a document, he never let go until the owner donated the item to the Historical Society.

The capstone of his career came in 1956 when he added two remarkable collections. The first was the Adams Papers, the manuscripts of Presidents John and John Quincy Adams and their family—a collection "beyond price and without peer." In historian-editor Lyman H. Butterfield's words: "No such assemblage of historical records touching so many aspects of American life over so long a period has ever been created and kept together by any other family in this country." The Adams family had begun to place segments of these papers on deposit at the Society for "safe keeping" in 1902. While permitting a few select scholars access to the documents, they maintained a rigid control. For all intents and purposes, it was a closed collection. In 1956, the Adamses deeded the collection to the Society, thereby making it available to all serious researchers. Riley's close relationship with the two key members of the Adams family trust, Thomas Boylston Adams and John Quincy Adams, was a key consideration in their decision.

Riley's second major acquisition in 1956 was the smaller but still imposing and profoundly significant collection, the Paul Revere Papers. The Revere family had placed these documents on deposit at the Society many years earlier, a practice Riley encouraged as an alternative if he could not persuade the owner to make the gift outright. The chances of acquiring a collection rose appreciably if the materials were placed in the physical custody of the Society. In 1956, Edward H. R. Revere, the owner of the papers, transmitted a deed of gift "remarkable for its brevity," together with a great many other Revere papers still in his custody. The "wolf" had made his kill.

While the Society's library had long held the reputation of being one of America's premier repositories, it achieved such Olympian heights in the Riley era that the compilers of the *Harvard Guide to American History*, an authoritative bibliographical reference, could declare that the Historical Society "houses the most important collection of American manuscripts outside the Library of Congress." When Riley became director, he appointed John D. Cushing, a Clark University Ph.D. in American history, as librarian. Until his untimely death in 1987, Cushing was also an extraordinarily successful collector of manuscripts.

Riley's legacy transcended manuscripts. He also collected antique furniture, paintings, and decorative arts. In accepting such artifacts, Riley was motivated as much by functional as by aesthetic considerations. He preferred objects which either could be used in the daily operation of the Society or enhanced "the beauty of our quarters." His annual reports reveal a high degree of selectivity. In 1973, for example, he recorded the following acquisitions: a Simon Willard banjo clock; a large partner's desk (which became the director's desk); a wag-in-the-wall clock; a desk that had belonged to Senator Charles Sumner; copies by Chester Harding of the Gilbert Stuart portraits of Paul and Rachel Revere; a marble statue of a child and tortoise (*Cupid Bound*) by Richard Greenough; and a number of silhouettes of prominent eighteenth-century Englishmen and British Americans. Riley closed this segment of his report with the comment: "I must admit that at times I felt that I had deserted my true love— historical manuscripts—for the world of antiques and art objects."

One other significant development occurred during the Riley era which related to the Society's holdings: there was a dramatic increase in loan requests from museums, historical societies, and other cultural organizations that sponsored exhibitions. From its founding, the Society had generously acceded to loan requests. In 1865, for example, it lent a portrait of Benjamin Lincoln to the Society of the Cincinnati, which was sponsoring a gala Fourth of July dinner. In 1876, it lent four portraits and other items to the Centennial Exposition in Philadelphia. And, in 1936, it provided Harvard College with an assortment of materials relating to the Cambridge institution for the Harvard tercentenary program. Before World War II, however, loan requests were few in number. After the war, a sudden proliferation of museums and historical societies led to a concomitant increase in exhibitions. The demand for high-quality historical materials, from paintings and decorative arts to manuscripts and rare books, grew steadily. Borrowing became a common practice.

Word of the Society's historical riches quickly circulated through the national network of museum and historical society directors and curators. What was more, they reported, the Society was a willing lender. The requests for loans flowed in at an ever-increasing rate, as Riley's reports indicate. In 1975, he cited loans to ten institutions, including such major museums as the Amon Carter Museum, the National Gallery of Art, the National Portrait Gallery, and the Museum of Fine Arts, Boston. The Boston museum had borrowed heavily from the Society for its major exhibition "Paul Revere's Boston, 1735–1818," which Riley called "our favorite exhibition (for we felt in part it was our own)."

All research institutions, including the Society, which collect twentieth-century historical sources face a common set of problems. First and foremost, they must contend with the factor of enormous volume. Whether a political or government figure, business leader or scientist, the modern history maker produces a tremendous body of documents. The technological revolution, from the carbon copy to fax machines, has abetted the paper explosion.

Consider this contrast between the past and the present. The personal and public papers of John and John Quincy Adams, which embrace all aspects of their long and active lives, including their presidencies, occupy a mere ninety linear feet of shelf space in the Society—

Stephen T. Riley

and both men were prolific writers in their respective periods. On the other hand, Leverett Saltonstall's papers, which relate almost entirely to his senatorial career, arrived at the Society in 1969 in a huge moving van in eight hundred cartons, which weighed nine tons, and occupied about seven hundred thirty-five linear feet of shelf space. Saltonstall's papers represent the rule, not the exception. The papers of modern presidents fill entire buildings, though these officials cannot serve beyond eight years. Few modern research libraries are blessed with sufficient free space to accommodate many collections of this magnitude.

These gargantuan collections also require a large staff for processing, cataloging, and the preparation of finding aids. To become usable to researchers, a collection must be brought under intellectual control.

While material from the seventeenth, eighteenth, and nineteenth centuries continues to arrive, the Society faces the timeless challenge of building representative collections within real physical space constraints. Formats ranging from photocopies and carbons to videocassettes and computer disks add to the complications. However, the Society has never shrunk from a challenge, and will continue to the best of its abilities to collect, preserve, and publish for the benefit of American historical scholarship.

Jeremy Belknap would no doubt be pleased at the success of today's Historical Society and its reputation in the international academic community. The seeds he planted in 1791 have been fostered by generations of collectors, librarians, and historians, and the holdings continue to strengthen as the Historical Society enters its third century of collecting.

Color Plates and Catalogue

*V M Galli in Floridam provinciam . secunda navigatione instituta duce Laudonniero, appulis-
sent, ipse comitibus quinque & viginti pyxidarijs in continentem descendit . salute ab Indis ac-*

1. Illustration from Theodor de Bry's *America*, 1590–1595 (no. 11)

11. *Mrs. Baker*, 1675 (no. 23)

III. Embroidery of Harvard Hall, eighteenth century (no. 45)

IV. *The Bloody Massacre perpetrated in King Street, Boston on March 5th, 1770* by Paul Revere (no. 48)

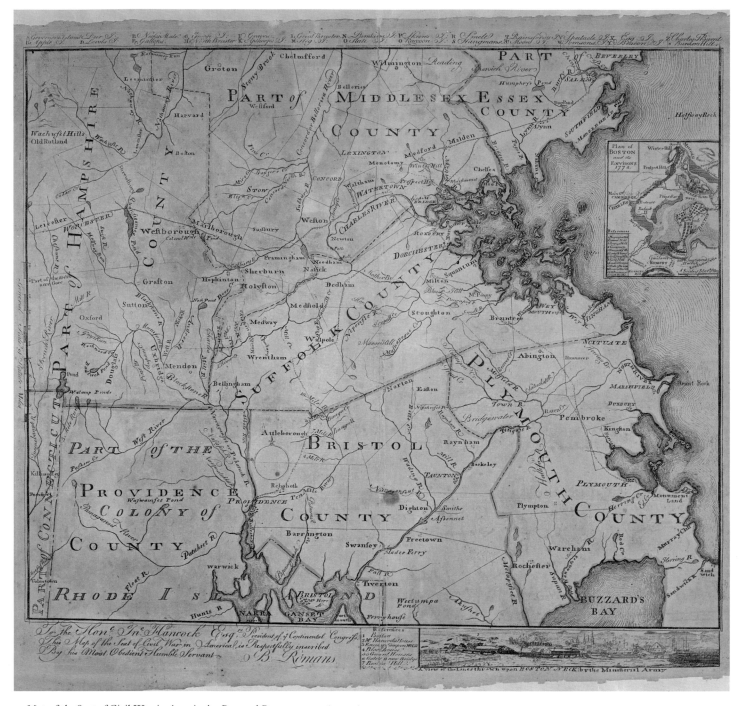

v. *Map of the Seat of Civil War in America* by Bernard Romans, 1775 (no. 56)

VI. *Gilbert du Motier, Marquis de Lafayette* by Joseph Boze, 1790 (no. 71)

VII. George Washington's Gorget (no. 86)

VIII. *Brook Farm* by Josiah Wolcott, 1844 (no. 138)

ix. Elizabeth "Mumbet" Freeman by Susan Sedgwick, 1811
(no. 144)

x. *Daniel Webster* by Sarah Goodridge, 1827 (no. 122)

1

1

Shem Drowne (1683–1776)
Indian Archer weathervane
Boston, ca. 1716
Hammered copper, traces of original gilding, amber-colored glass eye
H. 53¾ in. (136.8 cm), W. 46½ in. (118.2 cm), D. 1¾ in. (4.3 cm)
Gift of Emily Warren Appleton, 1876

The Indian Archer weathervane with traces of its original gilding and a curious amber-colored glass eye represents the Native American from the old colonial seal of Massachusetts Bay and was made to stand on the cupola of Boston's Province House, where it soon became a local landmark. In the nineteenth century, Nathaniel Hawthorne described the weathervane in his story "Drowne's Wooden Image" as "an Indian chief, gilded all over," which "stood during the better part of a century on the cupola of Province House, bedazzling the eyes of those who looked upward, like an angel of the sun." Hawthorne's "Legends of the Province House" went on to describe the bow and arrow "as if aiming at the weathercock on the spire of the Old South."

The Province House dated from 1679, and in 1716 the General Court purchased the large brick home nearly opposite the Old South Church as the official residence of the governor. As symbols of the government, the royal coat of arms (now also in the collections of the Society) was installed over the doorway, and the Indian archer weathervane graced the cupola. The first official resident was probably Governor Shute, and then Governors Burnet, Shirley, Pownall, Bernard, Gage, and Howe lived here in succession. Thomas Hutchinson had his own stately townhouse. In 1817 the state contributed the estate to the Massachusetts General Hospital, and the

hospital leased it for ninety-nine years to David Greenough (1774–1836), a builder and real-estate developer, who covered the half acre with various buildings. The Province House itself was turned into a tavern and was later destroyed in a fire in 1864. The land reverted to the hospital at the expiration of the lease in 1916.[1] Today, the original exterior steps leading to the mansion are still visible on Province Street as a reminder of this old focal point for colonial Boston.

Shem Drowne, the artisan who created this vane, was the best-known tinplate worker in early Boston. Born in Kittery, Maine, Drowne came to Boston as a young boy with his family. Several of Drowne's other vanes survive in the Boston area, including a rooster (1721) now on the First Church in Cambridge, Congregational; a swallow-tail banneret (1740) at the Old North Church; and his most famous, the grasshopper (1742) atop Faneuil Hall.[2] Drowne became unusually prosperous for an eighteenth-century artisan and owned property both in Boston and in New Hampshire.[3] One of his sons, Thomas, followed him in tinplate work, and his daughter Sarah married the Boston bookdealer Jeremiah Condy, who was also minister of the First Baptist Church, where Drowne himself was a deacon.

The Indian archer weathervane came into the possession of Henry Greenough of Cambridge, the son of developer David Greenough, and from him went to Dr. John Collins Warren, a founder of the Massachusetts General Hospital.[4] Dr. Warren placed it atop his house in Brookline, which in 1856 was inherited by his daughter, who presented the weathervane to the Society in 1876.

E.W.H.

1. *MHS Proceedings*, 1st ser., 15(1876–1877): 178–180.
2. Bishop 1981, p. 15.
3. SCP, 73:387.
4. Washburn 1939, p. 561.

2

Samuel Hill (ca. 1766–1804) and Joseph Callender (1751–1821), after Osgood Carleton (1742–1816). Vignette drawn by George Graham (fl. 1794–1812)
Map of Massachusetts Proper
Boston: Published by Benjamin & Josiah Loring, 1802
Engraving
32 in. (81.5 cm) x 47¼ in. (120 cm)
Inscribed: *Map / of /* MASSACHUSETTS *Proper /* COMPILED *from* ACTUAL SURVEYS */ made by order of the / General Court, / and under the inspection of Agents / of their appointment. / By Osgood Carleton.*
From the Archives of the Massachusetts Historical Society

In January 1795, the Massachusetts Historical Society applied to the General Court of Massachusetts "for the exclusive power of compiling a map, for the benefit of the Society, from the returns which may be made of plans in this State, ordered by the Legislature."[1]

The genesis of the first official map of the state was in 1791 when Osgood Carleton, one of the first professional mapmakers in America, suggested a regional map of southern New England based on town surveys. The

Historical Society helped persuade the Massachusetts General Court to pass a state mapping law in 1794 which required all towns in the state, including the District of Maine, to produce town surveys on a standard scale of 3300 feet to an inch by June 1, 1795, for use in producing an official map. Many of these detailed manuscript plans survive in the Massachusetts State Archives.[2]

For reasons that do not appear in surviving records, after a long delay, the General Court rejected the proposal by the Historical Society to publish a state map in favor of competitive bids from Boston commercial mapmakers. Osgood Carleton, one of the most active American mapmakers of the post-Revolutionary period, made the winning proposal in 1797. Born at Nottingham, New Hampshire, Carleton saw brief service as an artillerist in the British Army during the French and Indian War and fought at the Battle of Bunker Hill during the Revolution. Along with Richard Gridley, another early Boston mapmaker whose work is included in this catalogue (see no. 40), he was one of the few Americans trained in military engineering and mapmaking. After the Revolution, Carleton opened a school for navigation, mathematics, and cartography on Oliver's Dock in Boston. There he published navigation and mathematics textbooks as well as maps of Boston, Massachusetts, the District of Maine, New Hampshire, the United States, nautical charts, and a marine atlas.[3]

While the Historical Society was not the sponsoring agency for the map, it did remain intimately involved in the publication. In 1795, Carleton had drawn a map of Maine to accompany James Sullivan's *History of the Dis-trict of Maine*. Sullivan, then attorney general of Massachusetts, was also the first president of the Massachusetts Historical Society. The Society loaned manuscript maps from its own files to Carleton, and members of the Society served on the committee that inspected the engraved plates John Norman made for the map.

After many delays, the engraved plates for the official map were inspected by the state committee and judged unsatisfactory. Carleton and Norman took their rejected printing plates and from them published commercial maps of Massachusetts and the District of Maine. A new team of engravers and a new publisher took the information Carleton had re-compiled from the town surveys, after his original effort had been rejected. The official map was re-engraved by Joseph Callender and Samuel Hill and published by Benjamin and Josiah Loring in 1801. The 1801 edition was paid for by the state and distributed to the towns. A second edition was published at state expense in 1802 for the use of court officials, members of the legislature, and schools located in the commonwealth.

In 1800, while work on the map was still underway, a committee of members of the Historical Society and the American Academy of Arts and Sciences petitioned the legislature for the printing plates for the maps, for the use of the two societies. In 1801, the legislature granted a fourteen-year copyright, after copies were struck off for official use. The Society and the Academy were to share proceeds from ownership, but there is no evidence that either organization ever profited from the arrangement or retained the engraved plates.[4]

Mapmaking has been described as the art that became a science. The *Map of Massachusetts Proper* was published at a time when geographical data was increasingly available to cartographers. At the same time, in its final form, it represents the work of some of the most skillful Boston engravers and printers of the day. Since 1801, the Society has withdrawn from the mapmaking business in favor of map collecting. In the library of the Society are more than 5,000 early maps, nautical charts, city plans, views, and atlases, both manuscript and published, as well as a large number of modern maps, facsimiles, and redrawings to support research in American history.

P.D.

1. MHS *Proceedings*, 1st ser., 1(1791–1835): 81.
2. Danforth 1983, pp. 37–39.
3. Ristow 1985, pp. 68–70.
4. Danforth 1983, pp. 42–44.

3

The American Apollo, January 6, 1792. Vol. 1, No. 1, Part 1
Boston: Printed by Belknap and Young, 1792
Newspaper
12 p., 9¼ in. (23.5 cm) x 5½ in. (14 cm)
From the Archives of the Massachusetts Historical Society

In early discussions about the establishment of the Massachusetts Historical Society, founder Jeremy Belknap considered the "multiplication of copies" of manuscripts and books for access by future generations to be equally as important as the actual collection and preservation of original items. On November 1, 1791, Belknap stated in his *Circular Letter* (see no. 4) that he had received proposals for publishing documents in the *American Apollo*, a soon-to-be-published periodical, intended to cultivate the intellectual curiosity of post-colonial society. The publishers were a young team of Boston printers, Alexander Young and, not coincidentally, Jeremy's eldest son, Joseph Belknap.

On January 6, 1792, a permanent form of the Society's collections began appearing in the *American Apollo*. Four to eight pages were set aside every week for material from the Society on the "natural, political and ecclesiastical history of this country."[1] Jeremy Belknap alone was responsible for the selection of documents and preparation of copy. For the first issue, he chose documents relating to the victorious expedition of Massachusetts troops to Cape Breton in 1745, a selection designed to promote local patriotism (and the *Apollo*).[2] At the beginning the paper was popular, with 1200 Bostonians as subscribers at a cost of two dollars per year, although subscriptions dropped dramatically after the first quarter.[3] The May 11, June 15, and August 3, 1792 issues provided lists of donations to the Society by nonmembers, an attempt to publicize names and encourage future donations.[4] With financial assistance from the Historical Society, the *American Apollo* published the Library's collections from January 6 to September 28, 1792, thirty-nine numbers in all, 208 pages of published collections in volume one.[5] The printers supplied the Society with fifty complementary copies of each issue, thereby assuring a future for

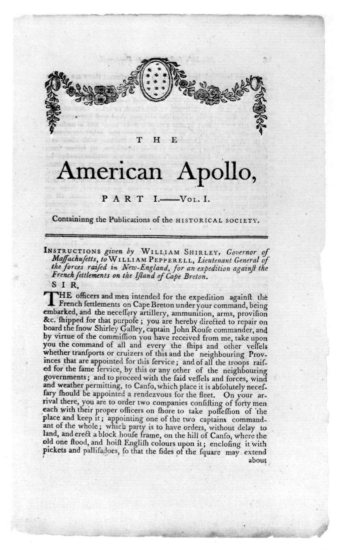

3

historical research in the event that original items were lost.

In September of 1792, the Society discontinued its weekly association with the newspaper in favor of a separate publication of the collections in monthly issues of twenty-four pages, which was still printed by the Apollo Press through September 1794.[6] Shortly after the Society's printing contract moved to the firm of Samuel Hall, the *American Apollo* ceased all publication.

The series which began in the *Apollo* in 1792 still appears on an occasional basis, publishing edited historical documents under the title of the *Collections of the Massachusetts Historical Society*.

M.E.C.

1. MHS *Proceedings*, 1st ser., 1(1791–1835): xx.
2. Tucker 1990, p. 127.
3. Ibid., pp. 125, 127.
4. MHS *Proceedings*, 1st ser., 1(1791–1835): 31.
5. Ibid., p. xxv.
6. Ibid., p. xxvi.

4

Jeremy Belknap (1744–1798)
Circular Letter of the Historical Society
Boston: Printed by Belknap and Young, 1791
Pamphlet
3 p., 8⅛ in. (21.7 cm) x 4⅞ in. (12.4 cm)
From the Archives of the Massachusetts Historical
Society

About ten months after the founding of the Historical Society, Jeremy Belknap drafted a *Circular Letter of the Historical Society*, dated November 1, 1791, for the purpose of announcing the formation of the Society, defining its objectives, and particularly for soliciting historical contributions for the library. The letter was the Society's first publication and in many ways its most important, establishing the new organization as a repository of historical material and stating that such collections would be accessible to the public. "Belknap's vision of the Society as a private organization endowed with a public responsibility . . . was not unusual"[1] for late-eighteenth-century Bostonians. As the *Circular Letter* stated: "Any person desirous of making a search among the books or manuscripts, may have access to them." This attitude of accessibility by the public to its intellectual heritage was a reflection of America's fight for democracy.

After stating the Society's function, Belknap indicated that collections would be published in the *American Apollo*, a local periodical of intellectual curiosities (see no. 3). Although the Society did not have a formal collecting policy, Belknap requested contributions in the following areas of colonial, revolutionary, and independent American history: town histories and genealogical records, wars and battles, personal narratives of suffering and captivities, histories of local churches, biographical memoirs, geographical, meteorological and topographical descriptions, census and vital records, modes of education, and commentaries on travel, navigation, manufacturing and commerce. The contributions could be in the form of "books, pamphlets, manuscripts, maps or plans," as well as "natural or artificial productions which may enlarge its museum."

The circular letter was sent to members, prospective members, friends, and "other gentlemen of public character"; it was later published in the *American Apollo*, and eventually revised and expanded for subsequent solicitations. Through repeated distribution of this circular letter and his constant personal persuasion, Belknap actively pursued the sources upon which organized historical research would rely. As a result, he successfully established the Massachusetts Historical Society as the institution to assume the responsibility of collecting, preserving, and making accessible material for American historical research.[2]

M.E.C.

1. Tucker 1990, p. 135.
2. Ibid., p. 141.

5

Catalogue of Books in the Massachusetts Historical Library
Boston: Printed by Samuel Hall, 1796
Pamphlet
40 p., 8⅞ in. (22.6 cm) x 5¼ in. (13.3 cm)
From the Archives of the Massachusetts Historical
Society

During the course of the first two meetings of the Historical Society in 1791, the founding members agreed that a record should be maintained and eventually published of books in the library. John Eliot, the first librarian, began keeping accession records at the second meeting in April 1791. This list probably served as the only catalogue until newly elected recording secretary Thomas Wallcut began a formal alphabetical listing of all titles. Through his diligent efforts, Wallcut completed the project around 1793; it remained the Library's working catalogue until, after a few years of discussion, the Society agreed to publication.[1]

The first published catalogue of the Library, entitled *Catalogue of Books in the Massachusetts Historical Library*, was printed for the Society in Boston by Samuel Hall in 1796. The 40-page catalogue consists of 1035 entries, including some duplicates, listed in single columns. It is an unsystematic, imperfect, alphabetical arrangement with a mixture of author/title entries; subject or genre entries; short, abbreviated or incomplete title entries; or a combination of any of the above descriptions. Place and date of

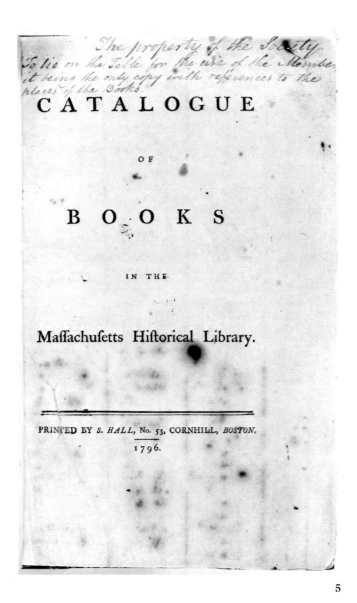

Belknap provided the single largest gift—171 titles, nearly 15 percent of the total catalogue.[3]

The 1796 catalogue includes a variety of subjects, mostly titles on political, social, economic, religious, and historical events of the time, relating to colonial and independent America. But there are also titles reflecting the personal interests of the donors, including histories of foreign countries, ordination and funeral sermons, medical essays, personal narratives on Indian captivities and wars, domestic essays on social behavior and child rearing, and analytical discourses on scientific phenomena.

This copy of the 1796 catalogue came directly from the librarian's desk, with manuscript notes on the cover indicating its purpose as the working catalogue: "The property of the Society to lie on the table for the use of the members; it being the only copy with references to the places of the books." Shelf marks were recorded at some unknown date beside the titles and bound at the beginning of the catalogue is an "Explanation of the marks," describing in detail the specific arrangement of books in the library.

As part of its bicentennial celebrations, the Society will publish a new edition of the 1796 catalogue, complete with full bibliographic annotations, which were begun by the late librarian, John D. Cushing.

M.E.C.

1. MHS *Proceedings*, 2d ser., 8(1892–1894): 325.
2. Ibid., p. 321.
3. Tucker 1990, p. 101.

publication are usually included, with volume number and size periodically supplied. The catalogue excluded unbound books and pamphlets, European publications without an American connection, and large collections of newspapers in the library. Inclusiveness also proved elusive due to problems with record keeping and borrowing privileges. A book sale recorded in 1796 and an agreement to exchange duplicates further complicated the compilation of a complete accessions record.[2] Despite these flaws, the 1796 catalogue reveals much about the original core of printed material in the library and is the unique example of a historical society collection in eighteenth-century America.

The first donors to the library were the original founders of the Historical Society, British subjects by birth, independent Americans by choice, ministers, historians, lawyers, librarians, and politicians by profession. Jeremy Belknap, John Eliot, James Freeman, Peter Thacher, James Sullivan, William Tudor, Thomas Wallcut, and James Winthrop began contributing books to the library at Belknap's request by the second meeting in 1791. Books were given from personal libraries and collections, with no indication that purchases were made specifically for donation. As membership to the Society grew additional donations were received, but Jeremy

6

Abraham Hayward (ca. 1734–1796) and William Blake
Windsor Chair
Boston, 1791
Pine, ash, and maple (?), green paint overpainted with black, metal bracing
H. 37 1/8 in. (94.3 cm), W. 24 3/16 in. (61.4 cm); Seat H. 17 7/8 in. (45.5 cm), Seat D. 14 3/4 in. (37.5 cm)
Purchased from Hayward and Blake, 1791

On June 30, 1791 the Historical Society convened at its first home, the Library Room of the Massachusetts Bank. The "Proceedings at the 3d meeting of Historical Society"—the first meeting held at the Bank—record a vote "that the Treasurer be desired to purchase twelve chairs, a plain pine table painted, with a draw & lock & key, also an Inkstand."[1] The secretary's notes further specified the chairs were to be "Elbow & Green."[2]

The purchase of these chairs is recorded in a receipt, dated September 1, 1791, at Boston, showing that "Willim Tuder Esqr Bought of Hayward and Blake twelve chairs for Society @ 8/" for a total of £4 16s. 0.[3] The painted table, complete with lock and key, had been supplied by Isaac Durell in July for 15 shillings.[4]

Before moving from the Bank to Faneuil Hall in the summer of 1792, the Society made at least three more purchases of furniture. The sum of £1 10s. was paid for "nine boxes calculated for books" to William Appleton; £2 14s. for "Making a Cabinet Compleat" to Hayward and Blake; and £1 for "five Case's to put Books in" to Abraham Hayward.[5]

6

1. Minutes of the Historical Society, June 30, 1791. MHS Archives.
2. Records of the Recording Secretary, MHS Archives, vol. 1, p. 16.
3. General Correspondence (Chiefly Financial), 1791–1860, MHS Archives.
4. Ibid.
5. Ibid., June 27, 1791; Jan. 30, 1792; March 30, 1792.
6. Kaye 1974, p. 283.
7. *NEHGR* 140(1986): 152.
8. *Independent Chronicle*, June 18, 1789.
9. MHS *Proceedings*, 1st ser., 3(1855–1858): 167.
10. Santore 1981, pp. 31, 35.
11. Ibid., p. 48.

Abraham Hayward was a Boston cabinetmaker with a shop located on Ann Street in 1789 and later on White Bread Alley.[6] By 1791 he was in the partnership of Hayward & Blake, probably with William Blake.[7] Blake was another local chair maker specializing in the popular Windsor style. He specifically advertised "Green Winsor Chairs" along with other pieces made at his shop in Fore Street including, "at a low price, Round-top chairs fanback Garden-Chairs, Soffas, stuff-seat Chairs, and a large Assortment of Dinning Chairs, painted equally as well as those made at Philadelphia."[8]

The Historical Society's original chairs were used until 1857, when the newly installed Dowse Library, with its elegant furnishings, displaced them. At that time, then President Robert C. Winthrop expressed his hope that the original furniture would "be sacredly preserved as memorials of our small beginnings."[9] This chair is the last remaining item from the original furnishings.

Windsor chairs were the basic utility chairs of the late eighteenth century. The style developed in England prior to 1720 and was brought to America a decade or two later.[10] The Historical Society's sack-back Windsor chair is a sturdy and elegant, if worn, piece. Its original green paint—the conventional color at the time it was made[11]—has since been covered with black. The matching pattern of the turned legs and arm supports is comparatively complex. The elbow rests are carved but have no scroll. Metal reinforcing rods were added probably during the nineteenth century.

H.J.C.

7

Gilbert Stuart (1755–1828)
James Sullivan (1744–1808)
1807
Oil on panel
33 in. (83.8 cm) x 26½ in. (67.3 cm)
Bequest of Richard Sullivan, 1908

James Sullivan served as the first president of the Massachusetts Historical Society, from its founding in 1791 until 1806. Before his unanimous election to this post, the then forty-seven-year-old jurist and politician had already had an illustrious career. Born in Berwick, Maine, on April 22, 1744, James was the fourth son of John and Margery Sullivan. His father, an Irish Catholic immigrant, was the local schoolmaster and also educated his own family in the classics and the Bible. Sullivan became apprenticed to his elder brother, a lawyer practicing in Durham, New Hampshire, and by 1767, he set up his own practice in Georgetown, Maine, before marrying

7

Mehitable Odiorne of Durham in 1768. He was appointed King's Attorney for York County and admitted to practice before the Superior Court in 1770.[1]

Sullivan participated in the Revolution on the local level as commander-in-chief of the militia and as a member of the provincial congress in both 1774 and 1775.[2] He was appointed as a Justice of the Supreme Court of Massachusetts in 1776. Because the court still rode circuit at that time, Sullivan chose Groton, Massachusetts, as a more central residence in 1778. He was then chosen to represent the town as a delegate to the Constitutional Convention (1779).[3]

In 1782 Sullivan again relocated, this time to Boston. Soon after his arrival there, he built a large and lucrative law practice in the capital and was elected a delegate to Congress in 1783.[4] Early in 1786, his wife died leaving him with the care of six children, but within the year Sullivan met and married the young widow Martha Simpson.

As a staunch Jeffersonian anti-Federalist, Sullivan was a friend and ally to John Hancock, whom he supported in Hancock's two unsuccessful bids for the vice presidency in 1788 and 1789. Sullivan received a great deal of public criticism for his unquestioned support of Hancock.[5] However, despite the negative press, in 1790 he was appointed attorney general of Massachusetts, a position he held for seventeen years. Sullivan ran for governor of Massachusetts several times, but he was not elected until 1807. Reelected in 1808, he died in office.

Sullivan had a long-standing friendship with Jeremy Belknap based on a mutual love of history and a desire to preserve documentary sources from the ravages of time and indifference. As a new member of the Brattle Street Church, Sullivan supported Belknap in his unsuccessful bid for the pulpit in 1783 and 1784. Although Sullivan was not directly involved in the planning stages of the Society, he was invited by the five original members (Belknap, Eliot, Thacher, Tudor and Winthrop) to join, when they decided to expand their group to ten members. It was at the second organizational meeting of the Society, on January 24, 1791 that the officers were chosen. As Louis L. Tucker points out, "Sullivan, a man of Olympian stature in Boston" was the "unanimous choice" for president.[6]

Soon after his election as president, Sullivan donated two 1692 pine tree coins, the first gifts which the Society received. He also contributed the royalties earned by two of his most important books, *History of the District of Maine* (1794) and *History of Land Titles in Massachusetts* (1801).[7] Like the other founding members, Sullivan donated important books from his own library to the Society's fledgling collection. It was largely through his effort that the Society was legally incorporated in 1794.[8] During his fifteen-year term as president, Sullivan presided over the Society in its first three homes.

When Gilbert Stuart painted James Sullivan, the artist had been in Boston for only two years. Already established as the town's premier portrait painter, he was in great demand by Boston luminaries. Although Stuart was over fifty and not always in the best of health, his painting ability had not diminished. This astute portrait of Sullivan, taken near the end of his life is characteristic of Stuart's late style. The artist used luminous color thinly applied to the canvas to give Sullivan both a wonderful intensity and a sense of dignity appropriate to his age and his position in society. The book which Sullivan holds, alluding perhaps to his love of history, or to his legal profession. Another version of this painting by Stuart and dating from the same year is now at the Museum of Fine Arts, Boston.[9]

S.R.M.

1. Sibley 1873, 15:300.
2. MHS *Collections*, 1:252.
3. Sibley 1873, 15:304.
4. Tucker 1990, p. 91.
5. Sibley 1873, 15:311.
6. Tucker 1990, p. 95.
7. Sibley 1873, 15:312.
8. Amory 1859, p. 356.
9. Oliver 1988, p. 100.

8

John Trumbull (1756–1843)
Christopher Gore (1758–1829)
London, 1802–1804
Oil on panel
29 in. (73.7 cm) x 24 in. (60.8 cm)
Purchased by subscription, 1844

Christopher Gore, the second president of the Massachusetts Historical Society (1806–1818), was born in Boston, the youngest son of John and Frances (Pinckney) Gore. His father, a heraldic and coach painter, also owned a prosperous "color shop" on Queen Street.[1] Gore entered Harvard at the age of thirteen, and it was there that he met two young men who would become close friends and colleagues, Rufus King (1755–1827) and John Trumbull. After graduating in 1776, Gore studied law and set up his own practice where he "rose rapidly in the public esteem as a sound lawyer . . . and as an honest man."[2] Appointed by Washington in 1789, Gore became the first United States Attorney for the District of Massachusetts and in the 1790s became active in the nation's new banking system as a director of the Boston branch of the Bank of the United States.[3]

Seven years later, Gore joined William Pinckney and his college friend John Trumbull as commissioners under the Jay Treaty to resolve war claims made by American citizens against the British. As a result, Gore and Trumbull spent eight years (1796–1804) together in London with Rufus King, who was then the United States minister to Great Britain. Returning to America in 1804, Gore resumed his law practice and his involvement in local politics as a state senator and representative. He also served one term as the governor of Massachusetts (1809–1810). After losing his bid for reelection to Elbridge Gerry, Gore retired from practicing law and moved to his summer residence in Waltham, Gore Place, considered "one of the most elegant in this part of the country."[4]

Despite Gore's desire to retire from public life, Governor Strong appointed him senator from Massachusetts in 1814 to fill an unexpected vacancy. Reluctantly, Gore accepted the position, which he held until 1816, when failing health led to a permanent retirement. After a long illness, Gore died at his home in 1829.

8

Trumbull painted this portrait while serving with Gore on the Jay Treaty Commission, depicting his friend as a middle-aged statesman, which belies the close relationship between the two. Trumbull chose a pyramidal, neoclassical composition which was a popular format for contemporary English portraits of men, although he has abandoned the fine colors of earlier portraits for a somber palette which is relieved only by the glowing white shirt and the rich red drapery. Taken together, the drapery, the column, and the books allude to Gore's classical education as well as his current position as a representative of the United States government. Another version of this portrait is part of the Trumbull Collection, Yale University Art Gallery.[5]

The multitalented John Trumbull came from a better-connected family than did Gore. His father, John Trumbull (1710–1785) served as the governor of Connecticut during most of the Revolution. An accident at an early age left the future artist blind in his left eye but did not deter his studies, and at the age of fifteen he qualified to enter Harvard as a third year student. Graduating in 1773, Trumbull later wrote that he had

> formed one and only one intimate acquaintance. It was with Christopher Gore of Boston, an amiable boy, my junior in years. . . . This was the commencement of a friendship which lasted through life.

Against his father's wishes, Trumbull wanted to be an artist and to study painting. However, the Revolutionary War altered his plans. Trumbull joined the first Connecticut regiment which arrived in Boston in May 1775. He captured Washington's notice after attempting to survey and draw a plan of the enemy's fortifications. Trumbull was rewarded for his efforts by serving for nineteen days in July 1775, as Washington's second aide-de-camp, an honor he referred to throughout his long life.[6]

After his service ended, Trumbull spent a year in Boston copying works of art before leaving to study in Europe.[7] Armed with a letter of introduction from Benjamin Franklin, Trumbull became a student of Benjamin West at the same time as Gilbert Stuart. Unfortunately, Trumbull's plans were again interrupted when he was arrested for high treason in 1780 for bearing arms against the Crown. After seven months in prison, Trumbull returned home to Connecticut.

As the end of the war approached, Trumbull returned to London to continue his studies with West and at the Royal Academy. It was at this time that Trumbull, inspired by his mentor West and encouraged by Thomas Jefferson, began his "national history" series of the American Revolution.[8] He became the first to paint the key episodes of American history as a means of conveying the values and lessons of the Revolution. The first painting he completed depicts the death of General Warren at the Battle of Bunker Hill (Yale University Art Gallery). In 1787, with Jefferson's assistance, Trumbull began work on his famous painting *The Declaration of Independence* (completed 1820, Yale University Art Gallery).

The years 1789–1794 were perhaps the artist's most productive.[9] He returned to America in order to paint the portraits of the Revolutionary heroes whom he planned to include in his history paintings. George Washington sat for Trumbull several times for *General George Washington at the Battle of Trenton* (1792, Yale University Art Gallery). Following this period of almost feverish activity, Trumbull spent ten more years in London as a commissioner for the Jay Treaty with Christopher Gore. He settled in New York in 1804, but soon returned to London for another eight years (1808–1816). Failing to establish himself there as a fashionable portrait painter, Trumbull returned in 1816 to New York, where he spent the next twenty years with mixed success. Although he obtained some important commissions, such as the four large paintings (1817–1824) for the Rotunda of the United States Capitol, Washington, D.C., he never equaled the promise of his early work.

In 1831 Trumbull gave his personal collection of paintings to Yale University in exchange for an annuity. The gallery which housed the paintings was designed by Trumbull and opened in 1832 as the first art museum to be connected with an educational institution in America.[10]

The Society has two manuscript maps of Connecticut which Trumbull made for his father in 1773. The Washburn Papers also contain a small group of letters from Gore to Trumbull. In addition, the Society owns a Trumbull portrait of Grenville Temple (ca. 1797), as well as Joseph Wright's portrait of George Washington (1784), which was completed by Trumbull in 1786.[11]

S.R.M.

1. Hammond 1982, p. 7.
2. Greenwood 1827, p. 9.
3. Hammond 1982, p. 83.
4. MHS *Collections*, 2d ser., 3:272.
5. Cooper 1982, p. 158.
6. Trumbull 1953, pp. xviii, 6, 10, 45.
7. Ibid., p. 44.
8. Sizer 1967, p. 7.
9. Ibid.
10. Ibid., p. xi.
11. Oliver 1988, pp. 101, 111.

9

9

Hiram Powers (1805–1873)
Robert Charles Winthrop (1809–1894)
Florence, 1871
Marble
H. 27 in. (68.2 cm), W. 16 ⅝ (42.2 cm), D. 14 ⅝ in. (37.1 cm)
Signed, on back: H POWERS / *Sculp.*
Gift of Elizabeth Mason Winthrop, 1918

Robert Charles Winthrop was born in 1809 into a family prominent in Massachusetts history since Boston's founding by Governor John Winthrop in 1630. His mother's family added descents from Governor James Bowdoin and Sir John Temple, the royal customs collector for New England. Robert C. Winthrop organized the tangible portion of this heritage as the Winthrop Papers and Bowdoin-Temple Papers, which are now at the Historical Society together with numerous paintings and other pieces of family memorabilia. Eleven generations are represented in this collection, which is one of the most comprehensive of its type in this country.

After graduating from Harvard in 1828, Winthrop read law in the Boston office of Daniel Webster and was admitted to the bar in 1831. He went into politics as a state representative from Boston, and served in the House for six years, including three as Speaker. From there he was elected to the federal Congress in 1840, and when the Whigs gained a majority in 1847 was elected Speaker. When Webster was appointed secretary of state in 1850, Winthrop was appointed senator in his stead. After being defeated for the position of governor of Massachusetts in 1851, Winthrop withdrew from politics.

Since 1839 Winthrop had been a member of the Massachusetts Historical Society, and in 1855 was elected pres-

ident, a position which he held for thirty years. During his tenure, the Society grew both in size—raising its statutory membership level from sixty to one hundred—and in stature, primarily through an increase in publications, to which Winthrop himself contributed heavily. His two-volume biography of Governor John Winthrop received critical acclaim at its publication.[1]

Powers modeled this bust in 1868 at Florence, during an extended European vacation by the Winthrops. The first marble, an undraped version now in the Harvard Portrait Collection, was completed in 1869 and displayed by Winthrop at the Boston Athenaeum upon its arrival. As the first bust was intended for Winthrop's stepson, George Derby Welles, a second was also ordered for Mrs. Winthrop. However, the second bust was to have drapery added, "both to make a little variety, & because she herself prefers a bust with drapery over the shoulders. She wishes it also to match another bust in our hall, which has a full drapery."[2] A plaster cast of the draped version was presented to the Historical Society in 1899 to replace an 1859 Winthrop bust by Henry Dexter which was considered "Weak in design and execution" and a "failure both as a work of art and as respects portraiture."[3] In 1918 Winthrop's daughter-in-law presented the marble draped version to the Society.

Hiram Powers made his early reputation in Washington, where he sculpted portrait busts of the nation's officials from 1835 until late 1837. It was, however, after he moved to Italy and established himself in Florence, that his real fame developed. There, the 1840s saw a new American school of sculpture developing around the expatriates Powers and Horatio Greenough.[4] Americans flocked to Powers's studio for portrait busts which provided a steady income while he began a series of idealized sculptures. The *Greek Slave* (1843) in particular brought Powers admiring reviews both in Europe and in America, where it was acclaimed, although the nude presentation was the object of debate.[5] The *Greek Slave* is considered a milestone in American art because it, more than any other single piece, spurred the public to discuss the work of an American sculptor.[6]

The Society also holds a marble bust of the philanthropist George Peabody (1868) by Powers, as well as a plaster cast of his bust of Jared Sparks.

E.W.H.

1. Mayo 1948, pp. 315–345.
2. Robert C. Winthrop to Hiram Powers, Brookline, Mass., Oct. 28, 1869. Hiram Powers Papers, AAA-SI, microfilm reel 1144.
3. MHS *Proceedings*, 3d ser., 1(1907–1908): 98.
4. Reynolds 1977, p. 94.
5. Crane 1972, pp. 169–269.
6. *DAB*.

10

Truman Howe Bartlett (1835–1923)
Samuel Abbott Green (1830–1918)
Paris, 1883
Bronze
H. 24 ⅞ (58 cm), W. 13 ⅞ in. (35.3 cm), D. 8 ¾ in. (22.3 cm)
Inscribed, on back: DR. S. A. GREEN, / MAYOR OF BOSTON. / *Made by THB, Oct. / 1882.*; beneath left shoulder: GRUET J^NE FONDEUR. / PARIS.; beneath right shoulder: MADE IN / BRONZE FOR / THE SAINT BO / TOLPH CLUB. / *1883.*
Gift of the sitter, 1883

Dr. Samuel Abbott Green was a leading member of the Massachusetts Historical Society for fifty-eight years, and is remembered at the Society today for his domineering personality as much as his scholarly contributions and direction of the library. A native of Groton, Massachusetts, and eventual historian of his native town, Green trained as a physician at the Harvard Medical School and in Vienna. He practiced medicine in Boston until 1861 when he entered the army as a surgeon during the Civil War, ending the war as a brevetted lieutenant colonel and acting staff surgeon in Richmond. After the war, he returned to his medical practice in Boston, became city physician, and served one term as the city's mayor (1882).

Among his many voluntary activities, Green became cabinet keeper (curator of the museum collection) of the Historical Society in 1860, a few months after he was elected to membership. In 1868 he added on the part-time position of librarian, a post he retained until his death in 1918. His zealous guardianship of the Society's collections became legendary and earned him the reputation of a "growling Cerberus" keeping away intruders. The eminent historian Samuel Eliot Morison, while a graduate student at Harvard, was even denied use of the card catalogue.[1] Green's stout figure and difficult personality were familiar fixtures at the Historical Society until old age and illness rendered his visits fewer and required two assistants to help him up the stairs to his office.[2]

This bronze bust was executed in the year Green served as Boston's mayor and portrays him as a large, vigorous, middle-aged man, with bare chest and bristling mustache. Another bronze casting of this bust is at the Saint Botolph Club in Boston, and in 1885 the sculptor presented a plaster cast of it to the Boston Public Library.[3]

Truman Howe Bartlett studied under Robert Launitz in New York and later studied in Paris, Rome, and Perugia. From his days working in Connecticut, the Wells and Clark monuments in Hartford are the best remembered examples of his work, along with the later *The Wounded Drummer Boy of Shiloh*. His bust of Dr. Green exemplifies the "characteristic Civil War-era academic naturalism" for which he was known.[4] Among his other portrait studies is the death mask of Bishop Phillips Brooks (1893), now in the collection of the Historical Society. For twenty-three years Bartlett was a modelling instructor at the Massachusetts Institute of Technology. During that period he wrote his best remembered work, *The Art Life of William Rimmer* (1882). Bartlett also ran a free school of modeling and drawing for the poor children of Boston for nine years.[5]

E.W.H.

10

1. Whitehill 1962, pp. 20, 21.
2. *MHS Proceedings* 78 (1966): 40.
3. Fine Art file, BPL.
4. Craven 1968, p. 428.
5. *Boston Transcript*, Feb. 18, 1922.

11

Theodor de Bry (1528–1598)
America, Parts 1–5
Frankfurt am Main: Theodor de Bry, 1590–1595
13 ⅛ in. (33.3 cm) x 9 ⁷⁄₁₆ in. (23.8 cm)
Bequest of Francis Russell Hart, 1938

They be all naked and of a goodly stature, mighty, faire, and as well shapen and proportioned of bodye as any people in all the worlde, very gentill, curtious and of a good nature.
—Jean Ribaut describes the Timucua Indians of Florida in 1563.[1]

Theodor de Bry's *America*, the first illustrated general account of the discovery and exploration of the Americas, is an extraordinary work. Firsthand narratives by explorers and detailed, hand-colored illustrations combine to tell Europeans of an exotic world previously unknown to them. Fortunately, de Bry was a reliable interpreter of the ethnological and natural history material from the narratives and illustrations placed in his hands by explorers. The Native Americans portrayed in de Bry's volumes were credible figures who could now be visualized by Europeans, and these images continued to be copied and reprinted until the eighteenth century.[2]

Dutch-born Theodor de Bry was forced to flee to Germany in 1570, during the religious wars in the Low Countries. A goldsmith who also worked as an engraver, de Bry employed his sons and their marriage relations in a family enterprise. After his death in 1598, they continued his great publishing project, *America*, which was finally completed more than thirty years later.

11 (see also color plate I)

The history and bibliography of de Bry's publications is extremely complicated. His work is divided into two main parts: the *Grands Voyages* (also known as *America* and covering the exploration of North and South America) and the *Petits Voyages* (Africa and Asia). *America* appeared in twenty-five parts that were published in fourteen folio volumes. They contain approximately 250 engraved illustrations and maps. The text is in German and Latin, the parts describing the early colonization of Virginia are also in English and French.[3] The first part of *America* is a reprinting of Thomas Harriot's narrative of Sir Walter Raleigh's failed Virginia colony, illustrated by engravings taken from the drawings of John White, the governor of the colony and a skilled watercolorist.

Part two is an account by Jacques le Moyne de Morgues (d. 1588), an artist attached to the disastrous French Huguenot settlement in Florida. In 1562, although wracked by religious civil war at home, France challenged Spanish claims to Florida. Jean Ribaut, a Huguenot and an experienced explorer, established a small fort, La Caroline, at the mouth of the Saint John's River in northern Florida in May 1562. Nearby, he erected a stone column to mark the annexation of Florida by France.

The first attempt at settlement failed; Ribaut returned to France and was temporarily exiled in England, where he published the account of the Timucua Indians cited above. A second expedition under Ribaut's lieutenant, René de Laudonnière, arrived in Florida in June 1564. This expedition included a staff artist—Jacques le Moyne. The illustration shown here is an engraving after

a watercolor by le Moyne. It shows Laudonnière at the site of the column erected by Ribaut, a column that was being worshipped and decorated as an idol by the Timucua Indians as described in Ribaut's work. While de Bry has Europeanized the features of the Native Americans, the composition and details are faithful to the original. Athore, the Native American chief, is very much the figure described in Le Moyne's explanatory text: "an extremely handsome man, intelligent, reliable, strong, of exceptional height, exceeding our tallest men by a foot and a half, and endowed with a certain restrained dignity. . . ."[4]

The rest of the brief story of the French colony is stark tragedy. The Spanish had resisted colonizing Florida until this time; now, with their seaborne line of communications threatened, they acted quickly to found their own colony in Florida and to raze the French settlement. An extra impulse to massacre was provided by the "heretic" religion of the French colonists. Pedro Menéndez de Avilez founded Saint Augustine, the oldest permanent European settlement in the United States; but the French garrison of La Caroline was slaughtered. Laudonnière and le Moyne were two of the few French survivors. Massacre was met by massacre. A French revenge raid in 1568 obliterated several Spanish posts, but in turn the Huguenot colony was extinguished. All that remains of Ribaut's "gentill, curtious" Timucua Indians in an Eden-like setting are le Moyne's depictions, as engraved by de Bry.[5]

This copy of de Bry's *America* is from the library

of Francis Russell Hart (1868–1938), whose strong interest in Central America and the West Indies grew out of his work on railways projects in Colombia, where he was general manager and later president of the Cartagena Railroad. He became a member of the Massachusetts Historical Society in 1920, and was elected the thirteenth president in 1937.[6]

The Hart Collection, a bequest to the Historical Society, consists of more than 900 books and pamphlets, along with research materials for Hart's books on the failed Scots settlement at Darien, on the Isthmus of Panama (1699–1701); and on the siege of Havana (1762). It also includes more than ninety early printed maps and atlases of the West Indies and Central America.

P.D.

1. Ribaut 1927, p. 69.
2. Quinn 1977, pp. 556–557.
3. Alexander 1976, pp. 7–10; Brown 1919, vol. 1, pt. 2:381–395.
4. Hulton 1977, p. 141.
5. Quinn 1977, pp. 258–261, 277–278.
6. Ford 1938, pp. 427–433.

12

John Winthrop (1588–1649)
History of New England (Volume 1, March 29, 1630 – September 14, 1636)
Manuscript
169 p., 7¼ in. (18.4 cm) x 5¾ in. (14.5 cm)
Gift of Francis B. Winthrop, 1803

Anno Domini 1630: march 29, mundaye.
Easter mundaye
Rydinge at the Cowes neare the Ile of wight in the Arbella, a Shippe of 350: tunes whereof Captaine Peter Milborne was master. . . .

These are the first lines of the first page of the most important single manuscript held by the Society, *the* basic document for the study of the history of the founding of Massachusetts. John Winthrop, the first governor of Massachusetts Bay, kept this journal as a personal record of his life and service, but also as a semiofficial history of the first nineteen years of the Bay Colony. Since the late colonial period, historians have used Winthrop's journal, first as a manuscript, and since 1790 in a variety of editions, for the study of the founding of Massachusetts.[1]

John Winthrop was forty-two years old when he began his journal. A landed Puritan gentleman who had been trained as a lawyer, Winthrop had considerable business and administrative experience when he was chosen first governor of the Massachusetts Bay colony, while still in England. The journal began as a day-by-day account of the voyage to America. Except when the weight of his work made it impossible for him to write regularly, that is how it remained through the first years of his governorship. Later, the journal became a much more self-conscious attempt to set down the history of important events in New England soon after they happened.[2]

The value of the journal to historians lies in the wealth of information not found in other surviving contemporary records that it provides concerning political and religious affairs in the first years of the new colony. Winthrop gives firsthand accounts, often extremely biased toward his own point of view, but substantial in detailing a range of events and figures in the early history of New England. William Bradford of Plymouth, John Cotton, Anne Hutchinson, and Roger Williams inhabit the pages of the journal; Antinomianism, Indian wars, witchcraft, and wolves are all described and discussed.[3]

The *History*, kept as a personal journal, was, in fact, very much a public document. It is different in character and content from Winthrop's personal correspondence from the same period and shows the reader only the often harsh public figure of the governor and lay magistrate. The private John Winthrop kept a personal spiritual journal during the same years he wrote the first volume of his *History*, and he had a wide-ranging correspondence with business associates, friends, and family that reveals a less solemn, more complicated man.[4]

The history of the manuscript of Winthrop's *History* and its publication is as tangled as the character and life of its author. The Winthrop family allowed early historians of New England, beginning with William Hubbard and Cotton Mather in the seventeenth century, to examine the journal, and manuscript extracts and transcriptions were made and used throughout the eighteenth century. In the course of this generous contribution to historical research, the family lost control of the entire journal. Volume three disappeared early in the eighteenth century, apparently when it was loaned to Thomas Prince, a Boston minister and antiquarian; and the remaining two volumes were in the hands of Jeremy Belknap, the founder of the Historical Society, at the time of his death in 1798. In 1790 Noah Webster, of dictionary fame, published the first edition of journals, which included only the first two volumes. The Winthrop family, which had recovered the actual volumes from Jeremy Belknap's heirs, gave them to the Historical Society in 1803. By a stroke of luck, the third volume of the manuscript was located in Thomas Prince's papers at the Old South Church and reunited with the first two volumes in the library of the Society in 1817. Good fortune, however, was soon followed by tragedy. James Savage, a Boston banker and librarian of the Society (and its future president), borrowed the journal manuscript to check his transcription for a new edition of the *History*, and the second volume, containing more than half the manuscript text, was destroyed in a fire at his office in 1825.[5]

However, Savage's 1825–1826 edition of the *History* is the best presently available to scholars, except for Winthrop's 1630 journal entries that appear in volume two of the Society's modern scholarly edition of the *Winthrop Papers*. Five volumes of edited Winthrop family papers, covering the years 1598 to 1649 have appeared to date. Work on a modern scholarly edition of the entire *History*, with Savage's transcription supplying the text for the lost second volume, soon will be completed.

The surviving volumes of John Winthrop's *History* are a vital but very small part of an extremely large collection of Winthrop family papers at the Society, which date from 1544 to 1963. In addition to English ancestral material and Governor Winthrop's pre-migration correspondence, there are the papers of his son, John Winthrop, Jr. (1606–1676), one of the most versatile figures in

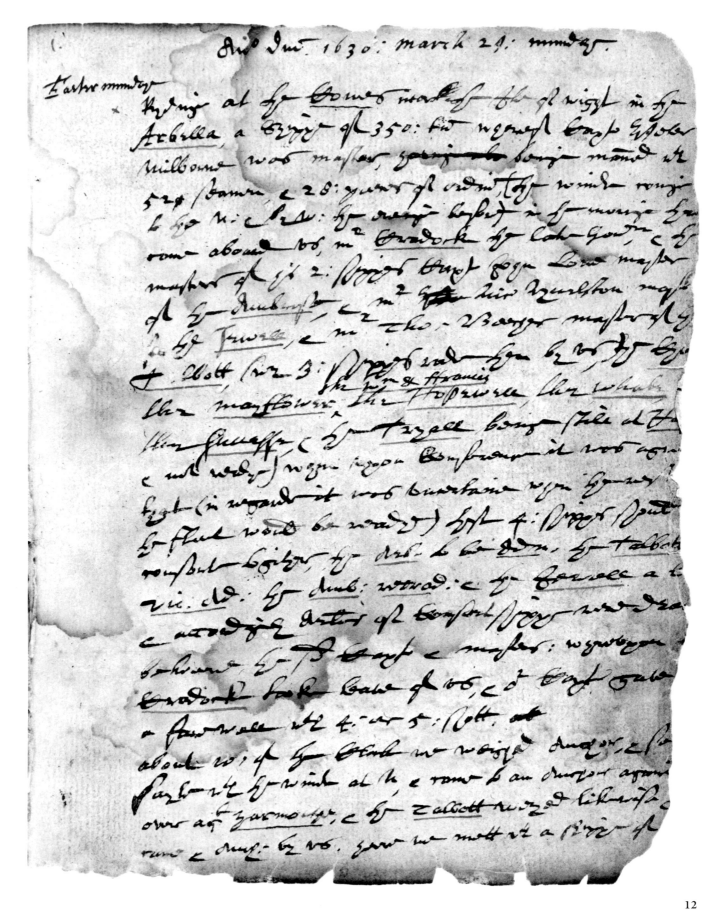

American colonial history, and eight descendant generations of Winthrop family members. These manuscripts
include correspondence, letterbooks, diaries, journals,
travel journals, speeches, account books, deeds, medical
records, publications, scrapbooks, and other papers.[6]

P.D.

1. Dunn 1984, p. 186.
2. Ibid., pp. 188–200.
3. Winthrop 1826.
4. Morgan 1958, pp. 13–14.
5. Freiberg 1969, pp. 55–61.
6. Ibid., p. 61.

John Foster (1648–1681)

An "ingenious mathematician" and schoolmaster, John Foster was the first printer in Boston and the first engraver in New England. He was born in Dorchester, where he taught school after he graduated from Harvard in 1667. On Christmas Day, 1674, just another working day in Puritan Boston, Foster purchased a printing press, which he moved to Boston and set up at the "Sign of the Dove" in 1675.[1]

Foster was unusual in that he had no apparent practical training as a printer. Samuel Green, a contemporary who printed at Cambridge, complained that Foster was a "young man that had no skill in printing but what he had taken notice of by and by." Because Green's complaint implied a lack of expertise on Foster's part, Isaiah Thomas, the first historian of American printing, postulated that Foster hired workmen to run his press. However, there is little contemporary evidence to resolve the question.[2]

The items that Foster printed were, for the most part, not very different from the products of Green's Cambridge press, which, by 1675, had issued more than 200 publications in the thirty-six years since printing was introduced to English America (see nos. 16, 46). The bulk of Foster's work consisted of almanacs that he wrote and printed, Massachusetts Bay government documents, for which he engraved a variant of the Indian seal, and sermons—his first publication was an execution sermon, preached for the soul of a condemned criminal by Increase Mather, the representative Puritan of his day—and books, pamphlets, and broadsides, including two contemporary histories of King Philip's War, one containing the map displayed here.[3]

Foster's printing career was influential but brief. He died of consumption in 1681, at the age of thirty-three. It has been said that had Foster lived longer and become more widely known, the range of his interests and accomplishments was so large that Benjamin Franklin might have been called a "second Foster." Along with the first portrait and first map printed in America discussed below, Foster has been credited with the earliest American medical imprint, Thomas Thacher's *Brief Rule . . . in the Small Pocks or Measels* (1677); and the first American collection of poetry, the writings of Anne Bradstreet. In his own day, Foster was memorialized in verse in two funeral elegies printed in Boston. One elegy, by Thomas Tileston, describes Foster's life and education and then continues:

> Adde to these things I have been hinting
> His skill in that rare ART OF PRINTING
> His accurate Geography
> And Astronomick Poetry;
> And you would say 'twere pitty He
> Should dy without an Elegie[4]

P.D.

1. Littlefield 1907, pp. 3–13.
2. Green 1907, pp. 19–22.
3. Ibid., pp. 19–22.
4. Sibley 1873, 2:225.

13

Attributed to John Foster (1648–1681)
A Map of New-England
Boston: Printed by John Foster, 1677
Woodcut
12¼ in. (31 cm) x 15⅞ in. (40.3 cm)
Originally published in William Hubbard (ca. 1621–1704), *Narrative of the Troubles with the Indians* (Boston, 1677)
Inscribed, upper right: A MAP OF / NEW-ENGLAND, / *Being the first that ever was here cut, and done by / the best Pattern that could be had, which being in / some places defective, it made the other less exact / yet doth it sufficiently shew the Scituation of / the Country, and conveniently well the / distance of Places. / The figures that are joyned with the Names of Places / are to distinguish such as have been assaulted / by the Indians from others.*; above measured scale: *A Scale of forty Miles.*
Gift of Robert C. Winthrop, Jr., 1895

The history of the mapping of New England *in* New England begins with a controversy. The first map known to have been published in the English colonies of North America, and probably the first map published in the Western Hemisphere, has been attributed to John Foster, who printed William Hubbard's *Narrative of the Troubles with the Indians* in which *A Map of New England* appeared. Foster is thought to have been the only man in Boston to have made woodcuts during that period. The difficulty arises because another version of the map, possibly also cut in Boston by Foster, was inserted in the London edition of Hubbard's work, retitled *The Present State of New-England*, that was published within a few months of the Boston edition.[1]

The two versions of the map have perplexed bibliographers for more than a century. The American edition of Hubbard's *Narrative* contains the version known as the "White Hills" map; in the other version, the White Hills of New Hampshire are identified as the "Wine Hills." The problem for historians of printing and map collectors has been to determine the order in which the maps were printed, and if they were cut by the same engraver—John Foster. After more than a century of examination these questions are not entirely settled; what is known is that the Historical Society's copy of the "White Hills" map is unique, as it contains a symbol for an unnamed town that appears on *no* other surviving copy of this version.[2]

Both versions are among the Massachusetts Historical Society's holdings of more than 5,000 historical maps and charts, 200 atlases that contain separately printed maps, and large collection of early printed books illustrated with maps.

Neither John Foster's rough woodblock map of New England, nor his crude portrait of Richard Mather (no. 14) can be fairly judged against the standard of European engraved portraiture and mapmaking of the late seventeenth century. However, they are not without rough charm. Fine arts were slow to develop in New England with its small, largely rural population. Self-taught in several fields, John Foster made considerable achievements during his brief career. His woodcut map, as

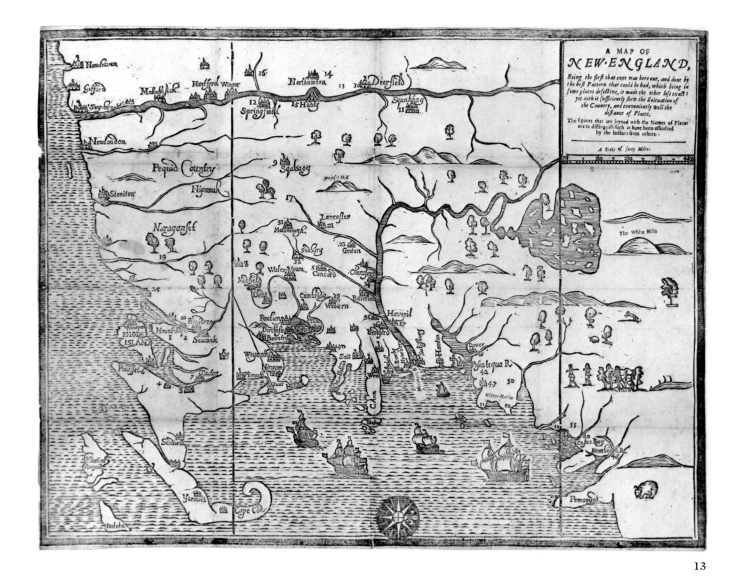

13

copied, proved satisfactory for the English edition of the work it illustrated.

P.D.

1. Holman 1960, pp. 53–96; Woodward 1967, pp. 52–61.
2. Wheat 1969, p. 144.

14
Attributed to John Foster (1648–1681)
Mr. Richard Mather
Printed after 1700
Woodcut
6 ⅛ in. (15.5 cm) x 5 ⅛ in. (13 cm)
Gift of Arthur Maynard Walter, 1807

This portrait of Richard Mather is one of six surviving impressions of the earliest-known American woodcut. It first appeared soon after Mather's death and at one time was thought to be an illustration for a memoir written by his son, Increase Mather, and published in 1670. The attribution of the woodcut to John Foster is based on a contemporary inscription—"Johannes Foster sculpsit"—on an impression of the print, inserted in a copy of the memoir held by Harvard University.[1]

The Harvard impression of the portrait is the only surviving example that definitely was printed in the sev-

14

enteenth century. The exact date of the Massachusetts Historical Society example is not certain, but the woodcut is printed on paper that bears a "Pro Patria" watermark, in common use early in the eighteenth century. The noticeable step in Mather's shoulders in the print probably was caused by printing from two separate blocks, one for the head and the other for the body, that were wet and had expanded at different rates. Woodblock prints were time-consuming to produce and often used over long periods, or reused to illustrate different subjects. The portrait of Richard Mather may have been cut on two blocks so that the separate body portion of the block could be joined to another head.[2]

The progenitor of a line of distinguished Boston clergymen (see nos. 27–29), the Reverend Richard Mather came to Massachusetts Bay in 1635 and held the pulpit of the church in Dorchester from 1636 until his death in 1669. John Foster's family were members of Mather's church and the young Foster had been baptized by him. Foster retained his strong connection to the powerful Mather family through his brief publishing career. His first and last publications were sermons by Increase Mather, one of the Massachusetts Bay censors, who approved and controlled all printing. Increase Mather and his son Cotton, along with John Eliot, the "Apostle to the Indians," received legacies from Foster's small estate at the time of his death.[3]

P.D.

1. Griffin 1958, pp. 1–7.
2. Holman 1960, p. 30.
3. Ibid., pp. 25–26.

15

John Josselyn (ca. 1608–1675)
New-Englands Rarities Discovered
London: Printed for G. Widdowes, 1672
114 pp., 5 13/16 in. (14.7 cm) x 3½ in. (8.8 cm)
Gift of Josephine Spencer Gay, 1918

Between the years 1663 and 1671, Englishman John Josselyn flourished as a keen observer and creative recorder of nature in New England. His book *New-Englands Rarities Discovered*, published in London in 1672, culminated an eight-year study in New England where he made it his "business to discover all along the Natural, Physical, and Chyrurgical Rarities of this New-found World."[1] His studies of the region's flora, including identification of several new genera, remained authoritative until 1785.[2]

Josselyn was born in Essex, England, about 1608 and, after a liberal education, became an accomplished scientist and physician, with a personal interest in natural history. His respect for the Royal Society (founded in 1660) and desire for its acknowledgment and approval led to his publishing botanical observations based on visits to his brother Henry in Maine, the first in 1638 and again from 1663 to 1671.

During the latter visit he compiled detailed notes and a few drawings on plants, herbs, fish, and mammals; interspersed with these descriptions were incredible stories on sea serpents, amazing medicinal cures from local folklore, and imaginative passages about wild beasts. Despite his scientific background and training, he "enthusiastically transmitted the myths and legends that continued to flourish alongside the New Science,"[3] and

New-Englands Rarities. 73
A Branch of the Humming Bird Tree.

15

in New England. Along with these sometimes humorous and poetic narratives are brief descriptions of Native Americans, written in a positive light otherwise unheard of in seventeenth-century literature.

After a brief description of Boston and New England, Josselyn's account turns to four sections on birds, beasts, fish, and serpents, then proceeds with plant species (a major part of the book) and a geological description of stones, minerals, metals and earths in section six. Descriptions of the plants were further enhanced by ten crude woodcuts based on the writer's drawings, including the first illustrated record of the development of a skunk cabbage. Although Stearns states that Josselyn published these woodcuts, they are not signed and there is no other evidence to indicate that he was also the cutter.[4] At the end of the natural history accounts are three short sections: some additional rarities, a description of a Native American "squa, in all her Bravery," and a chronological table of names and events in New England, including the first record of an earthquake in Boston in 1638.

Although "he had little, if any, conception of scientific botany, no ecological sense, little concern for plant structure, botanical system, or nomenclature,"[5] Josselyn's writing was respected by the scientific community and quite popular among the reading public. His book was the first major attempt at a systematic account of New England's botanical species.[6] Two years later he published

An account of two voyages to New England, a further elaboration on the scientific lore, local history, and general observations that were so common in *New England Rarities*. Both books were regarded as handbooks and travel guides for Englishmen anxious for knowledge about the New World.

M.E.C.

1. Josselyn 1672, p. 2.
2. Josselyn 1988, p. xiii.
3. Ibid., p. xvi.
4. Stearns 1970, p. 144.
5. Ibid.
6. Goodale 1900, p. 184.

16

Mamusse wunneetupanatamwe up-Biblum God
("The-whole holy his-Bible God")
Cambridge: Printed by Samuel Green and Marmaduke Johnson, 1663
Unpaged, 7 ⅛ in. (18.1 cm) x 5 ¾ in. (14.5 cm)
Gift of Mrs. Coffin, 1793

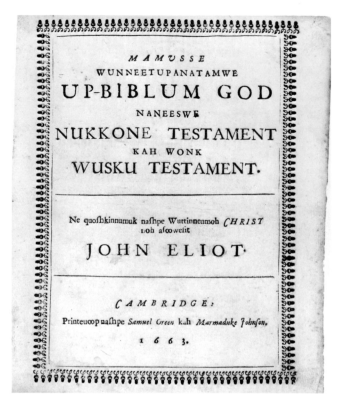

16

The Charter of the Massachusetts Bay Company, the founding document for the colonization of New England, describes "the principall ende of this plantation . . . to wynn and incite the natives of the country, to the knowlege and obedience of the onlie true God and Saviour of Mankinde. . . ."[1] Of the clergymen who participated in the attempt to evangelize the Native American population of New England, the chief missionary agent was the Reverend John Eliot (1604–1690), who earned the title of "Apostle to the Indians" through a lifetime of unceasing missionary effort. Eliot emigrated to Massachusetts Bay in 1631 and settled in Roxbury. For almost sixty years he served as minister of the local church and, in addition to his clerical duties there, in 1646 he began preaching to Native Americans in their own language, first locally and in 1651 at Natick, the first permanent "Praying Indian" settlement.[2]

While Eliot believed that all the indigenous population should be settled in permanent villages on the model of Natick and encouraged to adopt European ways, he thought that they should hear and read scripture in their own language and be served by Native American ministers. To accomplish this goal he embarked on an ambitious publishing plan; first by publishing a basic primer and Bible extracts in the Massachuset language spoken by Native Americans in eastern New England, and later a much larger project to translate and publish the entire Bible in Massachuset. The New Testament was printed separately in 1661, and the combined Old and New Testament published in 1663. The "Eliot Indian Bible" is a landmark of printing history. It is the first Bible printed in any language in North America and the largest single printing venture of the early colonial period.[3] Funds for the publication came from the Society for the Propagation of the Gospel in New-England and Adjacent Parts, an English missionary society that raised money for evangelical work in the colonies.[4]

The actual translation presented many problems as Eliot's knowledge of Massachuset was imperfect, and there were grammatical problems that could only be resolved by resorting to English words when there were no equivalent Massachuset terms. The scale of the project made it necessary to recruit Marmaduke Johnson, an English printer, to assist Samuel Green, the official printer for the colony, and to secure additional printing equipment. Two Native Americans played important roles in publishing the Bible. John Nesutan, a preacher who had studied at Harvard, assisted Eliot with the translation, and James Printer, a young Nipmuck who had been apprenticed to Green, assisted both with the translation and the printing.[5]

The "Eliot Indian Bible," however, symbolizes the tragic failure of the Puritan colonists to accomplish their "principall ende" to christianize the New England Native Americans and reshape their lives in the image of the colonists. During King Philip's War (1675–1676), most of the indigenous population of southern New England was killed, enslaved, or driven beyond the reach of the vengeful English colonists. Native American prisoners and Christian converts proved to be the most effective colonial forces, but this did not prevent the "Praying Indians" from suffering harsh treatment at the hands of the colonists. During the course of the conflict they were kept under guard on Deer Island in Boston Harbor, and in the turmoil of the war, most copies of the Eliot Bible were destroyed. James Printer took the side of King Philip against the colonists, although after his capture he returned to his printing craft. John Nesutan was killed while serving in the colonial forces against his own people.[6]

From the ashes of his life's work, at the age of seventy-two, Eliot began again. He lived long enough to see a corrected second edition of his Bible published in 1685. Some copies of this improved edition still were used by inhabitants of Mashpee, a Native American community on Cape Cod, until the nineteenth century, but the Christian Native American population, never large, did not recover from the effects of King Philip's War.[7]

The Historical Society's copy of Eliot's Bible lacks the English title pages and dedicatory material to King Charles II, who was sought as a patron for missionary activity; this absence indicates that the copy probably was intended solely for Native American use.

M.E.C.

1. Morison 1930, p. 289.
2. Ibid., pp. 291–297.
3. Amory 1989, p. 39.
4. Pilling 1891, pp. 127–184.
5. Winship 1945, pp. 208–244.
6. Amory 1989, pp. 41–42.
7. Morison 1930, pp. 315–319.

17
Wenceslaus Hollar (1607–1677)
Portrait of an Unknown Native American
Antwerp, 1645
Etching
4 ⅛ in. (10.5 cm) x 3 ⅛ in. (7.8 cm)
Inscribed: *Unus Americanus ex / virginia, / Ætat: 23 / W: Hollar ad viuum / delin: et fecit 1645*
Gift of J. Clinton Hooker, 1862

Native Americans held an exotic fascination for Europeans of the sixteenth, seventeenth, and eighteenth centuries. Early images came from discovery and exploration narratives, such as Theodor de Bry's *America* (no. 11). Later, tribal leaders crossed the Atlantic not as captives, but as honored emissaries from a foreign country. These visits provided the opportunity for formally trained artists to record the visitors in formal portraits and more popular prints.[1] In 1616 Simon van de Passe (ca. 1595–1647) engraved a likeness of Pocahontas (see no. 18) wearing fashionable Tudor-Stuart finery. A generation later Wenceslaus Hollar chose to portray his subject more realistically.

This unidentified twenty-three-year-old Virginia native was drawn from life by Hollar in the conventional half-length view used by European artists of that time. Carefully and proudly adorned with a headband of suspended animal claws, dangling bead earrings, and necklace of matching design, the subject engages the viewer with his gaze. The tribal marks tattooed around his eyes in parallel lines leave no doubt about the individual's exotic origins. The conventional format and style combine with the unusual subject to create a powerful impression.

Wenceslaus Hollar, a Bohemian artist from the city of Prague, worked in London as an engraver from 1637 to 1644 and enjoyed the favor of King Charles I during those years. Though the reasons for his departure are not clear, civil war had broken out in England, and by the end of 1644 Hollar was living and working in the city of Antwerp. This etching was done in 1645 but may reflect a drawing that the artist had taken while in England.

Hollar left a large body of work, greatly varied in subject matter. Devoted to recording the world around

17

him, he depicted many scenes, events, places and people of seventeenth-century Europe and England. Considered most successful with prospects or bird's eye views, Hollar's portraits from life, such as this etching of a Native American, also approach the highest quality in his work. According to Richard Pennington, "a very delicate, nervous etched line of great subtlety" accounts for Hollar's ability to suggest the "solidity of stone to his churches or a softness . . . to the long vista of a gothic cathedral."[2]

J.L.P.

1. Parry 1974, p.7.
2. Pennington 1982, p. xlix.

18
Mary Woodbury (ca. 1717–1747/48)
Pocahontas (1595–1617)
Boston, ca. 1730
Oil on paper
15¼ in. (38.5 cm) x 12½ in. (32.0 cm)
Gift of the grandchildren of Dorothy Lancaster Libby, 1931

Daughter of Powhatan, the powerful chief of the Powhatan confederacy, Pocahontas was born in Virginia in 1595. Captain John Smith credited her with saving his life in 1608, in what has become an oft-repeated story in American history. Captured by the English and held hostage at Jamestown in 1613, Pocahontas converted to Christianity and was baptized as "Rebecca." She married John Rolfe, an English settler, in 1614, and two years later they went to England. There, Pocahontas was enter-

18

5–12, 1714, lists the various arts included in a typical finishing school curriculum: "At the house of Mr. *James Ivers* . . . is now set up a Boarding School, where will be carefully Taught, Flourishing, Embroidery, and all Sorts of Needle-Work, also Filigrew, Painting upon Glass, Writing, Arithmetick, and Singing Psalm Tunes."

J.L.P.

1. *DAB.*
2. Mossiker 1976, pp. 275–278.
3. Parry 1974, p. 8.
4. Ware 1934, pp. 18, 33.
5. MHS *Proceedings* 64 (1930–32):346.

19
John Simon (1675–ca. 1755) after John Verelst (1648–1734)
Tee Yee Neen Ho Ga Ron, Emperour of the Six Nations
London, 1710
Mezzotint
16 3/8 in. (41.7 cm) x 12 1/8 in. (31 cm)
Inscribed, lower left: *I: Verelst pinx:;* center: *I. Simon Fec:;* right: *Printed & Sold by Iohn King at the Globe in the Poultrey London*
Gift of William Scollay, 1795

tained by the bishop of London, received by the king and queen, and accorded all respects due a princess.[1] Pocahontas, her two-year-old son, Thomas, and his nursemaid fell ill shortly before they were to board ship to return to America. Though they began the journey, Pocahontas became so ill the voyage was interrupted at Gravesend, England, where she died.[2]

This early eighteenth-century representation of Pocahontas shows the legend of the Native American princess turned English lady as conceived by a Boston schoolgirl. As Rebecca Rolfe, she wears flowers in her hair, beads at her throat, a lace collar, and ruffled cuffs, and she holds a flower in her hand. Only her dark hair remains to suggest her own cultural beginnings. Relations between the Native Americans and the first English settlers were extremely hostile when Pocahontas was a young girl, but, as Elwood Parry concludes that "no more appropriate or convincing image of the taming of the American forests could be imagined than the arrival of Rebecca Rolfe in England."[3]

Though some knowledge of modeling is apparent in the painting, the youthful, largely untrained artist realized her idea by the use of an overall, two-dimensional design. The delicacy of the lace collar and the tiny, bunched flowers in Pocahontas's hair convey the young girl's enthusiasm and admiration for her subject. Mary Woodbury was born in Beverly and married Dr. Benjamin Jones there in 1736/7.[4] According to family tradition, she made the picture during her residence at a Boston boarding school for young ladies in the 1730s.[5] The Society also owns a candle sconce done in quillwork by Mary Woodbury during the same period. Constructed of paper filigree, the sconce is decorated with gilded paper, wax, and mica to form a basket of flowers, a rooster, and a peacock.

An advertisement in the *Boston News-Letter* of April

19

Sa Ga Yeath Qua Pieth Ton King of the Magua

20

20

John Simon (1675–ca. 1755) after John Verelst (1648–1734)
Sa Ga Yeath Qua Pieth Ton King of the Magua
London, 1710
Mezzotint
16 ⅜ in. (41.7 cm) x 12 ⅛ in. (31 cm)
Inscribed, lower left: *I. Verelst pinx.*; center: *I. Simon
Fecit*; right: *Printed & Sold by Iohn King at the Globe in
the Poultrey London*
Gift of William Scollay, 1795

21

The Four Indian Kings
London, 1710
Broadside
8½ in. (21.5 cm) x 12½ in. (31.8 cm)
Purchased, 1919

The arrival of four Mohawk sachems in London in April
1710 succeeded the visit of the famous Native American
princess Pocahontas (see no. 18) by nearly a century. And,
like that earlier visitor, the "Indian kings" were met with
much interest by the general public and became instant
celebrities. The purpose of their visit was primarily political. The British colonies needed the support of the tribes
of the Five Nations of the Iroquois Confederacy, who
occupied the land between the St. Lawrence River and

Lake Erie in New York, in their continuing strife against
the French settlers of Canada. The British also sought
the sachems' cooperation with their plan to send mis-
sionaries to America to convert the Iroquois people to
Christianity. In exchange for their compliance and
aid, the Native Americans were to receive arms and soldiers to bolster their defense against the French.[1]

This carefully orchestrated visit was the brainchild of
three colonial leaders, Peter Schuyler (first mayor of Albany), Sir Francis Nicolson (governor of Maryland and
Virginia successively), and Peter Vetch (later governor of
Nova Scotia). The delegation included Tee Yee Neen Ho
Ga Ron, Emperor of the Six Nations; Sa Ga Yeath Qua
Pieth Ton, King of the Magua; Eton Oh Koam, King of
the River Nation; and Ho Nee Yeath Tan No Ron, King
of the Generethgarich. They sailed from Boston in February 1710, arriving in London in April. The four leaders
were outfitted by a London tailor before being received
by Queen Anne on April 10, when they each presented
her with a gift of wampum and gave a speech which was
translated by an interpreter. These speeches were printed
and distributed as a broadside.[2]

In addition, the excitement which their six-week
visit generated led to a number of ballads in their honor.
One such example, *The Four Indian Kings*, is about an
apparently apocryphal unrequited love between one of
the Native American kings and an English woman. This
supposed love ballad is, in reality, thinly disguised propaganda. The unnamed woman in question refuses to
receive the attentions of the "youngest" king unless he
converts to Christianity. As she states in no uncertain
terms in the last stanza: "If he will become a Christian, /
Live up to the truth reveal'd, / I will make him grant the
question, / Or before will never yield."

Following the presentation of the four sachems to
the queen, she commissioned John Verelst to paint full-
length portraits of them, which she had hung in Ken-
sington Palace (now at Writtle Park, near Chelmsford,
Essex, England). Of Dutch origin, Verelst came from a
family of artists, who included the still-life painter Simon
Verelst (1644–1721). John Verelst was primarily a portrait
painter whose known works date between 1698 and his
death in 1734. To commemorate their visit the engraver
John Simon made a set of mezzotints based on Verelst's
portraits. John or Jean Simon was born in Normandy of
a Huguenot family. He studied engraving in Paris before
moving to London during the early reign of Queen
Anne. Most of his works are portrait engravings after
Kneller and other prominent painters who were working
in England at the time.[3]

The four mezzotints of the Native American kings
were printed and distributed as a set in both England
and America. The format of the portrait is similar in each
depicting the sachem standing against a wild and imaginary forest background. Three of the four have a similar
pose, the right foot is forward and the left elbow is bent,
with the left hand resting on the waist. Only in the case
of Ho Nee Yeath Tan No Ron (not exhibited) is the position reversed. All four are represented with the totem or
animal symbol of their clan. In the case of Sa Ga Yeath
Qua Pieth Ton, for instance, a bear is shown to represent
the bear clan. In the same example, he holds a long rifle,
and he is depicted again in the background using it to
hunt. He is also the only one of the group to be decora-

THE FOUR INDIAN KINGS.

PART. I.

How a beautiful Lady conquered one of the Indian Kings.

ATTEND unto a true relation,
Of four Indian Kings of late,
Who came to this Christian nation,
To report their sorrows great,
Which by France they had sustained
To the overthrow of trade;
That the seas might be regained,
Who are come to beg our aid.

Having told their sad condition,
To our good and gracious queen
With a humble low submission,
Mixt with a courteous mein,
Noble they were all received
In bold Britain's royal court.
Many lords and ladies grieved,
At these Indian king's report.
Now their message being ended,
To the queen's great majesty;
They were further befriended
Of the noble standers by.
With a glance of Britain's glory,
Buildings, troops, and many things,
But now comes a pressing story,
Love seiz'd one of these four kings.
Thus, as it was then related,
Walking forth to take the air,
In St. James's Park there waited
Troops of handsome ladies fair,
Rich and gaudily attir'd,
Rubies, jewels, diamond rings.
One fair lady was admir'd
By the youngest of those kings.
While he did his pain discover,
Often fighting to the rest;
Like a broken hearted lover,
Oft he smote upon his breast.
Breaking forth in lamentation,
Oh, the pains that I endure!
The young ladies of this nation,
They are more than mortals sure.

In his language he related,
How her angel beauty bright,
His great heart had captivated,
Ever since she appear'd in fight.
Tho' there are some fair and pretty,
Youthful, proper, strait, and tall,
In this Christian land and city,
Yet she far excells them all,
Were I worthy of her favour,
Which is much better then gold,
Then I might enjoy for ever,
Charming blessings manifold.
But I fear she cannot love me,
I must ope for no such thing:
That sweet saint is far above me,
Although I am an Indian king.
Let me sign but my petition,
Unto that lady fair and clear:
Let her know my sad condition,
How I languish under her.
If on me, after this trial,
She will no eye of pity cast,
But return a flat denial,
Friends I can but die at last.
If a fail by this distraction,
Thro' a lady's cruelty;
It is some satisfaction
That I do a martyr die.
Unto the goddess of great beauty,
Brighter than the morning day:
Sure no greater piece of duty,
No poor captive love can pay.
O this fatal burning fever,
Gives me little hopes of life,
If so that I cannot have her
For my love and lawful wife.
Bear to her this royal token,
Tell her 'tis my diamond ring:
Pray her that it mayn't be spoken,
She'll destroy an Indian King.
Who is able to advance her
In our fine America,
Let me soon receive an answer,
From her hand without delay.
Every minute seems an hour,
Every hour fix. I'm sure;
Tell her it is in her power
At this time to kill or cure.
Tell her that you see me ready

To expire for her sake
And as she is a Christian lady,
Sure she will some pity take.
I shall long for your returning
From that pure unspotted cove,
All the while I do lie burning,
Wrapt in scorching flames of love,

PART II.

The Lady's Answer to the Indian King's Request.

I WILL fly with your petition
Unto that lady fair and clear,
For to tell your sad condition,
I will to her parents bear.
Show her how you do adore her,
And lie bleeding for her sake:
Having laid the cause before her,
She perhaps may pity take.
Ladies that are apt to glory
In their youthful birth and state,
So hear I'll rehearse the story
Of their being truely great.
So farewell, sir, for a season,
I will soon return again:
If she's but endow'd with reason,
Labour is not spent in vain.
Having found her habitation,
Which with diligence he sought,
Tho' renown'd in her station,
She was to his presence brought.
Where he labour'd to discover
How is lord and master lay,
Like a pensive wounded lover,
By her charms the other day.
As a token of his honour,
He has sent this ring of gold
Set with diamonds. Save the owner,
For his griefs are manifold.
Life and death are both depending
On what answer you can give,
Here he lies your charms commending
Grant him love that he may live.
You may tell your lord and master,
Said the charming lady fair,
Tho' I pity this disaster,
Being catch'd in Cupid's snare
Tis against all true discretion,
To comply with what I scorn:
He's a Heathen by profession,

I a Christian bred and born.
Was he king of many nations,
Crowns and royal dignity,
And I born of mean relations,
You may tell him that from me.
As long as I have life and breathing
My true God I will adore,
Nor will ever wed a Heathen,
For the richest Indian store.
I have had my education
From my infant blooming youth,
In this Christian land and nation,
Where the blessed word and truth
Is to be enjoy'd with pleasure,
Amongst Christians mild and kind,
Which is more than all the treasure
Can be had with Heathens wild.
Madam, let me be admitted
Once to speak in his defence;
If he here then may be pity'd,
Breath not forth such violence.
He and all the rest were telling
How well they lik'd this place;
And declared themselves right willing
To receive the light of grace.
So then, lady, be not cruel,
His unhappy state condole;
Quench the flame, abate the fuel,
Spare his life, and save his soul.
Since it lies within your power
Either to destroy or save,
Send him word this happy hour
That you'll heal the wound you gave.
While the messenger he pleaded
With this noble virtuous maid,
All the words then she minded
Which his master he had said.
Then she spoke like one concerned,
Tell your master this from me,
Let him, let him first be turned
From his gross Idolatry.
If he will become a Christian,
Live up to the truth reveal'd,
I will make him grant the question,
Or before will never yield.
Altho' he was pleased to send to me,
His fine ring and diamond stone,
With this answer pray commend me
To your master yet unknown.

ted with elaborate body paint. Three of the four bear weapons, and all four wear the red cloaks edged with gold which were designed for them in London prior to their audience with the queen.[4]

As the Emperor of the Six Nations, Tee Yee Neen Ho Ga Ron is different in several ways. Only he wears the black waistcoat and breeches designed in London, although he has added a Native American belt to his costume. His tomahawk lies on the ground in front of him, perhaps as a symbol of peace. Instead of a weapon, he holds a large sash of wampum. Saunders suggests that this recalls a line of the kings' speech to Queen Anne, which was translated as "we do here in the Name of All present our great Queen with these BELTS OF WAMPUM."[5]

S.R.M.

1. Parry 1974, p. 18; Bolus 1973, p. 5; Saunders 1987, p. 85.
2. Saunders 1987, p. 85; Bolus 1973, p. 5.
3. Bolus 1973, p. 9; Waterhouse 1981, p. 389; DNB.
4. Saunders 1987, p. 85.
5. Ibid.

22

Daniel Christian Fueter (1720–1785), engraver and maker
"Happy While United" Indian Peace Medal
New York, 1764
Silver, cast

Legend, obverse: GEORGIVS III. D.G.M. BRIT. FRA. ET. HIB. REX. F.D. around laurel-crowned military bust of young king, to right; reverse: HAPPY WHILE UNITED above an Indian and an Englishman shaking hands while seated on a bench; the Indian carries a peace pipe. At left, a tree shades the men; at right, three ships ride in the harbor behind them, and a small house sits on a promontory. In exergue: 1764. Suspension loop formed by crossed pipe and bird's wing. Marked on reverse in oval: DCF; in shaped cartouche: N:/YORK
D. 2 15/16 in. (75 mm)
Bequest of William Sumner Appleton, 1905

The practice of awarding peace medals to Native Americans was a natural extension of the European use of medals to commemorate treaties, battles, events, and persons.[1] The French and British colonial governments were especially competitive in the practice, as they depended on the support and assistance of the northern tribes of Native Americans to maintain and defend colonial territorial claims. To this end, they presented silver medals, hat bands, buckles, and gorgets to the important chiefs and warriors of various tribes in an effort to obtain their allegiance and to reward their services against the enemy.[2]

22

These silver ornaments were indicative of the owners' political loyalties and became important symbols for native warriors and issuing governments alike. As such, governments encouraged the exchange of old tokens for new; a practice which led to the creation of the "Happy While United" medal in 1764.[3]

The medal was one of two instigated by Sir William Johnson towards the close of the French and Indian War (1755–1763). Johnson, Commissioner for Indian Affairs in the British colonies, had assembled his Native American allies and joined Sir Jeffrey Amherst, commander in chief of the British forces, in the 1760 campaign against Montreal. The defeat of the French in this battle hastened the end of the war. Johnson determined to reward his loyal native allies and sent a list of names to Amherst, who commissioned the first medal, known as the "Montreal Medal," from New York City goldsmith Daniel Christian Fueter in 1761.[4]

The "Happy While United" medal was the second, which Johnson required to serve a different purpose. Once peace was declared between England and France (with France ceding her claims to Canada), her Native American allies, the "Western Confederacy" of tribes, had to choose between accepting English domination or fighting England and her allies, the Six Nations. Assisted by the French, the Ottawa warrior Pontiac (d. 1769) led some of the Shawnee, Delaware, Seneca, and other groups in armed resistance. In an effort to prevent the resistance from becoming widespread, Sir William Johnson issued an invitation to all tribes who had been allies of the French to assemble at Fort Niagara in July of 1764, to discuss peace treaties. Johnson knew that those who accepted his invitation would be wearing French medals, and he wished to have British tokens ready to exchange with them. Accordingly, he wrote to General Thomas Gage a month before the convocation, requesting that medals be made. Time was short, so Gage used the dies he had commissioned Fueter to make for "the Indians in Florida &c." and had sixty medals cast for Johnson's use. By June 26th Fueter had completed the order, and the medals were on the way to Fort Niagara, with Gage's comment that, although he could "not say much for the workmanship of them nevertheless they are finished by the best hand that could be found here."[5] The "Happy While United" medal occurs in two sizes and with three other dates: 1766 (which possibly refers to the peace treaty made with Pontiac), 1780 (which is combined with a different obverse and is not considered an Indian peace medal), and undated.[6]

In 1720, Daniel Christian Fueter was born in Bern, Switzerland, and worked there as a goldsmith until 1749 when his involvement in a conspiracy to overthrow the government resulted in a death sentence. He fled to London where he lived and worked until he brought his family to America in 1754. He worked in New York City from 1754 through 1779, when he was permitted to return to Bern, where he died in 1785.[7] Fueter was one of the few goldsmiths working in eighteenth-century America to make such European forms as flat shallow bowls and baking dishes, bread baskets and gold coral-bell rattles.[8] His medallic works are scarce today. Only six of his Montreal medals are known, and of the three presentation issues of the "Happy While United" medals, a total of twelve examples have been recorded.[9]

The use of peace medals continued into the late nineteenth century, with the United States government continuing the colonial tradition. The final medal designed for presentation to Native Americans was commissioned on May 19, 1890, under President Benjamin Harrison.[10] With examples dating from Britain's earliest issue (George I, 1714) to the Federal series of "Seasons" Indian medals (1796) and on to many of those struck by the United States Mint (1801–1890), the Indian Peace Medals form an important subset in the medal collection of the Massachusetts Historical Society.

A.E.B.

1. Prucha 1971, p. xiii.
2. Hodge 1907, p. 830.
3. Woodward 1933, p. 27.
4. Ibid., pp. 17, 20.
5. Ibid., pp. 26–28.
6. Fuld 1988, pp. 28–37.
7. Fales 1958, p. 65–66.
8. Flynt 1968, p. 65.
9. Fuld 1988, pp. 25–26, 35.
10. Prucha 1971, pp. 134–135.

23

Mrs. Baker
London, 1675
Oil on canvas
30¼ in. (76.9 cm) x 25 ⁵⁄₁₆ in. (65.9 cm)
Inscribed, above left shoulder: AO *1675 70*
Bequest of Elizabeth Welles Perkins, 1920

This portrait of Mrs. Baker represents the family matriarch in a group of eight paintings, which were executed in London between 1671 and 1675, and subsequently shipped to Boston. They were the gift of Nicholas Roberts of London (d. 1676) and his wife Elizabeth Baker Roberts (d. ca. 1700) to their daughter Elizabeth Roberts Shrimpton (ca. 1650–1713).[1] After marrying Col. Samuel Shrimpton (1643–1698) in England in 1669, Elizabeth immigrated to Boston with her American-born husband. Shrimpton was a prominent landowner, whose property included much of Beacon Hill, as well as Noddle's Island in Boston Harbor.[2] The two portraits of Nicholas Roberts and his wife Elizabeth were sent to Boston in 1674. In a letter to the Shrimptons dated October 10, 1674, Roberts wrote, "you will receive by Capt foster

23 (see also color plate II)

1. Oliver 1988, pp. 13–14, 85–86.
2. Dresser 1966, p. 20.
3. Shrimpton Collection, MHS.
4. MFA 1982, 3:456.
5. Morris 1926, p. 3.
6. Hall 1979, p. 126.

24

Anne Pollard (1621–1725)
1721
Oil on canvas
28 ⅝ in. (71.5 cm) x 23 ⅞ in. (60.5 cm)
Inscribed, lower left : *Ætatis Suæ 100 / & 3 months- / Apr. Anno 1721–*
Gift of Isaac Winslow, 1834

This portrait of Anne Pollard is a significant historical document and a prime example of colonial painting before John Smibert's arrival in Boston in 1729 brought an academically-trained portrait painter to the province.[1] According to the inscription below Pollard's right arm, the portrait was executed when she was 100 years old. Her origins are obscure and not even her maiden name is known, although according to her obituary, she was born at Saffron Walden in Essex, England.[2] She claimed to have arrived with the Winthrop Fleet of 1630 and to have been the first to jump ashore at Boston, but no contemporary substantiation of that story has been found.[3] About 1643, she married innkeeper William Pollard (d. ca. 1679), and they had thirteen children. The Pollards opened a tavern in 1659 near the present site of the Park Street Church, and Mrs. Pollard continued the business after her husband's death. When she died in Boston on December 6, 1725, at the age of 104, she left 130 descen-

case sewed up in canvas w'h your marke upon it in which is mine & your mother's picktures your mother is dun well & I leav you to give your judgment of mine." The portrait of Mrs. Baker, who was Elizabeth Shrimpton's grandmother, is mentioned as part of the larger group of six paintings, which were sent to the Shrimptons later. On May 3, 1675 Nicholas Roberts wrote "I have sent you in a case yours & your wifes picktures with your grand-mothers & your three sisters."[3]

Today, the portrait of Mrs. Baker hangs at the Society together with those of Nicholas Roberts, Elizabeth Baker Roberts, and Samuel Shrimpton. The current location of the portraits of the four daughters is unknown. The likenesses of Mrs. Baker and the two Robertses are considered to be the work of the same unidentified paint-er, who was probably working in London in the 1670s.[4] Of the three, Mrs. Baker's portrait is perhaps the finest. Her face shows an uncanny naturalism evident in the pouches under her eyes, the loose jowls and the promi-nent nose. However, the artist deftly highlights her still smooth skin and her delicate coloring.

Like the portrayals of Nicholas and Elizabeth Rob-erts, Mrs. Baker's portrait exemplifies middle-class prosperity, both in her dress and in her accoutrements. Her elegant but somber dress is relieved by the elaborate lace collar of a type known as tape and needlepoint, worked into a scroll pattern.[5] Other attributes of her position include the small book with an ornate silver clasp and the gold ring on her thumb. Color is added to the picture by the bouquet of flowers which rests on a small table to her right. Flowers, which were popular in seventeenth-cen-tury European painting, were a typical emblem for female sitters and often used to symbolize the ephemeral nature of life.[6] In this case, the flowers may be a comment on Mrs. Baker's advanced age of seventy.

S.R.M.

24

25

dants. Judge Samuel Sewall was one of her pallbearers, and he also presided over the reading of her will.[4]

The unidentified Pollard painter depicted the subject without idealization. The deeply shadowed and elongated features of the face are balanced by the softly modeled arm and hand with its gracefully attenuated fingers. The symmetry of Pollard's large white collar emphasizes the severity of her face. The rather primitive painting style indicates that the work was probably painted by an American, rather than a European artist. Furthermore, the porthole format, the position of Pollard close to the viewer, and the graceful hand holding a book suggest that the painter based his composition on European mezzotints after portraits by Kneller.[5] Due to stylistic similarities, about twelve portraits painted during the early 1720s have been ascribed to this artist. They include portraits of Henry Gibbs (ca. 1721, Art Institute of Chicago); Elisha Cook, Sr. (Peabody Museum, Salem); and Mary Gardner Coffin (Nantucket Historical Association).[6]

S.R.M.

1. MFA 1982, 3:475.
2. *New England Courant*, Dec. 11, 1725.
3. MHS *Collections*, 3d ser., 7:291.
4. Pollard 1960, pp. 47–48; *New England Courant*, Dec. 11, 1725; Sewall 1973, 2:1040.
5. Belknap 1959, p. 272.
6. Saunders 1987, p. 5; Craven 1986, p. 48.

25

Dorothy Quincy (1708/9–1762)
ca. 1720
Oil on canvas
30 in. (73.6 cm) x 25¼ in. (63.8 cm)
Bequest of Oliver Wendell Holmes, Jr., 1936

Born in Braintree in 1708/9, Dorothy Quincy was the daughter of Judge Edmund Quincy and his wife Dorothy Flynt. In December 1738, her marriage announcement in the *Boston Gazette* described Dorothy as "an agreable young Gentlewoman, with a handsome Estate.[1] Though her husband was from a more modest social background, Edward Jackson (1707/8–1757) became a substantial Boston merchant and owner of iron mills at Milton. He later bought the great Quincy estate at Braintree to keep it in the family.[2]

Dorothy and Edward had two children. Their son, Jonathan Jackson, became a well-known merchant in Newburyport and Boston, and his pastel portrait (ca. 1768) by John Singleton Copley is in the collection of the Historical Society. The Jacksons' daughter, Mary, married Oliver Wendell of Cambridge in 1762. She inherited the portrait of her mother, and the picture hung in the Wendells' Cambridge home. It was Mary's grandson, Oliver Wendell Holmes (1809–1894), physician and poet, who immortalized his ancestor in the poem, "Dorothy Q: A Family Portrait." Holmes recalled his boyhood impression of the painting:

> It was a young girl in antique costume, which made her look at first sight almost like a grown woman. The frame was old, massive, carved, gilded—the canvas had been stabbed by a sword thrust—the British officer had aimed at the right eye and just missed it.[3]

Holmes himself had the painting restored, and he ended his poem with a promise and wish for the painting's future:

> It shall be a blessing, my little maid!
> I will heal the stab of the Red-Coat's blade,
> And freshen the gold of the tarnished frame,
> And gild with a rhyme your household name;
> So you shall smile on us brave and bright
> As first you greeted the morning's light,
> And live untroubled by woes and fears
> Through a second youth of a hundred years.[4]

Though the painting has been dated in the early 1720s on the basis of the flat, linear style and the apparent age of the sitter, the artist is unknown, and the portrait has not been linked to other contemporary paintings. The

fresh, clear skin tones and the brilliant red shawl contrast dramatically with the dark background on the left. The color of her dress is unusual for this period, when most were red or blue, because green dye faded easily and was thus a more expensive choice. Along with the silken shawl, this special color illustrates the material success of the sitter's family. The exotic parrot locates the picture in the New World. The three-quarter length pose with Quincy's elbow leaning on the window sill, the long curl curving over her left shoulder and the landscape, airy and illusionistic compared to the rest of the picture, are all conventions of eighteenth-century English portrait painting. Used at this period in the colonies, they indicate a familiarity with English mezzotint engravings which were known in the New World.[5] John Smith's mezzotint after Kneller portrait of Margaret, Countess of Ranelagh, may have been the artist's print source for this painting. Dorothy Quincy's pose, hairstyle, and dress are all similar to those of the Countess.[6]

J.L.P.

1. *Boston Gazette*, Dec. 4–11, 1738.
2. Sibley 1873, 8:62.
3. Tilton 1947, pp. 5–6.
4. Holmes 1895, p. 187.
5. Craven 1986, p. 171; Troyen 1980, p. 52.
6. Phillips 1955, p. 144.

Salem Witchcraft Trials

Sir William Phips arrived in Boston from London in May 1692, as the newly appointed governor of Massachusetts Bay Colony and brought with him the province's new charter. Upon his arrival, he found to his dismay that over a hundred people accused of the crime of witchcraft had been jailed in Boston. The accusations had originated with several young girls in Salem Village (now Danvers, Massachusetts), who early in the new year had succumbed to fits and other hysterical actions and had begun to accuse people in the village of tormenting them through witchcraft. The "witchcraft hysteria" has been attributed to any number of causes, including the occult; the psychopathology of adolescence; the excesses of repressive Puritanism; mass hysteria; collective persecution; and, most recently, social and economic conflict among the villagers of Salem.[1] Whatever the true origins, most people took this crime very seriously; many had been executed for witchcraft in England and Scotland and throughout Europe in the seventeenth century. Witches were perceived as a real threat, and the Bible warned against them. It was unchristian not to believe in them.[2]

Since the court system had not yet been reorganized under the new charter, Phips appointed a special Court of Oyer and Terminer ("hearing and determining") to try the accused witches in Essex, Suffolk and Middlesex counties. The court, which first convened on June 2, was composed of Lieutenant Governor William Stoughton as chief justice, Nathaniel Saltonstall (later replaced by Jonathan Corwin), John Richards, Bartholomew Gedney, Wait Winthrop, Samuel Sewall, and Peter Sergeant.[3]

After thus disposing of the matter, the governor left Boston for Maine to fight the French and Native Americans. During the summer and early autumn, nineteen persons were executed for witchcraft, and one, Giles Corey, was pressed to death for refusing to answer his indictment. This refusal by Corey could have been a way of protecting his property for his heirs, as the property of capital offenders was subject to seizure by the Crown; but it was more likely simply "a protest—the most dramatic protest of all—against the methods of the court."[4] Those accused were convicted largely on the basis of "spectral" evidence, whereby witnesses claimed that specters or images of the accused tormented them, often in the company of the Devil and their familiars (attendant animals). While Cotton Mather and other ministers cautioned that spectral evidence was not sufficient to convict a person of witchcraft, Lieutenant Governor Stoughton insisted on its admission.[5] He quit the Superior Court of Judicature the following January when spectral evidence was no longer admitted, and eight convicted witches were reprieved by the Governor.[6]

Upon his return to Boston in the autumn, Phips quickly sensed that events had gotten out of hand. More and more people, including his own wife, were "cried out" by the hysterical witnesses, and people were beginning to question the methods of the court. Phips brought the sessions of the Court of Oyer and Terminer to an end in October. In November and December the General Court set special sessions of the Superior Court of Judicature to try the remaining persons indicted for witchcraft. Three of these were convicted but reprieved by the governor along with five others awaiting execution. Finally, he issued a general pardon and emptied the jails of the remaining accused "witches."[7]

K.H.G.

1. Boyer 1974, pp. 1–8.
2. Hansen 1969, pp. 1–5; Demos 1982, pp. 4–6.
3. Hansen 1969, pp. 120–122.
4. Ibid., p. 154.
5. Ibid., p. 123; Boyer 1974, pp. 9–11.
6. Hansen 1969, pp. 205–206.
7. Ibid., pp. 204–207.

26

Samuel Sewall (1652–1730)
Diary, February 11, 1684/5–October 13, 1703
Manuscript
Unpaged, 7⁹⁄₁₆ in. (19.2 cm) x 6 in. (15.2 cm)
Purchased from family of Rev. Samuel Sewall, 1869

Samuel Sewall served as one of the judges at the infamous Salem witch trials in 1692. This alone could have tarnished his reputation in the eyes of posterity. And yet, one historian thus characterizes him: "A strong, gentle, and great man was Samuel Sewall, great by almost every measure of greatness,—moral courage, honor, benevolence, learning, eloquence, intellectual force, and breadth and brightness."[1] He earned this alternate reputation by "two humane and heroic acts [that] set him apart for all time . . . ."[2] These were his public confession of guilt in the witchcraft tragedy, and his firm antislavery stance bolstered by the publication in 1700 of his tract *The Selling of Joseph* (see no. 141).

Born at Bishop Stoke, Hampshire, England, in 1652, Sewall came to America in 1661 when his family settled in Newbury, Massachusetts. Graduating from Harvard in 1671, he married in 1676 Hannah Hull, the daughter of John Hull, America's first goldsmith, the colony mintmaster, and one of its wealthiest citizens. The couple moved into John Hull's home in Boston, where Sewall soon settled as a merchant. In 1677 he became a member of the Third (Old South) Church in Boston. In 1691 Sewall was named a member of the Governor's Council; he was elected annually to the position until June 1725, when he declined further service. On December 6, 1692, he became a justice of the Superior Court of Judicature under the new charter and in 1718 was appointed chief justice, serving in that capacity until 1728. On January 1, 1730, Sewall died at his home in Boston.[3]

Sewall kept a diary from 1673 until a few months before his death in 1730. As one of the Colony's prominent citizens, he knew all the notables of his place and time, and wrote about them, as well as about all aspects of his own daily life and activities. Scholars have found countless uses for this diary in studies of early America, for while many Puritans kept diaries, "Sewall set down the fullest existing record of how life was lived in his time. . . . Because of his devotion to record-keeping, more details and facts of his life are preserved than for most of his contemporaries, and we have nearly everything, even his weight."[4] Two complete editions of the diary have been published. Between 1878 and 1882 the Historical Society issued the first one as part of its *Collections* series. In 1973 Farrar, Straus and Giroux published a two-volume edition edited by M. Halsey Thomas.

In the spring of 1692, the governor appointed Sewall as one of the magistrates to sit on the special Court of Oyer and Terminer, established to hear the cases of the accused witches in Essex, Suffolk, and Middlesex counties. Sewall occasionally made note of the trials and executions in his diary. The diary entry for August 19, 1692, notes the execution of five persons at Salem for witchcraft. The Rev. Cotton Mather pronounced that "they all died by a righteous sentence."[5] The diary entry for September 19 notes the curious case of Giles Corey, who was pressed to death "for standing mute."[6] Corey refused to answer his indictment for witchcraft. Under English law a man who refused to answer could not be tried, but could be tortured until he either answered or died. Corey was "placed upon the ground with gradually increased weight piled on him. It took him two days to die."[7]

In December 1696 Sewall drafted a proclamation for a fast day in Massachusetts Bay for all to do penance and make reparation for the sins of the witchcraft tragedy. On January 14, 1697, Samuel Sewall stood in his pew in church while Rev. Samuel Willard read Sewall's petition confessing to his guilt and asking pardon of God and men for his role in the tragedy. Each year after that Sewall set aside a special day for fasting and prayer for forgiveness of his sins in the matter.[8]

K.H.G.

1. Tyler 1878, p. 99.
2. Kaplan in Sewall 1969, p. 28.

Richard ... at ye House of Madam Usher.

Sept.r 4.th Major Richards accompanies his Bride
to our Meeting, morning, & Evening.
N. Mr. Randolph came to Town last Friday. ———

Giles Monday; Sept.r 19. 1692. a[b]t noon, at Salem,
Corey Giles Corey was press'd to death for standing Mute
press'd much pains was used with him two days one after
to death. another by ye Court & Capt Gardner of Nantucket
who had been of his acquaintance: but all in
vain. Tr 20. Now J hear from Salem that ab.t
18 years agoe, he was suspected to have Stamp'd
and press'd a man to death: but was cleared. Twas
not rememb'd till Ann Putnam was told of it
by J[n] Corey's Spectre ye Sabbath-day night
before ye Execution.

Sept.r 20. 1692. The Swan brings in a rich
french Prize, of ab.t 300. Tuns, laden w.th
Claret, w.t wine, Brandy, Salt, Linen
Paper &c.

26

3. Thomas in Sewall 1973, pp. xxiii–xxviii.
4. Ibid., p. v.
5. Sewall, Diary, Aug. 19, 1792.
6. Ibid., Sept. 19, 1792.
7. Hansen 1969, pp. 153–154.
8. Ibid., pp. 207–210.

27
Daniel Quare (1649–1724)
Watch
London, late seventeenth or early eighteenth century
Silver and brass
Diam. 2⁵⁄₆ in. (6 cm)
Inscribed on works: *D: Quare / London / 807*; inside case
cover: NO *807*
Gift of Elizabeth Anna Byles Ellis, 1893

This early timepiece was made by watch and clockmaker
Daniel Quare of London. A master clockmaker from
1671, Quare invented a repeating work for watches about
1680, and a number of examples of his long case clocks
and watches exist in collections in England, Germany,
and Austria, and at the Metropolitan Museum of Art,
New York.[1]

27

This watch belonged to the Puritan clergyman Cotton Mather (1662/3–1727/8) and, according to family tradition, was "carried by him among the Indians, who, hearing the ticking, were frightened and thought he carried the Devil in his pocket, and ran away from him."[2] The watch has a silver pear case with engraved silver dial with a second's bit; and chain-driven brass works with tulip plate posts and pierced balance cock. With the watch is a sharkskin leather case and fob strap with silver furniture including two seals, a key, and a button hook.

Cotton Mather was from birth a member of the highest religious and intellectual circles of the province as the son of Increase Mather and grandson of Richard Mather and John Cotton, three of the most exceptional clergymen in Puritan Massachusetts (see no. 14). He soon proved his own merit by entering Harvard College at the age of twelve and in 1685 was ordained at the Second Church of Boston as his father's colleague and remained there for the rest of his life.

While his father was in London to procure a new charter for the Province of Massachusetts in the late 1680s, Cotton Mather remained in Boston as one of the local leaders in the struggle against the administration of Governor Edmond Andros. His *Declaration of the Gentlemen, Merchants, and Inhabitants of Boston* (1689) served as a clarion call for the insurgents who overthrew Andros during the local ramification of the larger Glorious Revolution, which deposed King James II in England.[3] Increase Mather returned to Boston in 1692 with the new Massachusetts charter and was accompanied by the new governor, Sir William Phips. One of the first concerns of the Phips administration was the witchcraft accusations in Salem Village, and Cotton Mather again took a leading but controversial role (see no. 29).

The most outstanding intellectual of his generation, Mather published 388 books, sermons, and pamphlets, probably more than all previous New England ministers combined. Through these works and his oft-criticized self promotion, he became perhaps the best known man in America of his times. Awarded a doctorate in divinity by the University of Glasgow, he was also created a fellow of the Royal Society in London for his scientific investigation, becoming only the eighth colonial to be so honored by one of the most illustrious scientific bodies in the world.[4]

Although Mather considered the *Biblia Americana* to be his greatest work, he was never able to find backers to publish this massive anthology and commentary on American writings. However, the *Magnalia Christi Americana; or the Ecclesiastical History of New England from its First Planting* (1702) remains his best-known work.[5] Among his manuscripts at the Historical Society are sermon notes, correspondence, the manuscript for *Biblia Americana*, and his diaries from 1682 to 1724, the lengthiest surviving for any American Puritan.

E.W.H.

1. Baillie 1947, p. 261.
2. MHS *Proceedings*, 2d ser., 8(1892–1894):80.
3. Levin 1978, ch. 5.
4. Silverman 1984, pp. 197–198, 254.
5. Ibid., pp. 157, 236–237.

28

28
Peter Pelham (1697–1751)
Cotton Mather (1663–1728)
Boston, 1728
Mezzotint
14 ⅜ in. (36.4 cm) x 10 ⅛ in. (25.7 cm)
Inscribed, at bottom: *Cottonus Matherus / S. Theologiæ Doctor Regiæ Societatis Londinensis Socius, / et Ecclesæ apud Bostonum Nov-Anglorum nuper Præpositus / Ætatis Suæ* LXV, MDCCXXVII – P. Pelham ad vivum pinxit ab Origin Fecit et excud

The first mezzotint in America was executed in honor of America's most famous minister, Cotton Mather, shortly after his death in 1728. The engraver Peter Pelham had only arrived in Boston from London the previous year. As there were no portrait painters in Boston who met Pelham's artistic standards, he painted Mather's portrait himself from life preparatory to the engraving. While the oil painting (now in the American Antiquarian Society) displays Pelham's skill as a competent, but not brilliant painter, the mezzotint engraved after it is considered to be his finest work.[1]

In the portraits Mather is not represented as an ascetic cleric, but rather as an intellectual gentleman.[2] Only his black robes, cascading in baroque abundance, and his white collar indicate his profession. Pelham chose a simple oval format and posed his sitter against a neutral background in order to concentrate his attention on Mather's expressive face. The light falls directly on the minister, so his features have an almost photographic clarity. As rendered by Pelham, Mather was not handsome, but self-confident and strong featured. While not idealizing his sitter, Pelham portrayed Mather with great dignity which was appropriate to the minister's revered position in colonial society.

Mather died on February 18, 1727/8. Less than a week later, Pelham's "PROPOSALS For Making a Print in *Metzotinto*, of the late Reverend Dr. COTTON MATHER, by *Peter Pelham*" appeared in the *Boston Gazette*. In his proposals, Pelham requested that subscribers for the print pay five shillings—three shillings down as a deposit and two more shillings on receiving the print.[3] The Society has the only surviving receipt for a deposit on the Mather print; this was signed "By me Peter Pelham" and given to Benjamin Colman, the first minister of the Brattle Street Church and ironically a long-time Mather opponent, on March 19, 1728. Although Pelham promised the prints to subscribers within two months, they were not ready for distribution until June.[4]

Peter Pelham was born in London and at the age of sixteen was apprenticed to John Simon (see nos. 19, 20). Working under Simon, one of the leading mezzotint engravers in London, Pelham was "exposed to the best work of his day in both painting and mezzotint engraving."[5] By 1720, Pelham set up his own studio in London and during the next six years engraved about twenty-five portraits in mezzotint, including six after Sir Godfrey Kneller, the most influential portrait painter of this period. Despite Pelham's success in his chosen field, the competition among engravers working in London was intense. It was probably for this reason and to better support his growing family that Pelham immigrated to Boston in 1727.[6] Just two years later, in 1729, the portrait painter, John Smibert arrived in Boston becoming Pelham's neighbor and sometime business partner (see nos. 35 and 36). Between about 1734 and 1747, Pelham engraved six portraits after Smibert's paintings, including one of Sir William Pepperrell (see no. 42).

During the twenty-four years which Pelham spent in Boston, he completed only fifteen mezzotints. With the exception of one map, the *Plan of Louisbourg* (no. 40), all Pelham's engravings were portraits, and eleven of the fourteen portraits were images of ministers. Following his Cotton Mather print, Pelham used the same format for all of his portraits of ministers. However, his later prints are much more austere in style. It has been suggested that Pelham adapted his style to fit the more conservative tastes which he encountered in America.[7]

Although Pelham had no competition from other engravers, the market in America was such that Pelham had to find alternative sources of income.[8] In 1737 he set up a finishing school in Boston where "Young Gentlemen and Ladies may be Taught Dancing, Writing, Reading, Painting upon Glass, and all sorts of Needle Work."[9] Pelham is also credited with holding the first public music concert in America in 1731.[10] In 1748 he became the stepfather of John Singleton Copley (see no. 38) upon whose work Pelham made an early impact.

Other portrait engravings by Pelham in the Society's collection, which are not included in this catalogue, are of Rev. Benjamin Colman (1735), Rev. Thomas Prince (1750), Rev. John Moorhead (1751), and Thomas Hollis (1751).

S.R.M.

1. Oliver 1973, p. 135; Craven 1986, p. 142.
2. Craven 1986, p. 143

3. *Boston Gazette*, Feb. 26—Mar. 6, 1728.
4. *Boston Gazette*, June 10–17, 1728.
5. Craven 1986, p. 141.
6. Allison 1947, p. 441.
7. Ibid., p. 443.
8. Craven 1986, p. 148.
9. *Boston Gazette*, Jan. 16–23, 1738.
10. Oliver 1973, pp. 139–140.

29

29

Cotton Mather (1663–1728)
The Wonders of the invisible world
Boston: Printed by Benjamin Harris for Samuel Phillips, 1693
In three parts: 32 p., 151 p., 32 p., 5 7/8 in. (14.9 cm) x 3 7/8 in. (9.6 cm)
Gift of James White, 1792

Clergyman, author, and scholar Cotton Mather became known as the chief apologist for the Salem witchcraft trials with the publication of his *Wonders of the Invisible World* (1693). In other witchcraft cases and early in the Salem trials, he was known for his moderate approach, which called for careful investigation using scientific methods and punishments milder than execution for convicted witches and stressed the use of fasting and prayer to cure the afflicted. However, he seemed to abandon this position in the fall of 1692 when he defended the actions of the special Court of Oyer and Terminer in this book.

In 1688 Mather had cured through fasting and prayer two children in the Goodwin family who had been tormented by witchcraft, and had suppressed the names of several accused witches in the case.[1] At this time he felt that a crisis of religious belief was at hand, that the materialists or "Sadducees" would destroy belief in the invisible world, taking the concrete out of religion and leaving nothing but a "frame of mind." Because the Goodwin case seemed to Mather a convincing example of actual witchcraft, he published an account of it in *Memorable Providences, Relating to Witchcrafts and Possessions* (1689), hoping this book would "once and for all confute materialism and reestablish Christianity on the firm foundation of a real and concrete spiritual world."[2] Mather also preached a "Discourse on Witchcraft," warning his congregation to be careful of accusations of sorcery, as it was an easy matter to misinterpret certain signs and gestures and to accuse falsely one's neighbors.[3]

When the first outbreak of accusations occurred in early 1692 in Salem Village, Mather suggested placing ministers on the bench as a way of preventing the abuse of spectral evidence.[4] He wrote letters to one of the justices, his friend John Richards, warning against the use of such evidence, recommending a "credible" confession as a means to determine the guilty and suggesting lenient punishments.[5] After the conviction of Bridget Bishop on June 2, Governor Phips asked the ministers of Boston to advise him and the Council about procedures in witchcraft cases. "The Ministers' Return," an anonymous document actually written by Cotton Mather, paraphrases his warnings to Richards, with more emphatic condemnation of the use of spectral evidence. He noted that demons could appear in the shape of innocent persons, thus the specters would not necessarily be those of practicing witches.[6] That the judges, most of whom were friends of Mather, did not follow his advice, is obvious from the results of the trials that took place over the summer.

Just as popular sentiment turned against the methods of the court and the trials were brought to an end, Mather published a vindication of the court's actions. In *The Wonders of the Invisible World*, Mather offered a defense of the trials themselves and, by extension, of the new government which instituted them.[7] He considered the broader aspects of witchcraft and argued for the justice of the verdicts in the five trials he described, since in each one there was by contemporary standards enough evidence to convict a witch. None of the five was based solely on spectral evidence. Mather was probably motivated by personal friendship and reverence for the magistrates to write the book.[8] In his diary account of the affair, he wrote that "I saw in most of the judges, a most charming instance of prudence and patience, and I knew their exemplary piety, and the agony of soul with which they sought the direction of Heaven; . . . I could not but speak honourably of their persons, on all occasions."[9] Above all, it must be remembered that Mather certainly did believe that a plague of witchcraft had visited New England: "The devils, after a most praeternatural manner, by the dreadful judgment of Heaven took a bodily pos-

session, of many people, in Salem, and the adjacent places. . . ."[10]

The publication of the book led to much controversy (see no. 30), as it seemed to contradict Mather's earlier stance for moderation and leniency. Even today his role in the whole affair remains open to argument among historians.

K.H.G.

1. Hansen 1969, p. 23.
2. Ibid, p. 27.
3. Ibid.
4. Levin 1978, p. 168.
5. Mather to Richards in MHS *Collections*, 4th ser., 8:391–397.
6. Levin 1978, p. 208.
7. Silverman 1984, p. 111.
8. Hansen in Calef 1972, p. xii.
9. Mather 1911, p. 151.
10. Ibid., p. 150.

30

Robert Calef (1648–1719)
More Wonders of the Invisible World
London: Printed for Nathaniel Hillar and
Joseph Collyer, 1700
156 p., 6 ¾ in. (17.1 cm) x 5 in. (12.6 cm)
Gift of Elizabeth Belknap, 1858

Robert Calef was born in England and emigrated to America before 1689. He became a cloth merchant or weaver, and held several town offices in Boston and Roxbury.[1] However, he owes his celebrity to the publication in 1700 of *More Wonders of the Invisible World*, a response to Cotton Mather's *Wonders of the Invisible World* (see no. 29) and to the prevailing attitudes concerning witchcraft in New England. In his book, Calef sought to discredit the Boston ministers in general, and Increase and Cotton Mather in particular, whose opinions about witchcraft were well known through the publication of various treatises on the subject.

Calef's book contains Cotton Mather's "Another Brand Pluckt out of the Burning," a previously unpublished account of the case of Margaret Rule, whom Mather treated for witchcraft affliction in 1693 through fasting and prayer. Apparently Calef obtained his copy through a third party and published it without Mather's permission.[2] The book also includes an exchange of letters on the subject of witchcraft with Cotton Mather and other Boston ministers, letters and statements concerning the differences within the Salem Village Church after the trials, an account of the five trials from Mather's *Wonders*, and a "Postscript" which criticizes Mather's biography of Sir William Phips and reiterates Calef's assertions regarding witchcraft.

While this book gained Calef a reputation with historians as an enlightened defender of reason against superstition, it also contained inaccuracies and personal attacks against the Mathers and the other Boston ministers, asserting that they somehow instigated the witchcraft delusion and encouraged the magistrates to carry through the persecutions. Calef charged the ministers with endorsing

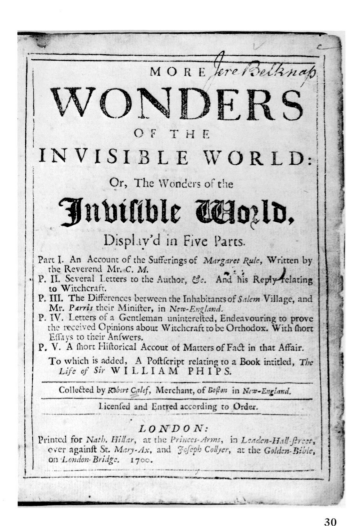

MORE *Jere Belknap*

WONDERS

OF THE

INVISIBLE WORLD:

Or, The Wonders of the

𝕵𝖓𝖛𝖎𝖘𝖎𝖇𝖑𝖊 𝖂𝖔𝖑𝖉,

Display'd in Five Parts.

Part I. An Account of the Sufferings of *Margaret Rule*, Written by the Reverend Mr. C. M.

P. II. Several Letters to the Author, *&c.* And his Reply relating to Witchcraft.

P. III. The Differences between the Inhabitants of *Salem* Village, and Mr. *Parris* their Minister, in *New-England.*

P. IV. Letters of a Gentleman uninterested, Endeavouring to prove the received Opinions about Witchcraft to be Orthodox. With short Essays to their Answers.

P. V. A short Historical Account of Matters of Fact in that Affair.

To which is added, A Postscript relating to a Book intitled, *The Life of Sir* WILLIAM PHIPS.

Collected by *Robert Calef*, Merchant, of *Boston* in *New-England.*

Licensed and Entred according to Order.

LONDON:

Printed for *Nath. Hillar*, at the *Princes-Arms*, in *London-Hall-street*, over against St. *Mary-Ax*, and *Joseph Collyer*, at the *Golden-Bible*, on *London-Bridge.* 1700.

30

the Salem court's methods; accused the Mathers of immodest conduct in the Margaret Rule case; criticized Cotton Mather's management of the Goodwin children; and in a number of different places accused him of inciting the population to a frenzy against witchcraft. One historian has suggested that Calef may have been opposed to the Mathers on political grounds, because they were strong supporters of the new charter, or perhaps on religious grounds, as Calef complained that the clergy acquired heathen superstitions through their classical educations.[3]

Calef's principal arguments concerning witchcraft and the handling of the trials in New England concerned the pervasive evil of the Devil, who would not refrain from using his power wherever he was able (thus, a witch could turn this power on and off), although since Scripture did not describe in any concrete terms what characterized a witch, people could not determine who was or was not a witch. However, Calef did not argue that witchcraft did not exist, since that would have been against Bible teachings, and his whole argument rested upon interpretation of Scripture. If he had not brought a personal attack upon the Mathers as well, if his purpose was true justice and not "to malign the Boston ministers and to make a sensation," his arguments may have carried more weight with learned persons of the time.[4] The historical virtue of the book lies in his account of the sufferings of the innocent, compared with Cotton Mather's defense of the injustice wrought at the Salem witchcraft trials.

This copy of *More Wonders of the Invisible World* was Cotton Mather's own, and bears a paraphrase from the Book of Job in his hand: "My desire is—that mine Adversary had written a Book. Surely I would take it upon my shoulder, and bind it as a crown to me." That Mather suffered personally at the hands of Calef is undoubted. Several entries in his diary and the passage from Job indicate how greatly he felt the weight of the accusations against him. While he and his father did not choose to dignify Calef's attack with a direct response, some of his supporters did in *Some Few Remarks upon a Scandalous Book* (1701), which included a letter from Mather in his defense written to his parishioners.[5]

Mather's copy of the book was later acquired by Jeremy Belknap and given to the Society's library by his daughter Elizabeth in 1858, along with a number of other Belknap items.

K.H.G.

1. Gummere 1967, p. 17.
2. Hansen 1969, p. 185.
3. Hansen in Calef 1972, pp. x–xi.
4. Poole 1886, p. 169.
5. Hansen in Calef 1972, pp. xii–xiii.

31

Salem Witch Bureau
Eastern Massachusetts, possibly Salem,
late seventeenth century
Oak and white pine with maple and walnut moldings
H. 41 in. (106.6 cm), W. 44 in. (114.2 cm), D. 20 5/8 in.
(52.5 cm)
Bequest of William H. Sumner, 1872

In his will, General William H. Sumner described this chest of drawers as "the Witch Bureau, from the middle drawer of which one of the Witches jumped out who was hung on Gallows Hill, in Salem."[1] Chests with three to five drawers have been popular since the mid-seventeenth century, providing flexible and portable storage.[2] This chest of drawers is similar in design and construction to a number of chests made in eastern Massachusetts, some of which are attributed to the Symonds workshop of Salem.

The distinctive upper front molding of the chest is cut with diagonal lines, and the band below has gauged notches. The lower molding extends around the sides. Applied paired spindles are turned in columnar lengths appropriate to the varying drawer sizes, and are ebonized. The top couple of drawers and the middle large drawer have panel designs symmetric about central pairs of spindles, while the other drawers have three panels. All the drawer panels are edged with red molding in bold geometric patterns.

The drawers hang on runners that are rabbeted into the stiles. The drawer fronts are rabbeted to accept the sides and bottoms. Double-pegged mortise-and-tenon joints link the stiles and rails. The sides of the chest are formed of four regular panels. The back has two horizontal panels with beveled edges.

With a single exception, the brass teardrop pulls with star-shaped plates appear to be original. The top of

the chest has been replaced. Ball feet probably originally supported the chest.

Chests of similar design are identified with eastern Massachusetts. Such chests have geometric patterned front panels, four-paneled sides, and distinctive upper moldings, cut with diagonal slashes above a band of gauged notches. They generally have ball feet and corbels.[3] The Salem Witch Bureau is included in a group of six chests thought to have been made in Salem, possibly in the Symonds workshop. Attributes frequently common to chests in this group include paired split spindles, a 2–3–2–3 configuration of panels per drawer level, and the same distinctive molding.[4]

John Symonds (bef. 1595–1671) was a joiner from Great Yarmouth, Norfolk, England, who immigrated to Salem, where he set up a shop. He trained his sons James (1633–1714) and Samuel (1638–1722) and a number of

other apprentices.[5] It is possible that one of the sons or apprentices made this fine chest.

The Historical Society's furniture collection includes several other seventeenth-century pieces, notably the Paine family cupboard from Essex County, a turner's chair from the Byles family, and a caned side chair from the Winthrop family.[6]

H.J.C.

1. Sumner 1861, p. 31.
2. Ward 1988, p. 123.
3. Randall 1965, p. 32.
4. Ward 1988, p. 131.
5. MFA 1982, 2:526; Forman 1971, p. 30.
6. Kane 1976, pp. 960–969.

32

32

John Hull (1624–1683) and Robert Sanderson (1608–1693),
designers and engravers
New England Shilling
Boston, 1652
Silver
Irregular hammered planchet; stamped, on obverse: NE;
on reverse: XII
D. 1 ⅛ in. (29 mm)
Bequest of William Sumner Appleton, 1905

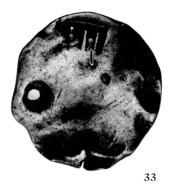

33

33

John Hull (1624–1683) and Robert Sanderson (1608–1693),
designers and engravers
New England Threepence
Boston, 1652
Silver
Irregular hammered planchet, pierced, stamped, on
obverse: NE; on reverse: III
D. ¾ in. (19 mm)
Bequest of William Sumner Appleton, 1905

These small coins represent an official acknowledgment
of New England's growing sense of identity as separate
from the mother country. The Massachusetts General
Court's act of May 26–27, 1652 establishing a mint in Boston, was an act of defiant trespass upon the Crown's prerogative to mint coins by a colony determined to regulate
its own economy without British interference. Considered a possession existing solely for the economic benefit
of the mother country, the Massachusetts Bay colony
was kept short of ready money in order to prevent trade
with England's competitors and enemies. New England provided raw materials in the form of naval supplies
and furs to England in exchange for manufactured goods,
bills of exchange payable only in London, and debased
coinage unacceptable to Europeans, that is, coins with

precious metal content below legal standards but not
necessarily counterfeit.[1] Initially this was not a problem,
as arriving immigrants carried enough coins and credit to
pay for their food and housing. However, in the late
1630s, when political troubles in England caused a halt in
immigration, the demand for food and services was so
far below the abundant supply that the colony experienced its first depression.[2] In August of 1640 Governor
John Winthrop lamented that "the scarcity of money
made a great change in all commerce."[3] King Charles I
and Oliver Cromwell were involved with England's political situation and resultant Civil War, so the Massachusetts Bay Colony was left to govern itself under the Royal
Charter granted in 1628/9.

New England had long practiced a barter system. At
different periods in its history grain, fish, furs, wampum,
and even musket balls were used as a legal medium of
exchange. To bolster this commodity trading, New England began an illegal trade with foreign markets. In exchange for lumber, dried and salted fish, and pipe staves
the province received cotton, wines, and Spanish gold
and silver. New England also received visits from free-
spending buccaneers and pirates so that, by 1652, there
was in circulation considerable coinage, a great deal of
which was counterfeit, clipped, and debased. At this
point the province seized the initiative to regulate its own
coinage. This led John Hull to write that "upon occasion of much counterfeit coin brought in the country, and much loss accruing in that respect . . . the General Court ordered a mint to be set up, and to coin it. . . .
And they made choice of me for that employment, and I
chose my friend Robert Sanderson, to be my partner, to
which the Court consented."[4]

Born in Market-Hareborough, England, Hull emigrated to Boston with his family in 1635. He learned the
craft of goldsmithing from his half-brother Richard
Storer, who had trained under London goldsmith James
Fearne and about whom little is known.[5] In 1647 John
Winthrop officiated at Hull's marriage to Judith Quincy
(1626–1695), which marked the beginning of his career as
a landholder and merchant. By 1655, using products from
his holdings and the bullion to which he had access as a
goldsmith, Hull had established himself as one of Boston's leading merchants.[6] Later, as an elected official with
wide-ranging commercial contacts, he was responsible
for outfitting the colony in preparation for the 1675–1676
war with King Philip.[7] John and Judith Hull's only surviving child, Hannah, married Samuel Sewall in 1675/6.
As the young couple lived with the Hulls, they figured
prominently in Sewall's diaries (no. 26).

Robert Sanderson served a nine-year apprenticeship
with William Rawlins of London before bringing his
family to Massachusetts in 1638. Given his unusually long
apprenticeship, the quality of his surviving work, and
Hull's extremely varied business interests, Sanderson is
believed to have carried on most of the work at the mint.[8]
Credited as colonial America's first silversmiths, the
partnership of Hull and Sanderson lasted from 1652 until
Hull's death in 1683.

The first act for the coining of money specified that
anyone could take bullion, Spanish coin or plate to be
melted down by mintmaster John Hull "to be cojned
into twelve penny, sixpenny, and threepenny peeces,
which shall be . . . stamped on the one side with NE, and

on the other side with the figure xiid, vid, & iiid . . . together with a privy marke which shall be appointed euery three months."[9] Created by striking both sides of a silver planchet with steel punches much like those used to make goldsmith's marks, these New England coins were minted only from June through October of 1652.[10] Because they were too easily counterfeited or clipped, the General Court issued an act providing for a more intricate design with lettering to discourage this tampering.[11] This Willow Tree coinage (1652–1660) evolved into the Oak Tree coinage (1660–1667) and then into the famous Pine Tree coinage (1667–1682), all of which bear the single date of 1652 although Hull and Sanderson continued to mint them until Hull's contract as mintmaster expired in 1682.[12] Ironically, the mint had effectively ceased operation by 1684 when the Massachusetts Bay Company's charter was revoked for, among other reasons, the violation of the Crown's prerogative to mint coins.[13]

The Massachusetts Historical Society sold the bulk of its coin collection (mostly foreign pieces) during the 1970s but retained its earliest American pieces. Among them are a Willow Tree twopence and sixpence, an Oak Tree sixpence, a contemporary counterfeit Pine Tree shilling, several of the early Washington cents, quarters and half dollars (1783–1796), and a couple of pattern coins of note (see no. 84).

A.E.B.

1. Breen 1988, p. 699.
2. McCusker 1978, p. 132.
3. Winthrop 1826, 2:18.
4. Hull 1857, pp. 145–146.
5. Buhler 1956, p. 13.
6. Kane 1987, pp. 33–35.
7. Clarke 1940, p. 170.
8. Kane 1987, p. 53.
9. Mass. 1854, 4, pt. 1:84.
10. Kane 1987, p. 50.
11. Ibid., p. 104.
12. Breen 1988, pp. 11–18.
13. Crosby 1875, p. 91.

34
Engraving attributed to John Coney (1655/6–1722)
Massachusetts Colony Bill of Credit, Two Shillings Sixpence
Boston, 1690/1
Engraving
5⁷/₁₆ in. (13.5 cm) x 4⅛ in. (10.4 cm)
Inscribed, recto: [scroll at indenture] / *No. (110* [ms.]*)*
20s / THIS *Indented Bill of Twenty / Shillings due from the Massachusets / Colony to the Possessor shall be in value / equal to money & shall be accordingly / accepted by the Tresurer and Receivers / subordinate to him in all Publick payments / and for any Stock at any time in the / Treasury Boston in New-England / February the third 1690 By Order of / the General Court* / Seal of the Colony of the Massachusetts Bay (an Indian holding a bow and arrow, with *Come over & help us* issuing in reverse from his mouth) / *Comĩtee* (signed Penn Townsend / Adam Winthrop / Tim Thornton). Verso: [scroll at indenture]
Gift of Henry S. Nourse, 1891

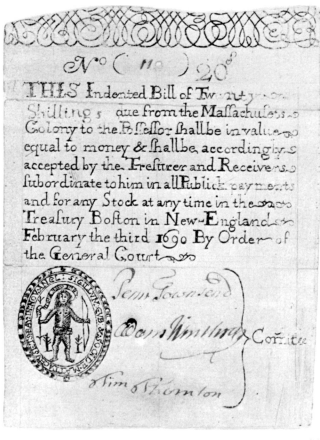

34

Five years after losing its colony charter (see no. 33), Massachusetts joined the rest of New England in King William's War (1689–1697). In the fall of 1690 a fleet was equipped and dispatched under Sir William Phips to take Quebec with the expectation that the resulting spoils would finance the campaign. The Phips Expedition was a dismal failure, and soldiers returning in November looked to an empty treasury for their pay. The threat of riots prompted the provisional government to pass an act on December 10, 1690, authorizing the printing of £7,000 in paper bills of credit, which were backed by taxes, excises, and fees that would be levied and collected later.[1] This was the first use of a government-backed paper money in the western world.[2]

Wary after their experience with their mint and anticipating a new charter, the colonials were careful to call their notes "bills of credit," not money. These bills promised the holder credit towards his taxes ("publick payments") or coin ("stock"), when available, from the treasury. An interesting feature of the note is the use of the seal of the Colony of the Massachusetts Bay, defunct since 1684. This followed an earlier precedent of printing legal documents with the governing body's seal, but since Massachusetts was between charters in 1690, the last official seal of the colony was used to indicate that the bills were official documents.

Initially, this first issue was met with such resistance that Cotton Mather was moved to publicly "wonder at the great indiscretion of our Countrymen who Refuse to accept that, which they call Paper-money, as pay of equal value with the best Spanish Silver."[3] By February 1690/1 it was clear that more bills were needed, so the government authorized another issue, and announced a five percent premium on all bills paid into the treasury for taxes.[4]

As with coins, counterfeiting and alteration became a serious problem from the start. This example is one of three known surviving bills of this second issue, all of which have been fraudulently raised in value from two shillings sixpence to twenty shillings. They were apparently altered by Robert Fenton and Benjamin Pierce who stood trial in Cambridge and Charlestown courts in 1691 for raising thirty-seven of such bills to ten- and twenty-shilling denominations.[5] As long as these raised bills passed unknowingly in payment of private debts, they were accepted. However, when bills were returned to the treasury in payment for taxes or for redemption in coin, denominations were matched against the numbered, indented stubs in the treasurer's books, then redeemed and destroyed. If the bills did not match the stubs, they were not redeemed and thus escaped destruction.

The Massachusetts Historical Society's note differs slightly from the others in letter spacing and style, ornamentation, and the seal. This example is blank on the verso, which indicates that it was issued prior to the act of July 2, 1692, requiring that all bills paid out be endorsed by either Jeremiah Dummer or Francis Burroughs.[6] In all, £40,000 worth of these bills were issued to settle the debts incurred during the Quebec expedition, and they circulated until they were retired in 1702.[7]

The engraving for these bills has been attributed to silversmith John Coney based on the similarity of style between them and the Massachusetts issues of 1702 and 1710, which he is known to have engraved.[8] Boston born and trained, Coney made his earliest known piece of plate in 1676, the year he turned twenty-one. Recent scholarship has determined that Coney served his apprenticeship under Jeremiah Dummer (1645–1718), who studied under mintmaster John Hull.[9] As a master silversmith, Coney trained many young men, the last of whom, Apollos Rivoire (1702–1754), trained his own son, Paul Revere.[10] The printing of the notes is tentatively attributed to the Greens at the press in Cambridge. After the Boston press burned in September 1690, Bartholomew Green joined his father, Samuel, Sr., in Cambridge, where they worked until the latter retired in 1692. As the Greens had the contract to print the act of December 10, 1690, it is possible that they also printed the bills.

This note is an example from the Society's extensive paper currency collection, which includes American colonial currency and fiscal paper, merchant's scrip, and private bank notes, all with a heavy concentration on Massachusetts, as well as National bank notes, United States fractional currency and legal tender, and emergency military scrip.

A.E.B.

1. Newman 1990, p. 158.
2. Hunter 1943, pp. 316, 361.
3. Mather 1971, p. 189.
4. Davis 1971, pp. 26–27.
5. Scott 1957, pp. 24–28.
6. Mass. 1869, p. 35.
7. Davis 1971, p. 27.
8. Clarke 1932, p. 10.
9. Kane 1987, pp. 113–114.
10. Federhen 1988, p. 65.

35

35

John Smibert (1688–1751)
Jane Clark (1722–ca. 1753)
1732
Oil on canvas
50 in. (128 cm) x 40¾ in. (103.4 cm)
Gift of Susan Minns, 1916

Jane Clark was born in Boston in 1722, the daughter of Jonathan and Mary (Phillips) Clark. In 1741 she married Ezekiel Lewis, a Harvard graduate who had joined the family merchant trade. The couple settled in Boston, where they were important members of the Old South Church. Jane Clark Lewis died young, in or shortly after 1753, leaving her husband and four children.[1]

When this portrait was given to the Society, it was attributed to Hogarth and dated 1739, but Blackburn was also suggested as the artist. The scholar William Sawitzsky first attributed the portrait to Smibert, an attribution accepted by Smibert expert Richard Saunders.[2] The date of 1732 is taken from John Smibert's notebook, where he notes "Ms. Clark—whole lenth" in September of that year.[3] The notebook, which contains a list of his portrait commissions from 1722 to 1746, is the property of the Public Record Office, London, and was published by the Historical Society in 1969. Since its publication, a number of portraits, formerly believed to be the work of other artists, have been attributed to Smibert.

Smibert was born in Edinburgh, Scotland, but moved to London in 1709 and there worked as a coach painter and made copies of paintings for picture dealers. His formal art training was at the academy operated by Sir Godfrey Kneller (1646–1723), the premier portrait painter in England during this period.[4] Kneller promoted a sophisticated and aristocratic style of portraiture in which it was more important to present the subject's exalted position in society than to show his or her individual character. Smibert returned to Edinburgh about 1716 and worked as a portrait painter for nearly three years before he embarked on a sojourn to Italy (1719–1722). During this trip Smibert copied masterpieces by Renaissance and Baroque artists as well as painting from life.[5]

Back in London in 1722, Smibert soon established himself as a professional portraitist. Between the years 1722 and 1728, Smibert completed 175 portrait commissions, averaging twenty-five per year.[6] In 1728, he accepted an offer from his friend Dean George Berkeley (1685–1753) to be part of a small group to establish a college in Bermuda. Smibert was to be the professor of art and architecture and set sail for America with Berkeley's group in September 1728. Landing in 1729, the group settled temporarily in Newport, Rhode Island, to await the arrival of the additional funds necessary for the establishment of the college. Soon after their arrival, Smibert began a group portrait of himself and his fellow travelers, now known as the *Bermuda Group* (Yale University Art Gallery). Completed in 1730, it is considered Smibert's masterpiece, and is the largest group portrait painted in America up until that time. In the same year Smibert also painted a smaller bust-length portrait of Berkeley, which is now in the Society's collection.

By May 1729 Smibert had moved to Boston, presumably to be better able to support himself by painting portraits in the more populous town. Sometime during Smibert's first winter there, he held an exhibition in his studio. Not only did he exhibit his own recent portraits, but also the copies he had made of masterpieces while in Italy, as well as some plaster casts of antique statues he had brought from Europe. This was the first "art exhibition" in America and the public's response was overwhelmingly positive. One spectator, Mather Byles, the young nephew of Cotton Mather, was so taken with the artist's work that he wrote an eighty line laudatory poem, "To Mr. Smibert on the Sight of His Pictures."[7] In 1730 Smibert married Mary Williams, the twenty-three-year-old daughter of Nathaniel and Anne (Bradstreet) Williams. The Society now owns Smibert's portrait of Mary Williams (1729), painted during his first year in Boston.

It was clear by 1731 that the money necessary to establish the college in Bermuda would never be forthcoming, and although Berkeley returned with his family to England, Smibert decided to remain in Boston, where he was already established as the town's foremost portrait painter. In 1734, Smibert extended his interests and opened a "color shop" in his home on Queen Street, where he began to sell "all sorts of colours, dry or ground, with oils, and Brushes, Fans of Several Sorts, the best Mezotints, Italian, French, Dutch and English Prints."[8] The shop seems to have been quite successful becoming a gathering place for artists as well as for those with an interest in art. Smibert continued to paint portraits until about 1746, and his American production totals 250 paintings during his seventeen years here.

Waldron Phoenix Belknap, in his pioneering work on the influence of English mezzotints on American colonial portraiture, suggests that the source for Jane Clark's pose is a mezzotint of Lady Essex Mostyn by John Smith after Kneller (1705).[9] Certainly, the landscape setting, which opens up to a vista on the right, and the position of Clark on an incline beside a tree suggest the print after Kneller. However, unlike his mentor, Smibert seems to have painted a realistic likeness. Posing in her sumptuous pink satin gown, Jane Clark seems somewhat stiff, but her basket of fruit, from which she offers an apple, serves to engage the viewer. Smibert used a similar landscape background in his portrait of James Bowdoin (1736, Bowdoin College Museum of Art).[10]

S.R.M.

1. Sibley 1873, 9:550; Thwing Catalogue, MHS.
2. Foote 1950, pp. 144–145.
3. Smibert 1969, p. 98.
4. Saunders 1987, p. 113.
5. Craven 1986, p. 153; Saunders 1987, p. 113.
6. Riley 1971, p. 162.
7. Ibid., p. 167.
8. *Boston Newsletter*, Oct. 10–17, 1734.
9. Belknap 1959, p. 305, plate XXXIII.
10. Saunders 1987, pp. 124–125.

36

36
John Smibert (1688–1751)
Peter Faneuil (1700–1743)
Boston, 1739
Oil on canvas
50 in. (127.5 cm) x 40½ in. (103 cm)
Gift of Charles Faneuil Jones and Eliza Jones, 1835

Perhaps the most striking of the eight portraits by or attributed to John Smibert in the Society's collection is the portrait of Peter Faneuil. The son of French Huguenot parents, Peter Faneuil was the eldest of their eleven children born in New Rochelle, New York. Following the death of his father in 1718, he moved to Boston, where his uncle Andrew Faneuil was a prosperous merchant and real-estate investor. Peter Faneuil entered the family business and upon his uncle's death in 1738 inherited the estate and became one of the richest men in Boston.[1] His sister Mary Ann Faneuil (1715–1790) managed his household for him, and in 1739 Smibert painted their portraits,[2] both of which are now in the collection of the Historical Society.

Faneuil was active in civic affairs, serving as a selectman for Boston and contributing to a number of causes. Today he is best remembered for financing the construction of Faneuil Hall, a combination market and municipal building. Begun in 1740, the structure was designed by John Smibert, his only known foray into architecture. The two-story brick structure had an open arcade on the first level which housed the market. The upper story contained a series of meeting rooms and municipal offices, including those of the board of selectmen.[3] As local historian A. E. Brown observed, "The house given by Peter Faneuil to the town of Boston was regarded as the greatest munificence the town had received."[4]

Upon the completion of the hall Smibert was commissioned by the town to paint a full-length portrait of Faneuil to hang there. At the first public meeting in the hall on September 13, 1742 it was voted: "That in testimony of the town's gratitude to Peter Faneuil, Esq., and to perpetuate his memory, that the Hall over the Market Place, be named Faneuil Hall, and at all times hereafter, be called and known by that name."[5]

Faneuil died in 1743, and the painting, as well as the building, became a fitting memorial to him. The finished portrait by Smibert hung in Faneuil Hall until 1761, when it was damaged by a fire, which also extensively destroyed the interior of the building. The current building, which is a substantial enlargement of Smibert's design, is largely the work of Charles Bulfinch (1763–1844).

This half-length portrait of Peter Faneuil exemplifies the increasing realism found in Smibert's portraits after his first years in Boston. The figure, which is slightly over life-size stands close to the spectator. His brown velvet coat and vest and ruffled shirt indicate his prosperity. Yet the richness of the fabric is understated rather than ostentatious. His serious expression and thoughtful stare indicate his sobriety and intelligence. The seascape glimpsed through the window on the ship indicates Faneuil's mercantile interests and is a typical convention from British portraiture. In fact, the composition suggests Smibert may have modeled Faneuil on Kneller's portrait of Dudley Woodbridge which was made into a mezzotint by John Smith (1718).[6] Two other half-length portraits of Faneuil by Smibert are known today. One is now in the collection of the Corcoran Gallery, Washington, D.C., while the other is privately owned.[7]

S.R.M.

1. Brown 1900, ch. 2–3.
2. Smibert 1969, p. 96.
3. Brown 1946, p. 62.
4. Brown 1900, p. 86.
5. Foote 1950, p. 81.
6. Belknap 1959, p. 138.
7. Oliver 1988, p. 40.

37

37
Joseph Badger (1708–1765)
John Joy, Jr. (1751–1813)
Boston, ca. 1758
Oil on canvas
40⅓ in. (102.3 cm) x 31 in. (78.5 cm)
Gift of Benjamin Joy, 1953

Born in 1751, John Joy, Jr., was the eldest son of a prosperous Boston builder and landowner who joined the 1759 military expedition to Quebec, where his abilities won him a commission. Early in the Revolution, the father was assistant engineer to the British troops under General Gage, but the whole family fled to England during the Evacuation of Boston in 1776. Though some members of the family remained in England, John Joy, Jr., returned home in 1783 with his wife, Abigail Greene of Boston, whom he had married in England in 1777. He worked as an apothecary and druggist in Boston during the 1780s, was called a merchant in the 1790s, and after 1805 listed himself as a physician in the *Boston Directory*. By the time of his death in 1813 Joy, now styled a gentleman, had accumulated a sizable estate including stores in Boston and a mansion house on Beacon Street next to John Hancock's home.[1]

The artist Joseph Badger, the son of a Charlestown tailor, was born in 1708. He married in 1733 and moved across the river to Boston two years later. In order to provide for his family, which grew to include nine children, Badger painted houses and signs and by the early 1740s he was painting portraits as well. Though Badger was largely self-trained, he did know and imitate the work of the painter John Smibert. Badger lived near Smibert's studio and shop and probably bought supplies for his own work there.[2] He had little competition in the years between Smibert's retirement in 1745 and the beginning of John Singleton Copley's career in 1753 as well as the appearance of Joseph Blackburn in the same year. Badger's twenty-year career as a portraitist produced 150 surviving works. Though none are signed, his style is well-defined and very recognizable.[3]

The major characteristics of Badger's work can be seen in his full-length portrait of John Joy, Jr., as a well-dressed child of about seven years. As in most Badger portraits, the subject faces the viewer directly with a sober and, in this case, sincere expression. The muted colors of Badger's palette can be seen in the young boy's soft brown curls, gray suit, and blue waistcoat; colors which are echoed in the more freely painted landscape of the background. The artist's careful modeling of the figure and methodically articulated buttons, gathered cuffs, and other details of the costume illustrate his desire to follow the example of academically trained artists like Smibert.

J.L.P.

1. Jones 1930, p. 185; Thwing Catalogue, MHS; Suffolk Probate file 24333.
2. Park 1917, pp. 158–201.
3. Saunders 1987, p. 191.

38

John Singleton Copley (1738–1815)
James Allen (1739–1808)
1768–1770
Oil on canvas
30 in. (76.5 cm) x 25 in. (63.5 cm)
Gift of Susan Allen, 1836

Born in Boston in 1739, James Allen was the older brother of Sheriff Jeremiah Allen (see no. 110) and the great-grandson of Parson James Allen, the largest holder of real estate in the history of the town. Though he entered Harvard College in 1756, Allen cut classes, played cards, and dropped out in the middle of his second year. Living on the proceeds of his family's real estate holdings, he wrote poetry but seemed indifferent as to whether it were published or not. Though some Bostonians questioned Allen's political sympathies, his patriotic poem *Lines on the Boston Massacre*, was carried to publication in Boston in 1772 by friends. His unpublished epic on the Battle of Bunker Hill is now lost.[1] Near the end of his life, Allen's personal behavior continued to intrigue the locals. In 1797, one contemporary claimed that "he is an Atheist & the popular report is that he keeps his coffin in his bed chamber & sometimes sleeps in it."[2] James Allen never married. He died in Boston in 1808.

John Singleton Copley's beginnings were modest. His parents emigrated from Ireland to Boston around 1736 and became the proprietors of a tobacco shop on

38

Long Wharf. Copley's father died shortly after his son's birth, and in 1748 the widowed Mary Singleton Copley married Peter Pelham, a local engraver (see no. 42). Young Copley learned to paint and engrave in his step-father's studio. Although he studied the work of other contemporary Boston painters, including John Smibert, Robert Feke (ca. 1705–ca. 1750), John Greenwood (1727–1792), and later, Joseph Blackburn (active 1753–1764 in America), Copley was greatly talented and ambitious and quickly learned to trust his own eye. By the time he reached his early twenties, he had established his reputation as a portrait painter, and some of the most illustrious inhabitants of the colonies came to him as sitters. Between 1753, the year he produced his first works, and 1774, the year he left the colonies to live and work in England, Copley produced approximately 350 paintings, most of them portraits.[3] Though portrait painting had made him a wealthy, and therefore respected man, he lamented that "Were it not for preserving the resemblance of particular persons, painting would not be known in the place. The people generally regard it no more than another useful trade . . . not as one of the noble arts in the world."[4]

By the late 1760s, when the Allen portrait was painted, John Singleton Copley had literally "climbed the hill." In 1769 he married Susanna Clarke and entered one of the elite mercantile families of the town. He built a house and began to buy other property on Beacon Hill near that of John Hancock, the richest man in town. Copley's marriage marked both a personal milestone and a change in his artistic style. The ebullient style of previous years, especially evident in the large, full-length portraits of youthful social scions, was replaced by a more restrained manner and a more somber palette.[5] The artist's strong, sober portrait of James Allen is representative of his smaller bust portraits of the late 1760s. Though

Allen was castigated in his own time as an eccentric was-trel, Copley portrayed him as a mature individual. Only a trace of youthful defiance remains in his intense gaze. Two rows of splendid gold buttons enliven the sitter's dark clothing and indicate his wealth. The artist's characteristic dramatic contrasts between light and shadow are emphasized here in the sharp definition of form against the darker colors of his palette.

J.L.P.

1. Sibley 1873, 14:245.
2. Dunlap 1969, p. 177.
3. Prown 1966, pp. 22, 97.
4. MHS *Collections*, 71:65–66.
5. Prown 1966, p. 61.

39

39
John Singleton Copley (1738–1815)
Samuel Danforth (1696–1777)
Boston, ca. 1758
Oil on copper
5 ⅝ in. (12.9 cm) x 4½ in. (10.5 cm)
Gift of Elizabeth and Mary Danforth, 1881

Judge Samuel Danforth was born in Dorchester in 1696, the sixth child of the local minister. He attended Harvard College as a scholarship student, graduating in 1715, and then kept school, first at Dorchester and later at Cambridge. In 1725 he married Elizabeth Symmes and brought his bride to Cambridge where he had bought a house on the east side of Dunster Street. In 1730 Danforth turned from teaching to surveying frontier towns for the General Court, dabbled in literary matters, and assisted Thomas Prince with his historical researches. In the following years Danforth became active in town government in

Cambridge, which in 1734 elected him to the Massachusetts House of Representatives. He was returned to that seat several times and in 1739 was promoted to the Council where he remained until 1774. Subsequently appointed register of probate by the royal governor, he rose to the post of judge of the Middlesex court of common pleas in 1741 and served for thirty-four years, the latter part of his term as chief justice.[1]

Always interested in medicine and science, Danforth had been successfully inoculated against smallpox in early experiments during the epidemic of 1721. In 1730 in the midst of another smallpox outbreak, his neighbors rebelled when he inoculated others and, frightened for their own health, demanded that the infected individuals be removed from the town. Newspaper attacks against Danforth at the time belittled him as "Madam Chemia," in reference to his notorious interest in alchemy long after it had been eschewed by most scientists.[2]

After 1770 Danforth ceased to be active in politics, though still a senior member of the Council. He was one of the Mandamus Councillors named in May 1774, but the mob actions of that spring convinced him to resign and he fled from Cambridge to his son's home in Boston for safety. Though the judge remained in Boston during the Revolution until his death in 1777, one of his sons fled to England and the other was arrested as a Tory.[3]

This unusually large miniature of Samuel Danforth was painted about 1758, midway through the judge's years of judicial service but relatively early in John Singleton Copley's career as a colonial portraitist. Copley produced the majority of his miniatures between 1758 and 1761. Though accomplishing successful miniatures using watercolor on ivory in later years, he departed from the "true miniature" of the English tradition in this early period by using oil on copper.[4] The year 1758 marked the ripening of the twenty-year-old's artistic genius, and these early miniatures are similar in style and technique to his full-size oil portraits.[5] The almost palpable reality he achieved is evident in his portrayal of Judge Danforth. The frontal pose, unusual for Copley's miniatures during this period, is relaxed and natural, the face and eyes are animated and communicate with the viewer. The amiable but dignified expression of Judge Danforth and Copley's lively, fresh color also help to fulfill another requirement of painting "in little," that is, achieving a great deal in a very small space.[6]

J.L.P.

1. Sibley 1873, 6:80–86.
2. Ibid., 6:83.
3. Ibid., 6:84–85.
4. Prown 1966, p. 29.
5. Craven 1986, p. 318.
6. Wehle 1927, p. 3.

Louisbourg

The capture of the French fortress of Louisbourg in Nova Scotia by a New England army in 1745 was the most celebrated feat of arms in American colonial history. For more than one hundred years, Nova Scotia, the maritime boundary land between Puritan New England and French Canada, was a battleground, and on three separate occasions (1654, 1690, and 1710) New Englanders attacked the French settlements there. In 1720, to protect their access to the Atlantic fisheries and trade, the French began construction of a great fortress city at Louisbourg on Cape Breton. Louisbourg protected French territory, but also posed a threat to, and a source of competition for, New England shipping and fishing. Puritan New Englanders feared French power in Canada, particularly as it instigated trouble with the Native Americans along the northern and western border.[1]

In 1744, the outbreak of King George's War led to French attacks on the New England outposts in Nova Scotia at Canso and Annapolis. Governor William Shirley of Massachusetts responded by planning a great colonial expedition to reduce Louisbourg and, he thought, finally end the threat to New England. Colonel William Pepperrell (see no. 43) was placed in command of almost 3,000 New England soldiers and a fleet of fifty-two colonial vessels, which set sail from Boston on Sunday, April 4, 1745.

Sailing on a Sunday was not accidental. The expedition against Louisbourg had been trumpeted by ministers in Boston as a protestant crusade against "Satanic" Catholic Canada. As with other crusades, the possibility of adventure and plunder appealed to the majority of the young soldiers and sailors, but almost all New Englanders believed in the righteousness of their purpose, and that the expedition had the blessing of the Almighty. A wave of fasting, religious revival and patriotic sermons reinforced this belief. Cynical Benjamin Franklin, a Bostonian by birth then living in Philadelphia, observed in a letter to a brother in Massachusetts that "in attacking strong towns I should have more dependence on *works*, than on *faith*."[2]

At first, the expedition truly appeared to have benefited from a divine blessing when it was joined at Louisbourg by a Royal Navy squadron under the command of Commodore Peter Warren from the West Indies. The understrength French garrison did not put up a strong defense, and the fortress was taken after a forty-nine-day siege and relatively little hard fighting. The extraordinary victory was greeted by popular celebrations throughout America and in England, but especially in New England, as the first major victory gained primarily by colonial troops (see no. 41).

The aftermath of the victory was not so happy. There had been considerable friction between the colonial troops and the Royal Navy during the siege, and the following winter, through incompetence and mismanagement, the New England garrison at Louisbourg lost more than 1200 men to disease, a far higher toll than actual combat casualties during the capture of the fortress.[3] The most bitter blow, however, came at the end of the war, when the Treaty of Aix-la-Chapelle returned "New England's conquest" to the French as part of the general peace settlement in October 1748. Ten years later,

in the next round of the French and Indian wars, Louisbourg would be captured again by another Anglo-American expedition, and this time the fortress was completely leveled, but a lasting sense of betrayal, and distrust for British imperial policy had already been planted in the minds of New Englanders in 1748.[4]

In addition to the engravings, broadside, and powder horn shown herein, the Historical Society holds several manuscript collections that document the Louisbourg campaign. These include not only the papers and manuscript diaries of ordinary soldiers and sailors, and collections of official documents and records, but also personal papers of Governor William Shirley and Sir William Pepperrell. The Pepperrell Papers were one of the first gifts to the Society, donated by founder Jeremy Belknap in October 1791, and published in 1889 in the *Collections of the Massachusetts Historical Society*.

P.D.

1. Rawlyk 1967, pp. xv–xviii.
2. Ibid., pp. 44–48; Benjamin Franklin to John Franklin, 1745, quoted in ibid., p. 57.
3. Leach 1977, pp. 36–54.
4. Rawlyk 1967, p. 158–159.

40

Peter Pelham (1697–1751) after Richard Gridley (1710–1796)
A Plan of the City and Fortress of Louisbourg
Boston: Sold by John Smibert, 1746
Mezzotint
17¼ in. (44 cm) x 21⅛ in. (53.8 cm)
Gift of George G. Wolkins, 1926

In the winter of 1745–1746, Richard Gridley, who had commanded the artillery train at the Siege of Louisbourg, drew this handsome map of the city and fortress. The skillfully executed map, dated February 5, 1745[/6], and dedicated to Governor William Shirley, "Captain General and Governor in Chief," documents the siege and includes an inset "Plan of the Harbour" and a profile of the fortifications.[1]

Gridley apparently placed his manuscript map in the hands of Peter Pelham, the Boston mezzotintist and music-school teacher who produced the elegant engraving, his only surviving nonportrait mezzotint. Advertised in the *Boston Gazette* on September 16, 1746, it was sold by John Smibert in Queen Street, Boston, as were many of Pelham's other engravings.[2]

Richard Gridley, a Boston surveyor and engineer, was introduced to military engineering and gunnery by John Henry Bastide, a young English military engineer serving in America who later would become chief engineer of the Royal Army. This lead to Gridley's appointment as both chief engineer and artillerist during the 1745 Louisbourg campaign. He supervised the construction of Pepperrell's siege works and the bombardment of the French fortress, personally firing mortar shells into the Louisbourg citadel, during the destructive bombardment that hastened its surrender.[3]

After King George's War, Gridley served as a regular officer in the British Army. He later served with the Massachusetts provincial artillery in the French and Indian War, including service at the second siege of Louisbourg in 1758. At the beginning of the Revolutionary War, Gridley was too old for active service, but few Americans had technical military training and experience; he was given command of the Massachusetts artillery regiment in May 1775, and later the same post, as well as that of chief engineer, in the Continental Army. In June 1775, Gridley planned the rebel works at the Battle of Bunker Hill, where he was wounded. In November 1775, because of his advanced age, he was replaced by Colonel Henry Knox as chief of artillery, but he continued as chief engineer until 1776 and planned the fortification of Dorchester Heights during the Siege of Boston. Gridley died in 1796, fifty years after he drew the plan of the French fortress of Louisbourg, a largely forgotten hero of the "late Important Expedition against that Place," the scene of much New England martial glory, and Gridley's own elegantly illustrated triumph.

P.D.

1. Wheat 1969, pp. 15–16.
2. Oliver 1973, pp. 154–155.
3. Abernathy 1967, pp. 96–99.

41

New England Bravery
Boston: Thomas Fleet, 1745
Broadside
12 ¾ in. (32.4 cm) x 5 ⅛ in. (20.6 cm)
Gift of the Saltonstall family, 1948

News of the victory at Louisbourg was celebrated in New England by bonfires, bell-ringing, fireworks, official announcements and proclamations, and also in song and verse. Contemporary newspaper accounts, pamphlets, and more ephemeral broadside announcements praised the military prowess of New Englanders. "New England Bravery," set to the tune of the old English ballad of Chevy-Chase, is only one of many contemporary accounts, unusual for the amount of specific detail about operations contained in the verses, but also for the large woodcut decoration at the head of the sheet.

Thomas Fleet (1685–1758), who worked "at the sign of the Heart and Crown in Cornhill" from 1731 to 1764, was one of Boston's most influential printers. As a young man, he had been one of the "Couranteers," who, with Benjamin Franklin, provided satirical material for James Franklin's *New England Courant* in the 1720s. Together with his sons, and followed by his grandsons, Thomas

New England Bravery.

Being a full and true Account of the taking of the City of *Louisbourg*, by the *New-England* Forces under the Command of the gallant General *Pepperell*, on the 17th of *June*, 1745.   Tune of, *Chivey-Chace*.

COme all *New-England*'s gallant Lads,
   and lend to me an Ear,
And of your Brethren's mighty Acts
   I will in short declare.
Brave PEP'RELL with three Thousand Men,
   (perhaps some hundreds more)
Did land the very first of *May*,
   upon *Cape Breton* Shore:
And tho' opposed by *Morepang*
   with full two hundred Men,
A handful of our gallant Lads
   did drive them back again.
Some few were taken Prisoners,
   and many kill'd out-right,
Which taught the *French* at *Louisbourg*
   New England Men can fight.
The *Monsieurs* all astonished
   to see our Armament,
Were griev'd to see that they must be
   within Stone Walls all pent.
In haste they call in to their Aid
   the Men upon the Isle,
Forgetting their own Poverty,
   (such Things would make one smile)
But what is vastly more absurd
   Than any thing like this,
They quitted the *Grand Battery*,
   the Glory of the Place.
Of which our *English* Lads did take
   Possession quietly,
And with the Guns did ever since
   the Enemy annoy.
They also did with mighty Toil
   their Batteries erect,
Against the Town and Citidel,
   which play'd with good Effect.
They sent such Showers of Bombs and Balls
   as made the *Frenchmen* quake,
And sputter out such Words as these,
   Those Dogs the Place will take.
Our Men did also batter down
   the West Gate and the Wall,
And made therein so large a Breach
   that to the *French* they'd call,
Come out, Jack Frenchman, *come to us,*
   and drink a Bowl of Punch,

Jack Frenchman *cries, you* English *Dogs,*
   come, here's a pretty Wench.
But by and by they change their Tones,
   and offer Terms of Peace,
Which if consented to they would
   surrender up the Place.
(For they were so severely maul'd
   by Cannon Shot and Shells,
That they no Place of Safety found
   on Platforms or in Cells.)
Their Island Battery likewise,
   on which they much depended,
Was so annoyed by our Men
   it could not be defended.
For they did wisely plant some Guns
   upon the Light House Point,
And also one good Mortar-Piece,
   which put them out of Joint.
Our Lads they fir'd so furiously
   into that Island Fort,
The Soldiers jump'd into the Sea,
   which made our Men good Sport.
Our Gen'ral upon this Success
   did send *Monsieurs* Word,
If they would not give up the Place,
   He'd put them to the Sword.
And now not daring to withstand
   the Force of all our Bands,
They gave up all their Fortresses
   into our *English* Hands.
With Beat of Drums and Colours spread
   the Seventeenth of *June*,
Our gallant Army marched in,
   'bout Twelve o'Clock at Noon.
The Gentlemen and Ladies too
   they did caress our Men,
For having them delivered
   from worse than Lion's Den.
They all are to be sent to *France*,
   with all the Islanders,
Which needs must ease our Countrymen
   of many Cares and Fears.
And all the Men are strictly bound
   (that is as we do hear)
Not to bear Arms against King GEORGE,
   at least for one whole Year.

Sold at the Heart and Crown in Cornhill, Boston.

Fleet later ran the most successful printing shop in eighteenth-century Boston. Their publications included books, pamphlets, broadsides, and also the *Boston Evening-Post*, the most important newspaper of its day, until it ceased publication at the beginning of the American Revolution.[1]

Even very successful New England printers were frugal with their time and materials; the same woodcut that illustrates this broadside celebration of the fall of fortress Louisbourg, was used more than thirty years later on a broadside titled *Two Favorite Songs Made on the Evacuation of Boston, by the British Troops, on the 17th of March 1776*.[2] Although not a finely drawn rendition of the Boston skyline, this woodcut is accurate in detailing specific buildings, including the lighthouse in the harbor.

At the Historical Society, *New England Bravery* forms part of a collection of more than 10,000 broadsides—advertisements, announcements, notices, proclamations, and the like—printed on one side of a sheet to be circulated or posted in the colonial and early national period.

P.D.

1. Pitre 1980, pp. 162–70.
2. Ford 1922, pp. 116–117.

42

Peter Pelham (1697–1751) after John Smibert (1688–1751)
Sir William Pepperrell (1696–1759)
Boston, 1747
Mezzotint
14 ¾ in. (38.6 cm) x 11 ⅛ in. (28.2 cm)
Inscription, at bottom: *Sir William Pepperrell Bart., Colonel of one of his Majesty's Regiments / of Foot, who was Lieutenant General and Commander in Chief of the American / Forces Employ'd in the Expedition against the Island of Cape Breton which was / happily Reduced to the Obedience of his Britanick Majesty June the 17, 1745 / J: Smibert Pinx: Sold by J. Buck in Queen street Boston P: Pelham fecit et ex: 1747*
Bequest of Denison Rogers Slade, 1923

The capture of the French fort of Louisbourg at Cape Breton prompted three commemorative mezzotints by Peter Pelham, who was at the time America's foremost engraver. The first to appear was an engraving of *A Plan of the City and Fortress of Louisbourg* (1746), printed six months after the on-the-spot drawing made by Richard Gridley (see no. 40). Along with the map, Pelham engraved portraits of the two heroes of the event, Governor William Shirley (1694–1771) and Sir William Pepperrell, both after paintings by Smibert which were executed in the summer of 1746.[1] While Smibert's oil portrait of Pepperrell (Essex Institute) is full-length, Pelham chose a three-quarter-length format for this mezzotint. Unlike the earlier engraving of Cotton Mather, it is not just Pepperrell's head, but his whole figure which dominates the space. Elegantly uniformed with his full wig tied into a pigtail at the back with ribbon, Pepperrell gazes at the viewer directly, but since his face is partly in shadow, his expression seems somewhat tentative. In his right hand he holds a rolled manuscript, perhaps representing the map of Louisbourg, which Pelham had engraved. Pepperrell's image is softened by the expanse of sky behind him,

42

as well as by the drapery, strategically opened to reveal the battle scene outside. His left hand points to the battlements and cannons below. Two cannonballs are seen near the horizon on the lower right side.

Compositionally, this work is very similar to the mezzotint of William Shirley engraved in the same year. Both men are represented in three-quarter length, both are positioned close to the viewer, and both men point to battle scenes in the background. This is the first instance in American history that a military event was commemorated by the commission of prints, imitating a practice that has had a long tradition in English art.[2]

S.R.M.

1. Oliver 1973, p. 155.
2. Saunders 1987, p. 141.

43
Seth Pomeroy (1706–1777)
Powder Horn
American, ca. 1756
Cow or ox horn, with wooden neck, pour spout, and base plug
L. 16 ¾ in. (42.5 cm), H. 11 ¾ in. (30 cm), D. 6 ⅞ in. (17.5 cm)
Signed: SCRIBED BY HIS FRIENDLY OFFICER MAI SETH POMEROY Inscribed: CAPTOR OF LOVISBOVRG / IVNE 16 1745 / MAI-GEN SIR WM PEPPERREL / HIS HORN / FOR THE 1756 CAMPAIGN / SCRIBED BY HIS FRIENDLY OFFICER MAI SETH POMEROY / *Hide not your Light beneath any Bushel / Let your light so shine before Men that they shall see your Good Works / The Year Now Near Gone / The Campaign Near Loss / Our Hope is with Anew Year New Plans and Supplies But Mostly in An Able Leader*
Gift of Mr. and Mrs. William Cahalan, 1987

This elaborately engraved American map horn is an extremely significant example of American folk art as well as an important historical document and vestige of colonial military history.[1] It is inscribed to Major General Sir William Pepperrell, military commander of the New England troops in the Louisbourg expedition, in honor of his expected role in the Crown Point campaign during the French and Indian Wars of 1754 through 1763.

The carefully executed design includes inscription and date within a laurel wreath and shield, bird's-eye view of the harbor and city of Louisbourg, coastal battery positions, and naval fleet. Supplementary embellishments include the British Union flag, the British Royal coat of arms bearing the motto "Dieu et mon Droit" (God and My Right), a French fleurs-de-lis flag upside down to symbolize the French defeat at Louisbourg, a compass, and a candle. A wide decorative border encircles the neck and base.

Seth Pomeroy, the engraver of this handsome horn, was the son of Ebenezer and Sarah (King) Pomeroy and born in Northampton, Massachusetts. It was in the Pomeroy family trade as blacksmiths and gunsmiths that Seth most likely learned the art of powder horn manufacture and engraving. He began his military career as a

member of the local militia and quickly rose from ensign to captain. In 1745, Pomeroy was commissioned as a major in the 4th Massachusetts Regiment under the command of Major General William Pepperrell in the expedition against the French fortress of Louisbourg during King George's War. Ten years later, he was a lieutenant-colonel of the western Massachusetts troops during the French and Indian War in the campaign at Crown Point on Lake Champlain. It was about the time of the Crown Point expedition that Pomeroy "scribed" this commemorative map horn for his senior officer Major General Sir William Pepperrell. When he returned to Northampton in 1756, he continued as head of the militia and was in command of the forts along the Massachusetts frontier. Although approaching the age of seventy years, Pomeroy remained active in the Massachusetts military into the Revolutionary war. He embraced the American cause for liberty, was elected a representative to the First and Second Provincial Congress, raised and drilled troops for the Continental Army, and fought at the Battle of Bunker Hill. Pomeroy's life-long military service ended abruptly in 1777 when he died of pleurisy while on his way to join the American forces in New Jersey.[2]

Sir William Pepperrell (1696–1759), the son of William Pepperrell and Margery (Bray) Pepperrell, was born into a prominent mercantile family at Kittery Point, Maine. He was a business partner with his father, trading lumber, fish, and imported European goods in Boston, and they quickly became one of the most wealthy and powerful families in the New England provincial colonies. In 1723, he married Mary Hirst, granddaughter of Samuel Sewall (see no. 26).[3]

Like Seth Pomeroy, Pepperrell joined the local militia at an early age and rose rapidly becoming colonel of all the troops of the Province of Maine in 1726. He later added civic position with his election to the Massachusetts General Court, appointment as chief justice of York County by Governor Jonathan Belcher, and election as president of the Massachusetts Provincial Council for eighteen years.

His victory as commander of New England troops at the conquest of Louisbourg in 1745 won him the reputation as the greatest popular hero of colonial Massachusetts and earned him a baronetcy from the king, making Pepperrell the first American to receive this honor. Commodore Peter Warren and Pepperrell served jointly as governors in Louisbourg, until they were relieved of duty by British troops in the spring of 1746. Pepperrell returned to Boston and resumed his political, military, and mercantile affairs.

With the outbreak of the French and Indian War in 1755, Governor Shirley proposed expeditions against French forts at Crown Point and Niagara. The Louisbourg army was reactivated as the Fifty-first Regiment, and Pepperrell looked forward to another contest with the French. Much to his disappointment, General Edward Braddock, commander of the British forces in the American colonies, refused to commission Pepperrell as commander of the Crown Point troops because it was "inconsistent" with his rank of major general. A second request for Pepperrell to command the Crown Point expedition was ignored by Governor Shirley.[4]

Pepperrell resumed his provincial duties, continued as President of the Massachusetts Council, and served as

A Prospect of the Colledges in Cambridge in New England

44

acting governor of Massachusetts until the arrival of Thomas Pownall in 1757. Failing health prompted him to return to the family mansion at Kittery, where he died in 1759.

The Pepperrell powder horn is a bittersweet testimonial to the Louisbourg victory and the aborted Crown Point command from a "friendly officer" who undoubtedly had hoped to serve once again in glory under his major general's command. It is one of eight powder horns in the Massachusetts Historical Society's museum collection. It accompanies the silver-hilted sword and scabbard worn by Pepperrell at the siege of Louisbourg in 1745. Seth Pomeroy's 1755 journal of the expedition against Crown Point is included in the Society's Francis Parkman Papers.

L.C.G.

1. Brown 1980, pp. 277–279; Wall 1931, pp. 3–24; Grancsay 1945.
2. *DAB.*
3. Ibid.
4. Fairchild 1976, p. 105.

44

Attributed to John Harris (fl. 1686–1739/1740) after William Burgis (fl. 1718–1731)
A Prospect of the Colledges in Cambridge in New England
1726
Engraving with hand coloring, first state
24½ in. (62.4 cm) x 19¼ in. (48.8 cm)
Inscribed, below print, in cartouche at center: *To the Honourable / William Dummer Esqr. / Lieutenant Governour of the Province / of the Massachusetts Bay in New England / this View is most humbly Dedicated / By Your Honours / Most obedient most humble Servt / W: Burgis*
Gift of William Scollay, 1795

The only known impression of the first state of William Burgis's view of Harvard College certainly ranks high among the Historical Society's treasures but was only accidentally discovered in the 1880s. Dr. Fitch Edward Oliver (1819–1892), the Society's cabinet keeper, reported to the February 1881 monthly meeting that the 1743 view of Harvard, published by William Price and given to the Society in 1795, was mounted on a wooden panel which had become warped and cracked and required attention. "On lifting it from the panel another engraving embracing the same view revealed itself . . . similar in character, but published at an earlier date." It was Oliver himself who connected this earlier print with Burgis's announcement for "A Prospect of the Colledges in Cambridge in New England, curiously engraved in Copper," which appeared in the *Boston News Letter* of July 26, 1726.[1]

William Burgis had a short but active working career as an artist. Little is known about his early life. He probably arrived in New York from London sometime in 1717. His first known work was a large panorama of New York, *A South Prospect of the Flourishing City of New York* (1717; published 1719–1720). In the inscription, Burgis's name appears as the designer and publisher, and the engraver has been identified as John Harris, who is also believed to have engraved the view of Harvard. Harris worked in London, where he specialized in architectural and topographical views after a number of artists.[2] During this early period of American printmaking, it was common practice to send drawings to Europe to be engraved and printed.

Burgis is believed to have been living in Boston in 1722. A small print of a view of Boston from that year might be his first work executed here. This view of Boston, which is now at the Essex Institute, was taken from Noddles Island and depicts an artist drawing in the right hand corner. If this is indeed the work of Burgis, then the figure may be a self-portrait. Burgis is definitely the artist for the later panoramic view, *A South East View of the Great Town of Boston in New England in America* (1725), which was also engraved by John Harris.[3]

This 1726 view of Harvard gives an accurate picture of the college as it appeared in the early eighteenth century. The three buildings are, from left to right: Harvard Hall (built 1672–1682), Stoughton Hall (built 1698–1700) and Massachusetts Hall (1718–1720).[4] All three buildings were constructed of brick, evident in the use of red wash for the hand coloring. Harvard Hall, the oldest of the three, replaced an original wood structure. The flag flying above the cupola on Harvard proclaims, "HC 1639," which is the date for the original building. The courtyard before the three buildings contains a lone elm tree and several men in academic gowns scurrying along.

The street, which is separated from the college by a plain fence, contains a great deal of genre details which enliven the view. On the left, for example, two horsemen trot past an elegant four-horse coach, while in the center, above the dedication to Lieutenant Governor Dummer by Burgis, a gentleman points out the buildings to a woman, while a dog looks on.

Since moving to Boston, Burgis resided at the Crown Coffee House which was located at the head of Long Wharf. His landlord, Thomas Selby, was involved in the production and sale of some of Burgis's prints. When Selby died in 1727, he left his widow, Mehitable, a large fortune. The next year, she and Burgis were married. However, because the estate was disputed by other Selby heirs, Burgis and his wife spent much of their life together involved in litigation.[5]

In the court records, Burgis listed his profession variously as a draftsman, painter, gentleman, and innkeeper, but never as an engraver. The only work which he inscribed as both designer and engraver is a mezzotint, *To the Merchants of Boston this View of the Lighthouse* (1729). In that same year, Burgis drew a map, *Plan of Boston in New England*, which was engraved by Thomas Johnston. According to Dunlap, Burgis left his wife in 1731 and returned to New York. However, two prints made of New York scenes, Fort George and New Dutch Church, date from 1729–1731 and 1731 respectively, indicating that Burgis may have been in New York before that date.[6] In July 1736, his wife unsuccessfully filed for divorce claiming that "her Husband William Burgess having got what he could of her estate into his hands about five years since left her, and has never returned to the Province again."[7] Nothing further is known of Burgis's life or his career as an artist after 1731.

S.R.M.

1. MHS *Proceedings* 18 (1880–1881):318–320.
2. Deák 1988, 1:44–45; Bail 1949, p. 21; *DNB*.
3. Holman 1973, pp. 58, 64, 65, 78.
4. Deák 1988, p. 49.
5. Dunlap 1918, 3:286; Edmonds 1915, pp. 46–47.
6. Holman 1973, pp. 58, 72–73, 79–80; Dunlap 1918, 3:286.
7. Edmonds 1915, p. 46.

45 (see also color plate III)

45

Attributed to Mary Leverett Denison Rogers (1701–1756)
Embroidery
Boston area, first half of eighteenth century
Silk, wool, and gilt-silver yarns on open plain-weave linen
7 3/4 in. (19.6 cm) x 9 7/8 in. (25.1 cm)
Inscribed, on banner: *euco*. A PRÆSEPIBUS RCEUT
Provenance unknown, in the Society's collection from about 1795

This early embroidered view of Harvard Hall at Harvard College shows the second building of that name, built in 1676 but destroyed by fire in 1764. Some of the architectural details of that building are confused with nearby Stoughton Hall (see no. 44) in this rendition.[1] The embroiderer also replaced the cupola with a swarming beehive and a variation upon a quotation from Virgil which roughly translates as "They keep out drones from these premises."[2]

Based upon this quotation which he found used in reference to Harvard among the Leverett family papers,

Harvard historian Samuel Eliot Morison in 1933 hypothesized that the piece was worked by Mary Leverett as a gift for her second husband.[3] Mary Leverett, the daughter and granddaughter of Harvard presidents, was born in the old parsonage in Cambridge where her father, John Leverett, served as pastor until his election to the Harvard presidency in 1708. She married her cousin Major John Denison of Ipswich in 1719, but he died five years later, and she was remarried in 1728 to another cousin, the Reverend Nathaniel Rogers, also of Ipswich. Both husbands were Harvard graduates. Although only fifty-five at her death, she survived all but three of her two Denison and eight Rogers children.

The piece is worked in the basic half-cross stitch or tent stitch, a decorative thread crossing diagonally the intersecting threads of the linen. The two large putti holding the beehive aloft are done in a technique resembling the stump work popular in the seventeenth century in which forms are padded or raised to produce a three-dimensional effect. The red color of the bricks contrasts richly with the narrow strip of blue, cloud-streaked sky and the dark roof.

J.L.P.

1. Bail 1949, p. 25.
2. Morison 1933, p. 68.
3. Ibid., pp. 68–70.
4. Sibley 1873, 5:527, 6:557.
5. Hanley 1969, p. 24.

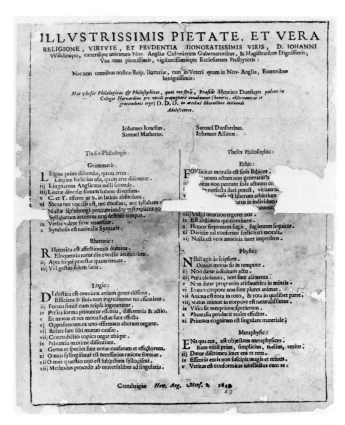

46

46

Harvard College
Theses
Cambridge: Printed by Stephen Daye, 1643
Broadside
12 in. (30.5 cm) x 9½ in. (24 cm)
Provenance unknown, in the Society's collection before 1860

Less than ten years after the arrival of Puritan colonists in Massachusetts Bay, Harvard College was established in Cambridge. Although it was officially founded in 1636, classes probably began in the summer of 1638, and that same year the college was named for John Harvard, who had left a bequest of money and his library to the new school. The training of ministers and the education of Native Americans converted to Christianity were important objectives, but Harvard was not limited to theological instruction. It was "to be a nursery of knowledge in these deserts and supply for posterity."[1]

A large proportion of the early Harvard graduates left New England for what seemed to be more promising careers in the West Indies or, until the Restoration, England. That, and disruptions in Harvard classes (there were no graduates in 1644 or 1648, and only a total of forty-five graduates before 1650) meant that Harvard was slow to become a true "nursery of knowledge."

Part of the medieval educational heritage brought to colonial New England was the tradition of college commencement exercises. At this ceremony, a series of propositions was presented based upon the undergraduate curriculum, which was dominated by the study of classical

subjects and authors. These theses were supposed to be defended in Latin, Greek, or Hebrew by any member of the graduating class "by the recognized rules of syllogistic disputation." Following the tradition of Edinburgh University, the theses presented at graduation were printed as broadsides and posted as public announcements.

No broadside copy of the theses for the nine members of the first graduating class (1642) survives. This thesis sheet lists speakers and topics at the second Harvard graduation in 1643 and was printed by Stephen Daye (ca. 1594–1668), the first printer in the English colonies of America. The *Bay Psalm Book* (1639–1640) is only earlier extant product of the Cambridge Press, the first press in the English colonies.[3]

There were only four graduates in 1643 to defend fifty-five subjects. Under the heading *Theses Philologic* are twenty-seven subjects in the categories of grammar, rhetoric, and logic. The second column, for *Theses Philosophic*, lists twenty-eight subjects in ethics, physics, and metaphysics. Printed directly above the list of topics are the names of the entire graduating class of 1643: John Jones (ca. 1624-ca. 1670), Samuel Mather (1626–1671), Samuel Danforth (1626–1674), and John Allin (1623–ca. 1682). All four became ministers. John Jones preached on the island of Nevis in the West Indies; Samuel Mather, a son of Richard and brother of Increase, returned to England; Samuel Danforth assisted John Eliot in converting Native Americans to Christianity; and John Allin became the minister at Woodbridge, New Jersey.[4]

This printed *Theses* provides information not only about the character and content of the curriculum offered at Harvard in 1643, but also the political situation in New England. To gain patronage from the loose confederation of other New England colonies, the *Theses* of 1643 was dedicated not only to Governor John Winthrop of Massa-

George Forrester. Loves to smoke & cook game.
Cushing. George Augustus, Lunenburg. A good musician. Chorister of the Hasty pud-
ding club when I was a member. Am
not acquainted with him.
Dana. Richard Henry. Cambridge. Went to sea after
being in College near Three years: left
on account of sickness wh. affected his
eyes. A good scholar, good looking, rosy cheeked. Son of Richard Dana (the poet of America)
nephew of Washington Allston (our great painter).
Dennis, Hiram Barret. Concord. Witty, idle, ambitious, dissipated considering
his poverty. Held a good many college
offices.

chusetts Bay, but to the governors and magistrates of the "united New England Colonies."[5]

The broadside displayed here is one of two surviving copies of the printed 1643 *Theses*. It was discovered in 1860 by Chandler Robbins, the recording secretary of the Historical Society, who, while examining the contents of a cabinet, came across "a small bundle of ancient papers in manuscript and type, amongst which were two printed broadsides"—this *Theses* of 1643 and a fragment of another from 1670.[6] The other copy is at the University of Glasgow.

Considering the ephemeral nature of broadsides (in this case the posted announcement for an event), the survival of this copy, in spite of its imperfections, is remarkable. Early broadsides are "among the rarest of early Americana, the greater number of them being known in single copies only." At the Historical Society it forms part of a large collection of early Massachusetts imprints.[7]

M.E.C.

1. Morison 1935, p. 160.
2. Morison 1936, 2:580.
3. Roden 1905, p. 36.
4. Sibley 1873, 1:77–101.
5. Morison 1935, p. 315.
6. MHS *Proceedings* 4(1858–1860):439.
7. Lane 1914, p. 304.

47
Amos Adams Lawrence (1814–1886)
Diary, February 28, 1834–April 13, 1836
Manuscript
168 p., 8 3/8 in. (20.7 cm) x 6 3/4 in. (17.1 cm)
From the Amos A. Lawrence diaries given by Mrs. Frederic Cunningham, 1927; Mrs. Augustus N. Hand, 1939; John S. Lawrence, 1950; and Paul C. Coolidge, 1989

Since its founding in 1636, Harvard College has been inextricably linked through its students to the intellectual, religious, and business history of Massachusetts. An ongoing series, *Sibley's Harvard Graduates*, sponsored by the Historical Society, chronicles the lives of these individual students. Harvard librarian John Langdon Sibley (1804–1885) compiled the first three volumes of biographical sketches, and later Clifford N. Shipton (1902–1973) masterfully carried on the series and brought the total number of volumes to seventeen and the classes covered through 1771. More recently, work has begun at the Historical Society to further this endeavor.

Within these individual biographies are the timeless tales of student days. In the eighteenth century, twelve- and thirteen-year-old college students were not uncommon, and neither were the concomitant problems of young boys away at school, practical jokes, growth and change, and even food fights. Asa Dunbar summarized his feelings in 1766 which led to one of the most famous student revolts in the eighteenth century. "Behold our Butter stinketh, and we cannot eat thereof! Now give us we pray thee Butter that stinketh not."[1] President Edward Holyoke put down this dining hall revolt, but food fights continued. In another celebrated incident, William Hickling Prescott was permanently blinded in one eye by a crust of bread flung by a fellow student (see no. 128).

The diary shown here was kept by Amos A. Lawrence, son of Boston businessman Amos Lawrence (see no. 120). Although Lawrence grew into a nationally respected businessman and philanthropist with particular interest in education and abolition, the diary of his college years records a wide range of schoolboy pranks from emptying a classmate's straw mattress and then setting the straw afire to an all-college hoax over the course of several days to confuse a visiting country bumpkin. Sometimes the pranks proved destructive, and one "gunpowder plot" during Lawrence's freshman year earned many of the students the punishment of rustication. The rustication procedure sent the offending students to live in the countryside usually with a minister who could individually supervise his behavior and continued studies. Although Lawrence was not personally involved in the explosive situation, President Josiah Quincy wrote to Amos's father that he was "young, very susceptible" and might be better served by some time in the country. His rustication was served at Bedford and Andover with Jonathan F. Stearns, a recent graduate, and proved so enjoyable that Lawrence extended his stay from six to eighteen months.[2]

When he returned to Cambridge, Lawrence wrote a brief sketch of each of his classmates to aid his memory in the future if he should ever lose the official printed catalogue. As private comments, his remarks were wide ranging and frank. Benjamin B. Appleton was "Unpopular in class. affects gentility. Walks a good deal in Wash[ing]ton street. not so bad as some suppose." On John Henry Eliot he wrote "My friend John wears spectacles. has a literary look. has lost some of his hair, wore a wig . . . ." Of Richard Henry Dana, later famous as author of *Two Years Before the Mast* (see no. 136), Lawrence remembered that he "Went to sea after being in college near three years: left on account of sickness wh. affected his eyes. A good scholar. good looking. rosy cheeked. . . ."

At the end of the last term in 1835 came commencement, and "all joined hands and danced around the Liberty tree, and in the afternoon they danced still more and drank pails of punch. Then, after a supper at Fresh Pond," they separated.[3]

E.W.H.

1. Cohen 1982, p. 179.
2. Lawrence 1888, pp. 12–13.
3. Ibid., pp. 24–25.

48
Paul Revere (1735–1818)
The Bloody Massacre perpetrated in King Street, Boston on March 5th, 1770 by a party of the 29th Regiment
Boston, 1770
Engraving with hand coloring
8 in. (20 cm) x 9 in. (22.8 cm)
Inscribed, lower right: *Engrav'd Printed & Sold by Paul Revere Boston*
Gift of William H. Keith, 1869

48 (see also color plate IV)

(No. 88.)

I Benjamin Church, jun. of lawful age, teftify and fay, that being requefted by Mr. Robert Pierpont the Coroner, to affift in examining the body of Crifpus Attucks, who was fuppofed to be murdered by the foldiers on Monday evening the 5th inftant, I found two wounds in the region of the Thorax, the one on the right fide which entered thro' the fecond true Rib within an inch and an half of the Sternum, dividing the Rib and feperating the cartilaginous extremity from the Sternum, the ball paffed obliquely downward thro' the Diaphragm and entering thro' the large Lobe of the Liver and the Gall-Bladder, ftill keeping its oblique direction, divided the Aorta Defcendens juft above its divifion into the Iliacs, from thence it made its exit on the left fide of the Spine. This wound I apprehended was the immediate caufe of his death. The other ball entered the fourth of the falfe Ribs, about five inches from the Linea Alba, and defcending obliquely paffed through the fecond falfe Rib, at the diftance of about eight inches from the Linea Alba ; from the oblique direction of the wounds, I apprehend the gun muft have been difcharged from fome elevation, and further the deponent faith not.
BENJ. CHURCH, Jun.

Suffolk, ff. Bofton, March 22. 1770. *Benjamin Church, jun. above-mentioned, after due examination, made oath to the truth of the aforefaid affidavit, taken to perpetuate the remembrance of the thing.*

49

49
A Short Narrative of the Horrid Massacre in Boston
Boston: Printed by order of the town of Boston, and sold by Edes and Gill and T. & J. Fleet, 1770
In two parts: 48 p., 83 p., 7 5/8 in. (19.3 cm) x 5 in. (12.7 cm)
Gift of C. C. Cunningham, 1966

On the evening of March 5 , 1770, an unruly crowd gathered in Boston outside the Customs House to taunt with jeers and snowballs the British soldiers standing guard. Reinforcements were called, unordered shots rang out, and when the smoke cleared three locals lay dead and another eight were wounded, two mortally. The Boston Massacre quickly became a rallying point for anti-British sentiment in the province, and the real indignation of the people was further inflamed by colonial propaganda, such as the two items exhibited here.[1]

Before the end of March, Paul Revere issued his engraving of the *Bloody Massacre perpetrated in King Street*. The original drawing was the work of Henry Pelham, John Copley's half brother. Somehow Revere obtained Pelham's picture and speedily produced his own engraving, which beat Pelham's to the street by a few days.[2] A letter from Pelham to Revere, written on March 29, 1770, angrily begins: "When I heard that you was cutting a plate of the late Murder, I thought it impossible as I knew you was not capable of doing it unless you coppied it from mine . . . ."[3] Though at quick glance the Revere and Pelham renderings of the Massacre may appear identical, there are small but discernible variations in the figures, buildings and sky.

Although colorful and dramatic, the scene portrayed is historically inaccurate and inflammatory. The picture shows a line of Redcoats with Captain Preston urging a point-blank volley into a defenseless crowd, when in fact there was no such organized military action and the civilians were an unruly mob of sixty. However, such a vivid representation of the viciousness of the British served as a powerful propaganda tool, and Revere, the ardent patriot, exploited the fact and added touches like the sign "Butcher's Hall" over the British-guarded Customs House. Appearing so soon after the event, the engraving was enthusiastically admired and widely circulated, and it continues even today to serve as the popular conception of an historical moment.[4]

Meanwhile, the town appointed a committee, consisting of James Bowdoin, Joseph Warren, and Samuel Pemberton, to investigate the "horrid Massacre." The committee report along with ninety-six depositions from witnesses was rushed into print and dispatched to England, to lay out the colonists' side of the story.[5] Copies in Boston were supposed to be suppressed until after the trials of the soldiers, to avoid influencing the juries, but were circulated before the trials began.[6] At the same time that the affidavits in this volume were being collected, depositions showing the soldiers in good light were being gathered and sent to England. These were published in London as *A fair account of the late unhappy disturbance at Boston in New England. . . .*

Shown here is the deposition of Dr. Benjamin Church on the autopsy on Crispus Attucks, "who was supposed to be murdered by the soldiers on Monday evening the 5th." Attucks, who went by the name Michael Johnson at the time of the massacre, was discovered after his death to be Crispus Attucks of Framingham, a "mollatto" who apparently escaped from slavery in 1750. According to local lore he was part African and part Native American of the Natick tribe. Regarded today as America's first black hero, Attucks led a group of sailors to the site of the riot but there was shot and thus became one of the first victims of the American Revolution.[7] Ironically, Dr. Church, who performed the autopsy, was later court-martialed for treasonously corresponding with the enemy in coded messages.

At the subsequent trials, the British Captain Thomas Preston and six of his men were acquitted of murder, while two soldiers were convicted of manslaughter, branded on the thumb, and released. The soldiers' defense was offered by John Adams and Josiah Quincy, Jr., while the prosecuting attorneys were Robert Treat Paine and Samuel Quincy. This copy of the *Short Narrative* belonged to Robert Treat Paine (1730/1–1814) and contains his notes on the grand jury depositions. Although a native of Boston, Paine was at this time living and practicing law at Taunton, Massachusetts. In 1774 he became a member of the Massachusetts delegation to the First Continental Congress in Philadelphia, where he served as chairman of the important munitions committee, but he is best remembered as a signer of the Declaration of Independence in 1776. In 1777 Paine returned to Boston, where he was elected the state's first attorney general, a position he kept until 1790 when he was appointed an associate justice of the Massachusetts Supreme Court.[8]

The papers of Adams, Paine, and the Quincy family are at the Historical Society and contain extensive information on the trials as well as on the Revolution that would follow.[9]

B.M.P., V.H.S.

1. Zobel 1970, ch. 16.
2. Brigham 1954, pp. 41–42.
3. MHS *Proceedings*, 2d ser., 8(1892–1894):227.
4. Brigham 1954, p. 41.
5. Adams 1965, p. 57.
6. Zobel 1970, p. 213.
7. Kaplan 1973, pp. 7–8.
8. Sibley 1873, 12:462–482.
9. Adams Papers 1965, 3:35.

50

Paul Revere (1735–1818)
North Battery Enlistment Certificate
Boston, ca. 1762
Copperplate
6¼ in. (15.8 cm) x 8 ⅛ in. (20.5 cm)
Signed: *P Revere Sculp*
Inscribed: *This may Certify all whom it may Concern; that the Bearer hereof / is an Inlisted* MONTROSS *at his* MAJESTY'S NORTH-BATTERY, *in Boston, under my Command. Given under my Hand this / In the / Year of his Majesty's reign.*
Provenance unknown, in the Historical Society's collection by 1877

This line-engraved copperplate for a North Battery enlistment certificate was cut by Paul Revere and is considered to be one of his first engravings. The view shows the North Battery fortification and unfurled British Union flag at the east corner of Boston's North End. The elaborate spire of Christ Church dominates the skyline, and the rolling hills of Charlestown extend beyond the Charles River in the background.[1] Small schooners sail in the tranquil breezes of Boston Harbor, while nude bathers dive from the North End wharves. The certifying inscription is cut so that the name of the enlisted montross, or artilleryman, the date, and the commanding officer can be easily inserted by hand.

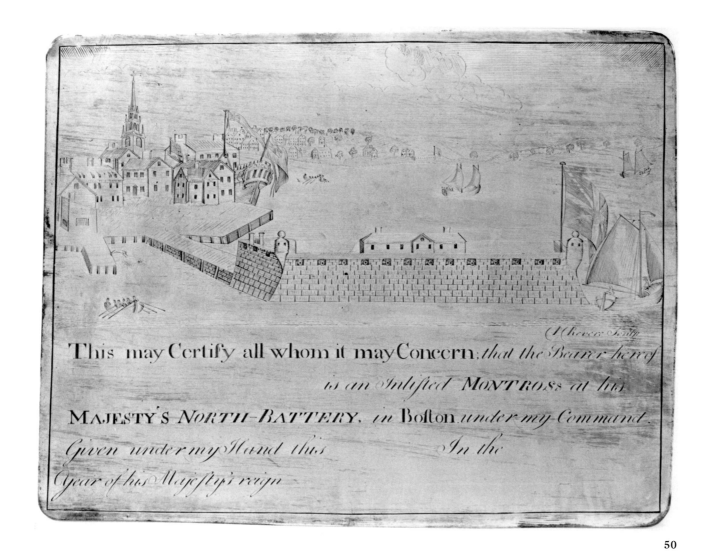

Paul Revere, ardent American patriot and gifted silversmith and engraver, was born in Boston, the son of Deborah (Hitchbourn) Revere and Apollos Rivoire, an early Boston silversmith who later changed his name to Paul Revere.[2] Soon after the death of his father in 1754, Revere inherited his business as well as a fully equipped silver shop.

Aside from Revere's most eminent craft as a master silversmith (see no. 104), he was also a favored engraver of heraldic and emblematic designs for the Boston elite.[3] He augmented his flourishing silver and engraving business by cutting a variety of embellished copperplates for the printing press. No commission was too large or too small for Revere's artistic eye and skillful hand. Revere engraved mastheads for the *Boston Gazette* and *The Massachusetts Spy* as well as a variety of everyday items including billheads for local taverns, advertisements and trade cards for local shopkeepers, bookplates, notifications, Masonic memberships, and military enlistment certificates, such as this North Battery copperplate.

With the coming of the Revolutionary War, political and patriotic scenes and inscriptions of American liberty became a favorite subject for copperplate engravers and their printmakers. Three later views of the harbor and city of Boston elaborately engraved by Revere, in 1770 and 1774, include a similar detail of the North Battery garrison, but omit the flying British standard.[4]

In addition to the Revere Family Papers, 1746–1965, which include the business records for Revere's silver workshop and copper foundry (see no. 52), the Massachusetts Historical Society holds a number of examples of Revere engravings. Among these are his most famous line engraving, *The Bloody Massacre perpetrated in King Street Boston on March 5th, 1770* (no. 48), and *Landing of the Troops*, issued the same year. Also in the collection are a number of prints engraved by Revere for various books and publications, as well as certificates and bookplates and the original copperplate for the Revere family crested bookplate. The Society's numismatic collection includes examples of currency notes he engraved from 1775 to 1779 for the Colony of Massachusetts Bay.[5]

L.C.G.

1. Brigham 1954, p. 11.
2. Leehey 1988, p. 15.
3. Fales 1973, p. 216.
4. Reps 1973, pp. 45–50.
5. Fales 1973, p. 219.

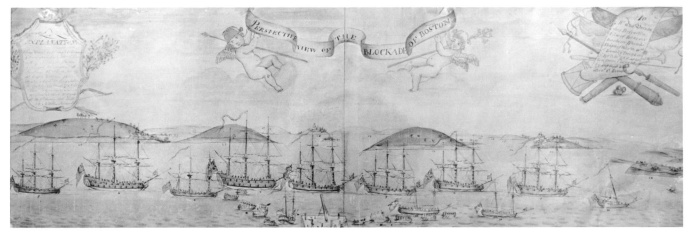

51

Christian Remick (1726–1773)
A Perspective View of the Blockad of Boston Harbour
Boston, 1768
Watercolor on paper
14 ⅛ in. (36.0 cm) x 62 in. (157.5 cm)
Gift of Henry Lee Shattuck, 1970

In early 1767 Boston began a boycott of British goods in protest against the Townshend Acts, a series of restrictive laws which included new taxes on paint, lead, tea, and paper. The town also sent out a circular letter to the other colonies protesting the new laws and calling for an inter-colonial conference on the matter. Following Boston's role in forcing the end of the Stamp Tax in 1765 and the more recent *Liberty* incident (see no. 70), any unrest in Massachusetts was seen as a threat to increasingly stringent British rule. As a show of force, the prime minister brought two regiments into Boston from Halifax in October 1768.

British warships lie at anchor off Long Wharf while their troops disembark in this carefully detailed bird's eye view of Boston harbor. The work both documents and protests against the newest act of tyranny by King George against the American colonies. Putti in military garb support the waving central banner citing the Magna Charta, the document symbolizing individual rights and the accountability of the king to the law for all English subjects.

In the upper-left corner the artist provides a legend naming the ships and points of reference in the landscape:

Explanation

1. Long Wharff	13. Govers Island
2. Mermaid	14. Dorcester Neck
3. Romney	15. Specticle Island
4. Launcestan	16. Long Island
5. Beaver	17. Galops Island
6. Bonetta	18. Nikses mate
7. Senegall	20. Sloop Liberty
8. Glasgow	21. Point Sherly
9. Martin	22. Aple Island
10. Landing the tropes.	23. Nodles Island
11. Tenders	24. Great Bruster
12. Castle Willam	

The inscription in the upper-right corner contains the title of the work, the date of the landing, and the artist's signature: *A / Perspective View of the / Blockad of Boston Harbour, / Islands & ca. men of war and / the landing the 29th and 14th / Rigiments on the first of Oct / ober 68, as taken from the end of / long wharff by:/ Christian Remich.*

The inscriptions are ornamented with figures of Native Americans, putti, a draped female figure symbolizing "charitas," and flags, weapons, and other eighteenth-century military devices. Self-taught, the artist relied on design and color in his work. Though derived from English and European models, the figures and objects are flat and one-dimensional.

Remick produced six known versions of this work, several dedicated to specific people. Though it bears no dedication, the provenance of this watercolor has been recorded by its previous owners and it is thus known that it was first owned by the royal governor in 1768, Thomas Hutchinson. The Massachusetts Historical Society owns a second, smaller version of this, and the Essex Institute also owns two versions. Another, dedicated to John Hancock, is owned by the Club of Odd Volumes, and one belongs to the New England Historic Genealogical Society.

Of the fourth generation of Remicks in this country, Christian Remick was born in Eastham on Cape Cod in 1726, oldest boy and fourth child in a family of nine.[1] By profession a sailor and master mariner, during the American Revolution he served on Massachusetts vessels. When not at sea he advertised for work as an artist. The following appeared in the *Boston-Gazette and Country Journal* of October 16, 1769:

> Christian Remich, lately from Spain, Begs Leave to inform the Public, That he performs all sorts of Drawing in Water Colours, such as Sea Pieces, Perspective Views, Geographical Plans of Harbours, Sea Coasts &ct. Also, Colours Pictures to the Life, and Draws Coats of Arms, at the most reasonable Rates. Specimens of his Performances, particularly an Accurate View of the Blockade of Boston, with the landing of the British Troops on the first of October 1768, may be seen at the Golden Ball and Bunch of Grapes Taverns, or at Mr. Thomas Bradford's, North-End, Boston.

Little, aside from the six views of the blockade, remains of Remick's work. It is known that he colored at least one engraving of the Boston Massacre for Paul Revere (Museum of Fine Arts, Boston).[2] When not at sea much of Remick's life was passed in Boston, though Harwich and Eastham claimed part of his time.[3] Christian Remick was admitted to the Boston almshouse on February 24, 1773, with his wife and two children. Only forty-seven years old, the artist died there two weeks later on March 10.[4]

J.L.P.

1. *NEHGR* 47(1893):475.
2. Brigham 1954, p. 48.
3. Cunningham 1904, pp. 12–13.
4. Records of the Boston Overseers of the Poor, MHS.

52

52

Paul Revere (1735–1818)
Letter to Jeremy Belknap, 1798
Manuscript
8 p., 9 in. (22.7 cm) x 7¼ in. (18.5 cm)
From the Archives of the Massachusetts Historical Society

"It was then young flood, the Ship was winding, and the moon was Rising." Thus Paul Revere poetically described the scene he remembered from the evening of April 18, 1775, as he set off across the Charles River from Boston for Charlestown. Along with William Dawes, Paul Revere helped to spread word that night that British troops were preparing to march from Boston, either to make prisoners of John Hancock and Samuel Adams at Lexington or to capture the munitions that the colonists had been secretly storing at Concord. The skirmishes that followed at Lexington and Concord on April 19 marked the outbreak of the American Revolution.

Upon reaching Charlestown, Revere obtained a horse from friends and set off for Lexington through Cambridge, but encountering several British soldiers, he was forced to elude them and ride instead through Medford. He alerted almost every house along the way that the British forces were assembled and marching. After reaching Lexington and warning Adams and Hancock, Revere and Dawes, joined by Samuel Prescott, decided to ride for Concord and alert the minutemen as they went. Revere was captured by British officers on the way but later released, whereupon he returned to Lexington in time to witness the opening volleys of the Revolutionary War.

Jeremy Belknap asked Paul Revere to write this ac-

count of his now-famous ride for the Society's library, and then published it in the *Collections* for 1798. Despite the early publication of this letter, Revere's role in Lexington and Concord was relatively unnoticed in history books until after his death in 1818. However, by 1863, when Henry Wadsworth Longfellow penned his highly romanticized ballad that cast Revere as a national hero, he had achieved historical and biographical recognition from a number of sources for his role in the events of April 18–19, 1775.[1]

During the war Revere rode express and printed money for the Massachusetts Provincial Congress, and in the fall of 1776, was commissioned lieutenant-colonel in charge of Castle Island in Boston Harbor, a post which he held through most of the war. After the war, as well as maintaining his silversmithing activities (see no. 104), Revere kept shop for six years as an importer of English goods, then principally hardware, until 1789. This early entrepeneur, also involved in numerous civic activities, then set up a foundry in Boston to supply metal ship fittings and in 1792 cast his first bell in Boston for the Old North Church. In 1800 he engaged to build a copper rolling mill in Canton, Massachusetts, to supply sheet copper for the hulls of ships, including the USS *Constitution*. A quaint figure known for wearing Revolutionary-era garb for the rest of his days, Paul Revere died in 1818 at the age of eighty-three.[2]

The Society also owns a draft and corrected copy of a deposition by Paul Revere giving an account of his ride, possibly prepared in 1775 at the request of the Massachusetts Provincial Congress, which was then gathering depositions from eyewitnesses to prove that the British fired first at Lexington. Revere never committed himself on that point, as he heard but could not actually see the first shot fired.

The Society holds a large collection of Revere family papers, which includes personal correspondence and records for the various family businesses. The collection contains primarily the papers of Paul Revere, his sons Joseph Warren Revere (1777–1868) and John Revere (1787–1847), and his grandsons Edward Hutchinson Robbins Revere (1827–1862) and Paul Joseph Revere (1832–1863).

K.H.G.

1. Morgan in Revere 1968; Forbes 1942, pp. 251–269.
2. Forbes 1942, chs. 8–10; Leehey 1988, pp. 15–33.

Prescott and Linzee Swords

53

Prescott Sword
Silver-hilted small-sword.
Blade, L. 29 ⅞ in. (75.9 cm), W. (at hilt) 1 ⁷⁄₁₆ in. (3.7 cm); L., overall 36 in. (91.4 cm)
Hilt: American, by Jacob Hurd of Boston (1702–1759), second quarter of eighteenth century; symmetrical, bivalve shell-guard, waisted at plane of blade (Norman's type 112); stamped, on inner side of the reverse shell: IHURD. Blade: plain, unmarked steel, hollow-ground, triangular section; inscribed, on obverse shell: *The Sword of - / Col. William Prescott*; on reverse shell: *and worn by him at the / Battle of Bunker Hill / June 17. 1775.*
Bequest of William Hickling Prescott, 1859

54

Linzee Sword
Small-sword for an officer of the Royal Navy.
Blade, L. 33 in. (83.8 cm), W. (at hilt) ¹³⁄₁₆ in. (2.1 cm); L., overall 39½ in. (100 cm)
Hilt: English, probably 1780s, gilded brass (Norman's type 112), engraved with laurel leaf sprays on either side of hafted arm panoply; inscribed, blade side of shell: *Sword of Capt. John Linzee R.N. / who Commanded / the British Sloop of War Falcon. / while / acting. against the Americans at the / Battle of Bunker Hill. June 17. 1775.*; other side, engraved with a overall with a jumble of naval colors, ordnance and short, foul anchors, hand and staff weapons of the period. Blade: German (Solingen), late eighteenth century; for about one-half length from tip, plain and highly polished; from this point, finely fire-blued and etched longitudinally with fire-gilt decoration of intertwined foliated strapwork, foliate tendrils, martial trophines and a gowned female figure with sword; etched, on both faces of *forté* just below the shoulders in gilded cartouche: *Me / Fecit / Sohlingen.*
Gift of Susannah Amory Prescott and Thomas C. A. Linzee, 1859

Colonel William Prescott (1726–1795) wore his sword when he commanded the provincial forces at the Battle of Bunker Hill on June 17, 1775. This was the first major military engagement of the Revolution, and troops from all over New England flocked to Charlestown to support the cause. From the nearby Mystic River, the British sloop-of-war *Falcon*, commanded by Captain John Linzee (1743–1798) cannonaded Prescott and his troops throughout the battle. Although the provincials lost the day, it was a costly victory for the British and became a legend in American military and patriotic lore.

Captain Linzee had earlier been in command of the sloop-of-war *Beaver* at Newport in 1772 when its tender, the schooner *Gaspee*, was seized and burned by Americans in a celebrated incident. He married Susanna Inman of Boston in 1772 and in 1792 resigned from the Royal Navy, returned to America, and permanently settled here with his family.[1]

The Prescott sword descended in the family to Colonel Prescott's grandson, the historian William Hickling Prescott. The Linzee sword, which probably dates from a period after the Battle of Bunker Hill (1780s), was given by Captain Linzee's son John Inman Linzee to William Hickling Prescott who married Linzee's niece Susan Amory. "The swords that had been worn by the soldier and the sailor on that memorable day came down as heirlooms in their respective families, until at last they met in the library of the man of letters, where, quietly crossed over his books, they often excited the notice alike of strangers and of friends."[2] One of these strangers was William Thackeray, who visited Prescott in 1852. Six years later he opened his novel *The Virginians* with the lines:

> On the library-wall of one of the most famous writers of America there hang two crossed swords, which his relatives wore in the great war of Independence. The one sword was gallantly drawn in the service of the king, the other was the weapon of a brave and honored republican soldier. The possessor of the harmless trophy has earned for himself a name alike honored in his ancestors' country and in his own, where genius like his has always a peaceful welcome.

The Prescott sword was bequeathed to the Historical Society by W. H. Prescott in 1859, but he returned the Linzee sword to his wife. However, so that the two swords should not be separated, Mrs. Prescott and her cousin Thomas C. A. Linzee also presented the Linzee sword to the Society.

Shortly after the swords came to the Historical Society, when the Prince of Wales (later King Edward VII) visited the Society's rooms on Tremont Street during his American tour in 1860, he glanced in passing at a number of artifacts on display but "he paused longer to learn the story of the two swords bequeathed to us by Prescott, now crossing each other over our folding-doors, as an emblem of good-will between England and the United States."[3]

E.W.H.

1. Linzee 1917, 2:520–549.
2. Ticknor 1864, p. 54.
3. MHS *Proceedings* 5(1860–1863):98.

The Siege of Boston, April 19, 1775 – March 17, 1776

On April 19, 1775, following the first combat of the American Revolution at Lexington and Concord, the victorious Massachusetts minutemen followed and harassed the British forces on their way back to Boston. By nightfall, a circle of American camps and redoubts had sprung up around the Boston peninsula and the 3500-man British garrison in the town, under the command of General Thomas Gage, found themselves besieged.[1] Within a week, volunteers from outlying regions of Massachusetts and the other New England colonies and numbering 20,000 men reinforced the American side. By June, the town of Boston was ringed on the west and south by nineteen rebel redoubts.

British reinforcements, under Sir William Howe, allowed Gage to plan an offensive. Two prominent vantage points near Boston remained unoccupied: Bunker Hill in Charlestown and Dorchester Heights (now South Boston). Gage decided to seize Dorchester Heights on June 13, but word of his plan leaked to the Americans, and they determined to seize Bunker Hill as a countermove.[2]

On the night of June 15–16, the rebel forces led by Colonel William Prescott and General Joseph Warren, passed over Bunker Hill, either by mistake or with the intention of being closer to Boston, and took Breed's Hill. During the night, the Americans erected a fortification, planned by Richard Gridley (see no. 40), that remained undetected by the British until first light.

On June 16, it took three frontal assaults and terrible British losses (nearly forty percent casualties) for the British to capture Breed's Hill. The Americans, who finally ran out of ammunition, were forced to retreat, but it was a costly British victory; they "could not afford to buy many hills at such a price." The town of Charlestown was burned during the battle, and the British occupied the peninsula and built a fort on Bunker Hill.[3]

While the siege continued, the Second Continental Congress meeting in Philadelphia formed a national army made up of troops from all the colonies—the Continental Army—to prosecute the war. George Washington was appointed commander in chief on June 15, and departed on June 23. He arrived in Cambridge on July 2 to take command of an untrained army, made up of troops, many of whose enlistments were to expire in six months.[4]

Although Washington wanted to launch an attack on the British at Dorchester Heights, his subordinates were reluctant to risk another major battle. There was no major fighting during the remainder of the winter, with the exception of artillery duels and skirmishes on Noddles and other islands in Boston Harbor. Washington used this period of virtual inactivity wisely. He recruited and trained the new Continental Army and completed the siege works. A supply of gunpowder was captured from British ships, and Henry Knox's men successfully dragged captured cannon from Fort Ticonderoga to Cambridge during the winter of 1775–1776 (See no. 57 for an account of the moving of the cannon). In March 1776, Washington was prepared to resume the offensive.[5]

From March 2 to 4, the American forces occupied and subsequently erected a fortification on Dorchester Heights. The American movements were witnessed by General Howe, who had succeeded Gage in command after the Battle of Bunker Hill. A gale delayed Howe's plans to attack the new American fort, a move for which Washington was well prepared, and on March 17, Howe decided to evacuate Boston, rather than risk another costly battle. After several days, the British sailed for Halifax, Nova Scotia, taking almost 1000 loyalists with them. Boston remained an important American base throughout the rest of the Revolution and was threatened by British naval forces, but there was no further fighting there.[6]

B.M.L.

1. Marshall 1976, pp. 4–5. For a more complete description of the Siege, see French 1934.
2. Greene 1911, p. 4.
3. Alden 1954, pp. 38–39.
4. Marshall 1976, p. 5.
5. Greene 1911, pp. 16–17.
6. Ibid, pp. 17–20.

55

William Wood after Richard Williams
A View of the Country round Boston
Boston, 1775
Ink and watercolor on paper
Four panels, each: 7 ⅛ in. (18.1 cm) x 18¼ in. (46.4 cm); total size: 7 ⅝ in. (19.4 cm) x 73 ¼ in. (186 cm)
Inscribed: *A View of the Country round Boston, taken from Beacon Hill, showing the Lines, Intrenchments, Redoubts, &c. of the Rebels, also the Lines and Redoubts of his Majesty's Troops. NB. These Views were taken by Lt. Wms. of the R.W. Fusiliers, copied from a Sketch of the Original by Lt. Wood of the same Regiment. The Original Drawings are now in the possession of the King.*
Gift of J. Carson Brevoort, 1859

These four panels, the first of which is pictured, provide a panoramic view from Beacon Hill, Boston, as seen by a British officer during the siege of 1775. Each panel includes a numeric key to the major military and civilian locations shown in the illustrations.

Panel #1 (east/southeast):	Panel #3 (west):
1. Boston Harbor	14. Works of the Rebels
2. Castle William	15. Ditto
3. Dorchester Neck	16. Town of Cambridge
4. Dorchester Meeting House	17. Works of the Rebels
5. Boston Common	18. Mount Whoredam

Panel #2 (south)

6. Boston Common
7. Our Lines
8. The Block House on the Neck
9. Rebels Intrenchments
10. Roxbury Meeting House
11. Rebels Intrenchments
12. Encampment of the Rebels
13. Hancock's house

Panel #4 (north):

19. Mt. Pisco, the strongest post of the Rebels
20. Lines & Encampments of ditto
21. Intrenchments of the Rebels
22. Our lines on Charlestown Heights
23. Encampment on ditto
24. Ruins of Charlestown
25. Redoubts taken from the Rebels
26. The Symmetry, armed Transport
27. Mystick River

The original scene, drawn and painted by Lieutenant Richard Williams of the Twenty-third Regiment of Foot (the Royal Welsh Fusiliers), is now in the collection of the British Library and includes a fifth panel not in the Historical Society's copy. The panel missing from this copy covers the north/northeast vista.[1] The drawing was probably made in the late summer or early fall of 1775 since numbers 22–25 show the remains of Charlestown which was burned after the Battle of Bunker Hill on June 17, because the British soldiers seen in panels 1 through 3 are wearing dress uniforms and not overcoats, and because the trees are still in full leaf.

William Wood was commissioned into the Royal Welsh Fusiliers as a lieutenant on February 8, 1773 and Lieutenant Richard Williams on May 13 of the same year.[2] In response to the anticipated rebellion by the Americans, the Fusiliers were sent to Boston in 1774 under the command of General Thomas Gage, who was appointed military governor. They were engaged in the first action of the war at Lexington and Concord and were among the units harassed on their return to Boston. Major General William Howe, later commander of the British forces in the thirteen colonies, was appointed colonel of the regiment on May 11, 1775. The Fusiliers were surrounded in Boston during the siege, were engaged at Bunker Hill, evacuated the city in March of 1776, and later fought in most of the significant battles of the war, including Brandywine, Germantown, Monmouth Courthouse, and Yorktown.[3]

For a map of Massachusetts during the Siege and a view of the American lines surrounding Boston from outside the city, see no. 56, Bernard Romans's *Map of the Seat of Civil War in America*.

B.M.L.

1. British Library 1975, pp. 56–57.
2. Great Britain 1775, p. 77.
3. Cannon 1850, pp. 89–94.

56

Bernard Romans (ca. 1720 – ca. 1784)
Map of the Seat of Civil War in America
Philadelphia: Printed by Nicholas Brooks, 1775
Engraving
17 in. (43.1 cm) x 21 in. (53.4 cm)
Inscribed: *To the Hone. Jno. Hancock Esqre, President of the Continental Congress, / This Map of the Seat of Civil War in America, is Respectfully inscribed / By His Most Obedient Humble Servant B. Romans.*
Provenance unknown, in the Historical Society's collections before 1800

Philadelphia, July 12, 1775. 'It is PROPOSED to PRINT, And in a few days will be published, A COMPLETE and ELEGANT MAP, from BOSTON to WORCESTER, PROVIDENCE and SALEM. Shewing the SEAT of the present unhappy CIVIL WAR in North-America. Author, BERNARD ROMANS . . . .'

The American Revolution saw a vast increase and improvement in the mapping of the colonies, largely for practical military purposes, but also for the graphic display of news of the war, both in England and in America. The presence of a large number of regular army officers with professional training or experience in mapmaking gave the British an advantage in this field. A small number of Americans (see entries for Richard Gridley, no. 40, and Osgood Carleton, no. 2), had formal cartographic training, but early in the war George Washington was forced to draw his own maps and plans to illustrate and coordinate army movements. For the most part, the American cause was dependent on European and ex-

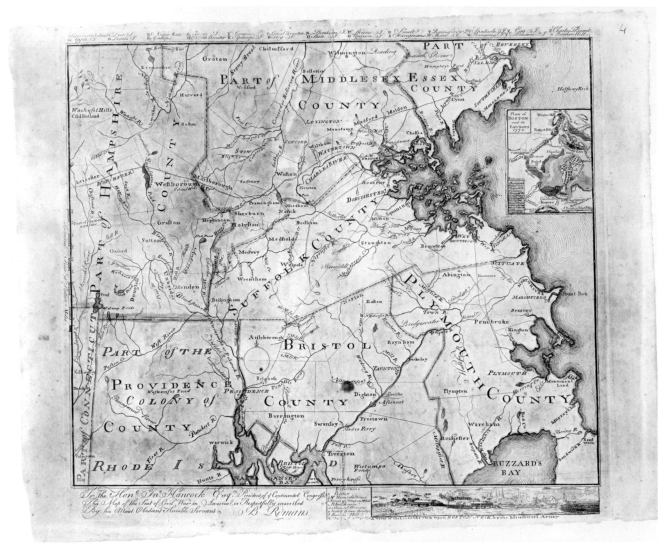

56 (see also color plate V)

British army officers for technical expertise. Bernard Romans, the cartographer of this, the first map printed in
America to show Massachusetts as an independent state,
was one of the small number of ex-British officers and
officials with technical training who gave their allegiance
to their new country.[2]

    Born in Holland about 1720, Bernard Romans had
some formal or practical training as an artillerist and
military engineer, but details of his early life and career
are obscure. In 1766, while engaged in trade, Romans
was shipwrecked off Florida. There, he secured employment as a surveyor for Georgia, and later in the British
colonial service for the Southern Department. His most
famous work was a natural history of Florida that accompanied an enormous twelve- by seven-foot map of that
colony, "an ornamental piece of furniture," as it was described in the *Boston Gazette* in 1774 when Romans came
to Boston to secure subscriptions and to arrange for Paul
Revere to engrave the map. Romans was a frequent contributor to Isaiah Thomas's *Royal American Magazine*,
published in Boston in 1774, and the same year was
elected a member of the American Philosophical Society,
the first learned society in America.[3]

    When the Revolutionary War began, Romans threw
his lot with the American cause; he was in Connecticut
when fighting began and joined the expedition from that
colony that took part in the capture of Ticonderoga. He

supervised the first efforts to remove the cannon from
the fortress (see no. 57). In the summer of 1775, Romans
was employed by the Committee of Safety in New York
to design fortifications for the Hudson River. In this, as
with much of his military career, Romans was unhappy
and unsuccessful. In spite of the war emergency, Romans
found time in the summer of 1775 to undertake the *Map
of the Seat of Civil War* showing Boston during the American siege. The inset view in the lower right corner of the
map shows the British lines on Boston Neck at approximately the same time Lieutenant Williams was making
his sketches (no. 55) from within the British lines, looking
in the opposite direction.[4]

    Despite contemporary newspaper advertisements
that claimed Romans was "the most able draughtsman in
America," and had been present at all of the "late engagements," there is no evidence that he was at Concord and
Lexington, or the Battle of Bunker Hill. His map of eastern Massachusetts is wildly inaccurate in many local
geographical details, but it well served its purpose of
graphically conveying information concerning the scene
of the fighting to the rest of the colonies.[5]

    Romans served in the Philadelphia artillery during
the abortive invasion of Canada in 1776, and in the construction of American defenses later in the war. He found
time during his military service to produce commercial
maps of Connecticut and the northern theater of military

operations, as well as a history of his homeland. According to his widow's pension request, written more than sixty years later, Romans was captured by the British in 1780 during another unlucky voyage, and died under mysterious circumstances at the end of the war.[6]

Although Romans's studies in natural history were not well thought of by the founders of the Society, his other work was collected for the library. Romans's history of his homeland, *Annals of the Troubles in the Netherlands* (Hartford, 1778), was one of the first gifts to the library of the Society in 1792, and this map joined it in the Society's collections within the first decade after its founding.[7]

P.D.

1. *Rivington's New-York Gazetteer*, Aug. 10, 1775.
2. Ristow 1985, pp. 35–47.
3. Phillips 1924, pp. 24–26, 45–50.
4. Ibid., pp. 81–82.
5. Advertisements from the *Pennsylvania Gazette* and *Rivington's New-York Gazetteer*, reprinted in Phillips 1924, pp. 81–83.
6. Phillips 1924, pp. 68–69.
7. MHS *Collections*, 5th ser., 3:57.

57

Henry Knox (1750–1806)
Diary, 20 November 1775–13 January 1776
Manuscript
30 p., 6 5/8 in. (16.8 cm) x 4 3/8 in. (11.1 cm)
From the estate of David Greene Haskins, Jr., 1927

8th. Went on the Ice About 8 oClock in the morning & proceeded so cautiously that before night we got over three sleds & were so lucky as to get the Cannon out of the River, owing to the assistance the good people of the City of Albany gave, In return for which we christen'd her - The Albany.

One of the most notable Revolutionary War generals in George Washington's army was Henry Knox of Massachusetts. Formerly a Boston bookseller and self-educated in military science, Knox rose from the civilian book trade to become the youngest American major general in the Continental Army. Knox's most remarkable achievement during the war was the establishment of a formidable artillery regiment, when virtually none existed, by retrieving the captured cannon from Fort Ticonderoga and dragging them 300 miles through the dead of winter to blast the British out of Boston.[1] This small and sketchy diary, hastily penned by the hand of Henry Knox, chronicles his incredible journey from Fort Ticonderoga and across the Massachusetts frontier to Westfield, Massachusetts, where he recorded his last entry just four days before reaching the Cambridge camp.

Born in Boston in 1750, Henry Knox was the seventh son of William Knox and Mary (Campbell) Knox. When his father abandoned the family in 1762, Henry at the age of twelve was apprenticed to a local bookseller. There he devoured the volumes that surrounded him, and he became most interested in military history and engineering science. At the age of twenty-one, the enterprising and sociable Knox opened his own book and stationery store in Boston. It quickly became a favorite meeting place for Boston patriots, British officers, and fashionable women.

57

One lively Tory lady, Lucy Flucker, caught his eye. Henry's staunch patriotism was well known and much to the displeasure of her father, Thomas Flucker, Royal Secretary of the Province of Massachusetts Bay, Henry and Lucy were married in 1774. That same year, the British Army took over the military occupation of Boston.[2]

In the fall of 1775, the besieged Boston was at a frustrating stalemate. General Washington was in need of big guns to contest the British troops and their imposing naval fleet. The Continental Army, however, had virtually no regular artillery company nor any impressive cannon except for a few unserviceable field pieces left behind by retreating enemy troops. Washington and John Adams were so impressed with Knox's energy and knowledge of military science that they advised Congress to immediately appoint him to succeed the ailing Richard Gridley as colonel of the Regiment of Artillery. Enterprising, energetic, and persistently optimistic, Henry Knox proposed the wild idea of undertaking the trek to Fort Ticonderoga to retrieve the cannon, captured by Ethan Allen and his Green Mountain Boys, to fortify Boston's Dorchester Heights. Washington immediately dispatched Knox to New York commanding that "The want of them [cannon] is so great that no trouble or expense must be spared to obtain them."[3] Exceedingly cold weather, snowstorms, and unexpected midwinter thaws were to compound this treacherous journey.

On November 16th 1775, Knox rode to New York City to order ammunition and then proceeded on to Fort Ticonderoga. For three days his troops disassembled fifty-nine brass and iron cannon, howitzers, mortars, and cohorns from their mounts and secured several tons of shot, 2300 pounds of bullet lead, and 30,000 gunflints.[4] They then hauled the over 119,000 pounds of guns and ammunition to the northern tip of Lake George for the beginning of an incredible 300-mile journey of unbearable winter hardship. The munitions were loaded onto a "Scow, Pettianger, and a Battoe," and Knox rushed to sail the lake before it froze. At Fort George, he wrote to Washington and promised him a "noble train of artillery."[5] For two weeks, Knox hired a convoy of New York teamsters with wagons, sleds, horses and oxen to transport the heavy ordnance down the western Hudson River shore. Holes were cut in the ice to strengthen the river crossing at Albany, but a few of the heavily laden sleds broke through and their vital cargo had to be dredged up from the icy river bottom.[6]

Knox's impressive artillery train, including "42 exceeding strong sleds" and "80 yoke of oxen," crossed the river and the weary teamsters labored eastward through the freezing weather and snow-covered forests of the New England Berkshires. Massachusetts wagonmasters replaced the New York teamsters at Springfield, and the convoy continued on to Washington's elated army at Boston. Generals Ward and Thomas directed 2,000 men and 400 oxen to position the guns at Dorchester Heights, and the British eventually evacuated the city on March 17th, 1776.[7]

Major General Henry Knox's formidable artillery regiment continued to exhibit skill, precision, and valor through all the major battles in the North. After the Revolution, Knox was appointed first secretary of war under the Constitution, drew up plans for the military academy at West Point, and was founder of the Society of the Cincinnati. Knox's brilliant military career ended abruptly in 1806 when he died at the age of fifty-six in Maine at his mansion Montpelier.

The major body of Henry Knox Papers, 1719–1883, on deposit at the Historical Society by the New England Historic Genealogical Society, contains over 12,000 items. Additional Knox papers owned by the Historical Society include this diary and a number of his letters among the papers of his correspondents. Also in the Historical Society's collections are the records of The Massachusetts Society of the Cincinnati, 1783–1883.

L.C.G.

1. Callahan 1964, p. 240.
2. Callahan 1958, pp. 16–32.
3. George Washington to Henry Knox, Nov. 16, 1775. Knox Papers, MHS.
4. Brown 1980, p. 300.
5. Henry Knox to George Washington, Dec. 17, 1775. Knox Papers, MHS.
6. Johnson 1976, p. 28.
7. Knox 1933, pp. 65–66.

58–68

United States Congress and French Académie des Inscriptions et Belles-Lettres, designers
Duvivier, Dupré, and Gatteaux of the Paris Mint, die engravers
"Comitia Americana" Medals
Paris, 1780–1789
Silver, die-struck
Gift of Peter Harvey, 1874

This presentation set of silver medals from George Washington's personal collection contains the first congressional medals issued. Months before declaring independence from Great Britain, the American Congress ("Comitia Americana") authorized the first of its medals to commemorate significant events and the men who

shaped them during the revolutionary war. This first medal, proposed by John Adams after hearing of the evacuation of British troops from Boston in March of 1776,[1] was created to honor George Washington, commander in chief of the Continental Army. This gold presentation medal is now in the Boston Public Library. Congress eventually commissioned ten more medals to mark the American efforts; eight of them belong to this special set, along with Dupré's famous medal of Franklin, and Franklin's own production, the "Libertas Americana" medal. Due to the exigence of war, there was a considerable delay between the time Congress authorized the medals and the time they were executed. Over the course of production, Robert Morris (minister of finance), Benjamin Franklin (minister plenipotentiary to France), David Humphreys (Washington's aide-de-camp and later secretary to the American commissioners negotiating treaties of commerce), and Thomas Jefferson (American minister to France) were all involved in the transactions. Jefferson summed up the events in a succinct fashion:

> Congress voted medals to several officers and directed Rob. Morris their minister of finance to have them made. He authorized Colo. Humphreys to have this done in Europe. Colo. Humphreys had contracted for some of them, had made some paiments, and left the whole business to be finished by me. I made contracts for the rest, and the whole of those named in Mr. Morris's list, were compleated and one medal either in gold or silver (according to the vote) was made for each officer and a set in silver for Genl. Washington.[2]

Following the advice of Morris, Humphreys contacted the Abbé Barthélémy of the Académie des Inscriptions et Belles-Lettres for assistance. Known as the "Petite Académie," it was an offshoot of the Académie Française, and at the time the "Comitia Americana" medals were struck its primary function was to devise appropriate inscriptions and designs for statues, medals, and other public art forms. The American Congress provided general instructions for legends and devices for each medal it authorized to be made; then, a committee of members of the Petite Académie designed the medals and mottos as requested; and once the final design was officially approved, the American agents contracted to have the dies engraved and the medals struck.

The medallists for this series were the finest in France. Pierre Simon Benjamin Duvivier, born to a family of distinguished medallists, was the engraver of coins at the Paris mint from 1774 until 1791, when he was succeeded by Augustin Dupré, who created the coinage for the French Republic. Nicolas Marie Gatteaux, medallist to Kings Louis XV and Louis XVI, was the son of a locksmith and also started as an engraver. His talent led to his introduction to the director of the Paris Mint, where he began to work in 1773. Extremely prolific, Gatteaux produced almost 300 medals in less than twenty years. Cornelius Vermeule has pointed out that, in their work for the United States Congress, these three artists "leaned toward the pictorialism of the grand French painting from the age of Louis XIV."[3] This is especially evident in the panoramic battle scenes, teeming with combatants.

This "set in silver" holds the place of honor in the Massachusetts Historical Society's numismatic collection. Jefferson brought the set home in a burled mahogany case, and presented it to George Washington in New York City around March 21, 1789.[4] After Washington's death in 1799, this set of medals passed to his nephew Robert Lewis.[5] The medals were offered for sale to the United States in 1827, but, according to Daniel Webster, "a constitutional question arose whether Congress could, without a violation of their duty . . . buy that little casket, a relic which came from General Washington's cabinet." When the issue was tabled, Webster stepped in and personally purchased the set.[6] From Webster the medals went to Peter Harvey, who presented them to the Historical Society in 1874.[7]

A.E.B.

1. Jefferson 1950, 16:54.
2. Ibid., 16:77.
3. Vermeule 1988, p. 80.
4. Jefferson 1950, 16:xxxv.
5. Webster 1977, p. 337.
6. Jefferson 1950, 16:xxxv.
7. MHS *Proceedings* 13(1873–1875):287–289.

58

58

Pierre Simon Benjamin Duvivier (1728–1819), engraver
"Washington Before Boston" medal, authorized March 1776
Paris, 1785–1789
Silver, die-struck
D. 2 11/16 in. (68 mm)
Legend, on obverse, around bust of Washington in profile, to right: GEORGIO WASHINGTON SVPREMO DVCI EXERCITVVM ADSERTORI LIBERTATIS; below bust: COMITIA AMERICANA; signed, below shoulder truncation: DU VIVIER / PARIS.F.; on reverse, above view of mounted Washington and his officers on Dorchester Heights, watching the British evacuation of Boston and American army's orderly advance: HOSTIBUS PRIMO FUGATIS; in exergue: BOSTONIUM RECUPERATUM / XVII. MARTII / MDCCLXXVI; signed on cannon barrel, at right: DUVIV.

On February 16, 1776, General George Washington, drawing from lessons of the Battle of Bunker Hill, used the element of surprise to force the British from Boston. The ground was too frozen to repeat the overnight digging of trenches, so, covered by diversionary bombardment, a breastworks was thrown up, which effectively surprised the British. Their commander, General William Howe,

initially planned to attack the Americans, but changed his mind shortly before a storm made his position untenable.[1] Congress awarded Washington this medal for his "wise and spirited conduct in the seige and acquisition of Boston."[2]

The medallic portrait of Washington was modeled after Houdon's bust from life, with the sculptor himself supervising the production of the medal, which caused extensive delay.[3] The final product was worth the wait: Duvivier created a medal of breathtaking simplicity and nobility. This has become the standard by which all medallic portraits of Washington are judged. Begun under David Humphreys in 1785, it was completed under Jefferson's supervision in 1789.

A.E.B.

1. Stefanelli 1973, pp. 5–6.
2. Loubat 1878, p. 3.
3. Jefferson 1950, 16:62.

59

Nicolas Marie Gatteaux (1751–1832), engraver
"Horatio Gates Victory at Saratoga" medal,
authorized November 1777
Paris, 1785–1787
Silver, die-struck
D. 2½ in. (56 mm)
Legend, on obverse, above civilian portrait bust, to left: HORATIO GATES DUCI STRENUO; in exergue: COMITIA AMERICANA; signed, along exergue line at right: N. GATTEAUX; reverse, above General Burgoyne surrendering his sword to General Gates: SALUS REGIONUM SEPTENTRIONAL; in left background the British forces are laying down their arms, while the American forces stand to attention before their flag, on the right; in exergue: HOSTE AD SARATOGAM / IN DEDITION. ACCEPTO / DIE XVII. OCT. MDCCLXXVII. Signed, on bottom of exergual line, at left: GATTEAUX F

In the fall of 1777 the American army, under Commander of the Northern Department Horatio Gates (1728–1832), was entrenched south of Saratoga, New York, on Bemis Heights. British general John Burgoyne, determined to winter his troops in Albany rather than retreat to Canada, tried twice to outflank the Americans and push through to Albany. The second time the British were forced to retreat to Saratoga, where the Americans surrounded

59

them. Burgoyne surrendered on October 17, 1777. The American victory was timely: Washington had suffered two defeats at the hands of the enemy, and Congress had been forced out of Philadelphia, the nation's capital. Gates's victory showed that the Continental Army, as inadequately trained and provisioned as it was, could beat the British and German regulars.[1]

In 1785 Humphreys provided Gatteaux with an engraved portrait of Gates, wearing the badge of the Society of the Cincinnati, as a model for this piece. This caused delays, since the badge was an anachronism and Jefferson felt that Congress would not wish to appear to be endorsing the society. The problem was settled by omitting the badge on the medallic portrait, which was completed in August 1787. This appears to be the first medallic representation of the "Stars and Stripes," as adopted by Congress on June 14, 1777.

A.E.B.

1. Stefanelli 1973, pp. 9–10.

60

61

62

60–62

These three medals were awarded for an action which took place at the American fort of Stony Point on the Hudson River, across from Peekskill, New York. Under General Sir Henry Clinton, the British took the fort, so Washington sent Brigadier General Anthony Wayne with a force of 1,350 men to retake it. As ever in Washington's plans, the element of surprise was crucial. On July 15, 1779, the American forces began their approach on foot, fourteen miles from the fort. In some places the road was so bad that they went single file. Within one-and-a-half miles of the fort, the Americans fell into battle formation. Two volunteer units, under Lieutenant-Colonel François Louis Tessiedre de Fleury and Major John Stewart, stormed the fort with fixed bayonets in unloaded muskets, "while Major Murfey amused [the British] in front."[1] De Fleury commanded the right column of volunteers and was the first to scale the walls of the fort. Stewart led the left column of volunteers. Both flanks had to coordinate their movements through British defenses and obstructions at night, keeping perfectly quiet to maintain the element of surprise. By the next day the fort had been taken with only fifteen American casualties. Washington had the fort dismantled on July 18.[2] While the operation was a success, it had more value as a morale booster than any strategic importance in the war.

A.E.B.

1. Loubat 1878, p. 20
2. Stefanelli 1973, pp. 12–17.

60

Nicolas Marie Gatteaux (1751–1832), engraver
"Anthony Wayne's Victory at Stony-Point" medal,
authorized July 1779
Paris, 1789–1790
Silver, die-struck
D. 2 ⅛ in. (54 mm)
Legend, on obverse, above Native American maiden (symbolizing southern United States) holding aloft a crown while extending a laurel victory wreath to General Wayne: ANTONIO WAYNE DUCI EXERCITUS; in exergue: COMITIA AMERICANA; signed at right, below Wayne's feet: GATTEAUX.; on reverse: STONEY-POINT EXPUGNATUM above panoramic view of fort, with American forces advancing under cover of fire provided by their cannon in foreground; in exergue: XV JUL. MDCCLXXIX; signed, on exergue line, at left: GATTEAUX

With the addition of the federal shield and a crocodile, Gatteaux transformed the eighteenth century-icon of a Native American maiden symbolizing the American continents into a representation of the southern United States.[1] The reverse side carries an astonishing wealth of detail, combining the depth of field and sense of movement for which Gatteaux was known. Benjamin Franklin intended to get this medal designed and struck, but the expense of the de Fleury piece prevented him from acting. It was not until 1789 that Jefferson finally completed this commission.

A.E.B.

1. Jefferson 1950, 16:xxxvii.

61

Pierre Simon Benjamin Duvivier (1728–1819), engraver
"DeFleury at Stony-Point" medal, authorized July 1779
Paris, 1780
Silver, die-struck
D. 1 ¹³⁄₁₆ in. (46 mm)
Legend, on obverse, above Mars standing in the debris of fort, trampling the flag which he has captured and raising sword with which he has vanquished his enemies: VIRTUTIS ET AUDACIÆ MONUM. ET PRÆMIUM; in exergue: D. DE FLEURY EQUITI GALLO / PRIMO SUPER MUROS / RESP. AMERIC. D.D.; signed, on fallen coping at left: DUVIVIER S.; on reverse, above an aerial view of fort at Stony Point, with British ships in the river below: AGGERES PALUDES HOSTES VICTI; in exergue: STONY-PT. EXPUGN. / XV JUL. MDCCLXXIX

The only medal in this set that does not feature a portrait of its recipient, this piece represents de Fleury (the first man over the walls at Stony-Point) as Mars, the Roman god of war. Duvivier's reverse is in sharp contrast to those on the same subject by Gatteaux (nos. 60, 62: Wayne and Stewart medals) and shows the fort and British ships anchored in the river beyond in distorted aerial perspective. Benjamin Franklin commissioned this medal in 1780. The first of the "Comitia Americana" series to be completed, it was given to de Fleury in 1783.

A.E.B.

62

Nicolas Marie Gatteaux (1751–1832), engraver
"John Stewart at Stony Point" medal, authorized July 1779
Paris, 1789–1790
Silver, die-struck
D. 1¹³⁄₁₆ in. (46 mm)
Legend, on obverse, above Native American maiden (symbolizing southern United States, with federal shield by her side and alligator at her feet), presenting a palm branch to Major Stewart: JOANNI STEWART COHORTIS PRÆFECTO; in exergue: COMITIA AMERICANA; signed at exergue, below Stewart's feet: GATTEAUX; on reverse, above view of Stewart, leading his men over an abatis with view of fort in background: STONEY-POINT OP-PUGNATUM; in exergue: XV JUL. MDCCLXXIX; signed, on exergue line, at left: GATTEAUX

Thomas Jefferson contracted with Gatteaux to make this medal in 1789. The final design shows the double column of American assault forces approaching the fort with British ships in the river beyond, while Stewart leads his men through enemy obstructions in the foreground.

63–66

In 1781, General Nathanael Greene's American forces in the south were facing Lord Charles Cornwallis's army. On January 17, at the Cowpens, South Carolina, British troops under Colonel Banastre attacked an American force of about 800 men under General Daniel Morgan. Under attack, the Americans fell back in an orderly withdrawal, then wheeled sharply on command and counterattacked. Morgan's strategy and the bravery of his forces were responsible for their success. Lieutenant Colonel Howard commanded the light infantry. After the Americans counterattacked, the British lines were thrown into confusion, upon which Howard ordered a bayonet charge that successfully routed the enemy. Lieutenant Colonel Washington, a distant relation of George Washington, commanded the Third Regiment of Dragoons, which covered the back of Howard's infantry. Upon hearing that American riflemen were being cut down by the British on the left flank, he charged them so ferociously that they broke and fled, as depicted on this medal.[1]

1. Stefanelli 1973, pp. 26–31.

63

Augustin Dupré (1748–1833), engraver
"Daniel Morgan Victory at Cowpens So. Car." medal,
authorized March 1781
Paris, 1785–1789
Silver, die-struck
D. 2 ¼ in. (56 mm)
Legend, on obverse, above Native American maiden with federal shield (United States) crowning Morgan with laurel wreath, with trophies of war in background: DANIELI MORGAN DUCI EXERCITUS; in exergue: COMITIA AMERICANA; signed, at bottom of exergue: *dupré f.*; on reverse, above battle scene showing exact moment of American army's charge into British ranks: VICTORIA LIBERTATIS VINDEX; in exergue: FVGATIS CAPTIS AVT CAESIS / AD COWPENS HOSTIBVS. / XVII. JAN. MDCCLXXXI.; signed, below a second exergue line: DUPRE INV. ET F.

Of the Washington-Webster "Comitia Americana" set, the Morgan medal is considered the finest example of the medallist's art. Dupré's close-up of the reverse battle scene successfully renders several planes in the field, giving this medal a sense of motion and power unmatched in this series.[1] Originally contracted by Humphreys in 1785, esthetic differences held up the effort until January 1789, when Jefferson approved the Académie's design. In 1838, when Congress authorized a gold restrike to be made to replace the original, which had been lost by Morgan, Daniel Webster loaned this medal to the secretary of war to have new dies made at Paris.[2]

A.E.B.

1. Loubat 1878, pp. xxi–xxii.
2. Julian 1977, p. 120.

63

64

65

66

64

Pierre Simon Benjamin Duvivier (1728–1819), engraver
"William Washington at Cowpens, S. Car." medal,
authorized March 1781
Paris, 1785–1789
Silver, die-struck
D. 1 ⅞ in. (47 mm)
Legend, on obverse: GULIELMO WASHINGTON
LEGIONIS EQUIT. PRÆFECTO above view of mounted
Washington leading his troops, with Victory above him;
in exergue: COMITIA AMERICANA; signed at exergue,
extreme right: DU V; on reverse, within a closed laurel
wreath: QUOD / PARVA MILITUM MANU / STRENUE
PROSECUTUS HOSTES / VIRTUTIS INGENITÆ / PRÆ-
CLARUM SPECIMEN DEDIT / IN PUGNA AD COWPENS /
XVII. JAN. MDCCLXXXI.

The design for this medal was prepared by the Académie
in December 1785, but was not implemented until Jefferson signed the contract with Duvivier in 1789.[1] Congress
awarded this medal to Washington because "in vigorously
pursuing the enemy with a handful of soldiers he gave a
noble example of innate courage at the battle of the Cowpens."[2]

A.E.B.

1. Stefanelli 1973, p. 29.
2. Loubat 1878, p. 46.

65

Pierre Simon Benjamin Duvivier (1728–1819), engraver
"John Eagar Howard at Cowpens, S.Car." medal,
authorized March 1781
Paris, 1785–1789
Silver, die-struck
D. 1 ⅞ in. (47 mm)
Legend, on obverse, above mounted Howard pursuing
enemy, with Victory flying alongside: JOH. EGAR. HOW-
ARD LEGIONIS PEDITUM PRÆFECTO; in exergue:
COMITIA AMERICANA; signed, at left: DU VIV.; on
reverse, within a closed laurel wreath: QUOD IN NUTAN-
TEM HOSTIUM ACIEM / SUBITO IRRUENS / PRÆ-
CLARUM BELLICÆ VIRTUTIS / SPECIMEN DEDIT / IN
PUGNA AD COWPENS / XVII JAN MDCCLXXXI

The Académie presented this design at the same time as
the William Washington medal, but the contract was not
agreed upon until Jefferson made the arrangements in
1789. Howard was awarded this medal "because by rush-
ing suddenly on the wavering lines of the enemy, he gave
a brilliant example of martial courage at the battle of
Cowpens."[1]

A.E.B.

1. Loubat 1878, pp. 48–49.

66

Augustin Dupré (1748–1833), engraver
"Nathanael Greene at Eutaw, S. Car." medal,
authorized October 1781
Paris, 1785–1787
Silver, die-struck
D. 2 ¼ in. (56 mm)
Legend, on obverse, around draped military bust, to left:
NATHANIELI GREEN EGREGIO DUCI COMITIA
AMERICANA; on reverse, above winged Victory trampl-
ing broken trophies of war: SALUS REGIONUM AU-
STRALIUM; in exergue: HOSTIBUS AD EUTAW / DEBEL-
LATIS DIE VIII SEPT. / MDCCLXXXI; signed, near sword
grip, at left: DUPRE

In September 1781 Green moved against the British (under
Lieutenant Colonel Alexander Stuart) at Orangeburg,
South Carolina. They retreated to Eutaw Springs where
Greene pressed his attack. Stuart's counterattack car-
ried the day for the British, but they were so weakened
by losses that they retreated to Charleston. Greene had
lost the battle, but won the campaign by keeping the
British in Charleston until Cornwallis surrendered at
Yorktown, six weeks later.[1]

In April 1785 the French Académie presented its design for this medal to David Humphreys, who contracted
with Dupré to make the medal that October. It was finished in 1787 and presented to Greene's widow.

A.E.B.

1. Stefanelli 1973, pp. 33–34.

67

Benjamin Franklin (1706–1790), designer and
Augustin Dupré (1748–1843), designer and engraver
"Libertas Americana" medal
Paris, 1782–1783
Silver, die-struck
D. 1¹⁵/₁₆ in. (47 mm)
Legend, on obverse, above head of Liberty, to left, with
unbound hair: LIBERTAS. AMERICANA.; pole supporting
Liberty cap set at angle behind her; in exergue: 4 JUIL.
1776.; signed, at truncation: DUPRE; on reverse, above
infant Hercules (United States), strangling two snakes
while Minerva (France) protects him from springing
leopard (Britain): NON SINE DIIS ANIMOSUS INFANS.; in
exergue: 17 1777 / OCT. / 19 1781; signed, at exergue line, at
right: DUPRE F.

The "Libertas Americana" medal was made to commemorate the surrenders of Burgoyne at Saratoga (1777) and
Cornwallis at Yorktown (1781). In a letter dated 1782 to
American Secretary of Foreign Affairs Robert Livingston, Franklin described his design for this medal.[1] The
drawing of Hercules, from which Dupré worked, has
been attributed to fresco painter Esprit-Antoine Gibelin
(1739–1813). The design for the obverse is attributed
to Dupré alone. The use of a liberty cap to symbolize the
eighteenth-century struggle for political freedoms has
been traced from printmaker and painter William
Hogarth to the American colonies, where it was so effectively used by engraver Paul Revere in his masthead for

67

the *Boston Gazette* that it became synonymous with the
American Revolution.[2] Dupré's conceptualization of
Liberty was so successful that the United States Mint
used the image, after a fashion, in its early coinage; and
Dupré used it again to symbolize the French Revolution
(1796). Even though Congress never officially sanc-
tioned this medal, Jefferson considered the "Libertas
Americana" to be an appropriate companion piece for
the "Comitia Americana" set. Indeed, Dupré's Liberty
has been called "one of the most effective and moving
works of art of the Revolutionary era."[3]

A.E.B.

1. Loubat 1878, p. 20.
2. Korshak 1988, pp. 69–70.
3. Ibid., p. 62.

68

68

Augustin Dupré (1748–1833), designer and engraver
"Benjamin Franklin" medal
Paris, 1786
Silver, die-struck
D. 1¹³/₁₆ in. (46 mm)
Legend, on obverse, around portrait bust, to left: BENJ.
FRANKLIN NATUS BOSTON. XVII JAN.; below:
MDCCVI; signed, at truncation: DUPRE F.; on reverse,
within a field framed by an oak wreath: ERIPUIT CŒLO /
FULMEN / SCEPTRUM QUE / TYRANNIS; below wreath:
SCULPSIT ET DICAVIT / AUG. DUPRE ANNO /
MDCCLXXXVI

This is the second medal in Washington's set which does
not bear the congressional imprint of "Comitia Americana." Jefferson intended to distribute sets of these medals
throughout Europe, and to omit an American of
the stature and popularity of Dr. Franklin would have

been unthinkable.[1] This medal, conceived and engraved by Dupré and dedicated to Franklin, shows the degree of esteem in which he was held by the French. The reverse epigram was composed in Franklin's honor by Turgot: "He drew fire from heaven and wrenched the sceptre from tyrants."[2]

A.E.B.

1. Jefferson 1950, 16:65.

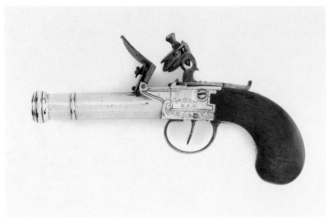

69

69

Flintlock-ignition pocket pistol
European, eighteenth century
Brass, steel, iron, and wood
Caliber: 13 mm (.51 cal.); barrel length (with chamber): 5¹/₁₆ in. (12.8 cm)
Inscribed, on one face: *Capt. J. P. Jones. / U.S.A.*; on other face: *Philadelphia / Oct. 10th 1776*
Gift of Theodore Chase, 1977

This eighteenth-century flintlock-ignition pocket pistol was presented to John Paul Jones in recognition of his commission as captain in the United States Navy in 1776. Although Jones's permanent captaincy was officially awarded on August 8th 1776, it was not until October 10th that the Continental Congress established the hierarchy of its officers in naval service. Jones was ranked eighteenth out of twenty-four on the seniority list, a placement which was not well received.[1]

The two-stage, untapered, circular-section brass "cannon" barrel of this European pistol is of moderate length. There are molded bands at the muzzle and about one-third the length toward the breech. The integral brass chamber with box-lock has a flat throat-hole cock with sliding-bar iron safety that also locks the steel and pan-cover closed. The pan and chamber are sparsely decorated with thin engraved lines, a punched repeated triangular border, and a spiraled basal border with voluted terminal. Screwed into the underside of the chamber is a deep, closed curved trigger-guard of flat-sectioned iron, lightly engraved with leaved motifs. The downcurving, short wooden grip appears to be an early-nineteenth-century replacement. The screws in the underside butt-strap and that securing the side-wall of the chamber are modern replacements.[2]

John Paul Jones was born in Scotland in 1747, the son of John Paul and Jean (MacDuff) Paul. The path to glory was the sea for this young gardener's son, and at the age of thirteen, the ambitious John Paul apprenticed on the brig *Friendship*, bound for Barbados and Virginia. Through persistence, force of character, and sheer merit, Paul was determined to improve his station in life. He dropped his Galloway brogue, taught himself English, cultivated his writing ability, and surrounded himself with gentlemen. By the age of twenty-one, he was the master of a merchant ship in the West Indies trade and had acquired the navigational skills to command a full-rigged cargo ship. An ill-fated incident changed his life and his name forever, when he was charged with the murder of a mutinous crew member in Tobago in 1773. Hiding incognito in the American colonies, John Paul emerged after twenty months in Virginia and subsequently adopted the name Jones to conceal his identity.[3]

In true gallant fashion, John Paul Jones declared himself "a free Citizen of the World in defense of the Violated rights of Mankind" and at the outbreak of the American Revolution embraced the American cause for liberty offering his services to the new colonial navy. With the assistance of his patron, Joseph Hewes, delegate to the Second Continental Congress from North Carolina and Chairman of the Marine Committee, Jones was commissioned a first lieutenant in the Continental Navy on December 7, 1775. In August 1776, he received his captaincy and was assigned his first independent command aboard the sloop *Providence*. There he distinguished himself as a resolute, skillful, and intrepid naval commander, capturing a horde of foreign vessels up and down the Atlantic coast.[4]

In 1777, Congress appointed Captain Jones to command the sloop *Ranger* and directed him to cruise the Irish Sea. Bold and daring raids along the British coast and the capture of the British man-of-war *Drake* heightened Jones's British reputation as a pirate.[5] His naval war fame, however, rests on the Battle of Flamborough Head between the British man-of-war *Serapis* and Jones's new command, the French ship, the *Bonhomme Richard*. Although the *Serapis* was far superior and outgunned the *Richard*, Commodore Jones audaciously sailed up to the *Serapis*, lashed the ships together from stem to stern, and prepared his crew for a vicious hand-to-hand battle. "I have not yet begun to fight!" was Jones's immortal cry to the British commander. Although Jones was victorious after the three-hour battle, what remained of both ships was nothing but "carnage, wreck and ruin."[6]

Throughout his life, Captain Jones was bitter and disappointed by the lack of American honors that he felt he so well deserved. Congress "thanked" Jones for his bravery and valor, but he never received the commission of rear admiral or the command of the *America* that he so desperately wanted. After the Revolutionary war, Jones entered the Russian navy to fight the Turks at the request of the Empress Catherine. His military engagements were successful, however, he left Russia following a personal scandal.

Jones's valor and victory, however, were well appreciated by the French. Louis XVI had honored him with the Ordre du Mérite Militaire in 1780. Other than on board ship, it was in the salons and boudoirs of

Paris that the Chevalier Jones spent his happiest days. With but few friends during the last two years of his life, he died alone in his Paris apartment at the age of forty-five in 1792. However, in 1905 Jones's remains were returned to America with an American naval squadron escort and later placed in the crypt of the Naval Academy chapel at Annapolis with full military honors.

The muster roll of the sloop of war *Providence*, Captain John Paul Jones's first commission, is in the Massachusetts Historical Society's collections.

L.C.G.

1. Sherburne 1825, pp. 26–27.
2. Blair 1983; Blair 1968; Brown 1980.
3. Morison 1959, p. 25.
4. Ibid., p. 33.
5. Miller 1974, p. 366.
6. Morison 1959, pp. 226–240.

70

John Singleton Copley (1738–1815)
John Hancock (1736/7–1793)
1770–1772
Oil on canvas
29½ in. (76.3 cm) x 24½ in. (63.7 cm)
Bequest of Henry Lee Shattuck, 1971

John Hancock, patriot, signer of the Declaration of Independence, and first governor of the Commonwealth of Massachusetts, was born in Braintree, Massachusetts, in 1736/7, the son of the Reverend John Hancock and his wife Mary Hawke. Upon his father's death, John Hancock at age nine went to live with his childless uncle, the wealthy Boston merchant Thomas Hancock, and his wife Lydia Henchman, in their mansion on Beacon Hill. After attending Boston Latin School and Harvard College, where he graduated in 1754, he learned the business of shipping and importing both on Hancock's Wharf in Boston and in London through his uncle's associates abroad. When Thomas Hancock died in 1764, his nephew inherited one of the largest business concerns and one of the greatest fortunes amassed in New England.[1] Able, ambitious and gregarious, the young merchant was also drawn to public life. His political career began at twenty-eight with his election to the office of selectman in Boston. Though his uncle's political ties were loyalist, John leaned toward the Whigs and gradually lost his faith in the ability of the royal ministry to provide just government for Massachusetts.[2]

At the time this portrait was painted in the early 1770s, John Hancock had been transformed by the *Liberty* affair from a member of the radical Whig party to patriotic hero. In 1768 Hancock's firm imported a large cargo of Madeira wine in the company sloop *Liberty* and smuggled it ashore to avoid taxes. There is little doubt that Hancock was a regular participant in the locally accepted smuggling activities, but this time the royal governor decided to make an example of the prominent Hancock and seized the *Liberty* as she was being reloaded for her next voyage. Townspeople rioted in protest of the seizure, and Hancock gained much prestige as the patriotic victim of English repression.[3]

70

Hancock sat for a large portrait by John Singleton Copley (City of Boston, deposited at the Museum of Fine Arts) in 1765, the year following his inheritance. Now, to demonstrate his solidarity with the Whig Party after a skirmish with the royal governor, he commissioned Copley to paint a matching full-length portrait of Samuel Adams (City of Boston, deposited at the Museum of Fine Arts), well-known leader of the Whig party and a zealous patriot, which he then hung side by side with his own in his parlor.[4] To further the patriot cause, the images of the two leaders were also displayed together before and after 1776 in Faneuil Hall, Boston's public meeting place.[5] About the same time he commissioned the Adams portrait, Hancock sat for the waist-length portrait in the collection of the Massachusetts Historical Society. A second almost identical portrait of John Hancock exists in a private collection.[6]

The Historical Society's portrait, like Copley's portrait of James Allen (no. 38), represents the more sober mood of the artist's work in the late 1760s and early 1770s. Hancock wears a short wig and an elegant black coat with gold embroidery and buttons. His face, showing the shadow of a beard, is strongly lighted and, along with his white collar, contrasts dramatically with the black suit and the dark brown background.

J.L.P.

1. Sibley 1873, 13:417.
2. Fowler 1980, p. 147.
3. Ibid., p. 87.
4. Miller 1936, p. 254.
5. Troyen 1980, p. 9.
6. Parker 1938, pp. 96–98; Prown 1966, p. 217.

71 (see also color plate VI)

71

Joseph Boze (1744–1826)
Gilbert du Motier, Marquis de Lafayette (1757–1834)
Paris, 1790
Oil on canvas
36 in. (92.1 cm) x 28½ (72.6 cm)
Gift of Mrs. John W. Davis, 1835

Born into an ancient and noble French family, Gilbert du Motier, Marquis de Lafayette, commenced his military career in the King's Regiment of Musketeers in 1771. With his marriage in 1774 to Adrienne de Noailles, the aristocratic young officer entered one of the most powerful and influential families in France, increasing both his social standing and his wealth. Stirred by the reports of the rebellious Americans fighting for liberty, he seized the opportunity to fulfill his dream of military glory, bought a ship and sailed for America. After his arrival in 1777, his pleasing manner and willingness to learn earned the twenty-year-old marquis an honorary commission as major general in the Continental Army. He was devoted to General Washington who became his mentor and father figure. Lafayette's courage and tenacity on the battlefield and his successful pleas for material aid for the Americans through correspondence and on furloughs to France established him as a hero. The fact that he left home and hearth to risk his life in a country not his own (and at his own expense) for the cause of liberty captured the imagination and admiration of Americans. Received as a hero in his homeland upon his return, and well-known for his liberal ideas throughout the western world, Lafayette played an important role in the political changes taking place in France. Appointed head of the Parisian Garde Nationale in 1789 after the storming of the Bastille, he ordered the prison leveled, and a few months later, sent the key to the Bastille to America as a tribute to Washington, his mentor and the man he considered the father of liberty.[1]

Commissioned by Thomas Jefferson in 1790 to be included in his gallery of American heroes, this painting by the French artist Joseph Boze represents Lafayette at the pinnacle of his career, a hero in America and France. Lafayette wears the uniform of the Parisian Garde Nationale (said to be of his design), with three medals decorating his lapel: on the right, the eagle of the Order of the Society of the Cincinnati, honoring French and American officers of the American Revolution, on the left, the Cross of St. Louis, presented to him by Louis XVI for his part in the American conflict, and, in the middle, the Medal of the Vainqueurs de la Bastille.[2] Though the red, white, and blue of Lafayette's uniform are also particularly appropriate for an American hero, the blue and red of Lafayette's jacket were the colors on the coat of arms of the City of Paris, and they became the symbol of the French Revolution.[3]

Joseph Boze, French portrait painter and miniaturist, counted Louis XVI, Marie Antoinette and members of their court among his sitters, and he was appointed official painter of the war under Louis XVI.[4] It has been suggested that the portrait of Lafayette does not appear to have been drawn from life. Jefferson's agent, William Short, remarked in a letter to Jefferson that Lafayette, though willing, never had a spare moment during this intensely active time of his life to sit for a portrait. Further, the French sculptor Houdon had recently completed a bust of Lafayette which Boze may have used as his model. The pose, turn of the head, wig and uniform are the same in both works.[5]

When President Jefferson died and his estate proved insolvent, his collection of paintings was exhibited in New York and at the Boston Athenaeum prior to a sale at Chester Harding's Boston gallery in 1835. This portrait was purchased at that sale and presented to the Historical Society the same year. Other paintings from Jefferson's collection which came to the Historical Society include a copy of a portrait of Christopher Columbus, and the portrait of George Washington by Joseph Wright and completed by John Trumbull.[6]

J.L.P.

1. Bernier 1983, pp. 23–41; Loveland 1971, pp. 8–10; Miller 1989, pp. 104–105.
2. Miller 1989, p. 105.
3. Bernier 1983, p. 202n.
4. Thieme 1948, 2:494–495.
5. Mongan 1975, pp. 90–94.
6. Oliver 1988, pp. 26, 111.

Benjamin Franklin (1706–1790)

The association of the remarkable Benjamin Franklin with Boston was brief. Born on Milk Street, the youngest son of a tallow chandler and soap boiler, Franklin worked for five years as a printer's apprentice and putative publisher in the shop of his brother, James Franklin, until he ran away to in 1723 to find great fame and considerable fortune as a printer, scientist, author, philanthropist,

THE
New-England Courant.

From MONDAY March 26. to MONDAY April 2. 1722.

Honour's a Sacred Tye, the Law of Kings,
The Noble Mind's Distinguishing Perfection,
That aids and strengthens Vertue where it meets her,
And Imitates her Actions where she is not,
It ought not to be sported with —————— Cato.

To the Author of the New-England Courant.

SIR, *Sagadahock, March 20.*

HONOUR is a Word that Sounds big and makes a most ravishing Entrance into Men's Ears, while a Just and proper Notion of it, is mistaken by most, and the Rules and Measures of it, are comply'd with but by few.

Hence it comes to pass, that some who make a conspicuous Figure in the World, (thro' their Ignorance of this Noble Principle,) falsly imagine themselves to be treading in the Paths of Honour, while they are but greedily pursuing their Ambitious Designs, and Impatiently Gratifying their Lusts of Pride and Covetousness.

Honour indeed, according to the vulgar Notion of it, is nothing more than an empty Name. The Actions of many Men, speak their Sentiments of it ; and render it Obvious, that they suppose it to consist only in Flattering Titles, and high Posts and Preferments, be they Acquir'd in the most Shameful and Dishonourable Ways. But how often do such Precipitate themselves into Open Shame ? and when they fondly imagine they have grasp'd the Airy Phantom, and arriv'd to the utmost Pitch of Honour, Behold, it Vanishes into nothing, perishes even in the using, and leaves a lasting Brand of Infamy on their Memory.

Now seeing nothing is more pernicious, than a Principle of Action not rightly apprehended, it may not be improper ; First, To hint at some Things, which have the Shadow and Appearance of Honour, but in reality are Infamous and Dishonourable ; and Then, to give some brief Description of this Superior Principle.

With respect then to Posts of Honour and Honourary Titles, (and some Men have no other Idea of Honour than what results from such Empty Names as these,) it may be said in the Words of an Ingenious Writer, "But whatever Wealth "and Dignities Men may arrive at, they ought to consider, "that every one stands as a Blot in the Annals of his Coun-"try, who arrives at the Temple of Honour, by any other "Way than through that of Vertue". He that advanceth himself to Posts of Honour, by cursed Bribery, or sordid Flattery, or any other base and unworthy Arts, lays his Honour in the Dust, and Exposes himself to lasting Infamy and Reproach. It is also highly Dishonourable for a Man, when any particular Accomplishment is requisite to Qualify him for Preferment, to climb thereto by Sham Pretences, and meer Imposture. He that will thus Impose on the World, it is no Wonder, if he Act by *Secret Commissions*, and carry on Designs in the Dark that are ruinous to his Country, and Infamous to himself. But the true Reason why Men are guilty of such Actions is, Their Breasts were never once warm'd with one single Spark of true Honour.

It is also Dishonourable, for men to rise to Places of Honour, by Calumny and Detraction, or other sordid Arts, which their Envy, Ambition, or Avarice prompt them to Improve, the more easily to undermine and supplant others, who are perhaps more Righteous and worthy of Honour than themselves.

But above all, how vile and inglorious is it, for Men hotly to pursue Preferment with this Design and View, that they may Squeese and Oppress their Brethren ; that they may Crush and Trample them in the Dust ? How amazing is it, that Men who pretend to Reason and Religion, should thus Desire to Act the Tyrant and the Brute ! May we not reasonably conclude of Such, that they never yet Entertain'd a Just Idea of true Honour. The Driving of such Men, is commonly like the Driving of the Son of *Nimshi* ; and to such a high Degree of impetuosity, do their Passions sometimes swell, that the Man is Dismounted, looses the Reins, and is Dragg'd whither the fury of the Beast directs.

Men of Arbitrary Spirits, what wont they comply with ? Through what Rules of Vertue and Humanity will they not

break, that they may attain their Ends ? Too many such there are, (says Mr. *Dummer*, In his Defence of the N.E. Charters, pag. 42.) who are contented to be Saddled themselves, provided they may Ride others under the chief Rider.

Men of Tyrannical Principles, with what abhorrence are they to be Look'd on, by all who have any Sense of Honour ? Such, it may be presum'd, had they Power equal to their Will, would soon, not only Sacrifice Honour, and Conscience, but even all Mankind, to their Voracious Appetites. They are to be Esteem'd, (as Dr *Cotton Mather* calls them) the Basest of Men. Such Sons of *Nimrod*, *Nero*, & old *Lewis*, are viler than the Earth they tread on ; it groans under them as an Intolerable Plague, and insupportable Burthen. Tyranny and Honour, cannot Reign together in the same Breast.

And (to mention nothing more) it is very Dishonourable, for Men to make rash and hasty Promises, relating to any Thing Wherein the Interest of the Publick is nearly concern'd, and then to say, they will retain their Integrity forever, or till *Doomsday*, pretending it is for fear of violating their Word and Honour. The Talents, Interest, or Experience of such Men (says one) make them very often useful in all Parties, and at all Times. They Ridicule every Thing as Romantick, that comes in Competition with their present Interests ; and treat those Persons as Visionaries, who dare stand up in a corrupt Age, for what has not its Immediate Reward annexed to it.

But let us now change the Scene, and see what true Honour Is. And no doubt, the reverse of what has been said is truly Honourable. True HONOUR, (as a Learned Writer defines it) is the Report of Good and Vertuous Actions, issuing from the Conscience Into the Discovery of the PEOPLE with whom we live, and which (by a Reflection on our selves) gives us the Testimony of what others believe concerning us, and to the Soul becomes a great Satisfaction. True Honour, (says another) tho' it be a different Principle from Religion, is that which Produces the same Effects. The Lines of Action, tho' drawn from different Parts, terminate in the same Point. Religion Embraces Vertue, as it is enjoin'd by the Laws of GOD ; Honour as it is Graceful and Ornamental to Humane Nature. The Religious Man fears, the Man of Honour scorns to do an ill Action. A Noble Soul, would rather die, than commit an Action that should make his Children Blush, when he is in his Grave, and be look'd upon as a Reproach to those who shall live a Hundred Years after him.

In a Word, He is the Honourable Man, who is Influenc'd and Acted by a Publick Spirit, and fir'd with a Generous Love to Mankind in the worst of Times ; Who lays aside his private Views, and foregoes his own Interest, when it comes in competition with the Publick : Who dare adhere to the Cause of Truth, and Manfully Defend the Liberties of his Country when boldly Invaded, and Labour to retrieve them when they are Lost. Yea, the Man of Honour, (when contracted sordid Spirits desert the Cause of Vertue and the Publick) will stand himself alone, and (like *Atlas*) bear up the Massy Weight on his Shoulders : And this he will do, in Spite of Livid Envy, Snakey Malice, and vile Detraction.

This is true Honour indeed : and the Man who thus Gloriously acquits himself, shall shine in the Records of Fame, with a peculiar Lustre : His Name shall be mention'd with Reverence in Future Ages, and all Posterity shall call him *Blessed*.

PHILANTHROPOS.

To the Author of the New-England Courant.

SIR,

IT may not be improper in the first Place to inform your Readers, that I intend once a Fortnight to present them, by the Help of this Paper, with a short Epistle, which I presume will add somewhat to their Entertainment.

And since it is observed, that the Generality of People, now a days, are unwilling either to commend or dispraise what they read, until they are in some measure informed who or what the Author of it is, whether he be *poor* or *rich*, *old* or *young*, a *Scholar* or a *Leather Apron Man*, &c. and give their Opinion of the Performance, according to the Knowledge which they have of the Author's Circumstances, it may not be amiss to begin with a short Account of my past Life and present Condition, that the Reader may not be at a Loss to judge whether or no my Lucubrations are worth his reading.

At the time of my Birth, my Parents were on Ship-board in their Way from *London* to *N.England*. My Entrance into this troublesome World was attended with the Death of my Father, a Misfortune statesman, and first citizen of Philadelphia.[1]

Franklin's various careers touch upon almost all aspects of the new nation. He was active in the drafting of and a signer of both the Declaration of Independence and the United States Constitution. His passion for self-improvement led him to write his *Autobiography*, a literary classic and America's first enduring best seller that has engaged and influenced writers ever since. At the end of his life, Franklin became active in the beginnings of the national movement for the abolition of slavery.[2]

The *Autobiography* provides insight into the two great themes of Franklin's life—first, printing here in Boston at the end of the Puritan era, and later, sometimes comical scientific research in mid-eighteenth-century Philadelphia. It was Franklin's work in these fields, as author and printer, and later as a scientist, that made him the first truly famous American, celebrated not only in colonial America, but in England and all of Europe as well.

P.D.

1. Wright 1986 is a modern scholarly biography of Franklin.
2. Franklin 1986, pp. xiii–xv.

72

The New England Courant, March 26–April 2, 1722
Boston: Printed and sold by James Franklin, 1722
Newspaper
2 p., 12 ⅜ in. (31.3 cm) x 7½ in. (19.2 cm)
Gift of Benjamin Burt, 1792

This is the only surviving copy of the issue of *The New England Courant* that contains Benjamin Franklin's earliest known writing. The *Courant*, Boston's third newspaper, was founded by Benjamin's brother James Franklin (1697–1735) in 1721. From its beginning it was a controversial publication. "The paper's lively, combative essays and verses," the editors of Benjamin Franklin's papers have observed, "were soon directed also against the clergy, the magistrates, the postmaster, Harvard College, men of wealth and property—in short, against the whole Massachusetts Establishment."[1]

Although Benjamin Franklin had less than two years of formal education when he was apprenticed to his brother's printing shop in 1718, according to the *Autobiography*, he "was anxious to try his hand" as an author. In order to avoid the laughter of the "Couranteers"—as his brother and the other contributors styled themselves—Franklin submitted his first essays by sliding them under the door, using the pseudonym "Silence Dogood." There was more than a little of Benjamin Franklin's life in the description that "Mrs. Dogood" gave of herself. Like much of the writing in the *Courant*, the fourteen Dogood letters owed their ironic style to Joseph Addison's *Spectator*.

At the same time that he embarked on his literary career, young Benjamin Franklin and his brother's anti-establishment newspaper became enmeshed in an early freedom-of-the-press controversy that elevated the teenage apprentice's rank. When James Franklin was fined, jailed, and forbidden to publish for libeling the Massachusetts colonial government, he named his sixteen-year-old brother Benjamin as publisher and continued the paper as before.[2]

The satirical columns in the *Courant* antagonized the Mathers, Increase and Cotton, the preeminent clergymen and scientists of colonial Boston, by attacking smallpox inoculation. Cotton Mather and his son Samuel, a recent Harvard graduate the same age as Benjamin Franklin, replied by describing the "Couranteers" as "the Hellfire Club." Judge Samuel Sewall, a political ally of the Mather party, was reminded of his unhappy role in the witchcraft hysteria of the 1690s (see no. 26), in a slashing literary attack that has been credited to Benjamin Franklin. To avoid censorship, the *Courant* appeared under Benjamin Franklin's name even after he abandoned his brother for Philadelphia and so continued until the paper failed and James Franklin left Boston for Newport in 1727.[3]

P.D.

1. Franklin 1959, 1:8.
2. Franklin 1956, pp. 6–7.
3. Ford 1924, pp. 336–353.

73

Benjamin Franklin (1706–1790)
Letter to [John Franklin?], Philadelphia, December 25, 1750
Manuscript copy
2 p., 12¼ in. (31 cm) x 7½ in. (19.1 cm)
Gift of Elizabeth Mason Winthrop, 1905

I have lately made an Experiment in Electricity that I desire never to repeat.

Franklin's scientific interest in electricity began in 1743 in Boston, when he was introduced to Dr. Archibald Spencer, who displayed and lectured on electricity here. Even before he retired from his successful printing business in 1748, which gave him leisure time to devote to his wide-ranging interests, Franklin conducted electrical experiments with a glass tube used to generate charges, and which his friend Peter Collinson of the Royal Society of London had donated to the Library Company at Philadelphia. Franklin's work, described in a series of letters to Collinson, was first published anonymously in *The Gentleman's Magazine* and later as a series of separate publications.[1]

This letter, written on Christmas Day 1750, is addressed to an unidentified family member, probably Franklin's brother John, who resided in Boston. It tells of a misadventure while attempting to experiment with electricity on a turkey. Franklin had several times electrocuted various fowl with his apparatus, but this time the experiment did not go exactly as planned:

> Two nights ago being about to kill a Turkey by the Shock from two large Glass Jarrs containing as much electrical fire as forty common Phials, I inadvertently took the whole thro' my own Arms and Body, . . . the flash was very great and the crack as loud as a Pistol; . . . I had a Numbness in my Arms and the back of my Neck, which Continued till the Next Morning but wore off. Nothing Remains now of this Shock but a Soreness in my breast Bone . . . . I am Ashamed to have been Guilty of so Notorious A Blunder; A Match for that of the Irishman, . . . who being About to Steal Powder, made a Hole in the Cask with a Hott Iron.

73

74

Edward Fisher (1730–1785?) after Mason Chamberlin
(ca. 1727–1787)
Benjamin Franklin (1706–1790)
Mezzotint
London, 1762 or 1763
13⅓ in. (33.8 cm) x 10 in. (25.8 cm)
Inscribed, in lower left: *[M.] Chamberlin pinxt*; in lower
right: *E. Fisher fecit*; in lower center: *B. Franklin of
Philadelphia L.L.D. F.R.S.*
Gift of Anna W. Storer, 1845

Benjamin Franklin was a frequent subject for eighteenth-
century artists, but the portrait by Mason Chamberlin
(Philadelphia Museum of Art), upon which this print
was based, was one of Franklin's personal favorites.[1] Although his career as a great statesman would come later,
Franklin was already famous as a printer, writer, inventor,
and scientist. By the time the Chamberlin portrait was
painted in 1762, Franklin had been in London since his appointment as agent from the Pennsylvania Assembly in 1757.[2]

Mason Chamberlin studied art under Francis Hay-
man (1708–1776), an important painter in mid-eighteenth-
century England, and then began to paint portraits "with
tolerable success, some of which possess great force and
semblance."[3] While most of Chamberlin's sitters hailed
from the middle class, he did occasionally paint more
famous subjects, such as Franklin (1762), two royal
princes (1771), and the eminent surgeon Dr. William
Hunter (1781). As a founding member of the Royal Academy in London (1769), Chamberlin exhibited there until
his death in 1787. However, the portrait of Franklin was
first exhibited at the Society of Artists (London) in

Franklin's embarrassment did not stop his scientific research. He had conducted his most famous, and far more
dangerous, experiment—flying a key from a kite during a
lightning storm—only a few months before his Christ-
mastime "Blunder." Reports of his experiments, finally
published under his own name, were greeted with great
interest in England and almost immediately translated
into French. Publication of his work on electricity earned
Franklin the reputation as America's most important
scientist of the colonial and early national period. In 1753,
the Royal Society of London awarded him the Copley
Medal, the most prestigious scientific prize of the day.
The same year, he received honorary degrees from both
Harvard and Yale and three years later was elected a fellow of the Royal Society.[2]

P.B.F.

1. Lemay 1964, pp. 199–216.
2. Cohen 1941, pp. 57–63, 126–127.

B. Franklin of Philadelphia L.L.D F.R.S.

74

1763. In that same year, Franklin, who was quite pleased with the portrait, commissioned a copy of it for his son, William (1731–1813), who had been recently appointed as governor of New Jersey.[4]

A print soon followed, and the engraver chosen was Edward Fisher, an Irishman, who had started his career as a hatter before taking up engraving and moving to London. During Fisher's years of artistic activity, between 1758 and 1781, he engraved over sixty portraits, including those of the famous actor David Garrick and the statesman William Pitt.[5]

Franklin's son ordered one hundred impressions of the print of his father to sell as a commercial venture, but Franklin himself used it to send to friends and correspondents, "it being the only way in which I am now likely ever to visit."[6] The Society's impression has a label attached to the back which states: "From Dr FRANKLIN / To M. Byles / Rec'd MAR. 15, 1764." Mather Byles (1706–1788), was a minister, poet, amateur scientist, as well as an overseer of Harvard College. Byles, who had known Franklin since they were boys together in Boston, was the driving force behind Harvard awarding an honorary degree to Franklin in 1753.[7] This print is the earliest copy known to have been given by Franklin to one of his friends.

In the print, as in the portrait, Franklin is depicted as a scholar interrupted from his writing. He is plainly dressed in a dark coat and vest with a white collar at his neck, his sleeve ruffles bent back. He is seated slightly turned in a chair in three-quarter view, close to the picture plane, but he gazes away from the viewer. The powdered wig sits upon an unidealized face in which every wrinkle and mole is evident.

The most interesting aspects of the image, is not the figure of Franklin, but the scene outside his window and the equipment beside him. Chamberlin and Fisher included depictions of three of Franklin's electrical experiments, which Franklin carried out between 1747 and 1753 (see no. 73). To the left are two bells. As he explained to a friend: "I erected an Iron Rod to draw the Lightning down into my House, in order to make some Experiments on it, with two Bells to give Notice when the Rod should be electrified."[8] The second experiment concerns two balls suspended from the bells and was recorded by Franklin's associate Ebenezer Kinnersley (1711–1778), in his published lectures of his electrical experiments (Philadelphia, 1752): "Suspend . . . two Cork Balls from silk Threads, & electrify them; & they will immediately separate & fly asunder to a great distance."[9]

The most dramatic experiment is seen outside the window, where a lightning storm has caused the ruin of several buildings. Franklin developed the lightning rod to prevent such destruction and gave instructions for its use in his *Poor Richard's Almanac* for 1753. Louise Ambler has noted that the structures pictured are not actually buildings but models which Franklin used to demonstrate the practical application of the lightning rod. Similar models designed by Franklin are preserved at Harvard University.[10] Thus, the print by Fisher serves both a didactic and a visual function, which may explain its enduring appeal to Franklin.

S.R.M.

1. Sellers 1956, p. 369.
2. Dorment 1986, p. 38.

3. Edwards 1808, pp. 121–122.
4. Dorment 1986, p. 38; Sellers 1962, p. 58.
5. Sellers 1962, p. 219; *DNB*, 7:56.
6. Sellers 1962, p. 58; Franklin 1959, 11:88–89.
7. Ambler 1975, p. 48.
8. Franklin 1959, 5:69.
9. Cohen 1941, p. 416.
10. Ambler 1975, p. 72.

75

Benjamin Blyth (1746–after 1786)
Abigail Smith Adams (1744–1818)
Salem, 1766
Pastel on paper
23 in. (58.5 cm) x 17½ in. (44.5 cm)
Gift of John Adams (1875–1964), 1956

76

Benjamin Blyth (1746–after 1786)
John Adams (1735–1826)
Salem, 1766
Pastel on paper
23 in. (58.5 cm) x 17½ in. (44.5 cm)
Gift of John Adams (1875–1964), 1957

John Adams was born in Braintree (now Quincy), Massachusetts, the son of Deacon John and Susanna (Boylston) Adams. He graduated from Harvard College in 1755, taught school and studied law in Worcester, Massachusetts, and returned to Braintree in 1758 to practice.[1] It was the next year that he visited the Weymouth home of Elizabeth (Quincy) Smith and the Reverend William Smith and met their daughters Mary and Abigail. Although he thought the sisters "Wits," he believed they lacked fondness and tenderness, comparing them unfavorably with another young woman.[2] Two years later, however, John Adams was devoting his full attention to Abigail Smith—"Miss Adorable"—as he demanded as many kisses from her as he had given: "two or three Millions at least." The two married on October 25, 1764, and lived in Braintree.[3]

John Adams pursued a career in law until his activities in politics and government took him away from Massachusetts. As a member of the Continental Congress, a peace commissioner, the first United States minister to England, first vice-president and second president of the United States, John Adams was away from home for extended periods, leaving Abigail the responsibility for managing the family farm and caring for their four children. Their correspondence, which survives today in the Historical Society, sustained their relationship during these long separations. Since its first publication by their grandson, Charles Francis Adams, in the nineteenth century, the letters have delighted and informed generations of readers.[4]

The pastel portraits by Benjamin Blyth, the earliest-known likenesses of the Adamses, were probably made in August or November 1766 when they visited relatives in Salem.[5] Pastels had become fashionable around Boston in the 1760s, and John Singleton Copley, colonial Boston's

75

76

preeminent portrait painter, experimented with pastel crayons as early as 1758. Blyth, a self-taught Salem limner, placed an advertisement for his services in the *Essex Gazette* of January 10–17, 1769:

> Benjamin Blyth Begs Leave to inform the Public, that he has opened a Room for the Performance of Limning in Crayons, at the House occupied by his Father, in the great Street leading towards Marblehead, where Specimens of his Performance may be seen. All Persons who please to favour him with their Employ, may depend upon having good Likenesses, and being immediately waited on, by applying to their Humble Servant, Benjamin Blyth.

Blyth was a young man of about twenty when he portrayed the Adamses.[6] Though his work does not exhibit brilliant technical skills, the portraits are pleasing representations of the newly married couple.

Two other Blyth pastels, both done in the 1770s, are in the Society's collection: those of Eunice Diman of Salem (1752–1796) and General John Thomas (1724–1776), along with Blyth's bill for the Thomas portrait, frame, glass, and box amounting to about six pounds.[7] Blyth later left Salem and is last known to have been in Richmond, Virginia, in 1786.[8]

C.W.

1. Adams 1961, 4:257.
2. Ibid., 1:108, 122.
3. Adams 1963, 1:2, 51.
4. Ibid., 1:xxi–xxii, xxxiii–xxxiv.
5. Oliver 1967, p. 2.
6. Foote 1958, pp. 67–69.
7. Ibid., pp. 73–74.
8. Little 1972, pp. 52, 57.

77

John Adams (1735–1826)
Diary, February 28–June 25, 1774
19 pp., 6½ in. (16.5 cm) x 4 in. (10.1 cm)
Gift of the Adams Manuscript Trust, 1956

The diary of John Adams, second president of the United States, is one of the great personal records of New England life and manners, the struggle to achieve independence, and the diplomacy of the Revolution. Adams began his diary by entering notes on a great variety of topics—his legal studies and cases, his reflections on man and nature, on history, on religion, on young women, on his friends' peculiarities, and his own moral and intellectual shortcomings—in fragile little paper booklets which he carried in his pocket as he traveled the court circuits from county to county or "dreamed away the day" as an obscure young lawyer in rural Braintree. Not until he began his record of debates in Congress in the fall of 1775—the third session he attended—did he indulge himself in a durable, store-bought blank volume in which to keep his diary. Even after that, there was no predicting how full and regular his entries would be. Thus his record of his decade of service in Europe, 1778–1788 (after which he virtually abandoned his diary), contains some of the most splendidly detailed and brilliantly written sequences and some of the most deplorably long gaps. Although John Adams did not boast of it, and perhaps did not realize it, he was one of the most gifted observers and recorders of human nature in action in the annals of literature.[1]

Exhibited here is an entry written at Ipswich, Massachusetts, where Adams, riding the circuit as one of the province's most active trial lawyers, was attending the Essex County Superior Court. Just eight days before

John Adams's diary is part of the massive Adams Papers collection, given to the Massachusetts Historical Society by the Adams family in 1956. The papers comprise over a quarter million manuscript pages of the letters and diaries of four generations of Adams husbands, wives, and children including John and Abigail Adams, John Quincy Adams, Charles Francis Adams, and Henry Adams. The Society microfilmed the entire collection on 608 reels, sets of which can be found in over ninety libraries in the United States and abroad. It also sponsors the Adams Papers editorial project, which is preparing a comprehensive documentary edition of the papers. To date, thirty-two volumes have been published by Harvard University Press.

R.A.R.

1. MHS 1969, pp. 25–26.
2. Adams 1977, 2:98–99.
3. Adams 1961, 2:96.
4. Adams 1963, 1:108–109.
5. Adams 1977, 2:99–100."

78
Abigail Smith Adams (1744–1818)
Letter to John Adams, March 31, 1776, completed April 5, 1776
Manuscript
4 p., 12 3/8 in. (31.4 cm) x 7 5/8 in. (19.6 cm)
Gift of the Adams Manuscript Trust, 1956

Abigail Adams's rich extant correspondence extends from 1761, her seventeenth year, to just before her death in 1818. In this half century she exchanged letters with a wide variety of correspondents, and turned her pen to an even wider variety of subjects. Men and women, sons and daughter, sisters, uncles, aunts, nieces, cousins, in-laws, friends from childhood, and a handful of non-related but brilliant public figures from several states were all treated to her acute observations and strong opinions upon matters of particular interest to her family, events in her hometown, issues that agitated all of Massachusetts, and major questions of national politics and international diplomacy. Interspersed with this commentary on the news were her general thoughts on education, history, and literature, and her insightful descriptions and comparisons of religion and social customs, and the staging of public events—festivals and parades, concerts and the theater—in Boston, London, and Paris.

At the center of this extraordinary woman's letter-writing career was her voluminous correspondence with her husband, John Adams. And the central theme of this correspondence was the Adamses' mutual concern for the political—and moral—state of their country. In the spring of 1776, after eighteen months of unusually voluminous correspondence with John, who was serving in the Continental Congress, Abigail was reaching the peak of her powers as a political analyst. Dazzled by her unexpected talents, John Adams wrote to her on May 27, 1776: "I think you shine as a Stateswoman of late, as well as a Farmeress. Pray where do you get your Maxims of State, they are very apropos [?]"[1]

Nothing Abigail ever wrote better exemplifies this

(June 17), he had been elected one of five delegates from Massachusetts to what became the First Continental Congress, scheduled to meet in Philadelphia on September 1.[2] This election began John Adams's twenty-seven-year career in national and international politics.

Adams entered his first recorded reaction to his election in his diary on June 20, while stopping over at Danvers, Massachusetts, on his way to Ipswich. He immediately began to reflect upon the difficulties of his, and America's, new assignment, but he resolved at the entry's close to "keep an exact Diary, of my Journey, as well as a Journal of the Proceedings of the Congress."[3] Adams kept his most anguished reflections about the challenge facing him out of his letters to his wife, Abigail (June 23),[4] and to James Warren (June 25),[5] but after a five-day gap in his diary, he turned again to confront the awesome task before him:

> I wander alone, and ponder.— I muse, I mope, I ruminate. —I am often in Reveries and Brown Studies.—The Objects before me, are too grand, and multifarious for my Comprehension.—We have not Men, fit for the Times. We are deficient in Genius, in Education, in Travel, in Fortune—in every Thing. I feel unutterable Anxiety.—God grant us Wisdom, and Fortitude!
>
> Should the Opposition be suppressed, should this Country submit, what Infamy and Ruin! God forbid! Death in any Form is less terrible.

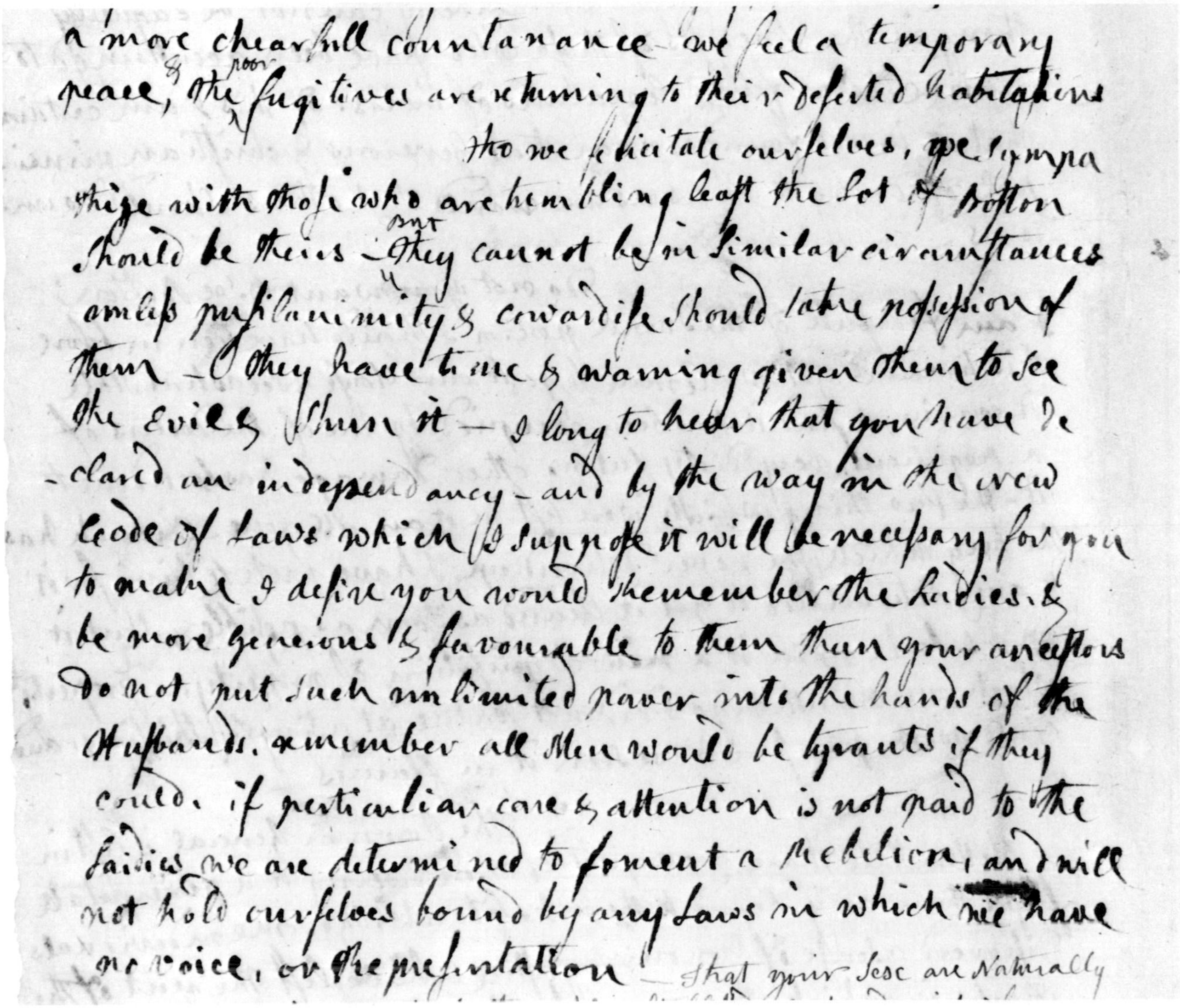

gift than her celebrated "Remember the Ladies" letter of March 31, 1776. The full passage shown here is worthy of quotation:

> I long to hear that you have declared an independancy— and by the way in the new Code of Laws which I suppose it will be necessary for you to make I desire you would Remember the Ladies, and be more generous and favourable to them than your ancestors. Do not put such unlimited powers into the hands of the Husbands. Remember all Men would be tyrants if they could. If perticuliar care and attention is not paid to the Ladies we are determined to foment a Rebelion, and will not hold ourselves bound by any Laws in which we have no voice, or Representation.
>
> That your Sex are Naturally Tyrannical is a Truth so thoroughly established as to admit of no dispute, but such of you as wish to be happy willingly give up the harsh title of Master for the more tender and endearing one of Friend. Why then, not put it out of the power of the vicious and the Lawless to use us with cruelty and indignity with impunity. Men of Sense in all Ages abhor those customs which treat us only as the vassals of your Sex. Regard us then as Beings placed by providence under your protection and in immitation of the Supreem Being make use of that power only for our happiness.[2]

In his reply to this remarkable letter, on April 14, John displayed both his embarrassment at Abigail's telling criticism, and his wit in deflecting it:

As to your extraordinary Code of Laws, I cannot but laugh. We have been told that our Struggle has loosened the bands of Government every where. That Children and Apprentices were disobedient—that schools and Colledges were grown turbulent—that Indians slighted their Guardians and Negroes grew insolent to their Masters. But your Letter was the first Intimation that another Tribe more numerous and powerfull than all the rest were grown discontented.—This is rather too coarse a Compliment but you are so saucy, I wont blot it out.

Depend upon it, We know better than to repeal our Masculine systems. Altho they are in full Force, you know they are little more than Theory. We dare not exert our Power in its full Latitude. We are obliged to go fair, and softly, and in Practice you know We are the subjects. We have only the Name of Masters, and rather than give up this, which would compleatly subject Us to the Despotism of the Peticoat, I hope General Washington, and all our brave Heroes would fight.[3]

Abigail's celebrated plea has drawn more serious attention from modern scholars, and has placed her, in the minds of many, in the role of a pioneering feminist. If by feminist one means a person convinced of the fundamental equality of women with men, and committed to improving the position of women in society and removing all inequalities before the law, then Abigail qualifies. The twentieth-century reader, however, should note that her concern was not with equality of political participation, which she did not advocate for women, but for equality before the law, particularly with respect to property rights and the right to the protection of the law within marriage. In this concern she anticipated the principal objectives of those who would campaign for women's rights in America in the several decades following the American Revolution.

R.A.R.

1. Adams 1963, 1:420.
2. Ibid., 1:369–370.
3. Ibid., 1:382. John Adams considered and justified the exclusion of women from voting in a letter to James Sullivan, May 26, 1776, in Adams 1977, 4:208–213.

79

79

John Edwards (1671–1746)
Tankard
Boston, ca. 1715
Silver
H. 8 in. (20.3 cm), W. 8 in. (20.6 cm), lip D. 4⅘ in. (12.2 cm), base D. 5⅘ in. (14.5 cm)
Marked on lid and to left of handle: crowned I E within shield
Gift of Margery Lee Sargent Adams, 1972

This silver tankard, a part of two presidential households, was first owned by the Reverend John Norton (ca. 1651–1716) of Hingham.[1] When Norton's daughter Elizabeth married John Quincy (1689–1767) of Braintree in 1715, the tankard began its 275-year association with the Quincy and Adams families. The Norton coat of arms[2] embellishes the front of the tankard and the names of subsequent owners are engraved on the sides:

This Tankard was / John Quincy's / then held in succession by / Norton Quincy, / by / John Adams, / by / John Quincy Adams, / and by him devised / to / Abigail Brown Adams./ February 23d. 1848. / to John Quincy Adams, / June 1889. To Fanny C. Adams / August 1894. / To / Arthur Adams / May 1911. / John Quincy Adams / Arthur Adams, Jr. / May 1943.

The tankard came into the Adams family through John Quincy's granddaughter Abigail Adams, and next descended to her son President John Quincy Adams, who was named for his great-grandfather.

John Edwards's family emigrated to America from England when he was fourteen. Probably apprenticed to Jeremiah Dummer (1645–1718), one of America's first native-born silversmiths, Edwards prospered in his work and became a respected member of the community, holding many public offices. Two of his sons, Thomas and Samuel, and his grandson Joseph also followed in this craft.[3]

American silver followed the style of silver imported from England. The early eighteenth century saw the richness and heaviness of Baroque design give way to simpler lighter form. American silver of this period emphasized plain surfaces and curving contours with little decoration other than engraving.[4] John Edwards's silver tankard exemplifies this American style in the simple lines of the straight tapering sides, stepped flat cover, applied molded base band and scroll handle. Edwards's mark, "I E" crowned within a shield, appears on the lid and to the left of the handle. From 1715 on this was Edwards's commonly used large mark.[5]

J.L.P.

1. MHS *Proceedings* 80(1968):141.
2. Bolton 1927, p. 122; *Heraldic Journal* (Boston), 13(1866):1.
3. Buhler 1972, 1:95.
4. Fales 1970, p. 16.
5. Buhler 1972, 1:95.

80

Eliza Susan Quincy (1798–1884)
Birthplaces of John Adams and John Quincy Adams
Quincy, Massachusetts, 1822
Watercolor and graphite on paper
6¼ in. (16 cm) x 8 in. (20.5 cm)
Inscribed in lower left: *E.S. Quincy jun. del.*; in lower right: *1822*
Gift of Eliza Susan Quincy, 1870

Eliza Susan Quincy, a prolific diarist, letter writer, genealogist, and artist was the quintessential well-bred New England woman of the nineteenth century. She was the eldest child of Eliza Susan Morton (d. 1850) and Josiah Quincy (1772–1864), who served as congressman from Massachusetts, state senator, mayor of Boston and president of Harvard during his long life. Elected to the Massachusetts Historical Society in 1798 Josiah Quincy remained a member for nearly sixty-seven years. During her more private, but equally useful life, Eliza Susan served as her father's collaborator on most of his important writings, including his two-volume *History of Harvard College* (1840). During 1823 and 1824, Eliza prepared a biography of her grandfather, also named Josiah

80

Quincy, which was published under her father's name in 1825. She also edited the biography of her mother which was privately printed in 1861. Her lifelong genealogical research on the Quincy family was published posthumously in 1884.[1]

The drawing exhibited is one of a series of nine watercolor drawings painted by Quincy in 1822, part of a two-volume bound memoir which Quincy presented to the Society in 1870. This remarkable document contains much of her early research on Quincy genealogy, letters, poems, and additional drawings. The watercolors were published as a portfolio by the Historical Society in 1975.

The memoir includes a description of this drawing in Quincy's precise handwriting. The small numbers in the bottom margin indicate that the house labeled (1) was the birthplace of John Adams and the second Adams home; and (2) was the birthplace of his son John Quincy Adams. Both are now part of the Adams National Historical Site in Quincy. Also indicated in the sketch is the school (3), which was run by Joseph Marsh and attended by her father and John Adams. In her description, Quincy notes that this view was taken from Penn's Hill, and "the heights of Dorchester and the City of Boston are seen in the distance." Although Quincy was probably more concerned with historical accuracy than artistic style, the total effect of the small landscape is quite charming.

The Society holds a large collection of Quincy family papers dating from 1639 onward.

S.R.M.

1. McCaughey 1974, p. 16; MHS *Proceedings*, 2d ser. 1(1884–1885):33; Howe 1946, p. 45; Quincy 1884, p. 146.

The Declaration of Independence

Perhaps the most sacred American historical document and certainly one of the most important, the Declaration of Independence has an interesting and complicated publication history. On June 7, 1776, Richard Henry Lee proposed a resolution to the Continental Congress, meeting in Philadelphia, "that all political connection . . . [with] Great Britain . . . ought to be, totally dissolved." The Congress did not immediately approve the resolution, but from its membership appointed a Committee of Five to draft a declaration of independence. The committee was made up of Thomas Jefferson, John Adams, Benjamin Franklin, Roger Sherman, and Robert R. Livingston. Jefferson prepared a rough draft that was circulated to Adams and Franklin and revised according to their recommendations. On June 28 the committee presented the revised draft to the Continental Congress that voted on July 2 to adopt the resolution for independence, which had been first proposed on June 7. On the following two days, July 3 and 4, the text of the Declaration was further revised and then authenticated. The Committee of Five was authorized to print the corrected text, and a manuscript copy was placed in the hands of John Dunlap, a Philadelphia printer, on July 4, 1776.[1]

P.D.

1. Jefferson 1950, 1:413–415.

81
Thomas Jefferson (1743–1826)
The Declaration of Independence
Manuscript copy
4 pp. (fragment of pp. 3–4 only), 12 ¾ in. (32.3 cm) x 8 ³⁄₁₆ in. (20.8 cm)
Gift of Mr. and Mrs. Alexander C. Washburn, 1893

Thomas Jefferson's revised draft of the Declaration of Independence was subjected to considerable congressional surgery before it was authorized and printed. Some of the changes were necessary: the text of the resolution for independence, approved after the Declaration was drafted, was appended to the Declaration. Some changes were political: Jefferson's attack on the slave trade was excised in order to gain unanimous support for the Declaration in Congress, and criticism of the English was more sharply focused on the king and his ministers. Other changes were more cosmetic but often felicitous: Jefferson's "inherent & inalienable rights" that "all men are endowed with" in the second paragraph of the Declaration became "certain unalienable rights" in the authorized text.[1]

Jefferson was extremely unhappy with many of the changes. He made several copies of the Declaration "as originally framed" by the Committee of Five in their presentation to Congress, and he sent them to close friends to show the travesty. As Richard Henry Lee, who originally had proposed the resolution for independence, commented Jefferson's manuscript had been "mangled." The copy displayed here was probably sent to Edmund Pendleton, a fellow lawyer and head of the Virginia Committee of Safety.[2]

The strength of the Massachusetts Historical Soci-

A Declaration by the Representatives of the United States of America in General Congress assembled.

When in the course of human events it becomes necessary for one people to dissolve the political bands which have connected them with another, & to assume among the powers of the earth the separate & equal station, to which the laws of nature & of nature's god entitle them, a decent respect to the opinions of mankind requires that they should declare the causes which impel them to the separation.

We hold these truths to be self-evident: that all men are created equal; that they are ... by ... with inherent & inalienable rights; that ... these are life, liberty & the pursuit of happiness; that to secure these rights, governments are instituted among men, deriving their just powers from the consent of the governed; that whenever any form of government becomes destructive of these ends, it is the right of the people to alter or to abolish it, & to institute new government, laying it's foundation on such principles, & organising it's powers in such form, as to them shall seem most likely to effect their safety and happiness. prudence indeed will dictate that governments long established should not be changed for light and transient causes: and accordingly all experience hath shewn that mankind are more disposed to suffer while evils are sufferable, than to right themselves by abolishing the forms to which they are accustomed. but when a long train of abuses & usurpations, begun at a distinguished period, & pursuing invariably the same object, evinces a design to reduce them under absolute despotism, it is their right, it is their duty, to throw off such government, & to provide new guards for their future security. such has been the patient sufferance of these colonies; and such is now the necessity which constrains them to expunge their former systems of government. the history of the present king of Great Britain is a history of unremitting injuries & usurpations, among which appears no solitary fact to contradict the uniform tenor of the rest, but all have in direct object the establishment of an absolute tyranny over these states. to prove this, let facts be submitted to a candid world, for the truth of which we pledge a faith yet unsullied by falsehood.

He has refused his assent to laws the most wholesome and necessary for the public good.

he has forbidden his governors to pass laws of immediate & pressing importance, unless suspended in their operation till his assent should be obtained; and when so suspended, he has neglected utterly to attend to them.

81

Conventions & Committees or Councils of Safety and to the several Commanding Officers of the Continental troops that it be proclaimed in each of the United States & at the head of the army."[1]

Dunlap rapidly printed a small number of copies of the Declaration on the night of July 4–5. On July 5, the first copies began to be distributed and independence was proclaimed in Philadelphia on July 8. News of the Declaration was spread at the speed of horse-borne riders throughout the colonies, and it was soon reprinted in newspapers and local broadside editions. In New York, the Declaration was read to Washington's assembled army on July 9; "Independency" was proclaimed "out of the balcony of the Town House" in Boston (no. 105) on July 18, to the ringing of bells, firing of cannon, and hearty cheers of the town's population.[2]

It is this rapidly produced but handsomely printed version of the Declaration that conveyed the news of the birth of a new nation and fixed July 4 as the national anniversary. The famous engrossed manuscript copy now at the National Archives was authorized and signed after the fact. This is one of only twenty-three known copies of the first Dunlap printing, the most important single printed document in American history.[3]

P.D.

1. Goff 1976, p. 4.
2. Henry Alline, Jr., letter to his family, Boston, July 19, 1776, MHS.
3. Carter 1967, p. 220.

ety's manuscript collections extends far beyond the borders of Massachusetts. One collection which came to Boston through family inheritance and to the Society by generous donation is a series of the personal papers of Thomas Jefferson, which include almost 10,000 pieces of correspondence; 400 architectural drawings (see no. 94); manuscripts of Jefferson's writings; the catalogue of his vast personal library; as well as manuscript estate and plantation records for his home, Monticello.

P.D.

1. Boyd 1943, pp. 31–35.
2. Ibid., p. 35.

82

The Declaration of Independence
Philadelphia: Printed by John Dunlap, July 4 or 5 , 1776
Broadside
18¹⁵⁄₁₆ in. (48.1 cm) x 15 in. (38.1 cm)
Provenance unknown, found in the library of the Massachusetts Historical Society

On July 4, 1776, the Committee of Five that had drafted the Declaration of Independence presented their corrected and approved text to the printing shop of John Dunlap (see no. 81), the publisher of *The Pennsylvania Packet*. Copies were to be sent to "the several Assemblies,

83

The United States Constitution, August 6, 1787
Philadelphia: Printed by John Dunlap and David C. Claypoole, 1787
8 numbered leaves, 15½ in. (39.5 cm) x 10 in. (25.4 cm)
Manuscript annotations by Elbridge Gerry (1744–1814)
Gift of James T. Austin, 1829

This copy of the first printed draft of the United States Constitution shows the evolution of the text as it was amended during the debates in the Philadelphia Convention of 1787. The notes are in the hand of Elbridge Gerry, a delegate from Massachusetts to the convention who refused to sign the completed Constitution.

The Constitutional Convention of 1787 changed the course of American history, but it had originally been planned only to modify the Articles of Confederation, the weak form of government of the United States during and after the Revolutionary War. Delegates slowly gathered in Philadelphia in May 1787. On May 25, when a quorum of delegates finally had arrived, George Washington was elected president of the convention, and the work began. Of an illustrious, ever-changing body of delegates, the most famous member was Benjamin Franklin. Notable in their absence were Thomas Jefferson and John Adams, who were both serving in diplomatic posts overseas.

After agreeing to go beyond their original stated goals and to reshape the government entirely, the delegates worked out a general plan for a new federal government. On July 26, 1787, the convention turned over previously debated resolutions to a Committee of De-

IN CONGRESS, JULY 4, 1776.

A DECLARATION

BY THE REPRESENTATIVES OF THE

UNITED STATES OF AMERICA,

IN GENERAL CONGRESS ASSEMBLED.

WHEN in the Course of human Events, it becomes neceſſary for one People to diſſolve the Political Bands which have connected them with another, and to aſſume among the Powers of the Earth, the ſeparate and equal Station to which the Laws of Nature and of Nature's God entitle them, a decent Reſpect to the Opinions of Mankind requires that they ſhould declare the cauſes which impel them to the Separation.

We hold theſe Truths to be ſelf-evident, that all Men are created equal, that they are endowed by their Creator with certain unalienable Rights, that among theſe are Life, Liberty, and the Purſuit of Happineſs--That to ſecure theſe Rights, Governments are inſtituted among Men, deriving their juſt Powers from the Conſent of the Governed, that whenever any Form of Government becomes deſtructive of theſe Ends, it is the Right of the People to alter or to aboliſh it, and to inſtitute new Government, laying its Foundation on ſuch Principles, and organizing its Powers in ſuch Form, as to them ſhall ſeem moſt likely to effect their Safety and Happineſs. Prudence, indeed, will dictate that Governments long eſtabliſhed ſhould not be changed for light and tranſient Cauſes; and accordingly all Experience hath ſhewn, that Mankind are more diſpoſed to ſuffer, while Evils are ſufferable, than to right themſelves by aboliſhing the Forms to which they are accuſtomed. But when a long Train of Abuſes and Uſurpations, purſuing invariably the ſame Object, evinces a Deſign to reduce them under abſolute Deſpotiſm, it is their Right, it is their Duty, to throw off ſuch Government, and to provide new Guards for their future Security. Such has been the patient Sufferance of theſe Colonies; and ſuch is now the Neceſſity which conſtrains them to alter their former Syſtems of Government. The Hiſtory of the preſent King of Great-Britain is a Hiſtory of repeated Injuries and Uſurpations, all having in direct Object the Eſtabliſhment of an abſolute Tyranny over theſe States. To prove this, let Facts be ſubmitted to a candid World.

He has refuſed his Aſſent to Laws, the moſt wholeſome and neceſſary for the public Good.

He has forbidden his Governors to paſs Laws of immediate and preſſing Importance, unleſs ſuſpended in their Operation till his Aſſent ſhould be obtained; and when ſo ſuſpended, he has utterly neglected to attend to them.

He has refuſed to paſs other Laws for the Accommodation of large Diſtricts of People, unleſs thoſe People would relinquiſh the Right of Repreſentation in the Legiſlature, a Right ineſtimable to them, and formidable to Tyrants only.

He has called together Legiſlative Bodies at Places unuſual, uncomfortable, and diſtant from the Depoſitory of their public Records, for the ſole Purpoſe of fatiguing them into Compliance with his Meaſures.

He has diſſolved Repreſentative Houſes repeatedly, for oppoſing with manly Firmneſs his Invaſions on the Rights of the People.

He has refuſed for a long Time, after ſuch Diſſolutions, to cauſe others to be elected; whereby the Legiſlative Powers, incapable of Annihilation, have returned to the People at large for their exerciſe; the State remaining in the mean time expoſed to all the Dangers of Invaſion from without, and Convulſions within.

He has endeavoured to prevent the Population of theſe States; for that Purpoſe obſtructing the Laws for Naturalization of Foreigners; refuſing to paſs others to encourage their Migrations hither, and raiſing the Conditions of new Appropriations of Lands.

He has obſtructed the Adminiſtration of Juſtice, by refuſing his Aſſent to Laws for eſtabliſhing Judiciary Powers.

He has made Judges dependent on his Will alone, for the Tenure of their Offices, and the Amount and Payment of their Salaries.

He has erected a Multitude of new Offices, and ſent hither Swarms of Officers to harraſs our People, and eat out their Subſtance.

He has kept among us, in Times of Peace, Standing Armies, without the conſent of our Legiſlatures.

He has affected to render the Military independent of and ſuperior to the Civil Power.

He has combined with others to ſubject us to a Juriſdiction foreign to our Conſtitution, and unacknowledged by our Laws; giving his Aſſent to their Acts of pretended Legiſlation:

For quartering large Bodies of Armed Troops among us:

For protecting them, by a mock Trial, from Puniſhment for any Murders which they ſhould commit on the Inhabitants of theſe States:

For cutting off our Trade with all Parts of the World:

For impoſing Taxes on us without our Conſent:

For depriving us, in many Caſes, of the Benefits of Trial by Jury:

For tranſporting us beyond Seas to be tried for pretended Offences:

For aboliſhing the free Syſtem of Engliſh Laws in a neighbouring Province, eſtabliſhing therein an arbitrary Government, and enlarging its Boundaries, ſo as to render it at once an Example and fit Inſtrument for introducing the ſame abſolute Rule into theſe Colonies:

For taking away our Charters, aboliſhing our moſt valuable Laws, and altering fundamentally the Forms of our Governments:

For ſuſpending our own Legiſlatures, and declaring themſelves inveſted with Power to legiſlate for us in all Caſes whatſoever.

He has abdicated Government here, by declaring us out of his Protection and waging War againſt us.

He has plundered our Seas, ravaged our Coaſts, burnt our Towns, and deſtroyed the Lives of our People.

He is, at this Time, tranſporting large Armies of foreign Mercenaries to compleat the Works of Death, Deſolation, and Tyranny, already begun with circumſtances of Cruelty and Perfidy, ſcarcely paralleled in the moſt barbarous Ages, and totally unworthy the Head of a civilized Nation.

He has conſtrained our fellow Citizens taken Captive on the high Seas to bear Arms againſt their Country, to become the Executioners of their Friends and Brethren, or to fall themſelves by their Hands.

He has excited domeſtic Inſurrections amongſt us, and has endeavoured to bring on the Inhabitants of our Frontiers, the mercileſs Indian Savages, whoſe known Rule of Warfare, is an undiſtinguiſhed Deſtruction, of all Ages, Sexes and Conditions.

In every ſtage of theſe Oppreſſions we have Petitioned for Redreſs in the moſt humble Terms: Our repeated Petitions have been anſwered only by repeated Injury. A Prince, whoſe Character is thus marked by every act which may define a Tyrant, is unfit to be the Ruler of a free People.

Nor have we been wanting in Attentions to our Britiſh Brethren. We have warned them from Time to Time of Attempts by their Legiſlature to extend an unwarrantable Juriſdiction over us. We have reminded them of the Circumſtances of our Emigration and Settlement here. We have appealed to their native Juſtice and Magnanimity, and we have conjured them by the Ties of our common Kindred to diſavow theſe Uſurpations, which, would inevitably interrupt our Connections and Correſpondence. They too have been deaf to the Voice of Juſtice and of Conſanguinity. We muſt, therefore, acquieſce in the Neceſſity, which denounces our Separation, and hold them, as we hold the reſt of Mankind, Enemies in War, in Peace, Friends.

We, therefore, the Repreſentatives of the UNITED STATES OF AMERICA, in GENERAL CONGRESS, Aſſembled, appealing to the Supreme Judge of the World for the Rectitude of our Intentions, do, in the Name, and by Authority of the good People of theſe Colonies, ſolemnly Publiſh and Declare, That theſe United Colonies are, and of Right ought to be, FREE AND INDEPENDENT STATES; that they are abſolved from all Allegiance to the Britiſh Crown, and that all political Connection between them and the State of Great-Britain, is and ought to be totally diſſolved; and that as FREE AND INDEPENDENT STATES, they have full Power to levy War, conclude Peace, contract Alliances, eſtabliſh Commerce, and to do all other Acts and Things which INDEPENDENT STATES may of right do. And for the ſupport of this Declaration, with a firm Reliance on the Protection of divine Providence, we mutually pledge to each other our Lives, our Fortunes, and our ſacred Honor.

Signed by ORDER and in BEHALF of the CONGRESS,

JOHN HANCOCK, PRESIDENT.

ATTEST.
CHARLES THOMSON, SECRETARY.

PHILADELPHIA: PRINTED BY JOHN DUNLAP.

tail made up of Edmund Randolph and James Wilson. The draft Constitution prepared by the committee was placed in the hands of John Dunlap and David C. Claypoole, Philadelphia newspaper printers who had served as the official printers for the Continental Congress and the Confederation Congress (see no. 82). Even though they were entrusted with what would have been a great newspaper story, Dunlap and Claypoole proved reliable and guarded their knowledge of the secret proceedings of the convention.[1]

From August 6 to September 8 the convention worked on the draft displayed here, making changes and

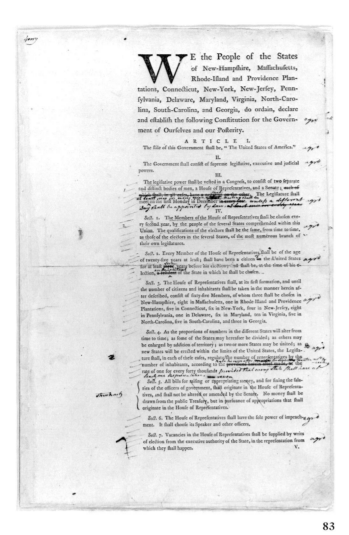

83

corrections. A Committee on Style then was appointed to prepare a second draft. The "penman of the Constitution," as we now know it, was Gouvernor Morris of New York, who followed the general principles listed in the Committee of Style's notes:

> In the draught of a fundamental constitution, two things deserve attention:
> 1. To insert essential principles only; lest the operations of government should be clogged by rendering those provisions permanent and unalterable, which out to be accommodated to times and events: and
> 2. To use simple and precise language, and general propositions, according to the example of the (several) constitutions of the several states. (For the construction of a constitution necessarily differs from that of law.)[2]

On September 12, the Committee of Style's draft was sent to Dunlap and Claypoole, who struck off more copies to be used for another round of changes and corrections by the entire convention. The final form of the Constitution is substantially different from the first printed draft as the twenty-three articles listed in the first draft became seven. "We the People of the States of New-Hampshire, Massachusetts, Rhode Island and the Providence Plantations . . . ," as this draft text begins, evolved into the simple, but more eloquent preamble: "WE THE PEOPLE of the United States . . . ." This was not only a stylistic change, there also was a practical reason. The Constitution would go into effect when ratified by nine of the thirteen states, but it was not clear

if, and in what order, individual states would come under the new national government.[3] On behalf of "WE THE PEOPLE . . ." the convention quickly reviewed the revised text, and on September 17, thirty-nine of the forty-two delegates present signed the engrossed document.

Elbridge Gerry, who carefully marked up both sets of printed copies as changes were made in the text, was born at Marblehead, Massachusetts, into a family of merchants and shipowners. His public career began long before the Constitutional Convention with his first election to the Massachusetts General Court in 1772. He was a signer of the Declaration of Independence and the Articles of Confederation, but refused to sign the Constitution and fought against its ratification in Massachusetts. Gerry later served as a member of Congress, governor of Massachusetts, and, at the time of his death in 1814, he was vice president of the United States under Madison. In spite of these achievements, Gerry chiefly is remembered as a "Grumbletonian" obstructionist who did not recognize the genius of the Constitution; and as a corrupt politician who gave the world the "Gerrymander," the practice of drawing political boundaries along party lines.[4]

The Constitution has come to be such a revered icon that it is difficult to remember that there were legitimate questions raised concerning the ratification. Gerry, one of the Massachusetts delegates to the Confederation Congress, had resisted the original call for a revision of the Articles of Confederation that led to the Constitutional Convention. On September 20, 1787, the day that the Constitution was presented to the Convention Congress, Gerry wrote to John Adams in London to explain why he had not signed. "Time must determine the fate of this production, which with a check on standing armies in Time of peace, & on an arbitrary administration of the powers vested in the Legislature, would have met with my approbation." Gerry's primary complaint was that there was no federal bill of rights. He was not alone in refusing to sign; like Gerry, George Mason cited the lack of a bill of rights; Edmund Randolph, the author of the first draft of the Constitution, did not believe that Virginians would approve of the final form, and also refused to sign.[5]

In addition to Gerry's annotated copies of the Constitution, the Society holds an extensive collection of Gerry manuscripts donated to the Historical Society by Russell Knight and Samuel Eliot Morison, and a large research collection of copies of Gerry manuscripts held in other repositories, gathered by George Billias for his biography of Gerry.

P.D.

1. Rossiter 1987.
2. Farrand 1937, 4:37–38.
3. Rossiter 1987, pp. 228–230.
4. Billias 1976.
5. Elbridge Gerry to John Adams, New York, Sept. 20, 1787, Adams Papers, MHS; Farrand 1937, 3:128–129.

84

84

Paul Revere (1735–1818), designer and engraver
Massachusetts State Pine Tree Penny
Boston, 1776
Copper
Inscribed, on obverse: MASSACHUSETTS STATE around
a pine tree atop a hill, with *1d* LM flanking the tree trunk;
on reverse: LIBERTY AND VIRTUE above the goddess
Liberty perched on a globe with an animal at her feet;
holding a staff in her left hand and a Liberty cap on a rod
in her outstretched right hand; in exergue: *1776*
D. 1¼ in. (31.8 mm)
Bequest of William Sumner Appleton, 1905

The Massachusetts 1776 Pine Tree Copper Penny was
virtually unknown until a grocer discovered this unique
pattern piece while excavating near Hull or Charter Street
in Boston's North End. Boston collector Jeremiah Colburn acquired the coin about 1852 and several years later
published an account of it in *The Historical Magazine*,
although he erroneously described the Liberty as "holding in her right hand an olive leaf."[1] In the same article
Colburn mentioned a "Janus Head" halfpenny in the
collection of Matthew A. Stickney and attributed the
dies for both coins to Paul Revere on the basis that there
were few engravers in the colonies capable of such
work. After revising his article, Colburn sent it to several
newspapers in 1858, but he neglected to correct his description.[2] Montroville Dickeson included the Pine Tree
Copper in his *Numismatic Manual* in 1859,[3] apparently
using the *Historical Magazine* as his source, because Liberty was still described as clasping an olive leaf. The coin
next appeared when John K. Curtis advertised "the
unique Massachusetts Copper Coin" in a sale to begin
February 11, 1861.[4] It was back on the market by December 1, 1862, when W. Elliot Woodward announced that he
would be offering "the unique Pine Tree Copper, from
the collection of Mr. Colburn, illustrated in Dickeson's
Manual" at an 1863 sale.[5] Boston numismatist William
Sumner Appleton (1840–1903) added the coin to his collection of American coins and medals.

Appleton also wrote about the coin, adding the information that it was one of two pieces prepared in 1776
as patterns for a proposed Massachusetts state copper
coinage.[6] While there is no mention of such a proposal in
the *Acts and Resolves of Massachusetts* from 1775 through
1778, Appleton deduced that the existence of a 1776 state
copper coinage in New Hampshire made it a viable assumption. Appleton correctly described the goddess
holding a Liberty-cap atop her pole; but he misread the
"d" as "c" in the obverse legend flanking the tree (1d

LM), which he interpreted as "one cent lawful money."[7]
Five years later, in 1875, Sylvester S. Crosby published
his monumental work on early American coins, using a
line drawing of the Pine Tree copper which incorporated
this error, yet the book's heliotype reproduction of a cast
from the coin clearly shows the "d."[8] Crosby also
linked the Pine Tree penny and the "Janus Head," more
appropriately named the "Massachusetts Halfpenny."
Half the size of the penny, the halfpenny features a reverse which is almost a mirror image of the Pine Tree.[9]
Still in the Stickney collection in 1875 and now in a private
collection, the halfpenny had been discovered with an
engraving and proofs of Revere's continental currency
notes, so Stickney attributed the coin to Revere.[10] The
1776 penny and halfpenny share a primitive vigor and
design and are clearly the work of one person. Recent
scholarship comparing lettering details with Revere's
engraved 1775–1776 currency and securities printing plates
confirms that Revere was the designer and engraver of
both coins. A Massachusetts state 1776 copper coinage
never materialized, probably due to the shortage of copper, so the two coins are considered pattern pieces and
are unique as such.[11]

Revere's design for the Pine Tree Penny borrowed
symbols from local and classical sources. The pine tree
alludes to both the Sons of Liberty flag from the Revolutionary era and to the earlier colonial pine tree coinage, representing Massachusetts's determination to govern herself.[12] The goddess of Liberty, freely adapted from
the Britannia of English coinage,[13] holds aloft the Pileus
cap, a symbol since the Roman Empire of a slave's man-
umission.[14] The animal at her feet is a watchdog, vigilant
in the service of its mistress.[15] All of these elements combine to create such an attractive coin, that several different copies have been made of the piece. None is from a
cast of the coin, and most mistakenly have "1 C LM" flanking the tree trunk. This leads to the conclusion that they
were made using Crosby's 1875 line drawing as a model.
Of the magnificent collection of American medals and
coins which William Sumner Appleton bequeathed to
the Society in 1905, the Massachusetts Pine Tree Copper
Penny remains the most requested research piece.

A.E.B.

1. Crosby 1875, p. 304; *The Historical Magazine*, Oct. 1857, p. 298.
2. *Boston Journal*, Nov. 25, 1858.
3. Dickeson 1859.
4. Curtis 1861.
5. Woodward 1862.
6. MHS *Proceedings* 10(1869–1870):294.
7. Breen 1988, pp. 59–60.
8. Crosby 1875, p. 303.
9. Breen 1988, p. 59.
10. Crosby 1875, p. 304.
11. Breen 1988, p. 59.
12. Ibid.
13. Vermeule 1971, p. 9.
14. Korshak 1988, p. 67.
15. Crosby 1875, p. 303.

85

85

George Washington (1732–1799)
1825–1835
Oil on canvas
67½ in. (171.5 cm) x 58 in. (147.7 cm)
Gift of Isaac P. Davis, 1840

George Washington was considered a larger-than-life figure during his lifetime, and this heroic image continued to grow after his death until he became the subject of legends. The cult surrounding Washington as the "Father of the Country" reached a climax in 1832 with the centennial of his birth. This monumental equestrian painting of Washington was probably done during this period.

By portraying Washington in the blue and gold uniform of commander in chief of the Continental Army, mounted on a white charger and brandishing a sword, the artist is making a nostalgic reference to Washington's Revolutionary War military victories. However, he appears here much older than he would have been during the war and bears a striking resemblance to Gilbert Stuart's much copied Athenaeum-type portrait (1795–1796; Museum of Fine Arts, Boston; National Portrait Gallery). Although anachronistic, it does conform with the image most Americans had of Washington in the nineteenth century.

Washington is rendered in a shallow, stagelike space, and he appears parallel to the picture plane, as if a relief sculpture. Romantic elements which enhance the subject include the darkened foreground, the broken tree on the right and the expressive cloud filled sky. It has been suggested that the horse soldiers behind the central figure of Washington represent specific individuals, perhaps Washington's aides-de-camp.

When given to the Society in 1840, the painting was titled *Washington Crossing the Delaware*, a popular subject for paintings of Washington.[1] However, it does not appear that any specific event was intended by the artist. Rather, Washington represents the American embodiment of the classical ideals of virtues.[2]

This painting hung at the Society for many years as the work of an unknown artist until the twentieth century, when it was attributed to John Vanderlyn (1775–1852) by John Marshall Phillips, curator of the Garvan Collection, Yale University Art Gallery. Early in his career, Vanderlyn studied with Gilbert Stuart for nine or ten months (1795–1796) when Stuart was painting his most famous portraits of Washington. Vanderlyn himself was later commissioned by Congress to paint a full-length portrait of Washington using Stuart's Athenaeum head (1832, House Chambers, United States Capitol). In 1796 Vanderlyn became the first American to receive formal artistic training in France studying under François-André Vincent, a follower of Jacques Louis David.[3] Like his teacher, Vanderlyn embraced neoclassicism and hoped to educate Americans and raise artistic standards through his history paintings.[4] Despite his early aspirations, Vanderlyn completed only a handful of history paintings, all of which are well documented. Two of his most significant works, *Marius Amid the Ruins of Carthage* (1807, De Young Museum, San Francisco) and *Ariadne Asleep on the Island of Naxos* (1814, Philadelphia Museum of Art) are much more sophisticated than *George Washington* in composition, style, and technique. Another painting attributed to Vanderlyn, *Washington and Lafayette at the Battle of Brandywine* (Gilcrease Museum, Tulsa), is identical in composition to the Historical Society's with the mounted figure of Lafayette superimposed in the foreground. However, the current scholarly opinion is that the Historical Society's painting is not the work of Vanderlyn, and the artist of this idealized portrayal of George Washington remains unknown.[5]

S.R.M.

1. MHS *Proceedings* 2(1835–1855):175–176.
2. Anderson 1980, p. 17.
3. Oedel 1981, p. 61.
4. Ibid., p. 4.
5. William Oedel in a telephone conservation, August 1990.

86

Gorget
American, 1760–1770
Gilt brass
5 ⅛ in. (13 cm) x 5 ⅛ in. (13 cm)
Bequest of Josiah Quincy, 1864

The military gorget is an ornamental and symbolic reminder of the neckplate on a suit of armor, and was originally worn in conjunction with a nape plate at the back of the neck. Between 1650 and 1700, the nape plate was gradually discontinued, and the gorget was worn lower, suspended by a ribbon from the neck, to accommodate the new fashion of lace cravats.[1] Officers wore the gorget as a symbol of rank, and it was generally inscribed with the royal coat of arms and the regimental number. A "Royal Warrant for the Regulation of the Colors, Cloathing, etc.," in 1743 proscribed gorgets to be "either gilt or silver, according as the lace of the uniform is either silver or gilt."[2] British officers used gorgets until 1803, but they

86 (see also color plate VII)

were discontinued in the United States after the Revolution.

This particular gorget belonged to George Washington as a colonel in the Virginia militia, and it appears in his 1772 portrait painted at Mount Vernon by Charles Willson Peale (Custis-Washington and Lee University).[3] Because of the piece's historical associations, it is considered to be the most interesting surviving example of an American gorget.[4] The crescent-shaped gilt brass gorget closely resembles British examples from the same period and is engraved in the center with the arms of Virginia.

When Washington's estate was divided, the gorget went to his wife's granddaughter Martha (Custis) Peter, who presented it in 1813 to Josiah Quincy, then retiring as congressman from Massachusetts. Quincy presented it the same year to the Washington Benevolent Society in Mrs. Peter's name, but when that society dissolved several years later, the gorget was returned to Mr. Quincy, who bequeathed it to the Historical Society in 1864, with the proviso that it could remain in the custody of his daughter Eliza Susan Quincy during her lifetime. She exhibited it at the Centennial Exhibition at Philadelphia in 1876 and then presented it to the Society in 1877.[5]

E.W.H.

1. Oakes Jones 1922, p. 253.
2. Pell 1937, p. 128.
3. Eisen 1932, 2:338.
4. Pell 1937, p. 130.
5. MHS *Proceedings* 4(1858–1860):44–46, 15(1876–1877):302–303.

87
Pair of Epaulets
Woven gilt lamé, yellow silk, white silk
ca. 1780
Each, 7¼ in. (18.4 cm) x 8¼ in. (21 cm)
Gift of David Humphreys, 1804

George Washington's personal fascination with uniforms and military insignia went back to his youthful days in the French and Indian Wars, when he designed his own regimental insignia.[1] His rank as commander in chief provided further opportunity for tinkering with uniforms and collecting accoutrements. One of his earliest general

orders issued at Cambridge decried the lack of uniforms, "and consequently many inconveniencies must arise, from not being able always to distinguish the Commissioned Officers, from the non Commissioned, and the Non Commissioned from the private."[2] To single himself out, he ordered "a light blue Ribband, wore across his breast, between his Coat and Waistcoat."[3]

Later in the war, distinguishing insignia became more sophisticated. Jonathan Williams, Jr., the continental agent at Nantes in France, sent Washington a "very handsome pair of Epaulets" in 1782, while Washington ordered himself "a pair of French Epauletts (gold)," although they need not be "of the largest and richest kind; because it is for a frock Coat they are intended," but "nor would I have them of the mean kind."[4]

The epaulets shown here were worn by Washington as commander in chief of the Continental Army during the siege at Yorktown in 1781 and on the day he resigned his military commission in 1783.[5] They appear in the John Trumbull painting *Washington Resigning His Commission* (United States Capitol).[6] This single act of relinquishing military power and returning to civilian life was of profound moment when it happened and provided a cornerstone for political development in this country separate from military strength. The heroic figure of Washington hearkened to the historic image of Cincinnatus, the Roman farmer who responded to a call to war but in peacetime returned to his civilian life and served as an inspiration for the Society of the Cincinnati.[7]

General Washington gave these epaulets to his aide-de-camp David Humphreys, who was one of the officers in attendance on him on the day of his resignation. Colonel Humphreys presented them to the Historical Society in 1804.[8]

E.W.H.

1. Flexner 1972, p. 416.
2. Washington 1985, 1:158.
3. Ibid., p. 115.
4. Washington 1931, 24:496, 26:243.
5. MHS *Proceedings* 1(1791–1835):178n.
6. Eisen 1932, 2:474.
7. Wills 1984.
8. MHS *Proceedings* 1(1791–1825):178n.

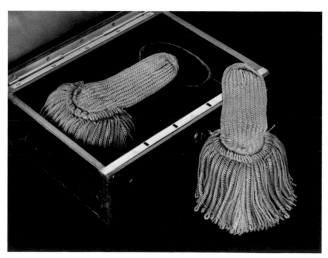

87

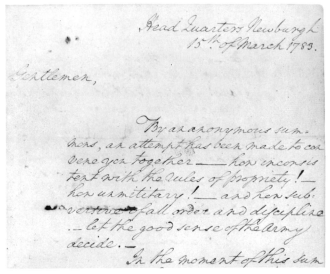

88

George Washington (1732–1799)
Newburgh Address
Newburgh, New York, March 1783
Manuscript
12 pp., 13 in. (33 cm) x 8 in. (21.5 cm)
Inscribed: *To the / General, Field & other / Officers / Assembled at the New Building / pursuant to / the General Order of the / 11th. Instant March*
Gift of William A. Hayes, 1821

George Washington delivered his Newburgh Address to confront one of the greatest challenges to his influence with the officers and soldiers of the Continental Army. In the waning months of the Revolutionary War, after the victory at Yorktown on October 19, 1781, when the army was restlessly ensconced in winter quarters at Newburgh, New York, the officers, long unpaid and apprehensive about arrearages, retirement pay, and other well-deserved concessions denied them by Congress, teetered for a moment on the brink of open revolt against the country and government for which they had fought so hard and long. That the balance fell in favor of peace and order was due to General Washington's great influence with and true affection for his officers and soldiers alike.[1]

For quite some time Congress had been indifferent to General Washington's pleas on behalf of his unpaid men. In March of 1783 an unofficial meeting of the officers was called, and an anonymous paper (later attributed to Major John Armstrong) was circulated urging the officers to *demand* concessions from Congress, rather than ask as they had in the past, with the implied threat that if their demands were not satisfied they would *compel* Congress to accede to them. Alarmed by these developments, Washington took control of the situation, cancelling the unofficial meeting and calling an official one for March 15.[2] There he read the famous address which is shown here in his own handwriting. He then presented a letter from a member of Congress to corroborate that body's good intentions, and as he began reading it he "made a short pause, took out his spectacles, and begged the indulgence of his audience while he put them on, observing at the same time, that he had grown gray in their service and now felt himself going blind."[3]

The address was brief, clear, and presented with great feeling; Washington exhorted his men to remain loyal and obedient, appealed to their patriotism, and offered his support for their cause. It was the most moving address he ever made, and afterwards the officers unanimously adopted a number of resolutions, including: "That the army continue to have an unshaken confidence in the justice of Congress and their Country . . . ; that His Excellency the Commander in Chief be requested to write to His Excellency the President of Congress, earnestly entreating the most speedy decision of that honorable body . . . ; that the officers of the American army view with abhorrence, and reject with disdain the infamous propositions contained in a late anonymous address . . . ."[4]

The Newburgh Address is bound together with a "Report of Proceedings in Meeting of the Officers assembled on 15th Mar. 1783," which was presided over by Major General Horatio Gates. The report is in the handwriting of Major Samuel Shaw, aide-de-camp to General Knox and secretary for the meeting, and is signed by General Gates. Also with the address are several letters testifying to the authenticity of the handwriting of Washington, and correspondence related to the gift of the address to the Society. The address was purchased about 1813 by William A. Hayes, a resident of South Berwick, Maine, from Captain Simeon Lord, also of that town. Captain Lord was an assistant to the adjutant general in the Continental Army from February 1, 1783, to the close of the war, and claimed to have acquired the address in his capacity there.[5]

K.H.G.

1. Flexner 1967, pp. 507–508.
2. Freeman 1952, pp. 431–433; Flexner 1967, pp. 503–505.
3. Shaw 1847, p. 504.
4. Horatio Gates, "Report of Proceedings in Meeting of the Officers assembled on 15th Mar. 1783." MHS.
5. William A. Hayes to Dudley Atkins Tyng, June 21, 1819. MHS.

89

Samuel Hill (active 1789–1803)
View of the triumphal ARCH *and* COLONNADE, erected in BOSTON, / in honor of the President of the UNITED STATES, *Oc 24. 1789.*
Boston, 1789 (from *Massachusetts Magazine*, vol. 2, no. 1, January 1790)
Engraving
5 3/8 in. (13.8 cm) x 8 1/8 in. (20.8 cm)
Inscribed, at top left: *No.I.*]; at center: *Massachusetts Magazine.*; at right: [VOL. II.; at bottom right: *Engraved by S. Hill*
Gift of Alice De V. Perry, 1978

View of the triumphal ARCH and COLONNADE, erected in BOSTON, in honor of the president of the UNITED STATES, Octr 24, 1789.

90

Procession. Boston, Oct. 19, 1789
Boston, 1789
Broadside
15 ³⁄₈ in. (39 cm) x 10 ¹⁄₈ in. (25.8 cm)
Provenance unknown

Washington was inaugurated as president in April of 1789 and in the autumn made a tour of the New England states of Connecticut, Massachusetts, and New Hampshire seeking public support for the new federal constitution. His personal charisma drew large crowds as he traveled through New Haven, Hartford, Springfield, and Worcester before reaching Boston, the climactic stop of his tour.[1] Washington was met by processions of citizens and honored at dinners wherever he went, but his patience with all the pomp began to wear thin as he approached another militia review in Boston. As he confided to his diary, he regretted that "this ceremony was not to be avoided, though I had made every effort to do it."[2]

Washington was met at the Boston town limits by Lieutenant Governor Samuel Adams. John Hancock, who was governor at the time, refused to greet the president, feeling that Washington should first call on him as head of the Commonwealth. Washington chose to ignore this slight, and in the end Hancock paid his respects to Washington, although not until the next day. Washington arrived on horseback, greeted by the selectmen of Bos-

ton, a group of children, and various state officials, but a conflict developed between state or municipal officials over whom should lead the procession in Boston. Washington, losing patience, was about to leave and enter the town by another route when it was decided that the selectmen would lead the way.[3]

The formal procession, as outlined in the broadside, was organized

> In order that we may pay our respects to him, in a manner whereby every inhabitant may see so illustrious and amiable a character, and to prevent the disorder and danger which must ensue from a great assembly of people without order.

The procession gathered at the Mall, which is now the Tremont Street side of Boston Common, and groups of citizens were arranged alphabetically by vocation. For each group, a white silk flag, a yard square, was designed with an insignia symbolizing its respective craft or trade. According to instructions:

> When the front of the Procession arrives at the extremity of the town, it will halt, and the whole will then be directed to open the column—one half of each rank moving to the right, and the other half to the left—and then face inwards, so as to form an avenue through which the President is to pass, to the galleries to be erected at the State-House.

Washington, with the various groups of dignitaries in his wake, followed this wall of people to the State House. There a triumphal arch spanned the street. Charles Bulfinch designed this temporary structure after one he

Procession.

BOSTON, OCT. 19, 1789.

AS this town is shortly to be honoured with a visit from THE PRESIDENT of the United States : In order that we may pay our respects to him, in a manner whereby every inhabitant may see so illustrious and amiable a character, and to prevent the disorder and danger which must ensue from a great assembly of people without order, a Committee appointed by a respectable number of inhabitants, met for the purpose, recommend to their Fellow-Citizens to arrange themselves in the following order, in a

PROCESSION.

IT is also recommended, that the person who shall be chosen as head of each order of Artizans, Tradesmen, Manufacturers, &c. shall be known by displaying a WHITE FLAG, with some device thereon expressive of their several callings—and to be numbered as in the arrangement that follows, which is alphabetically disposed, in order to give general satisfaction.—The Artizans, &c. to display such insignia of their craft, as they can conveniently carry in their hands. That uniformity may not be wanting, it is desired that the several Flag-staffs be SEVEN feet long, and the Flags a YARD SQUARE.

ORDER OF PROCESSION.

MUSICK.

The Selectmen,
Overseers of the Poor,
Town Treasurer,
Town Clerk,
Magistrates,
Consuls of France and Holland,
The Officers of his Most Christian Majesty's Squadron,
The Rev. Clergy,
Physicians,
Lawyers,
Merchants and Traders,
Marine Society,
Masters of vessels,
Revenue Officers,
Strangers, who may wish to attend.

Bakers,	No. 1.
Blacksmiths, &c.	No. 2.
Block-makers,	No. 3.
Boat-builders,	No. 4.
Cabinet and Chair-makers,	No. 5.
Card-makers,	No. 6.
Carvers,	No. 7.
Chaise and Coach-makers,	No. 8.
Clock and Watch-makers,	No. 9.
Coopers,	No. 10.
Coppersmiths, Braziers and Founders,	No. 11.
Cordwainers, &c.	No. 12.
Distillers,	No. 13.
Duck Manufacturers,	No. 14.
Engravers,	No. 15.
Glaziers and Plumbers,	No. 16.
Goldsmiths and Jewellers,	No. 17.
Hair-Dressers,	No. 18.
Hatters and Furriers,	No. 19.
House Carpenters,	No. 20.
Leather Dressers, and Leather-Breeches Makers,	No. 21.
Limners and Portrait Painters,	No. 22.
Masons,	No. 23.
Mast-makers,	No. 24.
Mathematical Instrument-makers,	No. 25.
Millers,	No. 26.
Painters,	No. 27.
Paper Stainers,	No. 28.
Pewterers,	No. 29.
Printers, Book-binders and Stationers,	No. 30.
Riggers,	No. 31.
Rope-makers,	No. 32.
Saddlers,	No. 33.
Sail-makers,	No. 34.
Shipwrights, to include Caulkers, Ship-Joiners, Head-builders and Sawyers,	No. 35.
Sugar-boilers,	No. 36.
Tallow-Chandlers, &c.	No. 37.
Tanners,	No. 38.
Taylors,	No. 39.
Tin-plate Workers,	No. 40.
Tobacconists,	No. 41.
Truckmen,	No. 42.
Turners,	No. 43.
Upholsterers,	No. 44.
Wharfingers,	No. 45.
Wheelwrights,	No. 46.
Seamen,	

N. B.—In the above arrangement, some trades are omitted—from the idea, that they would incorporate themselves with the branches mentioned, to which they are generally attached. For instance—it is supposed, that under the head of *Blacksmiths*, the Armourers, Cutlers, Whitesmiths and other workers in iron, would be included ; and the same with respect to other trades.

EACH division of the above arrangement is requested to meet on such parade as it may agree on, and march into the Mall—No. 1 of the Artizans, &c. forming at the South-end thereof. The Marshals will then direct in what manner the Procession will move to meet the President on his arrival in town. When the front of the Procession arrives at the extremity of the town, it will halt, and the whole will then be directed to open the column—one half of each rank moving to the right, and the other half to the left—and then face inwards, so as to form an avenue through which the President is to pass, to the galleries to be erected at the State-House.

IT is requested that the several School-masters conduct their Scholars to the neighbourhood of the State-House, and form them in such order as the Marshals shall direct.

THE Marine Society is desired to appoint some persons to arrange and accompany the seamen.

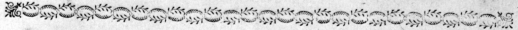

90

had seen in Milan three years earlier.[4] Eighteen feet high and twenty-one feet across, the triumphal arch dominates the engraving of the scene by Samuel Hill. Decorated with Ionic pilasters and rusticated to resemble stone work, the structure was replete with national symbolism. Thirteen blue stars painted across the entablature represented the states of the Union. This in turn supported an interlaced balustrade which was inscribed on one side: "TO THE MAN WHO UNITES ALL HEARTS; and on the other: TO COLUMBIA'S FAVORITE SON." A large panel contained the arms of the United States, together with those of the Commonwealth of Massachusetts and of France, above which the motto "Boston relieved March 17th, 1776" was inscribed in a laurel wreath.[5] Washington was impressed with the edifice, which he described in some detail in his diary:

> This Arch was handsomely ornamented, and over the Center of it a Canopy was erected 20 feet high, with the American Eagle perched on the top.

Also evident in the engraving is a colonnade in front of the west facade of the State House. Composed of six fifteen-foot columns, this structure was the work of Thomas Dawes (1731–1809), a craftsman-builder and civic leader. According to a contemporary account, the balustrade was hung with Persian carpets covered with thirteen roses. Above the colonnade, the female figure evident in the engraving represents Fortune.[6]

Samuel Hill, a self-taught artist, was active in Boston during the years 1789–1803. He was the principal engraver for *Massachusetts Magazine* during its six years of publication (1789–1794). His *View of the Triumphal Arch*, like many of his engravings, was made from his own drawings. Although lacking in sophistication, his work shows a great attention to detail and a close observation of his contemporary world. Hill also engraved book illustrations and some certificates, and was one of several engravers who worked on the *Map of Massachusetts Proper* (1801–1802) (no. 2).[7] He was in New York in 1803, but unfortunately no further details have been recorded about his life.

S. R. M.

1. Bostonian Society 1908, p. 75.
2. Washington 1925, p. 32.
3. Ibid., pp. 33–34n.
4. Kirker 1964, p. 102.
5. Washington 1925, p. 34.
6. Cummings 1973, pp. 182–183; Rothschild 1939, p. 162.
7. Parker 1979, p. 85.

91

Edward Savage (1761–1817) and David Edwin (1776–1841), after a painting by Edward Savage
The Washington Family
Philadelphia, March 10, 1798
Stipple engraving
21½ in. (54.6 cm) x 26½ in. (67.4 cm)
Inscribed: *Painted and Engrav'd by E: Savage. / The Washington Family. / La Famille de Washington. / George Washington his Lady, and her two Grandchildren by the name of Custis. / George Washington, Son Epouse, et Ses deux petits Enfants du Nom de Custis*
Gift of Catherine Colvin, 1921

This engraving, which provides a rare glimpse into Washington's domestic life, proved immensely popular and financially lucrative for Savage, as had the print *The Apotheosis of Washington* for John James Ballaret (see no. 93). In his 1857 lecture on "Washington and His Portraits" the artist Rembrandt Peale (1778–1860) observed,

> Mr. Savage, an Engraver, with the view of getting up a popular Furniture Print, painted his Picture of the Washington family, and published a large Mezzotint of it, which is known all over the United States—No engraving ever having a more extensive sale.[1]

Edward Savage was born and died in Princeton, Massachusetts, but he spent much of his life elsewhere. He began his career as a goldsmith before turning to painting, where his talent must have been considerable, because in 1789 he was commissioned by Harvard College to paint a life portrait of Washington. At the same time Savage began a large painting of *The Washington Family* (National Gallery of Art), which would serve as the model for the print of the same name. However, he delayed work on this project by going to London in 1791 to study painting under Benjamin West and to learn the art of stipple engraving. While in London, Savage published two portrait engravings of Washington, both based on the Harvard painting.[2]

On returning to the United States, Savage briefly settled in Boston where he married Sarah Seaver in 1794. By 1795, Savage was in Philadelphia where he remained for ten years before returning to his birthplace, Princeton, in 1805. It was in Philadelphia, then the country's capital, that Savage again turned to *The Washington Family* painting taking new sittings of George and Martha Washington, who had aged in the intervening years. It was probably at this time that Savage took the likeness, from life, of Washington's servant Billy Lee, who also appears in the composition. For the two remaining figures, Washington's adopted grandchildren, Eleanor Custis and George Washington Parke Custis, Savage used his original sketches. Savage explained to Washington that

> The likenesses of the young people are not much like what they are at present. The Copper-plate was begun and half finished from the likenesses which I painted in New York in the year 1789. I could not make the alterations in the copper to make it like the painting in Philadelphia in the year 1796. The portraits of yourself and Mrs. Washington are generally thought to be likenesses.[3]

In this print Washington is seated among his family, presumably in a room at Mount Vernon with the Potomac, visible through the window in the background.

THE WASHINGTON FAMILY.
George Washington his Lady and her two Grandchildren by the name of Custis.

La FAMILLE de WASHINGTON.
George Washington, sa Femme et les deux petits Enfants du Nom de Custis.

91

Although his uniform once again alludes to his earlier military accomplishments, the fact that his sword and hat rest on the table indicates his retirement from the Army. His arm rests affectionately on that of his grandson, whose own hand on the globe indicates that he, and not Washington represents the future. Martha points with her fan to a map, which is a plan for the new Capital City (Washington, D.C.). Edward Parry has noted that all the figures in the composition are named in the inscription with the exception of the servant Billy Lee, whose standing pose lends dignity to the family he serves.[4]

The print was published in March 1798, and was well received by the public and critics alike. For example, an article printed in the *Pennsylvania Gazette* of March 21, 1798, described the style as "evincive of the rapid progress of an elegant art, which has hitherto been in a very crude state in this country."[5] Although the print is signed by Edward Savage, there has been much controversy over whether or not he had the skill and training necessary to complete the complicated stipple engraving by himself. William Dunlap in 1834 claimed that the engraving was primarily the work of David Edwin. Edwin, an English engraver of acknowledged talent and training, was in Philadelphia by 1797, and it is possible that Savage had previously met Edwin during his stay in London when he studied stipple engraving. Wendy Wick suggests it is likely that the print was begun by Savage but completed by the more skilled Edwin.[6]

The Society owns several other prints by Savage including the beautiful engraving of *Liberty* (1796), as well as Savage's unfinished copperplate for *The Congress Voting Independence* after an unfinished painting by Robert Edge Pine which was completed by Savage. Charles Henry Hart considered this plate to be the last engraving on which Savage worked.[7] It is unclear why Savage did not continue producing these works celebrating the new republic and its heroes, but in 1805 he abandoned his career as an engraver and returned to Princeton. From 1809 onward he was a partner in the Poignaud and Plant Cotton Factory in Lancaster.[8] The Society's collection contains a miniature by Savage of one of his sons, a portrait of Joseph Warren after an original by Copley, and a portrait of Robert Treat Paine completed by John Coles, Jr.

S.R.M.

1. Eisen 1932, 1:308.
2. Hart 1905, p. 5; *American Art* 1976, p. 138.
3. Wick 1982, pp. 122–123.
4. Wills 1984, p. 188; Parry 1974, p. 53.
5. Wick 1982, p. 124.
6. Dunlap 1918, 1:381; Wick 1982, pp. 123–124.
7. Hart 1905, p. 14.
8. DAB.

92

92

Jonathan Maclie & Company
Handkerchief
Glasgow, early nineteenth century
Brown ink transfer print on plain-weave cotton with
hand-sewn rolled hem. Print, after unknown artist
19 ⅜ in. (49.2 cm) x 20½ in. (52.1 cm)
Inscribed: *Jno. Maclie & Co., Glasgow*
Gift of Samuel S. Shaw, 1908

After the unexpected death of Washington in December
of 1799, the American market was flooded with all
types of memorials. This was as much due to commercial
awareness on the part of some, as it was a reflection of
the public's outpouring of grief.[1] Among the more novel
mementos were cotton kerchiefs printed with death-
bed, mourning, or memorial scenes. The example shown
here is one of two Washington memorial kerchiefs in
the Society's collection.

The central motif was taken from a print by an unidentified artist which also appears on contemporaneous
Liverpool ware jugs.[2] A large gravestone towers above
the five figures. The plinth of the stone, which resembles
an Egyptian obelisk, is engraved with an eagle holding
the cap of Liberty in its beak, both obvious symbols of
America. On the base of the stone is a rather crude profile
of Washington in uniform, which bears some resemblance to Joseph Wright's 1790 portrait engraving. The
sides of the tombstone are inscribed:

> BORN / 1732 / FIRST / IN / WAR / FIRST / IN / PEACE /
> FIRST / IN / FAME — DIED / 1799 / FIRST / IN /
> VIRTUE.

To the right of the gravestone a winged personification of Fame, holds a handkerchief to her eyes, while her
trumpet dangles forlornly at her side. Kneeling in the
right corner is a Native American with bent head, who
has laid down his bow and tomahawk. To the left of the
tomb is a figure which appears to be a clergyman, offering either a eulogy or memorial prayer to Washington. A
uniformed male figure striding toward the group from
the left may represent either the Navy or a French officer.

The most ambiguous figure is the youth reclining on the
American flag at the base of Washington's grave. R. W.
Bingham identifies him as a personification of the Army
mourning the death of its commander.[3] In the foreground are the fasces (bound bundle of twigs), which
had become a symbol of the united colonies. The sword
and rifle allude to Washington's military genius.

In the background are a plow and house, perhaps
representing Mount Vernon and Washington's agrarian
interests. To the right a church steeple is evident, which
may symbolize Washington's honesty and piety. The
gravestone is framed by a willow tree and laurel tree,
both traditional symbols of death and resurrection, as is
the water in the left background.[4] Below this vignette is
the quotation "AND TAKE HIM ALL IN ALL WE SCARCE
SHALL LOOK UPON HIS LIKE AGAIN." Above this af-
fecting vision, within a sun burst is inscribed: "SACRED /
TO THE MEMORY / OF THE LATE GREAT & GOOD /
GEORGE WASHINGTON, First President of the Thirteen
United / STATES of AMERICA, / and Respectfully Addressed to the People. . . ." Circling the scene is a vine
entwined with a banner on which is inscribed the names
of the original thirteen states.

The body of the handkerchief is filled with quotes
from various named and unnamed sources eulogizing the
first great American hero. One of these, from the Marquis
de Chastellux, minister from the Court of France, honored the late president as "Brave without Temerity.
Laborious without Ambition. Generous / Without Prodi-
gality. Virtuous without Severity. And at the end / of a
Civil War (as at the End of Such a Life) He had nothing / Wherewith to reproach Himself!!!"

S.R.M.

1. Wick 1982, p. 66.
2. Deutsch 1977, p. 414.
3. Bingham 1927, p. 33; Lefevre 1939, p. 16.
4. Wick 1982, p. 70.

93

Jug
Staffordshire, England, early nineteenth century
Cream ware, with black transfer print after John James
Ballaret (ca. 1747–1815)
H. 10¼ in. (25.9 cm), W. 10 in. (25.4 cm), D. 8 in. (20.3 cm)
Inscribed, below print: *Apotheosis*; on tomb: *Sacred to the
Memory of / Washington. / OB 14 Dec AD 1799 / Aet 68*; in
cartouche below spout: *A Man Without Example, A Pa-
triot without Reproach*
Gift of Samuel A. Green

The "Apotheosis of Washington," one of several examples
of creamware in the Society's collection, is a good example of an inexpensive type of pottery, which was being
exported from England to America from the mid-
eighteenth century until about 1820. Although the pottery
was generically known as Liverpool ware (or creamware),
much of it was produced at various factories in Staffordshire, England. The technique for transferring a print
onto glazed pottery was developed by John Sadler in
Liverpool in 1748. This relatively simple method entailed
inking an engraved copperplate and printing it on thin

93

Cesare Ripa's *Iconologia* (reprinted by George Richardson, London, 1779). In the foreground Liberty, the symbol of America, forlornly leans on her spear. A realistically rendered Native American kneels in the lower right corner. Although a native was often used to personify the Western Hemisphere, this one probably also represents the Native American nation mourning the death of Washington. In the lower left is the national symbol of an eagle holding an olive branch and brandishing a banner inscribed, "E Pluribus Unum." The center of the print contains the most personal symbols relating to Washington. Dangling from the tomb are two medals, one from the Order of Freemasons, and the other from the Society of the Cincinnati representing the officers of the Continental Army. The sword, armor, and helmet lying below the tomb allude to Washington's military victories.[4] In this print, as in numerous other images of Washington which followed his death, he transcends his mortal position as the beloved first leader of the new country. With his death, both his life and his character came to embody the spirit of the new nation.

S.R.M.

1. Klamkin 1973, p. 12.
2. Jacobs 1977, p. 118.
3. Anderson 1980, p. 11.
4. Jacobs 1977, p. 124.

tissue paper. The wet print was then pressed or transferred onto the glazed pottery surface and fired in a kiln. For more elaborate pieces, the prints were also hand-enameled.[1]

The print used here was designed by John James Barralet and went through several printings in the nineteenth century. Barralet was born in Ireland and received his artistic training under James Mannin at the Dublin Society's school. He spent six years (1770–1776) teaching in London, where he also exhibited some of his drawings at the Royal Academy. Returning to Ireland, he worked as an engraver until he immigrated to Philadelphia in 1795. In 1799, Barralet engraved "General Washington's Resignation," in the neoclassical style in which he had trained.[2]

With the death of George Washington following soon after the publication of his resignation print, Ballaret turned his attention to creating a memorial print to honor the first president. The term *apotheosis*, which means the deification or glorification of a mortal by the gods and hence immortality, was quickly adopted for Washington along with a host of other classical allusions. In the seventeenth century, apotheosis scenes had been used to glorify the reign of a ruler, such as in the *Apotheosis of James I* (ca. 1629), designed by Peter Paul Rubens (1577–1640) for the ceiling of the banqueting hall at Whitehall, London.[3]

In Barralet's version, traditional allegorical figures are combined with the new American symbols to create a dramatic vision. Washington, whose head resembles the portrait by Gilbert Stuart (Athenaeum type), is depicted as rising from the tomb. The rays of light shining on his upraised head further emphasize this miraculous event. The figures assisting him are the personifications of Fame and Time. In the left middle ground are the traditional allegories of Faith, Hope, and Charity represented as three women, which Barralet most probably took from

94

Thomas Jefferson (1743-1826)
Monticello: Final Elevation of the First Version
Virginia, before 1771
Brown ink on laid paper
13 ⅞ in. (35.4 cm) x 7¼ in. (48.9 cm)
Gift of Thomas Jefferson Coolidge, Jr., 1911

Monticello was an architectural project which occupied Jefferson for most of his life. As his family home, Monticello was his most personal building design, which he supervised down to the smallest detail. Jefferson's expertise in design work bridged the gap between the gentleman architect of the eighteenth century and the professionally trained architect of nineteenth-century America.

When Jefferson attended the College of William and Mary, he was critical of the buildings which he observed in Williamsburg. As he later wrote in his "Notes on the State of Virginia," "the Genius of Architecture seems to have shed it's maledictions over this land."[1] In his own home, as well in his other architectural projects, Jefferson hoped to create a new style of architecture that would be expressive of the new nation. The choice of location for Monticello, on the top of a mountain, was in itself unusual for a plantation house. Jefferson's decision was based primarily on aesthetic rather than practical considerations.[2]

Monticello is one of the best-documented pre-Revolutionary buildings in America. Unique for their time, the detailed drawings Jefferson made of Monticello, beginning in about 1769, allow one to trace the genesis of his design. Since there was no formal training available to him, Jefferson learned about architecture through books. Andrea Palladio's (1508 1580) *Four Books of Ar-*

94

chitecture has always been considered to be the primary source for the design of Monticello. However, recent research indicates that for this first version Jefferson's main source was the English architect James Gibbs (1508–1580), who in turn drew upon Palladio's work in his two important volumes, *Book of Architecture* (London, 1728) and *Rules for Drawing the Several Parts of Architecture* (London, 1732). Using plates from Gibbs's books, Jefferson experimented with a square, then a rectangular floor plan before deciding upon the final cruciform floor plan for the design of the house.[3]

Typical of Jefferson's attention to detail, this elevation shows great precision. The facade is dominated by the two-story pedimented portico. The four columns, Ionic above and Doric below, divide the entrance into three bays. While the pedimented doors and windows on the second story echo the pediment of the porch, the straight arches over the doorway and first story-windows reflect the continuous entablature above. The flanking bays are both simple and contained. The two rather tall chimneys add a vertical element to what is otherwise a horizontal design.

Construction of this first version of Monticello began in 1769. Waddell has noted that while there is some doubt that the porticoes were ever completed, the existing evidence suggests that all of the columns were installed. In 1781, Jefferson added octagonal bays to the side elevations, but otherwise the appearance of the house resembled this drawing until Jefferson began his radical alterations in 1796.[4]

Jefferson's fascination with the field of architecture began while he was a student at Williamsburg, and, as he commented later in life, "Architecture is my delight and putting up, and pulling down, one of my favorite amusements."[5] Jefferson wholeheartedly embraced neoclassicism as the style appropriate to the new nation. The design of the Virginia State Capitol in Richmond (1785–1789) is considered the first true adaptation of a classical temple form in America.[6] His last major architectural project was the University of Virginia at Charlottesville (1817–1826), which he planned as an architecturally unified community. The library, a domed Rotunda, was based on the Pantheon in Rome. The Historical Society owns four hundred architectural drawings by Thomas Jefferson, which were given by Thomas Jefferson Coolidge, a great-great-grandson of Jefferson, as part of the larger Coolidge collection of Jefferson papers, begun by Coolidge's father and given to the Society in 1898. Many of the architectural drawings relate to Monticello, while others include houses he designed or remodeled for his Virginia neighbors, sketches for the Virginia State Capitol, and unexecuted designs for the President's House and the National Capitol in Washington.[7]

S.R.M.

1. Jefferson, "Notes on the State of Virginia," MHS.
2. Pierson 1976, pp. 291–292; Jefferson 1955, p. 79.
3. Waddell 1987, pp. 5, 10–11, 16; Jefferson 1976, p. 164.
4. Waddell 1987, pp. 18, 23, 24.
5. Quoted in Nichols 1961, p. 3.
6. Pierson 1976, p. 297.
7. Nichols 1961, pp. 33–48.

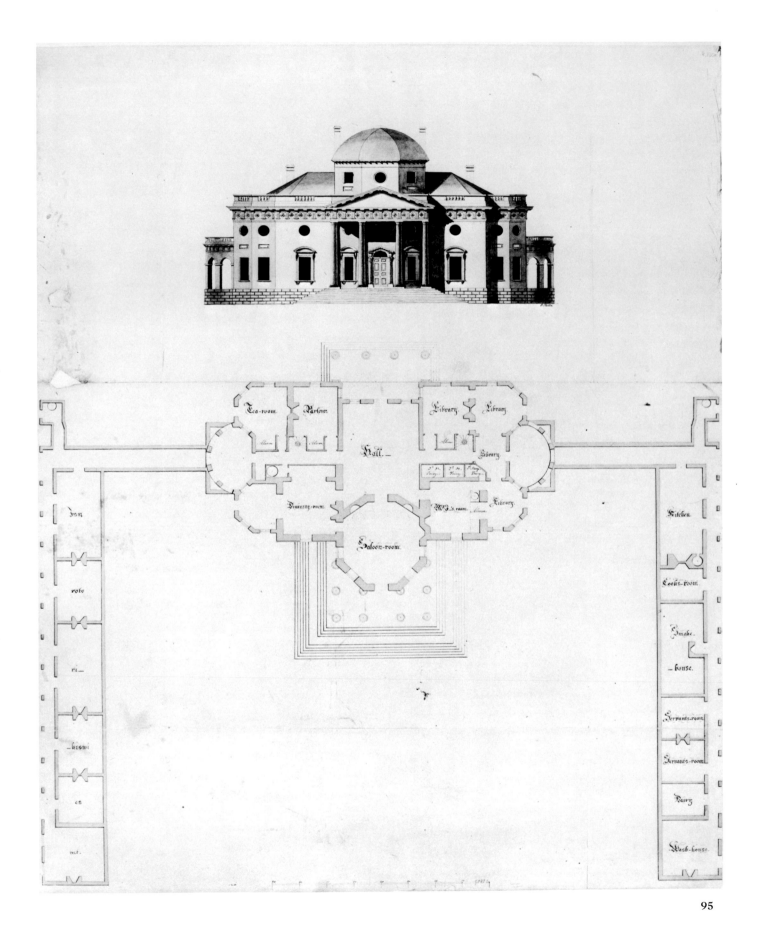

95

95
Robert Mills (1781–1855)
Study for Remodelling Monticello
ca. 1803
Ink and wash on paper
20¼ in. (51.6 cm) x 16 in. (41 cm)
Signed, lower right: *R. Mills*
Gift of Thomas Jefferson Coolidge, 1911

Thomas Jefferson returned to America from his five years in Paris as minister to France (1784–1789) impressed with the new styles of architecture he had seen there. The ostentatious chateaux of the rich had given way to elegant and intimate townhouses which epitomized French rococo architecture. One such example is the Hôtel de Salm (Paris, 1785–1787), which Jefferson observed being built along the banks of the Seine.[1] Several innovative features of architect Pierre Rousseau's (1751–1810) design are believed to have inspired Jefferson in his radical renovation of Monticello. These include the dome, the appearance of a single story, the use of a classical vocabulary for the decorative details and the general horizontality of the plan.

For two years, Jefferson was assisted with his renovations at Monticello by Robert Mills, who acted in the capacity of draftsman. Since Jefferson's plan for remodeling had already been established in 1796, Mills's study was more an exercise for the aspiring architect and showed little regard for practical considerations including cost. His design for the west facade of Monticello departs from Jefferson's conception in several ways. Mills's building is higher, his dome smaller, and his roof more pitched. Since the balustrade and entablature are lighter and more decorative than Jefferson's, they work against the emphatic horizontality of Jefferson's design.[2] Even more interesting are the two side arcades with pointed arches, years ahead of the Gothic revival in America. Mills's handling of wash shows a deft touch but his use of black to indicate voids harkens back to Gibbs. The floor plan of the house generally follows Jefferson's new design in which his private living quarters are on one side of the central reception area, and the public spaces are on the opposite side. As in Jefferson's finished design, the two small staircases are practically hidden from view.[3]

A native of Charleston, South Carolina, Robert Mills claimed to be the first American to receive professional training as an architect. Certainly, his early career seems like a deliberate attempt to obtain as much theoretical and practical knowledge as he could in the fields of architecture and engineering without traveling to Europe to complete his studies. Unlike many of the craftsmen-builders of his time, Mills attended the College of Charleston, where he probably specialized in classics. In 1800, Mills went to the new Capital City to work in the architectural office of James Hoban (1762–1831), an Irishman who had received the commission for the President's House. It was there that Mills met Jefferson who became president in 1801. Jefferson, for his part, allowed Mills access to his library at Monticello, which contained the best collection of architectural books in America. With letters of introduction from Jefferson, Mills made a tour of the eastern states to meet prominent architects, including Charles Bulfinch, and to sketch important buildings. With Jefferson's further assistance Mills obtained a position as an assistant to the English architect Benjamin Latrobe (1764–1820), one of the leading proponents of the Greek revival in America. During the five years he spent with Latrobe (1803–1808), Mills learned principles of engineering and construction which had previously been lacking in his training. Mills followed Latrobe in embracing the Greek revival as the first truly American style. In this, "Mills was merely true to his time in feeling that his architecture must be, above all, American." Like the French neoclassical theorists Boulée and Ledoux, Mills felt that architecture could be used as a means for social reform.[4]

During a long and successful career, Mills completed over 160 projects in Philadelphia, Baltimore, and Charleston. However, he is probably best known for the work he did in Washington, D.C., following his appointment as federal architect by President Andrew Jackson in 1836.

Surviving examples of his work are the United States Patent Office (1836–1840); the Treasury Building (1836–1842); and the Washington Monument (begun 1845–1852 but not completed until 1884).

S.R.M.

1. Pierson 1976, p. 298.
2. Hamlin 1944, p. 54; Kimball 1916, p. 68.
3. Bryan 1989, p. 5; Pierson 1976, pp. 301–303.
4. Hamlin 1944, pp. 53, 55; Dunlap 1918, 3:375; Bryan 1989, pp. ix, 3–4.

96

96
Charles Bulfinch (1763–1844)
Elevation of the First Harrison Gray Otis House, Boston
Boston, 1795–1796
Ink and wash on paper
6 1/8 in. (15.5 cm) x 5 5/8 in. (14.2 cm)
Inscribed: *Designed by C. Bulfinch about 1796 for Copley land / and excepting the second story windows, precisely the front of / what Mr. H. G. Otis called The Brick House on Lynde & Chamber / Street*
From the Harrison Gray Otis Papers

More than any other architect of his time, Charles Bulfinch was responsible for transforming the look of Boston in the early nineteenth century. He was also one of the first Americans to successfully progress from gentleman architect to professional architect. The son of a prominent Boston physician, Bulfinch was born into a wealthy and privileged family. After graduating Harvard in 1781 he became a clerk for Joseph Barrell (see no. 99), a successful local merchant. In 1785, Bulfinch made a grand tour of Europe which lasted nearly two years during which he nurtured a long-standing interest in architecture. His impressions from this trip made him realize the provincial nature of his native town. Soon after his return home Bulfinch began a series of designs which would eventually change the face of Boston and submitted as his first design one for a new state house, a project which was long delayed. His early projects include the Federal Street Theatre (1794), the domed Massachusetts State House on Beacon Hill (1795–1798), and the Tontine Crescent (1793–1794). The Tontine Crescent, which was modeled on residential crescents Bulfinch had observed in England, was significant as his first attempt at town planning in Boston. A room above the central arch of Tontine Crescent served as the third home of the Massachusetts Historical Society (1794–1833). Unfortunately, Bulfinch invested heavily in building the Crescent, and when the project failed in 1796 he was bankrupted. Until this point, all his architectural work had been done *pro bono publico*, but now he was forced to turn architecture from avocation to livelihood.[1]

Domestic architecture provided a new source for both commissions and expression. This drawing depicts the first of three houses Bulfinch designed between 1795 and 1805 for Harrison Gray Otis (1765–1848), a wealthy lawyer and real-estate investor, and a personal friend of Bulfinch. For the Cambridge Street house Bulfinch created a three-story symmetrical design in brick with a low-hipped roof. The emphasis of the five-bay facade is on the central bay. The tripartite entrance is echoed in the Palladian window on the second story and the arched window in the attic. The horizontality of the house is enhanced by white string courses separating the floors, decorative panels above the second-floor windows, and the dentil molding below the roofline. As in the case of Jefferson's design for Monticello (no. 94), the tall chimneys strike a discordant note.

The floor plan of the interior was symmetrical as well. A large central stair-hall divided the first story into two rooms on either side and an attached kitchen ell in the rear. As Kirker points out the interior was essentially colonial in character. He believes that the conservative floor plan was used because Bulfinch modeled the facade on the late colonial William Bingham house which he saw while visiting Philadelphia in 1789.[2] However, many of the decorative details of the interior owe their inspiration to the English architect and designer Robert Adam, whose country houses Bulfinch would have seen during his sojourn in England. Otis sold the house to John Osborn in 1801, and a colonnaded porch was added by the new owner. The house is now the headquarters of the Society for the Preservation of New England Antiquities, which acquired it in 1916.

The inscription on the drawing is believed to be in the hand of Sally Foster Otis.[3] This drawing is from the Society's extensive collection of Harrison Gray Otis Papers. The Society also hold a small collection of the personal papers of Charles Bulfinch.

S.R.M.

1. Pierson 1976, pp. 241–242; Kirker 1969, p. 78; MHS 1967.
2. Kirker 1969, p. 119.
3. Ibid., p. 118.

97

Samuel Blodget, Jr. (1757–1814)
Sketch of the East Front of the Capitol, Washington, D.C.
Washington, D.C., 1810
Ink and wash on laid paper (watermark 1797)
9 1/8 in. (20.7 cm) x 14 3/8 in. (26.5 cm)
Inscribed, across top: (in ink) *Sketch of the East front of the Capitol 376 feet* / (in pencil) *1810*; below, at right (in pencil): *Drawn by S Blodgett, 1810*
Gift of Mary Manning Howe, 1967

Samuel Blodget's sketch of the Capitol Building in Washington shows the original building as it looked until it was burned by the British during the War of 1812. The somewhat uninspired east elevation is the product of an architectural competition held to design the public buildings of the new capital. Dr. William Thornton's (1759–1828) design for the Capitol Building was selected, as modified by the French architect Stephen Hallet. The three-story mass is dominated by the central dome and projecting pavilion. An American eagle in the pediment flies above a two-story portico with six Corinthian columns which divide the structure into five bays. Below is a rusticated arcade which serves as the entrance. By contrast, the two smaller domes in the flanking pavilions appear to sink into the balustrade.

Samuel Blodget, Jr., is almost unknown today, and yet during the years of the Early Republic he was active in a variety of national endeavors. Blodget was born in Goffstown, New Hampshire, the son of the Samuel Blodget who drew the famous "Prospective Plan of the Battle Fought Near Lake George" (1755).[1] After serving in the New Hampshire militia during the Revolutionary War, Samuel, Jr., was reputedly involved in the East India trade in Boston where he earned a fortune. He then moved to Philadelphia where he married the daughter of the provost of the University of Pennsylvania, and there he founded the Insurance Company of North America in 1792.[2] Blodget soon realized the potential for further financial gain was possible with the construction of the nation's new capital, the Federal City (later Washington, D.C.) along the Potomac River, where he soon became active in real-estate speculation.

In 1792, an architectural competition was held for both the President's House and the Capitol building. Blodget tried to convince his friend Charles Bulfinch (see no. 96) that they should each submit a design. However, Bulfinch demurred for reasons of "modesty," and Blodget admitted that this "frightened me out of my Intention." The quality of the designs that were submitted by Americans underlined the paucity of trained native architects. Blodget, who had taught himself architecture from books, later changed his mind and did submit a design for the Capitol which was based on the Roman temple, the Maison Carrée in Nîmes, France, with the addition of a dome.[3] Jefferson later used the same building for his inspiration for the Virginia State Capitol in Richmond. The Commissioners of the Federal City invited Blodget to follow up his preliminary design with a complete set of drawings, but there is no evidence that he complied.

Although the commission for the Capitol was awarded to Dr. William Thornton, a young physician *cum* architect, the Commissioners recommended Blodget to President Washington as the Superintendent of Public

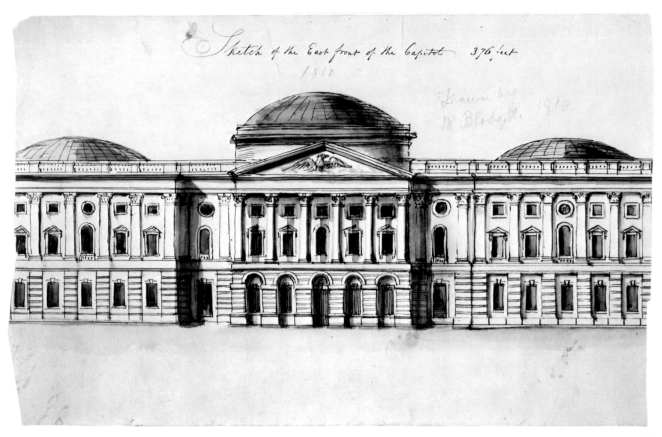

Sketch of the East front of the Capitol 376 feet
1810

Drawn by Mr Blodget 1810

Buildings. Although he knew little of Blodget, Washington agreed and following the appointment late in 1792, wrote that Blodget had "turned his attention (according to his own Account) to Architecture . . . and is certainly a projecting genius."[4] Unfortunately, the federal appointment was short lived. Blodget lacked the organizational skills and experience necessary for his job and became discredited when he could not refrain from local real-estate speculation.[5] Several unsuccessful lottery schemes completed Blodget's financial ruin, and he died in obscurity at a Baltimore hospital in 1814.

Some architectural projects which have been attributed to Blodget include the First Bank of the United States, Philadelphia (1795–1796, later the Girard Bank) and Blodget's Hotel, Washington, D.C. (1793). Recent research suggests that both buildings may actually be the work of James Hoban, who designed the President's House, Washington, D.C., and was the first teacher of Robert Mills.[6]

S.R.M.

1. MHS *Proceedings*, 2d ser., 5(1889–1890):416–417.

2. Butler 1976, p. 75; Tatman 1985, p. 76.

3. Seale 1986, 1:11, 29, 77.

4. Washington 1931, 32:244.

5. Ibid., 33:251.

6. Baigell 1969, p. 135.

The Early American China Trade

At the close of the Revolutionary War, new trade routes to the East were opened to American ships, no longer subject to the monopoly of the British East India Company. American merchants sought trade with the East Indies, and particularly with Canton, China, where other European countries already had firm footholds established. The New York ship *Empress of China* was the first American vessel to sail to Canton, and carried Major Samuel Shaw, son of a New England mercantile family, aboard as supercargo (purchase and sales agent). The ship arrived at the Whampoa anchorage of Canton in August 1784, with a cargo of ginseng, valued by the Chinese for its supposed restorative powers, and miscellaneous goods, which Shaw traded for a modest profit to the owners. Upon his return to Canton in 1786 as American consul, Shaw established the first American commercial house in Canton, Shaw and Randall. In 1786, the *Grand Turk* of Salem, commanded by Ebenezer West, became the first Massachusetts vessel to visit the Far East. She returned to Salem in May of 1787 with fabulous profits for her owners, whetting New England's appetite for the China trade.[1]

Great Britain traded for Chinese goods mainly with specie, something America could ill afford so soon after the Revolutionary War. While merchants could trade ginseng, which grew wild in New England, it had a limited market, and another commodity was sought for trade with Canton. This need was filled by the pioneering voyage in September 1787 around the Horn to the Northwest Coast of America by the ship *Columbia*, financed by a group of Boston merchants (see no. 98).

The *Columbia* traded with the Native Americans along the Northwest Coast for sea otter furs, and then continued on to China to exchange the furs, highly prized there, for tea, silks, and other wares to sell at home. This voyage established the highly profitable triangular Boston-Northwest Coast-Canton trade, which made many a fortune for Boston merchants.[2] Shipmasters soon discovered that sandalwood, also prized in China, could be obtained in the Sandwich Islands (Hawaii), a convenient resting place for crews worn out from the hard fur-trading life on the Northwest Coast and difficult conditions aboard ship.[3] Other trade goods eventually destined for the Canton market included beche-de-mer (sea slugs) and edible birds' nests, both delicacies in China; and sealskins, less valuable than sea otter furs, but still in demand. These items were collected en route to Canton, mostly in the southern hemisphere.

Fourteen American vessels had preceded the *Columbia* to Canton, and four of them belonged to the Salem merchant Elias Hasket Derby. New York, Boston, Salem, and to a lesser degree Providence, Philadelphia, Baltimore, and other East Coast cities all participated in some aspect of the China trade. While Salem ships never claimed a large share of the fur trade on the Northwest Coast, they did control a substantial portion of the old China trade. Most Salem ships carried miscellaneous cargoes eastwards around the Cape of Good Hope toward China, trading along the way in the East Indies for goods favorable on the Canton market. Salem also became the American and, for a time, the world emporium for the pepper trade.[4]

After the War of 1812, the fur trade declined, and by 1830 the sandalwood almost completely disappeared from Hawaii. However, by then Americans had sufficient commercial capital and specie to remain successful in the China trade, while continuing to seek new markets and products.[5] Opium, which the British had been selling to China for quite some time, became a trade commodity for the United States in the 1820s. Most of the American mercantile houses, except for Olyphant and Company of New York, participated in the opium trade.[6] The Opium War between Great Britain and China from 1840 to 1842 led to the opening of the treaty ports of Hong Kong, Shanghai, Amoy, Foochow, and Ningpo for foreign trade, which greatly increased the volume of trade between the United States and China.[7] As the textile industry blossomed in New England, cotton cloth also became a major import into China. The American China trade, led by the premier mercantile house of Russell and Company, continued to flourish through much of the nineteenth century.

The Massachusetts Historical Society has an important group of China trade manuscript collections, many of which were given by the China Trade Museum of Milton, Massachusetts, when that institution closed in 1984. Included are the Forbes Family Papers, a major collection of the family whose members were leaders in the nineteenth-century commerce with China, the papers of the wealthy Boston merchant Thomas H. Perkins, and logs and narratives concerning the voyages of the *Columbia*. There are many other collections as well, which document the China trade from 1784, when the *Empress of*

China sailed from New York City eastward to China, through the early twentieth century.[8]

K.H.G.

1. Morison 1921, pp. 44–46.
2. Ibid., pp. 46–47.
3. Latourette 1964, p. 44.
4. Morison 1921, pp. 84, 91.
5. Latourette 1964, pp. 54–55, 58.
6. Morison 1921, pp. 274–277.
7. Crossman 1973, p. 3.
8. MHS *Proceedings*, 100(1988):128–139.

98

Robert Haswell (1768–1801)
A Voyage Round the World onboard the Ship Columbia-Rediviva and Sloop Washington (September 1787–June 1789)
Manuscript
144 p., 12 ¾ in. (32 cm) x 8 in. (23 cm)
Gift of Rebecca Haswell Clarke Cummings, 1947

After the launching of the American China trade, merchants sought a commodity other than ginseng, which had a limited market, to trade in China for the tea, silks, and porcelain so much in demand at home. A group of Boston entrepreneurs, inspired by tales of Captain Cook's third voyage, decided there was profit to be made in trading for sea otter furs on the Northwest Coast of North America, and thence sailing to Canton to trade the furs, highly prized in China, for tea and other goods. They financed the adventure of the ship *Columbia Rediviva*, commanded by Captain John Kendrick, and the sloop *Lady Washington*, under Robert Gray, to sail around the Horn in search of fortune. The *Columbia* and the *Washington* departed in September 1787, and the *Columbia* returned to Boston in August 1790, becoming the first American-flagged ship to circumnavigate the globe. This voyage was not profitable to the owners for a variety of reasons, but undaunted they immediately launched a second voyage of the *Columbia*, under Captain Gray, in September 1790. The first voyage marked the birth of the highly profitable triangular Boston-Northwest Coast-Canton trade. Indeed, Boston so dominated this fur trade that all traders along the coast were referred to by the Native Americans as "Boston men."[1] The Northwest Coast fur trade enriched many Boston families until after the War of 1812, when other commodities replaced sea otter furs for import to Canton.[2]

This log, with a charming sketch of the two companion vessels, was kept by Robert Haswell, who joined the *Columbia* as third mate in 1787. Owing to differences with the irascible Captain Kendrick, the first mate, Simeon Woodruff, took his discharge at the Cape Verde Islands, and Haswell was promoted to the position of second officer. By the time the ship reached the Falkland Islands, however, he and Captain Kendrick were also at odds, and Haswell left the *Columbia* to become second officer of the sloop *Washington*. He remained with the sloop until July 1789 (when this log ends). Gray then took command of the *Columbia*, switching places with

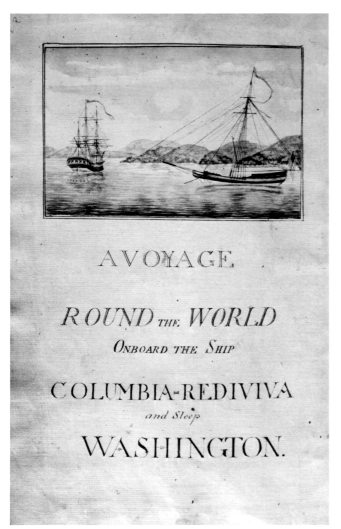

A VOYAGE

ROUND THE WORLD

ONBOARD THE SHIP

COLUMBIA-REDIVIVA

and Sloop

WASHINGTON.

98

Captain Kendrick, who remained with the *Washington* trading for furs along the coast. With Haswell as second officer, the *Columbia* sailed for Canton via Hawaii (then known as the Sandwich Islands) and then homewards around the Cape of Good Hope. She arrived in Boston on August 9, 1790.[3]

Haswell shipped out as first mate on the *Columbia* for her second voyage (September 1790 to July 1793), during which Captain Gray discovered and christened the Columbia River. This discovery served as the basis for American claims to the Oregon Country.[4] Thus, as historian Samuel Eliot Morison asserts, "On her first voyage, the *Columbia* solved the riddle to the China trade. On her second, empire followed in the wake."[5]

K.H.G.

1. Morison 1921, pp. 46–47.
2. Latourette 1964, pp. 54–55.
3. Howay 1941, pp. xvii–xviii.
4. Ibid.
5. Morison 1921, p. 51.

99
Design attributed to Joseph Barrell (1740–1804)
Dies attributed to Joseph Callender (1751–1821)
Columbia-Washington Medal
Boston, 1787
Copper
Inscribed, on obverse: COLUMBIA AND WASHINGTON. COMMANDED BY J. KENDRICK. around view of the ship and sloop sailing to left; on reverse: [star] FITTED AT BOSTON, N. AMERICA FOR THE PACIFIC OCEAN around text in field: BY / J. BARRELL, / S. BROWN, C. BULFINCH, / J. DARBY, C. HATCH, / J.M. PINTARD. / 1787.
D. 1 5/8 in. (41 mm)
Gift of Joseph Barrell, Samuel Brown, Charles Bulfinch, John Derby, Crowell Hatch, and John Marsden Pintard, 1791

Inspired by the British Royal Society's medals commemorating explorer James Cook's adventures, the Columbia-Washington medal was commissioned by Boston merchant Joseph Barrell to be sent on the first Pacific voyage of the ship *Columbia-Rediviva* and sloop *Lady Washington* in 1787 (see no. 98). The bill of lading for that voyage lists 300 medals entrusted to Captains John Kendrick and John Gray "to be distributed amongst the Natives on the North West Coast of America, and to commemorate the first American Adventure on the Pacific Ocean."[1] Considered the first die-struck medal issued after American independence, the Columbia-Washington token received considerable attention in contemporary newspaper accounts of the venture.

In spite of this notoriety, the origin of the medal remains obscure. While letters indicate that Joseph Barrell was solely responsible for its production, neither he nor the newspapers thought to mention the medal's designer, die-maker, or how many were struck in each metal used (pewter, copper, and silver). Early historians believed that architect Charles Bulfinch was the only member of the partnership with the necessary skills to design the piece;[2] but the hair- and painted jewelry that Joseph Barrell designed and had made for his family still exists as proof of his artistic ability.[3] The fact that there is no written evidence linking Bulfinch with the piece has led to the attribution of its design to Joseph Barrell. Boston engraver Joseph Callender has been suggested as the die-maker for the Columbia-Washington medal.[4] After apprenticing under Paul Revere, Callender went into business for himself and was listed as "Engraver" in the 1789 *Boston Directory*. One definite connection between Callender and the first voyage of the *Columbia* is the first set of dies which he made for the new Massachusetts 1787 cents and half cents which the *Columbia*'s partners obtained and shipped before the coinage was officially circulated.[5]

The striking of the medal was fraught with disasters. During the first striking the reverse die sank in, curtailing the number of medals shipped. Twelve days after the *Columbia* sailed, Barrell wrote that just as a new die was completed, "an Accident ruined it," and that another was in the making.[6] Among the known examples of the Columbia-Washington medal, those in silver and copper have an identical reverse which differs slightly from those in pewter, which have a rosette between "OCEAN" and

99

8. Joseph Barrell to Thomas Jefferson, Boston, Nov. 24, 1787, Thomas Jefferson Papers, MHS.

9. MHS *Collections*, 79:162.

10. Webb 1912, p. 353.

11. Revere Papers, MHS.

12. MHS *Proceedings* 1(1791–1835):25–26.

"FITTED," the "1" in the date has a serif, and the center text, while clearly by the same hand as the later version, is cramped and smaller. This fact and the testimony of an English mariner, who obtained pewter medals in Hawaii shortly after the *Columbia* sailed for Canton in 1789, indicates that the first striking was in pewter.[7] By November 24, 1787 Barrell was able to send presentation medals to John Adams and Thomas Jefferson, but again there is no record of the metals involved.[8] A contemporary account mentioned that twelve silver medals were struck, one of which was sent to George Washington,[9] but only five are known today (Massachusetts Historical Society; Oregon Historical Society; Henry F. DuPont Winterthur Museum; and two private collections). Apparently this silver striking was a disappointment to Barrell, for he advised one recipient that if he "let a Silver smith file and polish the edges of your [copper] Medal and have it properly cleaned, it will look better than the silver one."[10] Barrell seems to have followed his own counsel, for in Paul Revere's Waste Book there is an entry dated 1789 which charges Barrell five shillings "to repairing the edges of 10 Copper medals."[11] The same entry credits Barrell with depositing five ounces one pennyweight of silver, and charges him fifteen shillings for making six silver blanks for medals. It is possible that Barrell had his remaining silver medals from the 1787 striking melted down for a restrike.

In 1791 Joseph Barrell, acting on behalf of the merchants involved in the venture, presented this copper medal to the newly established Massachusetts Historical Society.[12] Close examination shows that the medal has been cleaned and the edges treated as described above, perhaps by Paul Revere himself. It has long been treasured as the nucleus around which the Society's medal collection has grown. With William Sumner Appleton's great numismatic collection in 1905, the Society received a silver specimen of the Columbia-Washington medal; and in 1962 completed the set with the Nash-Halsey pewter medal, inherited from James Briggs, who built the Ship *Columbia*.

A.E.B.

1. Columbia-Rediviva 1966; Joseph Barrell to John Adams, Boston, Nov. 24, 1787, Adams Papers, MHS.

2. Vietor 1962, p. 3.

3. Mary Barrell to Worthington C. Ford, Milburn, N.J., July 10, 1892, Barrell-Webb Papers, MHS; Fales 1987, pp. 642–649.

4. Vietor 1962, pp. 5–6.

5. Columbia-Rediviva 1966; Joseph Barrell to John Adams, Boston, Nov. 24, 1787, Adams Papers, MHS.

6. Webb 1912, p. 350.

7. Quoted in Vietor 1962, p. 1.

100

Thomas Handasyd Perkins (1764–1854)
Journal kept on the ship Astrea from San Jago towards Canton in China (March 22–September 11, 1789)
Manuscript
167 p., 7¾ in. (19.7 cm) x 6¼ in. (16 cm)
Gift of William Thaw Whitney, 1966

Learn from Mr Hayward who went on board the Ship in Company with us, that she is the Pigot, Capt. Balentine, for the hither Indies, out only 19 days from London. The Pigot spoke a small Ship 3 days since which was 10 weeks from Canton in China & nine days from St. Helena—we think he shoots with a long Bow—

Preparations going forward for shaving, *as we are nearly on the Equator* . . .

Thomas Handasyd Perkins was born in 1764 in Boston, the son of James Perkins, a well-to-do Boston merchant, and Elizabeth (Peck) Perkins. When James Perkins died in 1773, Elizabeth took charge of his countinghouse and carried on a large foreign trade that was later continued by her sons James and Thomas H. The young T. H. Perkins shipped out in 1789 as supercargo (purchase and sales agent) aboard the Salem ship *Astrea*, owned by Elias Hasket Derby and commanded by Perkins's brother-in-law Captain James Magee.[1] Upon his return, Perkins began to finance various shipping ventures to the East Indies and China, and eventually became "the first of Boston Merchants, both in fortune and public spirit." He established in 1803 Perkins and Company, the most famous American merchant house in Canton in the early period of the China trade. This was absorbed in the late 1820s by Russell and Company, which came to dominate American trading interests in China in the nineteenth century.[2]

Perkins's journal describes a portion of the *Astrea's* voyage from San Jago or St. Iago (Santiago in the Cape Verde Islands) to Canton, March 22 to September 10, 1789. The entry for April 2, shown here, describes meeting other ships at sea. At the bottom Perkins notes, "Preparations going forward for *shaving*, as we are nearly on the Equator." This refers to certain comical rituals observed in crossing the equator, whereby "green" deckhands were roundly abused by their fellows as an initiation to life at sea. The Perkins papers at the Massachusetts Historical Society also include a volume of memoranda kept at Batavia, where the *Astrea* was in port from July 13 to August 18, with detailed descriptions of the trade there and the customs of the inhabitants.

The *Astrea* sailed in February 1789 from Salem for Batavia and Canton with a miscellaneous cargo which took almost a year to assemble, including ginseng, butter, beef, salmon, rum, codfish, flour, tar, spermaceti candles, bar iron, wine, beer, and snuff. Derby intended that part of her cargo be sold at Batavia to purchase sugar, coffee, from St. Iago towards Canton in China

Winds	Remarks on Thursday April 2. 1789
West	

Small wind — at 3 OClock, Cap.
Bofetts boat came with an invitation to Cap. Magee, the Doctor
& myself to pass the afternoon with
him — which we did, much to
our pleasure & at the great expense
of his porter — learn from mr
Hayward who went on board the
Ship in Company with us, that she
is the Pigot, Cap. Balentine, for
the hither Indies: out only 19 days
from London — the Pigot spoke a
small Ship 3 days since which
was 10 weeks from Canton in China
& nine days from St. Helena — we
think he shoots with a long Bow —

Preparations going forward for
shaving, as we are nearly on the
Equator — At Meridian Cap. Bofett
came on board to take part of our Beef
Thermo. 83. after Showers —

100

nutmeg, and pepper. Perkins and Captain Magee were allowed five percent of the outward and two-and-a-half percent of the homeward cargo for their trading purposes. They reached Batavia on July 13 and discovered another Derby ship, the *Three Sisters* commanded by Captain Benjamin Webb, and very discouraging trading prospects.[3] They were not allowed to trade without a permit from the governing council of Batavia, because of a monopoly by the Dutch East India Company.[4] Perseverance on the part of T. H. Perkins eventually secured the permit, but trade was dull and the Americans lost money in the transaction. In his journal for August 10, Perkins lamented, "For these 10 days past employed in sacrificing our cargo."[5]

In September 1789 the *Astrea* arrived at the Whampoa anchorage of Canton. By October, there were four Derby ships in Canton: the *Astrea*, *Three Sisters*, *Atlantic*, and *Light Horse*. The plethora of American ships at Canton caused a glut of American goods on the market and drove up the price of tea. The Derby shipmasters and supercargoes decided to sell the *Atlantic* and *Three Sisters*, a not-uncommon practice, and loaded the remaining two ships with tea and other Chinese goods for home.[6] The *Astrea* and *Light Horse* departed Whampoa in January 1790. *Astrea's* return cargo was tea, nankeens (a type of cloth), and silk.[7] She arrived in Salem on May 31, the *Light Horse* following later in the month after nearly being dashed upon the rocks at Marblehead. An oversupply on the American market forced Derby to warehouse much of his tea for future sale rather than sell at a loss. While the Derby ships were away, Alexander Hamilton imposed a new duty system which gave no special consideration to ships already loaded with cargo, and this placed a heavy financial burden on Derby. He accordingly petitioned Congress for permission to pay duties on the tea as it was sold, which Congress granted, thus initiating the bonded warehouse system.[8]

K.H.G.

1. Seaburg 1971, pp. 19, 22–23, 43.
2. Morison 1921, pp. 49, 66, 274.
3. Phillips 1947, pp. 52–53, 55.
4. Peabody 1912, p. 87.
5. Perkins, Memoranda, Aug. 10, 1789.
6. Seaburg 1971, pp. 52–54.
7. *Astrea* manifest, Jan. 25, 1790.
8. Phillips 1947, p. 57; Seaburg 1971, p. 56.

101

Grand Chop of the Ship Astrea
Canton, China, January 1790
Broadside, completed in manuscript
29 3/4 in. (75.5 cm) x 21 5/8 in. (55 cm)
Gift of George Edward Cabot, 1922

All foreign traders approaching Canton, the only port open to international trade before 1840, were obliged to observe a complex series of customs and formalities. When a ship reached the Portuguese colony of Macao, a permit and pilot were secured to take the ship to Whampoa on the Pearl River, the anchorage for Canton, beyond which foreign ships were not allowed to progress. The ship and its cargo then had to be sponsored by one of the co-hong, a group of usually twelve senior merchants who paid a substantial fee to the emperor for a monopoly on all international trade. The shipmaster or supercargo in charge of the ship's cargo employed a linguist, or custom-house clerk, to manage all transactions and communications between the custom house officers and the foreign merchant, and a comprador was hired to act as steward and purser for the ship and the merchant's household. At Whampoa the Hoppo (superintendent of customs) or his deputies came aboard to receive presents and measure the ship for taxes. Finally, the merchandise was transported upriver in sampans (lighters) to Canton. It was there stored in a "factory" or warehouse hired from one of the hong merchants, who oversaw the trade procedures.[1] The strange laws and customs of Chinese trade led to the creation of Boston mercantile agencies at Canton to ease the way for American traders. The first of these was Shaw and Randall, established by Major Samuel Shaw of Boston in 1786.[2]

The formalities for shipping cargo out of Canton were similarly complex. Permits or "chops" were issued at Canton, examined and countersigned at Whampoa; dues, fees for pilotage, and bribes were paid, and when all was in order, the final Canton port clearance, or "Grand Chop," was issued to the ship. Everything with a government stamp or seal became known as a chop to foreigners, and this was the grandest of them all, "a formidable-looking document . . . ornamented with curling dragons."[3] This document enabled ships to depart from

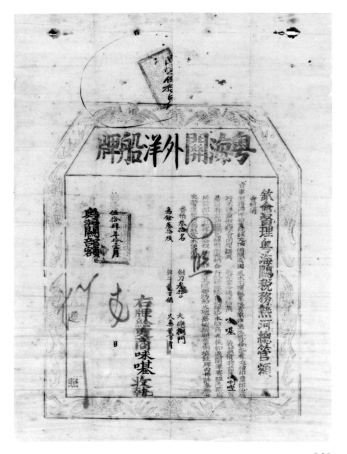

101

102

Dinner plate
Jingdezhen, China, 1795
Porcelain, painted
Diam. 9¼ in. (23.5 cm); H., 1 in. (2.54 cm)
Bequest of Ebenezer Thayer, 1884

This plate is from a Chinese tea service presented to Martha Washington by A. E. van Braam Houckgeest about 1796. The service was made and decorated in China using a design probably devised by van Braam himself, as adapted from the sunburst and chain used on the paper currency issued for the Continental Congress in 1776. The central decoration, on a white ground, contains the monogram "MW" in black on a red-gold field surrounded by a green wreath. From the wreath project sunburst rays, a sign of hope frequently associated with the early republic. Running across the rays is a pink banner with the motto "Decus et Tutamen Ab Illo" ("Honor and Defense come from it"). The rim has fifteen green ovals linked together by gold rings; inside each oval is the name of one of the states of the union including the recent additions of Vermont and Kentucky. Outside of this chain is a blue, black, and gold snake with its tail in its mouth, symbolizing eternity. The entire plate is edged with a gold band. When this plate was given to the Society in 1884, Dr. George E. Ellis, the Society's vice president, noted that it was broken in two pieces "strangely corresponding, as it severs the names of the States, with the line marked between those which seceded and those which held to the Union. The line of fracture divides the name of Maryland nearly equally. This, too, is significant."[1]

Martha Washington gave away at least one piece from the service to Julien Niemcewicz, the Polish traveler, in 1798, but in 1802 bequeathed the main service to her grandson George Washington Parke Custis, describing it in her will as a "set of tea china that was given me by Mr. Vanbram every piece having MW on it." Mr. Custis gave this plate to his half sister Mrs. Eugenia Stuart Webster. She gave it to Ebenezer Thayer of Brooklyn, New York, originally from Boston, who bequeathed it to the Society in 1884.[2] Another piece is said to have

the Whampoa anchorage and continue down river.

The grand chop shown here was issued to the Salem ship *Astrea*, whose supercargo Thomas H. Perkins kept a journal of part of the voyage to China in 1789 (see no. 100), and who retained this document. The *Astrea* obtained her grand chop in early January 1790, but was so overloaded with cargo and extra crew that she delayed her departure from Whampoa until January 22 so as to build an extra shack on deck to shelter the men.[4]

The grand chop states that all proper duties have been paid for the ship and should not be required again if the ship is driven into another port by contrary weather. It also lists the number of crew members, swords, cannons, guns, bullets, and gunpowder aboard ship, and the date of issue.[5]

George Edward Cabot, the donor of this document, was the great-grandson of Thomas Handasyd Perkins. He gave a large collection of T. H. Perkins papers to the Society, as well as papers of another China Trade merchant, Samuel Cabot, Perkins's son-in-law.

K.H.G.

1. Latourette 1964, pp. 22–23; Williams 1863, pp. 160–161.
2. Morison 1921, p. 66.
3. Williams 1863, pp. 167–168.
4. McKey 1962, p. 77.
5. Williams 1863, p. 168; Museum of Fine Arts, Boston, Asiatic Department translation, 1990.

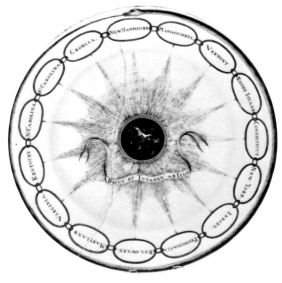

102

been given to LaFayette as a souvenir during his 1824 tour of the country. Mr. Custis in 1857 left the rest of the set to his daughter Mary Custis Lee, the wife of General Robert E. Lee. Family tradition speaks of barrels of china being rolled down the hill from Arlington House to the United States Patent House during the Civil War; and although many pieces were damaged during this exercise and otherwise, the "States" tea service remains one of the most popular items in porcelain collections. A line of "Martha Washington China" was sold at the American Centennial Exposition in Philadelphia in 1876, and commercial reproductions of the van Braam set soon followed.[3]

Other pieces from the original set are now in the White House Collection, the Diplomatic Reception Rooms of the State Department, the Wintherthur Museum, the National Museum of American History, Smithsonian Institution, the Collections of the Ladies of Mount Vernon, and the Metropolitan Museum of Art, New York.[4]

Andreas Everadus van Braam Houckgeest, a Dutch merchant formerly in the employ of the Dutch East India Company, served as the Dutch consul to North Carolina, South Carolina, and Georgia in 1783 and was naturalized as an American citizen the following year. In 1790 he returned to China as the Head of Canton operations for the Dutch East India Company and in 1794 went as one of the firm's ambassadors to congratulate the Emperor Qian Long in Peking on the sixtieth anniversary of his accession to the throne. Van Braam later told the story of this embassy in a detailed account published in two volumes. At the end of 1795 van Braam left Canton for the United States aboard the *Lady Louisa*, with a vast collection of furnishings and works of art. Among the items on the cargo manifest lists "a Box of China for Lady Washington." He settled in Pennsylvania with his impressive collection which included nearly 2,000 watercolor views of Chinese life and architecture which he had designed, commissioned, and collected. He lived on a Pennsylvania estate, which he named "China's Retreat," but soon landed in debtor's prison having left "all his good sense and all his prudence" in China, according to a contemporary. In 1798, van Braam took his collection to London, where part of it was sold at Christie's in 1799. He later returned to Holland where he died in 1801.[5]

E.W.H.

1. MHS *Proceedings*, 2 ser., 1(1884–1885): 255.
2. Detweiler 1982, pp. 151, 158; *MHS Proceedings*, 2d ser., 1(1884–1885):255.
3. Detweiler 1982, pp. 158, 195.
4. Gordon 1987, p. 184; Woodhouse 1935, p. 186; Mudge 1981, fig. 112.
5. Detweiler 1982, p. 151; Loehr 1954, pp. 179–193.

103

103
Solomon Loud (1787–1833)
Workbox
Boston, early nineteenth century
Satinwood, silver, brass, and mother-of-pearl
L. 7 in. (15 cm), W. 4 in. (11.2 cm), D. 3 in. (8.7 cm)
Gift of Helen Guild, 1957

Mary Clarissa Loud's little workbox exemplifies the distinct influence the China Trade had upon American decorative arts in the early nineteenth century.[1] Along with teas, silks, and porcelain, American merchants imported Chinese-made goods such as portrait and landscape paintings, elaborately carved ivory and mother-of-pearl fans, puzzles and gaming counters, silverware, textiles, and furniture. Chinese artisans inexpensively produced western-style as well as Chinese-style furniture and decorative objects for the American market.[2] The presence of these items in American households also inspired local craftsmen to incorporate elements of Chinese design into their own work. For example, the very popular lacquerware boxes were exported to America from 1785 to the mid-nineteenth century, and the most common types of lacquerware were the sewing box and lap-desk.[3] These boxes appear to have inspired the Loud workbox.

From its pagoda shape to its use of exotic materials, this workbox clearly shows a Chinese influence. Made of satinwood, the box was crafted sometime in the early nineteenth century by Solomon Loud for his daughter Mary Clarissa. A small nailhead trim decorates the hinged curvilinear lid. A mother-of-pearl keyhole is accompanied by an attached key. On the inside of the lid is a mirror, and the interior of the box has two compartments. The first compartment is a removable drawer fitted with a number of sewing implements, which include a slender glass bottle for smelling salts, a pair of scissors, a thimble, four star-shaped mother-of-pearl bobbins used for delicate lacework, an ivory bodkin, and a sterling-silver buttonholer. Underneath this drawer are scattered other objects including a spool of red ribbon, a heart-shaped pincushion with one side tooled in leather with embroidered flowers, an ivory bodkin, an ivory-handled buttonholer, a pair of scissors in a leather case, an ivory-handled eyelet, and a portable quill pen.

Solomon Loud was a Boston cabinetmaker who specialized in mahogany furniture. By 1820 he owned a sizable shop in Court Street where he employed eleven men. His business was not confined to the local area as evidenced by an 1822 notice in the *New York Evening Gazette* which advertised that Loud "manufactures and has for sale an excellent assortment of Furniture and chairs in the approved modern style, which will be sold low for cash or approved credit."[4] He was a member of the Ancient and Honorable Artillery Company of Massachusetts from 1821 to 1833. Loud died in 1833, leaving an estate appraised at $3,218.67.[5]

S.W.F.

1. Denker 1984.
2. Crossman 1973, pp. xi–xii.
3. Ibid., pp. 178–180.
4. Talbott 1974, pp. 40–44; *New York Evening Gazette*, Feb. 8, 1822.
5. Talbott 1974, p. 43.

104

Paul Revere (1735–1818)
Urn
Boston, ca. 1800
Silver, with ivory spigot handle
Inscribed, on front: TO / PERPETUATE / *The Gallant defence / Made by / Capt.* GAMALIEL BRADFORD. / in the Ship Industry on the *8th of July 1800 / when Attacked by four French Privateers / in the Streights of Gibraltar. / This* URN *is Presented to him* / *by* / SAMUEL PARKMAN.; marked, in rectangle on side of plinth: REVERE
H. 19 in. (48.2 cm), W. 10¼ in. (26 cm), Diam. (rim) 6½ in. (16.5 cm)
Gift of Helen Ford Bradford and Sarah Bradford Ross, 1933

Presented by "Merchant Prince and Federalist Grandee"[1] Samuel Parkman (1752–1824) to Captain Gamaliel Bradford (1763–1824), this urn by Paul Revere is rich in associations with the Massachusetts Historical Society. Samuel Parkman, one of the investors in the ship *Columbia's* second voyage on the northwest fur trade (1790–1793),[2] was the grandfather of historian and Society member Francis Parkman. Gamaliel Bradford, descendant of the Plymouth Colony's Governor William Bradford and of John Alden, himself became a member of the Historical Society in 1794. The action for which he received this silver urn was a dramatic engagement with privateers during America's undeclared maritime war with the revolutionary government of France.

After service with the Continental Army, during which he saw action at Saratoga (1777) and wintered in Valley Forge (1777–1778), Gamaliel Bradford decided upon a career at sea. He made his first voyage to France in 1784 and worked his way up in rank until, in November of 1799, he captained the ship *Industry* on a voyage to Italy. The *Industry*, presumably owned by Samuel Parkman, was a letter of marque, a private ship licensed to capture and confiscate foreign merchant ships. As tensions between the United States and France grew, attacks by such privateers increased on both sides. On this trip the *Industry* carried twenty-four men, two mates (one of whom was Gamaliel's brother, Gershom), and a passenger, to whom is owed the details of the engage-

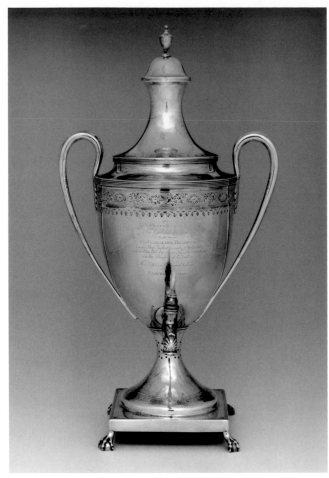

104

ment.[3] On the return voyage, after a small skirmish with two French privateers, the *Industry* arrived on July 8, 1800 at the Straits of Gibraltar, where she was attacked by four French privateers. The *Industry* returned fire as soon as they were within range. Three hours into the battle Captain Bradford was hit in the thigh, but before he was taken below deck, Bradford instructed his men to continue fighting and not allow the French to board. Gershom Bradford then took command and continued to fight for another two and a half hours. According to the passenger, Bradford's crew followed his orders with "determined courage."[4] The privateers abandoned their attack on the *Industry* in search of easier prey, leaving her badly damaged but with her cargo intact. The next day (July 9) the *Industry* hailed H.M.S. *Swiftsure*, whose captain Benjamin Hallowell supplied them with medical supplies and his surgeon's mate to care for Bradford. It took the *Industry* ten days to reach Lisbon, where Bradford underwent amputation of his leg. He later returned to the sea until 1809, when he retired. In 1813 he was appointed warden of the state prison, a post he held until his death in 1823.

Revere began working in the neoclassical style towards the end of the revolution. Adept at assimilating new styles, and reinterpreting them, Revere had an ease in this vernacular, evident in the shape of the piece. From its body, derived from the Greek amphora, to the finial, which echos the shape of the urn, it has a graceful sweep and flow. During the period that this urn was made, Revere's shops were not only producing tea- and coffeepots, trays, spoons, and Masonic medals, but also providing copper fittings for ships and buildings, rolling sheet copper, and casting bells, attesting to Revere's considerable abilities as artisan, innovator, and man of business.[5]

A.E.B.

1. Doughty 1962, p. 1.
2. Howay 1941, p. 461.
3. Bradford 1958, pp. 30, 35.
4. United States 1935, 6:126–128.
5. Skerry 1988, pp. 51–58.

105

James Brown Marston (1775–1817)
Old State House
Boston, 1801
Oil on panel
37½ in. (95 cm) x 51 in. (129.2 cm)
Purchased by subscription, 1879

This painting shows the eastward side of the Old State House as it looked at the turn of the eighteenth century, just a few years after the "new" State House on Beacon Hill became the seat of Massachusetts state government. On this site a Town House was erected in 1658 — a building which served as the center of civic life until it burned to the ground in 1711. A second structure replaced that one, but it too burned in 1747. Again, from the ashes arose another building, the present architectural landmark called the Old State House.[1]

For the next half century the building was used by governors, councils, and the General Court. The open square, shown in this painting as a place of social and commercial activity, was the scene of many memorable events, including the Boston Massacre which occurred there on March 5, 1770 (see no. 48). The balcony above the large door looked toward the harbor, and behind it was the Council Chamber where John Hancock was inaugurated as the Commonwealth's first governor. It was from this balcony that the first public reading in Boston of the Declaration of Independence was delivered on July 18, 1776. Later, on April 23, 1783, the Proclamation of Peace, marking the end of the Revolutionary War, was read from the same spot.[2]

At the beginning of the nineteenth century the Old State House was subdivided and fitted for shops and offices. In 1830 its owner, the City of Boston, took it over as City Hall. After ten years it reverted to commercial use, and by 1880 there were more than fifty professional and business people working there. At last, in 1882, the newly formed Bostonian Society installed a museum in the Old State House and assumed the once and future responsibility for the building's restoration and maintenance as an historical site.[3] One of the present-day threats to the continuing health of the building is from the rumbling of the subway trains that run beneath its basement, and a major structural restoration of the building is currently underway to prevent further damage.

In Marston's depiction of the Old State House as the centerpiece of a lively urban scene, the details of costume and occupation afford a pleasant impression of city life in 1801. It shows the building painted ochre with white trim and with an imposing grand staircase. The

105 (see also frontispiece)

building to the right where the sign "Union" appears was originally the home of John Apthorp, remodeled by Apthorp's grandson Charles Bulfinch in 1799 to be the location of the Union Bank.[4]

The artist James Brown Marston, a native of Salem, was in the commercial painting business in Boston from at least 1803.[5] Like many artisans, he became a member of the Massachusetts Charitable Mechanics Association, an organization of master craftsmen. Marston was also active in the military, as a captain in the state militia and a member of the prestigious Ancient and Honorable Artillery Company.[6] Little is known of Marston as an artist. His only other located painting is a portrait of Governor Caleb Strong (1807), also at the Historical Society.

V.II.S.

1. Howe 1946 (2), pp. 18–32.
2. Harris, 1982, pp. 198–204.
3. Chase 1982, pp. 31–48.
4. Kirker 1969, p. 368.
5. Salem 1924, 2:58; *Boston Directory*, 1803.
6. Buckingham 1853, p. 73; Roberts 1898, 2:1318.

106

Philip Harry (active 1843–1857)
Brimstone Corner (Tremont Street, South)
Boston, ca. 1843
Oil on canvas
13 ⅔ in. (34.6 cm) x 15 ⅔ in. (39.7 cm)
Gift of Henry Lee Shattuck, 1969

107

Philip Harry (active 1843–1857)
New South Church and Green (Summer Street)
Boston, ca. 1843
Oil on panel
13 in. (32.7 cm) x 15 in. (37.8 cm)
From the estate of B. Loring Young, 1964

These two delightful views of Boston were part of a series of street scenes painted by Philip Harry shortly after his arrival in Boston. Unlike most of Harry's other work, these paintings are well known through their reproduc-

106

tion as part of a set of four tinted lithographs entitled *Boston Street Scenes*, published in 1843.

In Harry's view of *Brimstone Corner*, the Park Street Church, which still stands today, is barely discernible along the right edge. Below its steps sit two women, one with a basket. Across the street is the entrance to the Boston Common, where two women are about to enter. The view up Tremont Street seems to be an accurate rendering of the cityscape, which was dominated by red-brick, low-rise residences. Harry's use of shadow to add visual interest is particularly effective.

In the *New South Church*, his shadowing in the foreground is even more dramatic. The bow-fronted buildings provide a framework for a lively street scene. Here a peddler with cart on the left is balanced by a pair of finely dressed women on the opposite side of the street. The center of the canvas is filled with small groups of strollers. However, the highlight of the scene is Bulfinch's granite New South Church (1814; destroyed 1868) in the background.[1] The stately three-story spire adds a strong vertical element to the composition. Both paintings by Harry display his ability to observe a myriad of urban activities as well as a sensitivity to the built environment of Boston in the early 1840s.

Little is known about the artist's background and training. Philip Harry, believed to have been a native of Cornwall, England, was living in Hartford, Connecticut, in 1841, and in Boston by 1843, when he worked on the "Streets of Boston" series. He noted in his diary for November 8, 1843, "Worked at finishing City Views," the four scenes which were reproduced in the popular litho-

graphs.[2] The first lithograph of the series, called simply "Tremont Street" is undated. It was printed by Thayer and Company and based on a Harry painting now at the Sawyer Free Library, Gloucester, Massachusetts. Harry himself was responsible for the lithography for the other three views which were all printed by the Boston firm of Bouvé and Sharp in 1843. The view of *Brimstone Corner*, number two in the series, was titled *Tremont Street, South*, while the view of the New South Church, *Summer Street*, was number four. The other lithograph, number three, is also called *Tremont Street*, and was taken from the original painting by Harry, now part of the Karolik Collection, Museum of Fine Arts, Boston.

During the same year that Harry worked on his "Streets of Boston" series, he showed twenty works at Harding's Gallery in Boston and the next year exhibited at the Fourth Exhibition of the Massachusetts Charitable Mechanics Association as well as the American Art Union. In 1844 the Boston Athenaeum included some of Harry's paintings in their annual exhibition of local artists.[3]

While Harry primarily painted landscapes, he also tried his hand at portraits and history painting. His surviving diary indicates that in January 1844 he traveled to New York and visited Thomas Cole, William Sidney Mount, and Caleb Bingham, three of the most important American painters of the period.[4] On his return from New York, Harry and his wife settled in Cambridgeport, Massachusetts, until they relocated to New York in 1846. Harry's two final diary entries indicate that he moved to Washington, D.C., in 1852. He exhibited some

paintings at the Washington Art Association in 1857.[5]
During the Civil War, he worked as a clerk in the war
department and probably died in Washington sometime
after the war.[6]

S.R.M.

1. Kirker 1969, p. 282.
2. Annotated transcript of Harry's diary made by Maxim Karolik, Object File, Department of Paintings, MFA.
3. Harry, Diary, Nov. 13, 17, 1843; Groce 1957, p. 196.
4. Harry, Diary, Jan. 26, 1844.
5. Groce 1957, p. 296.
6. Victor Harrie to Maxim Karolik, Apr. 23, 1952. Document File, Department of Paintings, MFA.

108
John Henry Bufford (1810–1870)
The Taking Down of Beacon Hill : Beacon Hill from Derne St.
Boston, 1857–1858
Chromolithograph
22 ⅛ in. (56.2 cm) x 15 ¾ in. (40.3 cm)
Purchased by the Society with the Savage Fund, 1879

109
John Henry Bufford (1810–1870)
*The Taking Down of Beacon Hill : Beacon Hill
from the Present Site of the Reservoir Between Hancock
and Temple Streets*
Boston, 1857–1858
Chromolithograph
22 ⅛ in. (56.2 cm) x 15 ¾ in. (40.3 cm)
Purchased by the Society with the Savage Fund, 1879

As Boston's population grew in the early nineteenth
century, so did the town's need for usable land. While
large-scale landfills provided a solution, they also permanently altered the area's topography. Earth from Boston's
three hills filled ponds, marshes and estuaries, and in
particular between 1811 and 1812, Beacon Hill provided
the fill for the Mill Pond and the construction of Charles
Street. These excavations were sketched from various
viewpoints around the hill by J. R. Smith. The original
drawings, done in ink and pale watercolor washes, are
owned today by the Boston Public Library. Bufford
noted on the chromolithographs that the drawings were
"done on the spot." The artist was possibly John Rubens
Smith (1775–1849), born in England and son of the English engraver John Raphael Smith. Known to be working
as an engraver in Boston in 1811, Smith moved to New

BEACON HILL FROM BERNE ST.

108

109

York by 1816 and spent much of the rest of his life working there as a portrait painter, engraver, and drawing teacher.[1]

The Beacon Hill Memorial Column appears in each of Smith's drawings at the summit of the hill. Designed by the architect Charles Bulfinch, it was erected in 1790 to commemorate the American Revolution. Constructed of stuccoed brick and stone, the sixty-foot-high Doric column and pedestal was topped by an American eagle made of gilded wood and set to serve as a weathervane. It replaced the old-style "beacon" first ordered by the General Court in 1634–1635, a utilitarian timber mast firmly anchored at the base and fitted at the top with a crane to carry a bucket of combustible material lighted as necessary.[2]

Together with Bulfinch, the ubiquitous Jeremy Belknap coauthored the inscriptions, carved on slate

tablets and set into the four sides of the pedestal, listing the events which led to the American Revolution and the securing of independence from Great Britain exhorting Americans to "forget not those who by their exertions Have secured to you these blessings." Though the memorial column was demolished along with the summit of the hill in 1811, a granite reproduction was approved in 1899 and placed behind the east wing of the new State House. The original tablets were placed in the new pedestal where they can be viewed today.[3]

John Henry Bufford, son of a New Hampshire sign painter and gilder, began his career in lithography in 1829 as an apprentice of the Pendleton brothers, the pioneers of the medium in Boston. By midcentury Bufford had developed into a prolific and successful lithographic artist and a major printer and publisher of prints. After participating in several partnerships, he opened his own firm in 1850 on Washington Street.[4]

In 1857–1858 the lithography firm of J. H. Bufford issued a series of five chromolithographs based on J. R. Smith's drawings of the *Taking Down of Beacon Hill*. The general title of the series, "Old Boston," indicates a nostalgic look back to the removal of some of the landmarks of earlier times and the beginnings of nineteenth-century growth and industrialization. One of the first Boston lithographers to experiment with printing in color in the 1840s, the series illustrates the bright, clear color Bufford had achieved by the 1850s.[5]

J.L.P.

1. Whitehill 1968, ch. 4; Hitchings 1975, p. 111; Fielding 1974, p. 339.
2. Stanley 1963, p. 25.
3. Kirker 1969, pp. 33–35.
4. Tatham 1976, pp. 47–51.
5. Hitchings 1975, p. 111.

Gilbert Stuart (1755–1828)

Of all the American artists in the new republic, probably none has had as great an influence on nineteenth-century portraiture as Gilbert Stuart. A native of Kingston County, Rhode Island, Stuart became the protégé of Cosmo Alexander (1724?–1772) during the Scottish painter's sojourn to Newport in 1769 and accompanied him on a brief journey to the south and then to Edinburgh in 1771. Stuart's hopes to be a portrait painter were dashed when Alexander died suddenly in 1772, leaving his student without any connections or means of support. After arriving home destitute and in poor health, Stuart was able to obtain portrait commissions from some of the wealthy Newport residents. However, his career was again interrupted, this time by the approach of the Revolutionary War. After his father fled to Nova Scotia as a loyalist, Stuart decided to journey to London in 1775 to study under Benjamin West (1738–1820).

West, a noted history painter, operated an informal American academy of art in London, where he trained many of the most distinguished artists of the period including John Singleton Copley and John Trumbull.[1] It was during his five years with West that Stuart's mature style developed, combining the naturalism of his earlier works with a new sophistication. After this training,

Stuart was able to obtain commissions independently and in 1781 he left West to establish his own studio. Fame came to Stuart after the success of one portrait, *The Skater* (National Gallery of Art, London), which received much attention and praise when it was exhibited at the Royal Academy in 1782. This full-length portrait of William Grant depicts him skating, a novel activity in an otherwise formal portrait.

Despite Stuart's success, his extravagant life style and inability to manage the business aspect of his profession plagued him throughout his life. In 1787, he abandoned his lucrative career in London for Dublin, mainly to escape his creditors.[2] Stuart became as popular in Dublin as he had been in London, but in 1793, he decided to return to the United States. His stated reason was that he had a great desire to paint the president, George Washington. He did hope that a successful portrait of the great man would make his fortune, but he was also again evading debtor's prison.[3]

When Stuart arrived in New York, his talent was quickly recognized, and he received portrait commissions from well-known patrons, including John Jay and Aaron Burr. It was Jay who gave him an introduction to Washington, and soon after his arrival in Philadelphia in 1795, Stuart wrote to the President requesting a sitting.[4] As *The Skater* had established his reputation in London, the three portraits which Stuart painted of Washington from life, secured his reputation in America. The unfinished Athenaeum bust (Museum of Fine Arts, Boston, and National Portrait Gallery) is considered to be the definitive image of Washington.

Stuart next spent a brief period in Washington, D.C., where he painted the portraits of James and Dolley Madison and other political notables. Stuart's arrival in Boston followed an invitation made by Massachusetts Senator Jonathan Mason, who promised Stuart commissions of his own family with others to follow. In 1805, Stuart settled in Boston where he spent the last twenty-three years of his life. Despite his erratic behavior and increasingly untidy appearance, Boston was honored by his presence. His ideas and his taste became the last word in all matters of art. As Washington Allston observed, "Stuart's word in the art is law and from his decision there is no appeal, and so say all good painters of America."[5] The four portraits by Stuart in this exhibition all date from his Boston period. Of the remaining five portraits by Stuart in the Society's collection, only the unfinished portrait of Abigail Adams (1800) predates his arrival in Boston.

Stuart was criticized by his contemporaries for failing to finish many of his portraits, but even so his output was remarkable. He painted the most famous Americans of the federal period from John Adams to Thomas Jefferson. Once in America, Stuart no longer signed his works because he felt that his style was immediately recognizable. As Dunlap related, "When asked why he did not put his name or initials, to mark his pictures, he said, 'I mark them all over.' "[6] Like West before him, Stuart was interested in training American painters. Many important nineteenth-century artists passed through his studio, including John Vanderlyn, Thomas Sully, and Sarah Goodridge.

S.R.M.

1. Whitley 1932, p. 35.
2. Gilbert Stuart 1967, p. 22.
3. Whitley 1932, p. 84.
4. Ibid., p. 91.
5. Ibid., pp. 121–122, 204.
6. Gilbert Stuart 1967, p. 31.

110

110

Gilbert Stuart (1755–1828)
Jeremiah Allen (1750–1809)
Boston, ca. 1808
Oil on panel
30 in. (70.9 cm) x 22½ in. (57.2 cm)
Gift of Susan Allen, 1836

The self-satisfied bachelor which Gilbert Stuart presents in his portrait of Jeremiah Allen provides an interesting contrast to Copley's introspective portrait of Allen's brother James (no. 38). Jeremiah was born in 1750 on the same day that his father, a Boston merchant and local politician, died.[1] Jeremiah Allen became the first high sheriff for Suffolk County, serving under governors John Hancock and James Bowdoin. In this position, he was responsible the enforcement of Boston laws. One of his most controversial acts was the closing of an illegal theater in Boston in 1793 under Hancock's orders at which time the "audience sympathized with the actors, and amid great excitement, in which Hancock's portrait was torn from the stage-box and trampled under foot, the play ingloriously ended." Allen lived in a stone house, which was considered the oldest of its type in Boston. Located on the corner of Beacon and Somerset streets, the house had been built by his great-grandfather, the Reverend James Allen of First Church, Boston.[2]

Taken near the end of Allen's life, this portrait represents someone who appears comfortable with himself and content with his position in the world. Like Stuart's portrait of Sarah Lloyd Borland (no. 111), Allen is painted in half length and situated close to the viewer. He gazes out with a contemplative expression. The slouch of his position, as well as the indirect lighting which leaves part of his face in shadow, gives the painting a sense of immediacy. His clothing is rich, the blue velvet coat with brass buttons set off by the yellow waistcoat and white shirt. Allen's high coloring is even more florid than that typical of Stuart's style. Charles Pinckney Sumner, who became sheriff in 1825, related this anecdote about his predecessor, "He was a rich and moral old bachelor, of whom it was once jocularly said in his presence and hearing that 'the sheriff knew very well how to arrest men and to attach women.' "[3]

S.R.M.

1. Sibley 1873, 8:540–549.
2. Drake 1971, pp. 261, 363.
3. Loring 1852, p. 330.

111

111
Gilbert Stuart (1755–1828)
Sarah Lloyd Borland (1762–1839)
Boston, ca. 1818
Oil on panel
27 in. (68.6 cm) x 21¼ in. (53.8 cm)
Bequest of Katherine Abbott Batchelder, 1977

An older, yet dignified woman of affluence is the image of Sarah Lloyd Borland painted by Gilbert Stuart in 1818, when Borland was fifty-six years old. She was the daughter of Sarah and Dr. James Lloyd of Boston. Her father,

a prominent local physician, was an early advocate of smallpox inoculation. Sarah married Leonard Vassall Borland at Trinity Church, Boston, in February 1785. They had six children, born between the years 1787 and 1798.[1] Leonard Vassall Borland, who was a Boston merchant, sold a small house, which had been built by his grandfather, and the large parcel of land on which it stood in Braintree (now Quincy) to John Adams in 1787. Enlarged over the years, the Old House became the family home of Presidents John Adams and John Quincy Adams. Leonard Borland died on board the ship *John Jay* on its return trip from Batavia to Boston in 1801. Sarah Borland lived in Boston until her death in 1839.[2]

This incisive portrait of Sarah Lloyd Borland shows Gilbert Stuart at his best. The half-length figure is seated close to the picture plane and she looks with an intelligent expression directly at the viewer. While not idealized, her smooth skin and rosy complexion add vivacity to her rather plain features. Mrs. Borland's costume is restrained, but the elaborate collar and turban, set off with the red patterned shawl, reflect the American taste for exotic fashion due to the rise of trade with the Near and Far East. One of Stuart's biographers astutely observed about the artist's late work:

> Though he rarely allowed sumptuous patterning to affect telling characterizations, and felt a special sympathy for older persons, whose decline is viewed with lofty dignity, Stuart's portraits of women had become his most satisfying works.[3]

This portrait of Sarah Lloyd Borland certainly attests to Stuart's continuing skill as a portrait painter in the years following his arrival in Boston.

S.R.M.

1. Thacher 1828, p. 363; Lloyd 1927, pp. 895–896.
2. Adams 1928, p. 4; Lloyd 1927, p. 895.
3. Mount 1964, pp. 278–279.

112
Gilbert Stuart (1755–1828)
Edward Everett (1794–1865)
Boston, 1820
Oil on canvas
30 in. (76.1 cm) x 25 in. (63.9 cm)
From the estate of Thomas Dowse, 1856

Eulogized as the "First Citizen of the Republic," Edward Everett was one of America's most popular orators, second only to his longtime friend Daniel Webster. Upon his graduation from Harvard with the highest honors in 1811, Everett became a Latin tutor at the college while preparing for the ministry. In 1813 he became the minister of the Brattle Street Church, the largest and most fashionable church in Boston. His sermons were noted for their erudition, classic style, and literary allusions, but the responsibilities of the position proved to be excessive for a young man of nineteen, and he turned to a more scholarly life. Everett accepted the new professorship of Greek literature at Harvard in 1815, and in preparation for this appointment, he traveled to Europe to continue his studies. In 1817 he became the first American to receive a doctorate from the University of Göttingen before returning to Harvard and teaching in 1819. Everett was

112

vember 19, 1863, preceding the now immortal two minute address of President Abraham Lincoln (see nos. 152–153). Everett died on January 15, 1865, just months before the close of the Civil War.

Gilbert Stuart's portrait of Edward Everett was taken in 1820, when Everett was twenty-six years old, the same year he was elected as a member of the Massachusetts Historical Society. Like several Stuart portaits, including his famous sketch of George Washington, this painting is unfinished. Nonetheless, Stuart has captured the intensity and intelligence of the young Harvard professor. This painting hung for many years in the library of Thomas Dowse of Cambridge (1772–1856), a friend of Everett's and an avid book collector who donated his collection to the Historical Society.[5] This portrait is similar to a somewhat earlier portrait of Everett (ca. 1815) by Stuart now at Harvard University.

S.R.M.

1. Dana 1865, p. 7; Frothingham 1925, p. 22; Yanikoski 1987, p. 10.
2. Loring 1852, p. 525.
3. Yaniskoski 1987, p. 28.
4. Ibid., pp. 38–43.
5. MHS *Proceedings*, 3(1855–1858):169.

considered to be an inspiring teacher by his students, who included Ralph Waldo Emerson, Robert C. Winthrop, and Charles Francis Adams.[1]

Everett's career as an orator was launched when he delivered the 1824 Phi Beta Kappa address at Harvard to a large audience which included the aged French general Lafayette. According to a contemporary, "When published, it received greater favor than any oration ever delivered at this ancient seat of learning."[2] In November of the same year, Everett was elected to Congress, a position to which he would be reelected four times. Following his years in Washington, he was elected governor of Massachusetts for four terms beginning in 1835. During his tenure, he was instrumental in setting up the nation's first successful state board of education and normal school system.[3]

With the aid of Secretary of State, Daniel Webster, Everett was appointed ambassador to England serving from 1841 to 1845. On his return to Boston in 1846, Everett was elected Harvard's eighteenth president. Unfortunately, he found that the changes which he had hoped to implement at his alma mater more difficult to institute than he had anticipated, thus leading to his resignation at the end of 1848. However, he continued his interest in education by working for the establishment of Boston's free public library, the first in the nation. After Webster's death in 1852, Everett served briefly as Secretary of State. The following year, Everett was elected senator from Massachusetts. He retired from this position in 1854 after receiving harsh public criticism for missing (due to illness) the vote on the decisive Kansas-Nebraska bill.[4]

Retired from elected office at the age of sixty, Everett continued to work for the causes in which he believed. His hopes to preserve the Union were dashed with the outbreak of the Civil War, but he spent the remaining years of his life working for the northern cause. His last important speech, was delivered at Gettysburg on No-

113

Chester Harding (1792–1866)
Grace Fletcher Webster (1781–1828)
Boston, 1827
Oil on canvas
38 7/8 in. (98.8 cm) x 28 in. (71.3 cm)
Gift of Benjamin Joy, 1953

Born at Hopkinton, New Hampshire, in 1781, Grace Fletcher was the daughter of the Reverend Elijah and Rebecca (Chamberlain) Fletcher. Educated at Atkinson Academy in Atkinson, New Hampshire, she taught school at Boscawen and Salisbury not far from her birthplace. She first met Daniel Webster (see no. 122) in 1805 at church in Salisbury, his hometown. They married in 1808 and enjoyed an especially affectionate and companionable relationship.[1]

Chester Harding finished this portrait of Grace Fletcher Webster at age forty-six in December 1827, just before the Websters left Boston for Washington, D.C. En route, they stopped in New York, where Mrs. Webster became very ill and died on January 21, 1828. Regarding the painting as a last keepsake, her husband wrote to a relative that "I cannot tell you how I value it. It was a most fortunate thing, that we had it done."[2]

Harding painted Grace Fletcher Webster during the height of his popularity in Boston. This life-sized, half-length portrait depicts Mrs. Webster "as a fashion plate of the period," wearing the costume, complete with matching pearl-gray hat and pelisse, that she had worn two years earlier when her husband delivered the address at the cornerstone laying for the Bunker Hill Monument."[3] However, a good likeness was always Harding's primary concern, and he succeeded in maintaining the sitter's individuality in spite of her elaborate dress.[4]

Born into a poor but respectable farming family in Conway, Massachusetts, Chester Harding spent the early years of his life working at various times as a hired hand,

a peddler, a furniture maker, a tavern owner and a sign maker in his native state and New York and Pennsylvania.[5] He stumbled onto his own vocation in 1818 at age twenty-six by attempting to paint his wife's portrait. "Frantic with delight"[6] at his success, Harding continued

to paint and developed his native ability solely through practice and observation. Though he began his professional career in Kentucky and Missouri, where he ventured into the woods to find and paint the legendary Daniel Boone at age eighty-six (1820, Massachusetts His-

torical Society), Harding found his most appreciative
audience when he traveled east to Boston. Throughout
his career, the artist rented a large room when he arrived
in a new location. Here he displayed exact replicas of his
previous works for the public to view. In Boston, as many
as fifty people a day visited his exhibit, and the number
of those wanting to sit to the artist grew so large a waiting list had to be compiled.[7]

In addition to the portraits of Mrs. Webster and
Daniel Boone, the Massachusetts Historical Society owns
ten other portraits by Harding: of Caleb Strong (ca.
1822), Paul Revere (ca. 1823), and Rachel Walker Revere
(ca. 1823), all three copies after Gilbert Stuart; Joseph
Story (ca. 1828); Daniel Webster (1830; and ca. 1830);
Charles Lowell (ca. 1833); Leverett Saltonstall (ca. 1836);
David Cobb; and Redford Webster.[8]

J.L.P.

1. Fuess 1930, 1:101, 347.
2. Lipton 1985, p. 94.
3. Hart 1897, p. 629.
4. Lipton 1985, p. 15.
5. Lipton 1981, pp. 46–47.
6. White 1890, p. 38.
7. Lipton 1981, p. 47.
8. Oliver 1988.

114

John Miers (1758?–1821)
James Bowdoin (1726–1790)
Ink on plaster
3 ⅜ in. (8.6 cm) x 2 ⅜ in. (6.1 cm)
From the estate of Clara Bowdoin Winthrop, 1973

James Bowdoin was born into Boston's circle of successful Huguenot families which included the Reveres and
Faneuils. After graduating from Harvard and following
his father's death, "Jemmy" took over the family business,
extending it through trading contacts in the West Indies
and by developing frontier land in Maine. He became
a successful investor in overseas merchant ventures and
soon added the trappings of a Boston mansion, which
quickly became the center of local society. Among his private activities was a keen interest in science, particularly astronomy. He corresponded with Franklin on scientific matters and in 1781 became a founding member
and the first president of the American Academy of Arts
and Sciences.

Drawn into politics, Bowdoin was serving in the
Council by 1757, and he continued there as an increasingly
powerful force through the Revolution. Despite recur-
ring bouts of ill health he remained active in a wide array
of activities from serving as president of the state constitutional convention to becoming first president of the
Massachusetts Bank and one of the first Bostonians to
invest in the China Trade. When John Hancock decided
not to continue as governor in 1785, the General Court
chose Bowdoin as his successor after a contested election.
Although overwhelmingly reelected the next year, Bowdoin faced a public opinion landmine when he decided
to use military force to crush the populist insurrection in
the western part of the state. Shays's Rebellion spelled
the end of Bowdoin's political career, and John Hancock

114

returned to the governorship.[1] As one French visitor
remarked at the time: "Bowdoin is more esteemed by
men of education; Hancock is more loved by the
people."[2]

This silhouette represents Governor Bowdoin in his
old age and may well be posthumous as is the portrait by
Christian Gullagher (Bowdoin College Museum of Art)
which it closely resembles. One sees the patrician statesman who was described by a contemporary as "a tall,
dignified man . . . dressed in a gray wig. . . . His face was
without color, his features rather small for his size, his
air and manner quietly grave."[3]

Comparatively few artists painted silhouettes on plaster, and the popularity of this medium diminished after
1800. However, because of the enormous production of
the Miers Studio, examples exist in most British collections.[4]

John Miers has been called not only the finest and
most widely known profilist of the eighteenth century,
but also among the finest profilists in the history of the
art. A native of Leeds in the north of England, Miers
followed his father as a retailer of paints, but by the time
of his marriage in 1781 had expanded his trade to include
gilding, painting coaches, and rendering profiles. His
success in silhouettes led him in 1791 to London where he
established a studio at which he was assisted by several
colleagues and soon had a thriving business. John Field
was employed to paint the majority of profiles from about
1793, and another unidentified artist worked in the Miers
studio during the 1790s. Miers himself continued active
in the business until his health failed about 1820 but
painted few silhouettes after 1800, and from that time
Fields was virtually the only profilist at the studio.[5]

The Bowdoin-Temple collection of family papers
which descended into the Winthrop family through
Governor Bowdoin's granddaughter, Mrs. Thomas Lin-
dall Winthrop (Elizabeth Bowdoin Temple), are now
at the Historical Society along with the companion
silhouette of Bowdoin's son-in-law, Sir John Temple,
also from the Clara B. Winthrop estate.[6]

E.W.H.

1. Sibley 1873, 11:514–550.
2. Brissot 1964, p. 105.
3. Kershaw 1976, p. 87; Sibley 1873, 11:544.
4. McKechnie 1978, p. 614.
5. Ibid., pp. 624–629.
6. MHS *Proceedings* 85(1973): 152.

lace collar, a shirt front, or (in the case of Mrs. Bromfield) a bonnet. A number of additional Bache silhouettes are in the Society's collection, notably those which came in 1987 with the Wigglesworth Family Papers.

The little volume which contains this painted profile is a commercially produced volume with sheets of black paper interleaved throughout to allow hollow-cut silhouettes to be contrasted. This particular volume, from the collection of Eliza Susan Quincy (1798–1884), contains a number of silhouettes and profiles as well as portrait engravings and some physionotracings by C. B. J. F. de Saint-Mémin of friends and relatives of the Quincy family.

E.W.H.

1. Quincy 1850, p. 4.
2. Tracy 1852.
3. Carrick 1928, pp. 59–71; Groce 1957, p. 18.

115

115
William Bache (1771–1845)
Ann Roberts Bromfield (1749–1828)
Black ink with white opaque watercolor on white paper
4 ⅛ in. (10.7 cm) x 3¼ in. (8.4 cm)
Inscribed: *Mrs. Ann Bromfield*; embossed, above three rosettes: BACH'S PATENT
Bequest of Eliza Susan Quincy, 1884

Ann (Roberts) Bromfield was born in 1743, daughter of Robert Roberts, a Welshman who settled at Newburyport, and his wife Sarah Woodbridge. Her university-trained father "bestowed" on her "great advantages of education, of which she had the disposition and power to avail herself."[1] She married John Bromfield in 1770 in Newburyport and had five children, including John Bromfield, Jr., the prominent Boston merchant and philanthropist. The family moved from Newburyport to Bradford about 1780 and then to Boston in 1782, to Charlestown in 1787, and later returned to Newburyport. Among the Bromfield Family Papers at the Historical Society is her comprehensive collection of household receipts from 1807 to 1816. In 1824 Mrs. Bromfield moved to Maine to live with a daughter and died there in 1828.[2]

William Bache, the silhouettist, was an Englishman who settled in Philadelphia as a cutter of profiles about 1793. Like many profilists, Bache led an itinerant life, wandering from the West Indies to New England. In 1812 he moved to Wellsboro, Pennsylvania, where he kept a general store after the loss of his right arm. He worked both in hollow-cut silhouettes (see no. 116) as well as profiles painted in black ink. His finely detailed silhouettes were further enhanced with the addition of white opaque watercolor to accentuate accessories, such as a

116

116
William Bache (1771–1845)
Thomas Barnard (1747/8–1814)
ca. 1800–1810
Hollow-cut white paper, black paper backing
6 ⅝ in. (16.8 cm) x 5 ¾ in. (14.5 cm)
Embossed, at lower left: *Bache's Patent*
Gift of Mary Stacy Beaman Holmes, 1954

The Reverend Mr. Thomas Barnard was born in Newbury in 1747/8, the son of a minister of the same name who was pastor to the First Congregational Society of Salem, and his wife Mary Woodbridge. He was a first cousin of Ann Roberts Bromfield, whose profile by Bache is also shown (no. 115). After graduating from Harvard in 1766 and studying theology, young Barnard was almost asked to join his father as colleague, but the parish chose another candidate. A minority of the congregation continued to support Barnard and withdrew to form the North Congregational Church of Salem, where he was ordained in 1773 and remained until his death in 1814. Although not a member of the Massachusetts Historical Society, Barnard donated a set of Joseph François Lafi-

117

118

tau's *Moeurs des Sauvages Américains,* and he was active in a wide array of charitable societies.[1] He was remembered by a colleague as "of a corpulent habit & rather inactive, but generally cheerful & social."[2] In this silhouette Barnard appears in a broad-brimmed hat with his hair pulled back into a queue, already old fashioned by this time.

E.W.H.

1. Sibley 1873, 16:316–322.
2. Bentley 1905, 4:289.

117
Mary Locke Craft (1783–1843)
Possibly Charlestown, Massachusetts, 1810
Etched gold leaf on glass
6 ⅛ in. (15.9 cm) x 5¼ in. (13.5 cm)
Gift of Rhodes Robertson, 1970

118
Elias Craft (1781–1872)
Possibly Charlestown, Massachusetts, 1810
Etched gold leaf on glass
5 ⅞ in. (15.1 cm) x 5¼ in. (13.5 cm)
Gift of Rhodes Robertson, 1970

Elias Craft of Newton and Mary Locke of Lexington were married in 1806, and spent their first several years together farming in Newton. Afterwards they moved to Charlestown, where Mary raised a family of eight children, while Elias worked as a teamster in an express business. For a number of years he also worked at the state prison in Charlestown.[1]

Examples of this type of silhouette are unusual in this country.[2] The image is etched into gold leaf and then backed with black to throw the profile into sharp contrast. These companion pieces show the most elegant type of portrait that most working-class families could afford.

E.W.H.

1. Crafts 1893, p. 256.
2. Carrick 1928, p. 72.

119
Anson Dickinson (1779–1852)
Abigail May (1754–1824)
1823
Watercolor on ivory
3¼ in. (8.3 cm) x 2 ⅝ in. (6.7 cm)
Signed, at lower right: *A. Dickinson / June 1823*
Gift of Abigail Adams Eliot and Martha May Eliot, 1971

120
Anson Dickinson (1779–1852)
Amos Lawrence (1786–1852)
1823
Watercolor on ivory
3¼ in. (8.5 cm) x 2 ⅝ in. (6.8 cm)
Signed, at lower right: *A. Dickinson / June 1823*
Gift of Andrew Oliver, 1963

Portraits in miniature, one of the most personal and private of art forms, emerged in the sixteenth century. Originally meant as keepsakes to be secreted away in a drawer, tucked into a pocket or worn as jewelry, the tiny ovals could be looked at anytime or place. In the early eighteenth century, ivory was substituted for the traditional base of vellum over card. Though the nonabsorbent, slippery ivory needed light sanding and degreasing before watercolor would adhere properly, it offered a unique translucency when properly used. The artist needed a steady hand and keen vision for the exacting work, which often began with a graphite sketch. The portrait was then built up with transparent washes of color. Either a hatching technique of parallel or crossed lines or a stippled application of small dots was used to fill out the background.[1]

These two portraits painted "in little" by New England miniaturist Anson Dickinson in the same month feature the rectangular-shaped ivory housed in a leather case and the dark colors popular in the 1820s and 1830s. At this time, miniatures were larger and more often intended for exhibit on the parlor table rather than for keeping to oneself for private contemplation.[2] Both of these miniatures illustrate Dickinson's facility for fine

119

120

founders of the Boston Asylum for Female Orphans, she also acted as a director of that institution. Friends described her as "lovely in person and character, and distinguished for her benevolence and practical good sense."[4] Two copies of this miniature were commissioned shortly after the original was finished, perhaps indicating the artist's success in achieving a likeness. The subject's solemn, dark clothing is old-fashioned for this time, but it suits her calm and dignified manner. Her pose is the same one the artist used most often for male sitters such as Amos Lawrence.[5]

A native of Groton, Massachusetts, Amos Lawrence moved to Boston and established his own dry goods business there in 1807. The firm of A. & A. Lawrence, founded in association with his brother Abbott, became a highly successful enterprise. Later in his career, he played a leading role in the development of the New England textile industry with his establishment of a cotton factory in Lowell in 1830. In addition to his business interests, Mr. Lawrence became particularly well known for his widespread philanthropy and his special interest in education.[6]

The artist Anson Dickinson grew up in the small Connecticut village of Milton and was apprenticed to the Litchfield silversmith Isaac Thompson. According to Dickinson's own record book, he began his career as a miniaturist in 1803. He traveled the eastern seaboard almost constantly for forty years and painted as many as 1500 miniatures. Largely self-taught as a painter, Dickinson used techniques of composition, including the high placement of his figures and employing a light-colored background to contrasting the subjects, which resemble those of the Connecticut artist Elkanah Tisdale (1768–1835), who may have taught Dickinson the intricate technique of miniatures. In New York in 1804, he sat for his own portrait with the famous miniaturist Edward Greene Malbone (1797–1807), who obliged his younger colleague with a discount in his fee.[7]

J.L.P.

1. Strickler 1989, pp. 13–14.
2. Ibid., p. 15.
3. Dearborn 1983, p. xxiv.
4. MHS *Proceedings* 80(1962):184.
5. Dearborn 1983, p. 84.
6. MHS *Proceedings* 75(1964):124.
7. Dearborn 1983, p. 21.

121
Edward Greene Malbone (1797–1807)
Elizabeth Peck Perkins (1798–?) and Nancy Maynard Perkins (1801–1887)
Boston, 1805
Watercolor on ivory
4¼ in. (10.9 cm) x 3 in. (8.9 cm)
Gift of Elizabeth Welles Perkins, 1921

Elizabeth and Nancy Perkins were the daughters of Samuel Gardner Perkins and Barbara Cooper Higginson who married in Boston in 1795. Their mother, a noted beauty of the period, was described as being "always striking in her person, and very brilliant in conversa-

modeling and the integration of the ivory's transparency with the skin tones. The background is completed with Dickinson's characteristic stippling technique.[3]

Mrs. May sat for Dickinson at age sixty-nine. Bostonian Abigail May married her distant cousin, a wealthy local merchant, Colonel John May, when she was nineteen and together they had eleven children. One of the

121

composed of tiny, precise cross hatchings of separate brush strokes of translucent watercolor. This was a time-consuming and painstaking process, involving the use of extremely small brushes, a microscope, and a reducing glass through which the size of the sitter would be reduced.[6]

Malbone had a short but distinguished career as a miniature painter, and today he is considered one of the foremost practitioners of the art. He was born in Newport, Rhode Island, and became interested in drawing at an early age, possibly learning to paint by observing scenery painters at the local theater. Several writers have also suggested that Samuel King (1748/9–1819), the painter and instrument maker, may have given Malbone some informal instruction.[7] It was also at Newport that he met Washington Allston, who would become a close friend and colleague. At the age of fourteen, Malbone ran away to Providence and set himself up as a professional miniature painter, and for several years he lived the life of the itinerant painter, traveling from Providence to Boston, to Philadelphia and New York. In 1801 Malbone journeyed with Washington Allston to London, where they spent time studying masterpieces in the museums and studying art at the Royal Academy.[8] They also met Benjamin West, who said of Malbone's portrait of Allston (Museum of Fine Arts, Boston): "I have never seen . . . a miniature that has pleased me more."[9]

When Malbone returned from England in the autumn of 1801, he entered the most productive period of his career. In Charleston, he painted eighty-nine miniatures in only seven-and-a-half months (1801–1802). His last period of great artistic activity was the sixteen months he spent in Boston from 1804 to 1805. It was at the end of this period that the portrait of the Perkins sisters was painted.

Due to failing health, Malbone sailed to Jamaica at the end of 1806 but died on May 7, 1807, at a cousin's house in Savannah, Georgia, on his return voyage. Of his untimely death at the age of twenty-nine, his friend, the miniature artist Charles Fraser wrote: "It has deprived his county of an ornament which ages may not replace. It has left a blank in the catalogue of American genius which nothing has a tendency to supply."[10]

S.R.M.

tion."[1] Their father was the younger brother of Boston's merchant prince Thomas Handasyd Perkins (see no. 100). Samuel Perkins supervised the family's sugar and coffee export business in Santo Domingo in 1785 and after his marriage became a partner with Higginson & Company in Boston and later president of the Suffolk Insurance Company. The family spent their winters at their house in High Street, Boston, and their summers in Brookline, Massachusetts.[2]

Neither Elizabeth nor Nancy Perkins married, and they spent their adult years with their father at Brookline in the family house which was later the home of H. H. Richardson, the noted architect. Their younger brother, James Handasyd Perkins, remembered Nancy as "one of the strongest minded, and most clear, determined disinterested women I ever knew." By contrast, the elder sister, Elizabeth, was recalled by an acquaintance "as extremely handsome and quite coquettish . . . she had all the men at her feet."[3]

This miniature by Malbone is the only known group portrait painted by him. It was commissioned by Samuel Perkins in 1805. Malbone recorded it in his account book as "Mr. Perkins 2 children—pd. ($) 109."[4] For the double portrait Malbone chose a rectangular-shaped ivory, larger than the oval discs he usually used. It was probably meant to be displayed on a table top in a leather case, now missing. The delicate palette is typical of his work after 1800. No doubt, the lightening of his colors was due in part to the influence of the graceful and elegant Federal style.[5] The two young girls are posed close together in order to fit into the confines of the ivory. The elder sister, Elizabeth, is seated on a bench or ledge, holding a rosebud loosely in her hand. Four-year-old Nancy stands alongside, leaning her head on her sister's arm. They are dressed identically in Empire-style peach-colored gowns with ruffled necklines. The soft tone of their dress is echoed in the delicate coloring of their faces. The family resemblance is unmistakable. The landscape, glimpsed through the open window on the left, includes a feathery tree and a fragile blue sky.

Close examination of the miniature reveals some aspects of Malbone's working method. The portrait is

1. Cunningham 1907, p. 22.

2. Ibid., p. 19.

3. Cunningham 1907, pp. 22, 194; MHS *Proceedings*, 2d ser., 2(1885–1886): 306.

4. Tolman 1958, p. 45.

5. Strickler 1989, pp. 15, 96.

6. Tolman 1958, p. 70.

7. Dunlap 1918, 1:137; Gourley 1963, p. 11.

8. Harding 1989, p. 15; Bolton 1927 (2), p. 92; Tolman 1958, p. 29.

9. Washington Allston to Charles Fraser, Charleston, August 25, 1801, quoted in Tolman 1958, p. 26.

10. *Charleston Times*, May 27, 1807. Reprinted in Tolman 1958, p. 60.

(see also color plate X)

122
Sarah Goodridge (1788–1853)
Daniel Webster (1782–1852)
Boston, 1827
Watercolor on ivory
3 ⅜ in. (8.7 cm) x 2 ¾ in. (7.2 cm)
Gift of Thomas Lee, 1864

123
Sarah Goodridge (1788–1853)
William Warland Clapp (1826–1891)
Boston, ca. 1838
Watercolor on ivory
3 in. (7.3 cm) x 2 ⅛ in. (5.5 cm)
Gift of Mrs. J. Howard Means, 1967

Sarah Goodridge, one of American's most distinguished and prolific miniature painters, worked in Boston between 1820 and 1850. Born in Templeton, Massachusetts, she was the sixth of nine children born to Ebenezer and Beulah (Childs) Goodridge. According to her sister and fellow artist, Eliza Goodridge Stone (1798–1882), Goodridge showed an early propensity for drawing and in school "was a general picture-maker for her school mates, and from memory sketched likenesses."[1]

Largely self-taught, Sarah Goodridge began by working with chalk and watercolor and then worked briefly on large-scale oil portraits before turning to the miniature watercolor format. Her professional career commenced in 1820 when she settled permanently in Boston and opened her own studio. According to Eliza, she was almost immediately successful. "From that time forward, she had as much as she could do."[2]

Goodridge's career was aided immensely by her association with Gilbert Stuart, which began soon after she opened her studio. Introduced by a mutual friend, Stuart was pleased with Goodridge's work, invited her to visit his studio, and soon became her mentor. Stuart once painted a miniature of Henry Knox (Worcester Art Museum) to demonstrate the proper technique to Goodrich and also allowed her to paint a miniature of himself (1825,

Museum of Fine Arts, Boston), which his daughter Jane declared "the most life-like of anything ever painted of him in this country."[3] Goodridge also executed a number of miniatures after Stuart's oil portraits.

Both Goodridge and her sister Eliza employed a stippling technique, scarcely visible in the sitters' faces but noticeable in the backgrounds. Goodridge also used a green underpainting for the faces to give them a sharp focus and a sculptural quality.[4] Another characteristic feature of her portraits is frequent use of a blue or green background.

Although she spent her entire working career in Boston, Goodridge did make two professional visits to Washington, D.C., in 1828 and again in 1841–1842.[5] She retired in 1850 due to failing eyesight, moved to Reading, Massachusetts, and died during a Christmas visit to Boston in December 1853.

In addition to the two miniatures shown here, there are several others in the Society's collection which are attributed to Goodridge, including those of Jane Winthrop (1819), Edward Everett, Margaret Dawes Eliot, and Hannah Hawkes (ca. 1850).

In 1827, Goodridge painted this miniature of Daniel Webster, shortly after his election to the Senate. The first of seven Webster miniatures that Goodridge would paint, it also marked the beginning of a long-term friendship between the two. Their surviving correspondence, some of which is in the Webster papers in the Historical Society, indicates that they were friends during most of Goodridge's working career, and she seems to be one of the people to whom the impecunious Webster turned to for loans of money.[6]

Webster, at age forty-four, was at the peak of his career, and his expression is self-assured to the point of arrogance. Even in the miniature format, his great presence is evident. Using a bust-length presentation, Goodridge followed her usual convention and has concentrated almost totally on the face of her subject. Goodridge portrays her sitter with dignity but does not idealize his features, as the receding hairline and lines around the mouth attest. Unlike her later work, Goodridge gives little attention to the light background which does not serve to enhance the image.

Daniel Webster, the great statesman and orator, was one of the best-known public figures in the nineteenth century. The son of a successful farmer and prominent citizen in Salisbury, New Hampshire, Daniel had "more talent for books than for farming" and so was sent to Phillips Academy at Exeter and on to Dartmouth. After college, Webster practiced law near his hometown for several years, before relocating in 1804 to Boston, where he worked in the law office of Christopher Gore.

Two years later, Webster returned to Portsmouth, New Hampshire, to marry Grace Fletcher (no. 113) and to begin what would become a lucrative law practice. Allying himself with the Federalists, Webster was elected to Congress in 1813. Several years later, he was back in Boston, practicing law where the potential for financial success was even greater than it had been in Portsmouth. Apparently, "no matter how much Webster earned, it was never enough to support his extravagant habits and wasteful ways."[7]

After six years of building up an important law practice, Webster returned to Congress, this time as a repre-

123

sentative for Massachusetts. In 1827 he was elected to the Senate, but this political triumph was dampened by the death of his wife. Less than two years later, he married Caroline Le Roy. As senator from Massachusetts for more than twenty years, Webster was known for fiery oratory and his adherence to the traditional values of home, patriotism, religion, and a reverence for the past.[8] In later years, he was a strong advocate for the Union and its preservation. In his famous 1830 Senate debate with Robert Hayne, Webster said "the union of the States is essential to the prosperity and safety of the States. I am a unionist, and, in this sense, a national republican. I would strengthen the ties that hold us together."[9]

In 1836, Webster was the Whig candidate for president. Although disappointed in his lifelong desire for the executive office, he did serve as secretary of state under Presidents Harrison and Tyler (1841–1843). He was a member of the Massachusetts Historical Society from 1821 until his death. Webster died at his home in Marshfield, Massachusetts, in 1853.

This portrait was painted for the writer Eliza Buckminster Lee, who was a friend of Webster. Given to the Society by her husband, Thomas Lee, this miniature was considered "one of the best likenesses of Mr. Webster ever taken."[10] The Society also owns what is probably the last miniature of Webster painted by Goodridge, an unfinished work dating from the mid–1840s.[11]

Executed during the peak of Goodridge's career, the miniature of William Warland Clapp as a young boy is a fine example of her work. Seated in a brown velvet armchair or settee, young William has a very serious expression. His face, with his light brown hair, large blue eyes, and soft complexion, is exceedingly well painted. Although the linen collar and bow at his neck display Goodridge's skill in rendering textures, she gave less attention to the rest of Clapp's dark shirt. Goodridge's use of stippling is evident in the blue and brown background which harmonizes well with Clapp's coloring. As Goodridge's sister Eliza said of her work, "Heads, and heads only she loved to paint."[12]

Upon his death, in December of 1891, *The Boston Post*

aptly proclaimed William Warland Clapp to be the "Dean of the Boston Press." He was the son of Hannah W. Lane and William Warland Clapp, a journalist who founded the *Boston Advertiser* in 1813 and was later editor of the Boston *Saturday Evening Gazette*. William Clapp was educated in Boston but spent several years in Paris to complete his education. At the age of twenty-one, he succeeded his father as editor of the *Gazette*, a position he held until 1865.

Clapp also became involved in the civic affairs of Boston, serving on the Common Council and on the Board of Aldermen, as well as one term as a state senator. During the Civil War, he was an aide to Governor Banks and also on the staff of Governor Andrew. In 1865, Clapp became the editor for the *Boston Journal*, a position he held until several months before his death. As a writer in the *Boston Post* noted, "In politics, Col. Clapp was an uncompromising Republican, and the whole strength of the Journal was directed in support of that party."

Since his early days in journalism, Clapp had an enduring interest in the theater, and he wrote or adapted several plays, as well as a series of articles for the *Gazette*, later reprinted as *A Record of the Boston Stage* (Boston, 1853). Clapp's later years were almost exclusively devoted to journalism, and he served as the president of the New England Associated Press. Writing about Clapp and his career, a colleague noted that he was "just, fearless, upright and honorable."[13]

S.R.M.

1. Mason 1879, p. 78.
2. Ibid., pp. 79–80.
3. Strickler 1989, pp. 64, 80; Morgan 1939, p. 61.
4. Strickler 1989, p. 63.
5. Mason 1879, p. 81.
6. Barber 1982, p. 24.
7. Ibid., pp. 29, 33–34, 96.
8. Ibid., p. 36.
9. Quoted in Peterson 1987, p. 173.
10. MHS *Proceedings*, 8(1864):4.
11. Barber 1982, p. 24.
12. Mason 1879, p. 80.
13. *Boston Post*, Dec. 9, 1891; *Boston Evening Transcript*, Dec. 9, 1891.

124

Caroline Negus (1814–1867)
Catherine Sargent (1774–1852)
Boston, ca. 1840
Watercolor on ivory
3 ½ in. (8.9cm) x 3 ⅞ in. (9.7cm)
Gift of the Wigglesworth Family, 1987

Catherine Sargent was born in Gloucester in 1774, daughter of Epes and Dorcas (Babson) Sargent. She became active in the abolition movement along with her sister Henrietta, and they both became friends of William Lloyd Garrison and his family. She never married and died in her hometown in 1852 at age seventy-eight.[1] Garrison wrote in her obituary for the *Liberator*: "the cause of the stricken slave, and of all identified with him by complexion, has lost one of its truest and best friends. Her sympathies were constantly affected, and her charities actively exercised, in behalf of the poor, the outcast, and the oppressed, without regard to color or race."[2]

Portrayed in her late sixties, Catherine Sargent sits squarely before the viewer, a sober and dignified woman of the mid-nineteenth century. The treatment of the sitter is highly individualized according to the well-known American desire for a truthful likeness, although Negus's realism is extreme compared to most other painters of her day. Careful attention is paid to the sitter's elaborate white lace day-cap and collar which contrast dramatically with the dark color of her plain dress and the simple stippled background.

Born into a family of painters, miniaturist and crayon artist Caroline Negus worked in Boston in the 1840s and 1850s. Her father, Joel Negus, was a sign painter, surveyor, and schoolmaster in the Connecticut Valley early in the nineteenth century. Her brothers, Joseph and Nathan, worked as itinerant painters in New England and the South. Both, however, died young. As early as 1842 Caroline participated in the first exhibition of the Boston Artist's Association, exhibiting three works, two portraits and a head, after the miniaturist Malbone. She also exhibited at the National Academy and at the Boston Athenaeum. Her drawings of botanical subjects were used for an early series of chromolithographs done in Boston by William Sharp and published in Morris Mattson's medical herbal *The American Vegetable Practice* of 1841. In 1844 the artist married the noted historian Richard Hildreth of Boston.[3]

Miniature painting was considered an appropriate artistic expression for women who were often denied more ambitious careers. Like Caroline Negus, Anna Claypoole Peale of the famous Philadelphia family of painters, the Goodridge sisters, Eliza and Sarah, of Massachusetts, and Sarah Frothingham of New York City all had successful careers as miniaturists.[4]

J.L.P.

1. Sargent 1923, p. 12.
2. Garrison 1971, 4:210n–211n.
3. Groce 1957, p. 467; Boston 1842; Hitchings 1975, pp. 103–104.
4. Bolton-Smith 1984, p. 9.

124

125

125
Richard Morell Staigg (1817–1881)
Stephen George Perkins (1835–1862)
Boston, 1845
Watercolor on ivory
3 ¾ in. (9.2 cm) x 3 in. (7.3 cm)
Inscribed, at lower right: *Staigg / 1845*; at lower left:
R.M.S. / *1845*
Gift of Elizabeth Welles Perkins, 1921

126
Richard Morell Staigg (1817–1881)
James Savage (1784–1873)
Boston, 1849
Watercolor on ivory
4 ¼ in. (10.8 cm) x 3 ¼ in. (8.3 cm)
Inscribed, at lower right: *R. M. Staigg, 1849*
Gift of Mr. and Mrs. J. William Middendorf II, 1970

The miniaturist Richard Morell Staigg emigrated to America with his parents in 1831 at the age of fourteen, having already worked as an architect's assistant in England. He settled in Newport and was encouraged by his teacher, the well-known American painter Washington Allston, to take up miniature painting. Staigg first exhibited in Boston in 1841, and though he worked in Baltimore, New York, and Newport, most of his work was done in Boston. During his travels abroad in 1856 and 1857, Stephen George Perkins, (painted at age ten by Staigg) carried examples of the artist's work to London. The miniatures were admired, and the following year two of his portraits were exhibited at the Royal Academy.[1]

In the two portraits shown here, the most admired characteristics of Staigg's work can be seen. His contemporary H. T. Tuckerman described his portrayal of children as "delicate as it is truthful."[2] Lips slightly parted in concentration, the ten-year-old Stephen George Perkins gazes to his left, seeming to be captured in a quiet moment rather than posed by the artist. Staigg's rendering of the boy's rumpled suit, tousled brown curls and

126

1. Groce 1957, p. 5 98; Tuckerman 1967, p. 445.

2. Ibid., p. 446.

3. Harvard 1906, p. 218.

4. Wehle 1927, p. 67.

5. MHS *Proceedings* 16(1878):117–153.

127

Hannah Child (1794–1809)
Sampler
1805
Silk yarn on open, plain-weave linen
21½ in. (55 cm) x 17¼ in. (44 cm)
Inscribed: *While through Lifes various scenes I stray / May virtuous Friendship chear my way / May Wisdom strew my paths with flowers / And Blessings Crown my fleeting hours / Hannah Child's work wrought in the / eleventh year of her age* A.D. *1805*
Gift of Edward E. Loud, 1967

Hannah Child, who stitched this sampler when she was ten years old, was born in 1794, one of the eleven children of Daniel and Rebecca (Richards) Child of Newton, Massachusetts. Virtually nothing is known about her short life apart from this sampler, but combined with the fact that she died in Boston, it suggests that Hannah may have been attending one of the town's several female academies when she died in 1809 at the age of fourteen.[1]

As early as the sixteenth century, samplers were used throughout Europe as pattern records of embroidery techniques.[2] This kind of needlework became a well-established tradition in colonial America and flourished until the mid-nineteenth century. The dramatic increase in the volume of samplers produced during the Federal period was due to new educational opportunities for young girls. Privately run female academies provided a genteel education for young ladies who learned reading, writing, cyphering, music, and needlework.[3] Recent surveys of American samplers from this period show how design and composition varied from region to region and from school to school, ranging from elaborate pictorial representations of townhouses, farms, and pastoral scenes to simpler genealogical records and script alphabets. By the 1840s, samplers declined both in number and in workmanship as taste and the curricula in female academies changed.

Hannah Child's workmanship bears striking resemblance to groups of samplers from Lexington, Concord, and Boston schools, which date from the 1790s up to 1808, the date of this example.[4] Each sampler follows the same general format although Hannah Child's use of an architectural centerpiece sets it apart from the others. The sampler's primary colors are blue, green, and yellow done in cross, seed, pulled and drawn, gathered, and laid stitches. Above the verse are two lines of script alphabet. The middle section depicts a gazebo, house, cottage and gardens under a blue sky with sun, moon and clouds framed by a border of geometric insects and flowers. Below this scene is a cartouche with the following: "Hannah Child's work wrought in the eleventh year of her age A.D. 1805."

Other needlework pieces at the Society include a view of Harvard Hall (no. 45); coats of arms of the Pier-

soft pink cheeks support Tuckerman's assertion.

Born in Boston in 1835, Stephen George Perkins was the son of Stephen Higginson Perkins and Sarah Seaver (Sullivan) Perkins. He graduated from Harvard College in 1856. After traveling in Europe, he returned to Boston and was admitted to the Scientific School at Harvard to study mathematics. Upon the outbreak of the Civil War, he was commissioned as a first lieutenant in the second regiment of Massachusetts Volunteers in 1862 but was killed at the battle of Cedar Mountain, Virginia, in the same year.[3]

The artist's portrayal of James Savage at age sixty-five exhibits Staigg's reputation for capturing with characteristically broad brush strokes, the easy self-assurance and dignified bearing of distinguished older sitters.[4] Born in Boston in 1784, the son of Habijah and Elizabeth (Tudor) Savage, James Savage graduated from Harvard College in 1803 and was admitted to the bar in 1807. Savage served several terms in the Massachusetts legislature and founded "The Provident Institution for Savings in the town of Boston" in 1816. Also important for his work as an antiquarian, Savage compiled the *Genealogical Dictionary of the First Settlers of New England* and edited an authoritative edition of the *Journal* of Governor John Winthrop (no. 12). He was a member of the Harvard board of overseers, and a founder of the Boston Athenaeum. Elected to membership in the Massachusetts Historical Society in 1813, he served in a number of capacities including as the fifth president from 1841 to 1855 (no. 134). James Savage died in Boston in 1873.[5]

Though in the traditional oval shape of the miniature, both these portraits are of the larger size that became popular in the nineteenth century. These family keepsakes were less personal and were meant to be placed on a tabletop or shelf rather than kept in a pocket or worn as jewelry.

The Society owns a number of other works by Staigg, including a crayon-and-chalk portrait of Edward Everett and miniatures of Sarah Ellen Francis (1841), Daniel Webster (1844 and 1846), and Elizabeth Welles Perkins (1845).

J.L.P.

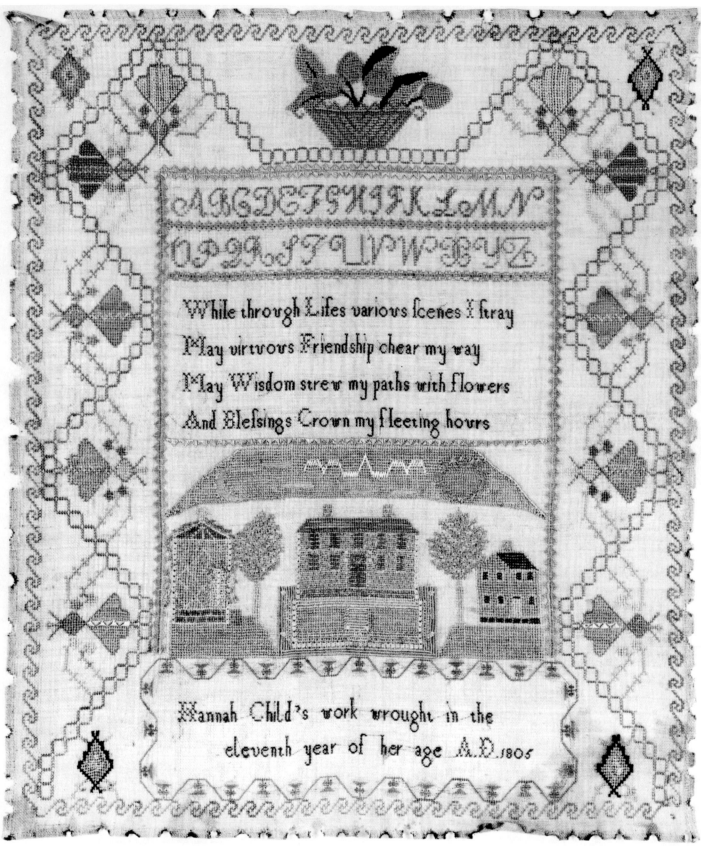

127

pont and Blanchard families; Lydia Little's mourning picture (ca. 1803); and a genealogical sampler (1827) done by Hannah Child's younger sister, Hannah Richards Child.

S.W.F.

1. Child 1881, p. 407; *Independent Chronicle*, Jan. 30, 1809.
2. Bolton 1921, pp. 1–2.
3. Ring 1975, pp. 38–39.
4. Krueger 1978.

128

Joseph Alexander Ames (1816–1872)
William Hickling Prescott (1796–1859)
1844
Oil on canvas
23¼ in. (59 cm) x 19 in. (48.4 cm)
Gift of Marian Lawrence Peabody, 1974

Historian of Spain's Golden Age, William Hickling Prescott spent his childhood in Salem, Massachusetts. His father was Judge William Prescott; his grandfather was Colonel William Prescott, hero of Bunker Hill (see no. 53). Young William attended Harvard and planned to read for the law in his father's office after graduation. Lively, witty and favored by all who knew him, his fortunate circumstances were interrupted by an accident during his third year at college. As he was leaving the dining room, a hard crust of bread flung playfully by another student struck Prescott's left eye resulting in a permanent loss of vision in that eye. After this trauma, he also experienced decreasing vision and painful inflammations in his sighted eye. William spent many months convalescing in a darkened room, attended by his mother and read to by his sister (see no. 129).[1]

Although he managed to finish school and entered his father's office, problems with his right eye forced the young man to give up his plans to become a lawyer. Though it was not necessary for him to earn a living, he wanted a useful life and determined to turn his efforts toward a literary career.[2] During this same period, Prescott married Susan Amory of Boston. He brought her home to his father's house where they raised their family and remained until the judge's death in 1844.

After six years of studying European history and literature with the aid of hired secretaries who read to him for many hours each day, he chose Spanish history as his field. After ten more years of study, he published *The History of the Reign of Ferdinand and Isabella, the Catholic* in 1837. It was an immediate success in Boston and earned acclaim in England as well.[3] *The Conquest of Mexico* (1843), *The Conquest of Peru* (1847) and three volumes of a history of Philip II were completed in the author's lifetime. Prescott related history as an exciting story in the romantic tradition of Sir Walter Scott whom he admired.[4] Fanny Appleton Longfellow wrote of *The Conquest of Mexico*, "It has the fascination of a romance and cannot be left. . . . Mr. Prescott seems to have seen it all with his own eyes."[5] In compiling these volumes, he introduced modern historical research methods including careful documentation and the use of multiple archives.[6]

This oil sketch of Prescott was described by the historian himself in his correspondence. In March 1845, a year after he sat for the popular Boston portraitist Joseph Ames, Prescott wrote to his English publisher to explain that he was sending two portraits of himself by Ames from which he wished one engraving to be drawn. Quipping that he didn't wish to be engraved

> with two heads like double-headed Janus, but the first is a sketch done in a few sittings and considered by my friends and those not my friends as a perfect likeness. The other is . . . a very rich and elaborate painting, but the likeness is generally thought by no means the equal to the first. They are both painted from me by the same artist. . . . He wishes the engraver to follow the head of the sketch and the fig-

128

> ure, costume, etc., of the finished portrait. The artist's name is Ames, and pray be careful that his name appears as the painter on the engraving. I would rather have an eye left out—and one of mine is only good to look at, for I can't see with it-than his name. . . .[7]

These instructions were followed by the engraver William Greatbach for the print which serves as a frontispiece for the 1847 American edition of Prescott's *Biographical and Critical Miscellanies*.

Self-trained and native to New Hampshire, Joseph Alexander Ames counted such luminaries as Ralph Waldo Emerson and Daniel Webster as sitters as well as Prescott.[8] A contemporary of the painter related that

> one of these . . . attracted the attention of Washington Allston who praised it for its fine color, which was one of Ames' strong points; and the favorable criticism was the means of starting the fame of this afterwards celebrated portrait painter whose power was genius, and genius alone, for he studied with no one.[9]

Though he worked and exhibited mainly in Boston, Ames was known in other eastern cities. He traveled to Italy in 1848, where he painted Pope Pius IX.[10] The Historical Society also owns a full-length portrait by Ames of Daniel Webster (prob. 1852) in a relaxed pose at his farm in Marshfield, Massachusetts, as well as a head-and-shoulders study for the same portrait.

J.L.P.

1. Prescott 1925, pp. ix–xi.
2. Ibid.
3. Ibid., p. xi.
4. Prescott 1838, pp. 431–474.
5. Longfellow 1956, pp. 103–104.
6. Allan Nevins, in Gardiner 1969, p. ix.

129

7. Ibid., p. 534.
8. Clement 1880, 1:14–15.
9. Ibid.
10. Fielding 1974, p. 7.

129

Ralph Wedgwood, Jr.
Noctograph (Stylographic Manifold Writer)
London, ca. 1816
10¼ in. (26.2 cm) x 17⅝ in. (45 cm), open
Red morocco leather folder; inside front cover: advertisement of manufacturer, Ralph Wedgwood, Jr.; in center: ivory stylus, held by strap; inside back cover: writing device, consisting of 16 horizontal brass wires; stamped in gold within rectangle on outside of front cover: *W.H. Prescott / London*.
Gift of William Amory, 1873

Following a brief and unsuccessful venture in his father's law practice, William Hickling Prescott went on The Grand Tour of Europe between 1815 and 1817.[1] While visiting London in 1816, he purchased a writing aid for the blind, which had been newly patented by its inventor, Ralph Wedgwood, Jr. Prescott immediately wrote home that the stylographic manifold writer, or noctograph, was "a very happy invention for me."[2] Years later, he described the noctograph to a friend:

> It is a simple apparatus, often described by me for the benefit of persons whose vision is imperfect. It consists of a frame of the size of a sheet of paper, traversed by brass wires, as many as lines are wanted on the page, and with a sheet of carbonated paper, such as is used for getting duplicates, pasted on the reverse side. With an ivory or agate stylus the writer traces his characters between the wires on the carbonated sheet, making indelible marks, which he cannot see, on the white page below. This treadmill operation has its defects; and I have repeatedly supposed I had accomplished a good page, and was proceeding in all the glow of composition to go ahead, when I found I had forgotten to insert a sheet of my writing paper below, that my labor had all been thrown away, and that the leaf looked as blank as myself. Notwithstanding these and other whimsical distresses of the kind, I have found my writing case my best friend in my lonely hours; and with it I have written nearly all that I have sent into the world the last forty years.[3]

With the aid of this device Prescott wrote his famous histories including the *Conquest of Mexico*, a sheet of which is shown here inserted into the noctograph. During his prolific career, Prescott used only two noctographs, both of which are now in the Society's collection.[4] The Prescott Papers include noctograph manuscripts for several of his histories, along with his correspondence with family and colleagues. Another noctograph frame is also at the Society in the Francis Parkman Collection.

S.W.F.

1. Gardiner 1969, pp. 21–23.
2. Ticknor 1864, p. 123.
3. W. H. Prescott to George E. Ellis, June 1, 1857, George E. Ellis Papers, MHS.
4. Ticknor 1864, p. 123n.; MHS *Proceedings*, 78(1966):157.

of butchery begun. *We had not gone a mile, when the prairie in front was literally black with buffalo. 2. and I put after them, driving them up the hills on the right. The mare brought me upon the rear of a large herd. In the clouds of dust I could scarcely see a yard, and dashed on almost blind, amidst the trampling of the fugitives. Their numbers became gradually visible, as they shouldered along.*

130

130

Francis Parkman (1823–1893)
Oregon Trail Notebook, June 16–September 2, 1846
Manuscript
Unpaged, 6 ⅛ in. (15.6 cm) x 4 in. (10.1 cm)
Gift of Elizabeth P. Cordner, 1942

131

Francis Parkman (1823–1893)
The California and Oregon Trail
New York: G. P. Putnam, 1849
448 p., 7 ⅞ in. (19.8 cm) x 5 ⅜ in. (13.5 cm)
Inscribed: *Rev. G. E. Ellis from his friend F. Parkman, Jr.*
Bequest of George E. Ellis, 1895

The historian Francis Parkman was born in Boston in 1823, the son of the Rev. Francis Parkman, minister of the New North Church in Hanover Street. Parkman was high-strung as a child, and his parents sent him to live with his maternal grandfather, Samuel Hull, in comparatively rural Medford. In that country setting he developed an abiding love for natural history and the outdoors. Parkman later attended the Chauncy Hall School in Boston and Harvard College, where he graduated in 1844. He spent a large part of his free time out-of-doors, and was a great sportsman and athlete, taking his vacations from school in the northern woods, and maintaining journals of his experiences which later served as the source material for some early writings.[1]

Parkman first broke into print in the *Knickerbocker Magazine* in 1845, with some tales based on his experiences in the northern woods. Then, in the early spring of 1846 his cousin Quincy A. Shaw invited Parkman to accompany him on a hunting expedition in the far west. At St. Louis they engaged Henry Chatillon, an expert Rocky

Mountain trapper, as guide. In May 1846 the party started on the Oregon Trail, the major route westward across the country from the Mississippi River. Parkman joined up with a roving band of Oglala Sioux warriors, with whom he spent three weeks hunting buffalo and living on the trail in the manner of the Native Americans. Parkman recorded his adventures in three notebooks, one of which is shown here, and later used these notes as the basis for his popular adventure narrative *The California and Oregon Trail* (later simply *The Oregon Trail*).[2]

When he returned from his Western sojourn, worn out with dysentery and the general hardships experienced among the Sioux, Parkman suffered a complete breakdown and continued to be plagued throughout his life by various "nervous disorders" and physical disabilities. Due to his failing eyesight, he was forced to dictate his narrative for *The California and Oregon Trail* to Quincy Shaw and other willing assistants.[3] The book first appeared in serial form in the *Knickerbocker*, the first installment in February of 1847 and the last in February of 1849. The narrative was so popular that it substantially boosted sales of the magazine. The first edition of the book, shown here, was published in 1849, and is to this day his best-known work. Parkman has been criticized for not placing his story in the historical context of the great Westward Expansion, but he weathered this criticism, and the story remains a fascinating adventure narrative in the romantic tradition.[4]

Parkman's great lifetime achievement was the multi-volume history *France and England in North America*, the last volume of which appeared shortly before his death. Although he formulated the plan for this comprehensive work while still in college, the first two volumes (*History of the Conspiracy of Pontiac*) did not appear until 1851. Francis Parkman died in 1893, shortly after the final volume in the series, *Half-Century of Conflict*, appeared in print. Today, just short of a hundred years after his death, Parkman's voluminous output, remarkable considering his disabilities, still marks him as one of the foremost writers of American history.

Francis Parkman was a resident member of the Massachusetts Historical Society from 1852 until his death in 1893. His personal papers were given to the Society between 1885 and 1942 by Parkman and his descendants.

K.H.G.

1. Morison 1955, pp. 7–10.
2. Ibid., pp. 14–15.
3. Wade in Parkman 1947, pp. 385–386.
4. Doughty 1962, p. 152.

THE California & OREGON TRAIL.

131

132

133

132
Felix Octavius Carr Darley (1822–1888)
Sketch for the Frontispiece of The California and Oregon
Trail
ca. 1849
Black and gray wash with graphite on paper
7½ in. (18.9 cm) x 6 in. (15.3 cm)
From the Francis Parkman Papers

133
Felix Octavius Carr Darley (1822–1888)
Sketch for the Frontispiece of The California and Oregon
Trail
ca. 1849
Black and gray wash with graphite on paper
7½ in. (19.1 cm) x 5¼ in. (13.2 cm)
From the Francis Parkman Papers

Felix Octavius Carr Darley was probably the most popular American illustrator during the mid-nineteenth century. The youngest child of a large theatrical family, Darley was the son of two successful English actors, who had performed in New York and Boston before settling in Philadelphia. At the age of fourteen, Darley was apprenticed as a clerk for the Dispatch Transportation Line. However, his first love was drawing, and he spent most of his leisure time sketching. Largely self-taught, he copied works by old masters, as well as anatomical illustrations in order to gain an understanding of human and animal forms. The contemporary influences on Darley were primarily European artists, such as the English sculptor and illustrator John Flaxman (1755–1826); the German illustrator Frederick August Moritz Retzsch (1779–1857); and the French painter and illustrator Emile-Jean-Horace Vernet (1789–1863). However, the American artist George Catlin (1796–1872), who was an important

chronicler of Native American life, also exerted a strong influence on the young artist.[1]

Darley was able to abandon his commercial career in 1841, after his sketches attracted the attention of Thomas Dunn English (1819–1902), a prominent Philadelphia writer and critic.[2] Darley began his career as a designer by illustrating local magazines, such as *Graham's Lady's and Gentleman's Magazine* and *Godey's Lady's Book*. In 1843, some of his drawings were published in two autonomous works, *Scenes in Indian Life* and *In Town and About: or Pencillings and Pennings*. Both these works captured the essence of his style: realism, humor, action, and a distinctly American point of view. Tuckerman, writing about Darley in 1867, also noted his talent as a satirist: "the idea of being caricatured by Darley, may well add to a sensitive man's horrors of life. . . . Two or three lines suffice Darley to metamorphose his fellow-creatures, while he preserves their identity."[3]

In 1848, Darley relocated to New York City, an important center for publishing, and there his reputation was further enhanced through some commissions for book illustrations from prominent authors. He became the definitive illustrator for the works of Washington Irving, beginning with *Rip Van Winkle* (1848), *The Sketchbook* (1848) and *The Legend of Sleepy Hollow* (1849). For Francis Parkman's *The California and Oregon Trail* (1849), Darley's designs were worked into wood engravings with tint-block backgrounds by engraver Benjamin Childs (1814–1863).[4]

Darley augmented his income by designing vignettes for bank notes during the mid-1850s. During the same

period, he was commissioned to design the illustrations for a thirty-two-volume set of the complete works of James Fenimore Cooper, a writer who combined adventure and romance with American patriotism.[5] Although his popularity declined following the Civil War, Darley continued to work and exhibit his drawings until his death in 1888. An obituary summed up the artist as "a noble and lovable character, full of earnest aspiration and faithful endeavor to accomplish his best work but with remarkably little of mere personal ambition."[6]

In these two preliminary sketches for the frontispiece of Parkman's book, a Native American on horseback is the central figure. In both instances the tepees below, the animal skull in the foreground, and the craggy mountain in the background evoke the American Southwest. The second drawing is closer to the finished design with the central figure returning to his village and the buffalo grazing in the distance.

S.R.M.

1. Darley 1978, pp. 1, 4, 5.
2. Ibid., p. 6.
3. Tuckerman 1967, p. 475.
4. Bolton 1951, p. 155.
5. Darley 1978, pp. 12–13.
6. *American Architect and Building News*, 23(1888):178.

134

John Adams Whipple (1882–1891)
Members of the Massachusetts Historical Society
Boston, May 17, 1855
Salt print (crystallotype)
8⁵⁄₁₆ in. (21.1 cm) x 16 ¾ in. (40 cm)
From the Archives of the Massachusetts
Historical Society

In a letter from Robert Charles Winthrop to Edward Everett dated May 15, 1855, the newly elected president of the Historical Society requested Everett's presence at the studio of crystallotypist John Adams Whipple on the following Thursday to honor, through a group portrait, the presidency of James Savage, who had just left that office at the Society after serving for fourteen years. "Our idea," wrote Winthrop, "is to group the members around Mr. Savage so as to make the picture complimentary to him, and commemorative of his administration."[1]

Charles Francis Adams recorded his impressions of the sitting in his diary for May 17, 1855: "we met at Whipple's room at twelve o'clock, and the gathering was one not a little curious as embracing much of the best talent of the state, and a high literary character. . . . I sat on one end of the semicircle where I had a fine opportunity to observe the varying expression of all the men. He made us sit for three successive impressions and would of have had more but for Mr. Savage's refusal to stay longer."[2]

James Savage is seated in the center of the photograph with the Society's balloting box, the samp bowl of King Philip (see no. 135), before him.

The photograph is printed in a rich brown tone, and the image itself has been heavily retouched. Artists were often employed by photographers for the purpose of retouching, tinting, and painting photographs. In this case, shirt fronts have been enhanced with white pigment, and black ink was used to define the tablecloths, shoes, trousers, jackets, hats, and eyes.

Twenty-six of the sixty members of the Society are pictured, and together they represent the outstanding figures of mid-nineteenth-century Boston. Seated, left to right, are: Charles Francis Adams (1807–1886), Reverend Joseph Barlow Felt (1789–1869), Nathan Appleton (1779–1861), Reverend William Jenks (1778–1866), John Chipman Gray (1793–1881), Jared Sparks (1789–1866), Josiah Quincy (1772–1864), James Savage (1784–1873), Lemuel Shaw (1781–1861), Edward Everett (1794–1865), William Hickling Prescott (1796–1859), Daniel Appleton White (1776–1861), David Sears (1787–1871), Abbott Lawrence (1792–1855), Reverend George Washington Blagden

(1802–1884), and George Ticknor (1791–1871). Standing, left to right, are: Reverend Chandler Robbins (1810–1882), Charles Deane (1813–1889), Richard Frothingham (1812–1880), Nathaniel Bradstreet Shurtleff (1810–1874), Joseph Willard (1798–1865), Reverend William Parsons Lunt (1805–1857), Reverend Samuel Kirkland Lothrop (1804–1886), Reverend George Edward Ellis (1814–1894), George Stillman Hillard (1808–1879), and Robert Charles Winthrop (1809–1894).

John Adams Whipple was born in 1822 at Grafton, Massachusetts. He was part of the first generation of American daguerreotypists-photographers and was one of Boston's premier photographers throughout his thirty-year career (1844–1874). He became interested in the daguerreotype process upon reading about Daguerre's process during the winter of 1839–1840. He successfully duplicated the process and then moved to Boston where he began to manufacture chemicals for the daguerreotype process. After the chemicals took an adverse effect on his health, Whipple stopped the manufacturing aspect of his career and moved behind the camera.[3]

In 1844, with the help of his photographic assistant William B. Jones, Whipple began experimenting with paper photographs using glass as a negative. This process was later known as crystallotype and patented on June 25, 1850. On December 18, 1849 Whipple, again in collaboration with Jones, began an attempt to daguerreotype the moon from the Harvard University observatory, an experiment that was not fully successful until March 14, 1851. From this site, they also daguerreotyped the star Alpha Lyra, the planet Jupiter, and a partial solar eclipse. They made about seventy daguerreotypes in all. Of these, the observatory now owns four images of the moon, four of a partial solar eclipse, and one of the planet Jupiter which was taken in 1858. To honor his pioneering lunar work, a peak on the moon's surface is officially known as Mount John Adams Whipple. Among other accomplishments, Whipple was in 1852 the first to daguerreotype a graduating class at Harvard. He retired from photography in 1874 and became a bookseller and publisher of religious books.[4]

This Whipple crystallotype is just one example from the Historical Society's vast photographic collection. The collection is particularly strong in portraits and spans the entire history of photography including the earliest daguerreotypes in Boston (ca. 1839–1840), early paper photographs of North Conway, New Hampshire (ca. 1853), the Civil War cartes-de-visite and albumen photographs, family snapshots, and modern political photographs.

H.C.S.

1. Edward Everett Papers, MHS.
2. Adams Papers, MHS.
3. Robinson 1980.
4. Pierce 1987, pp. 105–106.

135

135
Attributed to the Wampanoag
Bowl
Southeastern Massachusetts, 1655–1675
Elm burl
H. 7 in. (17.8 cm), W. 14 3/8 in. (36.5 cm), D. 13 1/8 in. (33.3 cm)
Inscribed, in gilt: *A Trophy / from the Wigwam of King Philip / When he was Slain in 1676 / by Richard. Presented, by Elezr / Richard, his Grandson*
Gift of Isaac Lothrop, 1804

Traditionally known as "King Philip's Samp Bowl," this carved elm burl is a fine example of Algonquian craftmanship. Samp, or *nasaump*, the Algonquian term for the porridge made from ground Indian corn, was served in such bowls which were generally carved from hardwood knots or burls using crude flints, scrapers, and stone adze blades. Seven Algonquian bowls are known to exist, all monumental in size with ornamental handles depicting animal heads.[1] This bowl was one of the earliest gifts to the Society and has been an important object in the Society's collections for nearly 200 years.[2] In 1803 Isaac Lothrop, one of the first members of the Society and register of probate for Plymouth County,[3] purchased the bowl from Eleazer Richard for eight dollars. Less than a year later, Lothrop gave the bowl to the Society at which time members voted to have the bowl inscribed.[4] The inscription, lettered in gold, inaccurately notes that one Richard killed King Philip. Lothrop's receipt from Eleazer Richard simply claimed that the samp bowl "was a portion of the trophy assigned to Eleazer Richard great-grandfather of the subscriber who made one of the party that terminated the existence" of King Philip.[5] His identity is uncertain, but he may have been one Eleazer Rickard of Plympton, Massachusetts.

Metacomet, or King Philip as he was more popularly known among colonists, was the second son of Massasoit, sachem of the Wampanoag tribe of southeastern Massachusetts and one of the New England Native Americans who established peaceful relations with the *Mayflower* pilgrims. In 1662 King Philip succeeded his brother,

Wamsutta, as Wampanoag chief and tried to preserve the peaceful coexistence between Indians and Englishmen, which his father had established forty years earlier. But the colonists' growing need for land strained these relations. Gradually, the accord between the Native Americans and colonists disintegrated, as King Philip united the fractious New England tribes against the expanding population of colonists. With the outbreak of war in June 1675, Philip's plans for a Native American nation to rival the English one seemed possible.

King Philip's united nation, however, was short-lived. Tribal disputes divided the people, eroding what power they had mustered. Inevitably, the Native Americans were no match for the well-armed colonists. In August 1676 a volunteer company under the command of Captain Benjamin Church ambushed King Philip's encampment in the marshes near Mount Hope. During this skirmish Philip was fatally shot by a Native American volunteer.[6] Although King Philip's War lasted little more than a year (1675–1676), it resulted in the destruction of many colonial towns and the almost complete extermination of Native Americans in New England. Many who survived either fled to tribes in the West or were transported as slaves to the West Indies.[7]

King Philip's samp bowl took a place of pride at the Society not only as a rare Native American artifact with a unique history, but also as a ceremonial object. Throughout much of the nineteenth century, the bowl was used for balloting with corn and beans at Society meetings.[8] It appears in the center of the 1855 photograph of members (no. 134).

Other objects relating to King Philip's War collected in the early years of the Society include Captain Benjamin Church's sword, worn the day Philip was killed, and a flintlock from the rifle reputedly used to kill Philip. Manuscript collections, notably the John Davis Papers, contain a number of accounts of King Philip's War and discussions of Native American relations during that period.

S.W.F.

1. Willoughby 1935, pp. 260–262.
2. MHS *Proceedings*, 1st ser., 1(1791–1835):163, 168, 7(1863–1864):177.
3. MHS *Proceedings*, 2nd ser., 3(1886–1887):384; MHS *Collections*, 2nd ser., 1(1814):258–260.
4. MHS *Proceedings*, 1st ser., 1(1791–1835):163.
5. Ibid., 163n.
6. Church 1975, p. 153.
7. Hodge 1907, pp. 690–691; Leach 1958, pp. 236–237.
8. MHS *Proceedings*, 1st ser., 1(1791–1835):163n.

136
Richard Henry Dana (1815–1882)
Two Years before the Mast
Manuscript
307 p., 10 in. (25.4 cm) x 8 in. (20.3 cm)
From the Richard Henry Dana Papers

Richard Henry Dana, Jr., the son of poet and essayist Richard Henry Dana and Ruth C. (Smith) Dana, entered Harvard in 1831 but was forced to abandon his studies after two years due to eye trouble resulting from a bout

with measles. Convinced that a sea voyage and hardy outdoor life would cure his eyesight, Dana signed on as a common sailor on the brig *Pilgrim*, commanded by Francis A. Thompson, bound from Boston for California to trade on the coast for hides. The brig sailed from Boston on August 14, 1834, rounded Cape Horn, and arrived at Santa Barbara on January 14, 1835. There, after sixteen months of trading up and down the coast, Captain Thompson received orders to exchange ships with Captain Edward H. Faucon of the *Alert*. Consequently, Dana returned to Boston aboard the *Alert* on September 22, 1836. The voyage had succeeded in strengthening his eyesight and in building his character in other ways, as noted by his biographer Charles F. Adams: "He went away a town-nurtured, college stripling of nineteen; he returned a robust man of twenty-one. The heroic treatment to which he had recourse settled the difficulty with his eyes; thereafter they gave him no more trouble."[1] Dana returned to Harvard and graduated in June 1837 at the head of his class, whereupon he immediately entered law school.

During his few leisure hours at sea, Dana kept brief notes in his journal and then expanded them into a full account of the voyage.[2] This account was subsequently lost at the wharf in Boston with his trunk containing all his possessions collected on the voyage. Later, during law school, Dana reconstructed his account from the brief journal entries, which fortunately were not left in the trunk. He read the manuscript (shown here) to his father and to his uncle-by-marriage, the artist and poet Washington Allston, who advised him to publish it. He turned to Harper's of New York for this project, with William Cullen Bryant to help him negotiate a contract. The book was published in 1840, the year Dana was admitted to the bar. For "one of the most successful American books of the century, and the best book of its kind ever written," Dana received only a flat fee of $250 and two dozen printed copies from Harper's.[3]

Dana's purpose in writing the book was to give an account of sea life "before the mast," or from the view of the common sailor, and to ensure that this much-maligned segment of society would be treated with justice in the future. An English edition soon appeared, and his London publisher paid him an honorarium greater than his fee from Harper's. Other foreign editions followed, and Dana was much celebrated at home and abroad for his work. In fact, when he returned to California on a visit in 1859, he found (somewhat to his astonishment) that he was a celebrity there, and that almost everyone had read the book, it being the only work available for many years that described the California coast in some detail.[4] In 1868, the original copyright expired, and he brought out a revised "author's edition" under a much more lucrative arrangement with Houghton Mifflin Company. This edition contained an added chapter, "Twenty-Four Years After," which described the 1859 visit and updated information on the crew of the *Pilgrim* and other characters mentioned in the original book.[5]

Soon after the book's publication, Dana began to specialize in admiralty cases in his law practice, and he went on to a distinguished career in law. In 1841, he published his manual *The Seaman's Friend*, which became a standard work on maritime law. While Dana was opposed by nature to the excesses of the abolitionists, he allied slowly until she was lost in the hollow between. She was undisturbed for some time until the noise of our bows gradually approaching roused him, & when turned lifting his head he stared upon us for a moment, & then spread his wide wings & took his flight. ——

—— Chap. 6

Monday Nov 19th. This was a black day in our calender. At seven o clk in the morning, it being our watch below, were aroused from a sound sleep by the cry of "all hands ahoy! a man overboard!" This unwonted cry sent a thrill of fear through the mind of every one, & hurrying on deck we found the vessel hove flat aback with all her studding-sails set, for the boy who was at the helm left it to throw something overboard, & the carpenter, who was an old sailor, knowing that the wind was light, put the helm down & hove her aback. The watch on deck were lowering away the quarter boat, & I got on deck just in time to heave myself into her as she was leaving the side, but it was not until out upon the wide Pacific in our little boat that I knew whom we had lost. It was George Ballmer, a young English sailor, who was prized by the officers as an active & willing seaman, & by the crew as a lively, hearty fellow & a good shipmate. He was going aloft to fit a strap round the maintopmast head for ringtail halyards, & had the strap & block, a coil of halyards, & a

himself with the Free-Soil movement in politics, and was the attorney for the defense of the persons involved in the rescue of the fugitive slave Shadrach in Boston (1851), and in the Anthony Burns case (1854). Upon witnessing Shadrach's rescue in Boston, Dana noted in his diary for February 15, 1851, "How can any right-minded man do else than rejoice at the rescue of a man from the hopeless, endless slavery to which a *recovered fugitive* is always doomed."[6]

Dana was elected a resident member of the Massachusetts Historical Society in 1858. While in Rome writing a treatise on international law, he died suddenly of pneumonia in 1882.

The large collection of Dana Family Papers at the Massachusetts Historical Society consists primarily of the papers of four generations of the Dana family: diplomat and jurist Francis Dana (1743–1811), Richard H. Dana (1787–1879), Richard H. Dana, Jr., and attorney Richard H. Dana (1851–1931). Richard Henry Dana, Jr.'s papers include correspondence, legal papers, diaries, and other miscellaneous volumes. The Society also holds the logs kept by Captain Edward H. Faucon (who exchanged ships with Captain Thompson in California) for the ship *Alert* from November 28, 1834 to May 20, 1835, and the brig *Pilgrim*, May 21, 1835 to July 6, 1837.

K.H.G.

1. Adams 1895, 1:14.
2. Dana 1911, p. xii.
3. Adams 1895, p. 26.
4. Dana 1911, p. 468.
5. Adams 1895, pp. 25–27.
6. Dana Family Papers, vol. 151, MHS.

137
Margaret Fuller (1810–1850)
Letter to James Freeman Clarke, Groton, Massachusetts,
April 12, 1836
Manuscript
4 p., 9 7/8 in. (25 cm) x 7 7/8 in. (19.9 cm)
Gift of Alice de V. Perry, 1985

When that blush does not come naturally into my face I do not drop a veil to make people think it is there. All this may be very "unlovely" but it is I.

Transcendentalist author, literary critic, editor, teacher, reformer, and revolutionary, Margaret Fuller had a brief but extraordinary life, which has inspired feminists since the nineteenth century. Interpretations of her work by generations of historians and literary critics help to demonstrate changes in views of the role and status of women since her death in 1850.

(Sarah) Margaret Fuller was born in Cambridgeport, Massachusetts, the daughter of a lawyer and social critic, Timothy Fuller, who provided her with a rigorous classical education at home but, as she later described it, "no natural childhood." Intellectually precocious, young Margaret soon entered the circle of writers growing up in Cambridge and Concord—the participants in the New England literary renaissance and related Transcendental movement of the 1830s and 1840s. Among her friends and colleagues were Ralph Waldo Emerson, Nathaniel Hawthorne, George Ripley, Henry David Thoreau, and James Freeman Clarke, a young Unitarian minister from Boston who moved in 1833 to Louisville. There, beginning in 1836, he published the *Western Messenger*, a Transcendentalist literary journal. Clarke helped Fuller develop her

137

literary career and published her early essays and poems.[1]

In 1836, when Fuller wrote the letter displayed here to Clarke, she was living in Groton, Massachusetts, where her family had moved in 1833. She planned to write a biographical study of Goethe, the romantic hero of her age, and was concerned about how to deal with Goethe's mistress, Christiane Vulpius, an affair that scandalized puritanical New Englanders. Fuller yearned to be free from provincial Groton, and provincial America as well: "How am I to get the information I want unless I go to Europe [?]" she asked Clarke.[2]

After the death of her father, Fuller was forced to abandon her travel plans and begin teaching to support her family. She continued her course of self-study, translated works by and about Goethe for George Ripley's *Specimens of Foreign Literature* series, and edited the *Dial*, the leading Transcendentalist periodical. During this time she supported herself by holding a series of "Conversations" (private classes) in Boston that gained a wide audience and influence. Her fame grew with the publication in 1843 of *Summer on the Lakes*, her "poetic impression" of America, and in 1845 of *Woman in the Nineteenth Century*, an impassioned and forceful argument for women's rights. Fuller's time spent at Brook Farm and her radical views are satirized in the character of Zenobia, the bluestocking reformer in Nathaniel Hawthorne's *The Blithedale Romance* (see no. 140).[3]

In 1846, Fuller at last was able to make her long-delayed trip to Europe as foreign correspondent for Horace Greeley's *New York Tribune. In* 1847 she settled in Rome, where she met and fell in love with the Marchese Giovanni Ossoli, a young Italian nobleman who supported the republican revolution underway in Italy. Their child, Angelo, was born in 1848; they apparently married the following year. When Rome fell to counterrevolutionary forces in 1849, they fled first to Florence and then to America, but they were shipwrecked and drowned off Fire Island, New York, in 1850.[4]

Fuller's concern with the relationship between Goethe's private life and public writings poignantly foreshadowed the difficulties that her friends, including James Freeman Clarke, faced when they published her letters in their *Memoirs of Margaret Fuller Ossoli* soon after her death. They eliminated almost all details of her personal life, and, in doing so, reduced her to a rather cold figure of Olympian intellect. A more serious problem for them was that in Italy she had lived with Ossoli, and the circumstance and date of their marriage was, at least, clouded.

Only brief extracts of Fuller's letters to Clarke, as published in the *Memoirs*, were available until 1985, when a treasure trove of almost ninety Fuller letters, together with a manuscript journal and poetry were found in a cache of James Freeman Clarke papers, which were donated to the Historical Society. The complete letters place Fuller's musings on art, literature, and philosophy in the context of her warm personal friendship with Clarke, and make her a more three-dimensional "human," but no less remarkable, figure.

B.M.P.

1. Fuller 1983, 1:30–37.
2. Ibid., 1:37–38, 248n.
3. *DLB*, 1:67–69.
4. Deiss 1969.

Brook Farm

Brook Farm, the best-known utopian experimental community in America, was founded by George and Sophia Ripley in the spring of 1841. A former Unitarian minister, Ripley was editor of *The Dial*, the principle journal of Transcendentalism, and his ideas for Brook Farm combined the theories of individual self-reliance from New England Transcendentalism with more radical social reforms of the time. He envisioned the community as one in which manual and intellectual labors would be united. In a letter to Ralph Waldo Emerson, the leading light of the Transcendental movement, Ripley explained his goals:

> Our objects, as you know, are to insure a more natural union between intellectual and manual labor than now exists, to combine the thinker and the worker as far as possible in the same individual . . . [where] thought would preside over the operations of labor, and labor would contribute to the expansion of thought.[1]

The practical application of these objectives came in the form of an agricultural community, located on 170 acres of poor-quality farmland at West Roxbury, near Boston.

To pay for the farm and supplies, shares were sold at $500 each, and stockholders could withdraw their initial investment with interest due by giving one year's notice to the trustees. Nathaniel Hawthorne, a fellow Transcendentalist, was one of the original subscribers to the community but later withdrew (see nos. 139, 140). A number of other leading Transcendentalists, including Emerson and Margaret Fuller, were frequent visitors to Brook Farm but never became members.

Membership in the community was granted by the vote of established members after the purchase of shares, in return for which individuals received free tuition in the community's school or five percent annual interest and one year's board in return for 300 days of labor.[2] The work of members was centered around the six major activities of teaching, farming, working in the manufacturing shops, domestic endeavors, work on the build-

138 (see also color plate VIII)

ings and grounds, and the planning of cooperative recreation projects. Social activities included picnics, lectures, boating parties, music, and dancing.

Throughout 1842 and 1843, the community thrived and in one year was visited by as many as 4000 guests, many simply curious Boston residents. The most successful ventures of Brook Farm were the school and the recreational aspect. The school attracted students from the south, Cuba, and the Philippines and was respected as a preparatory school by Harvard and even by the Unitarians against whom many of the Transcendentalists had rebelled.[3]

At the end of 1842 and throughout 1843, the community at Brook Farm underwent some significant changes. Ripley had become extremely interested in the writings and theories of François Marie Charles Fourier which had been translated and introduced in America in 1840 by Albert Brisbane, who would soon join the Brook Farm circle. Ripley felt that the farm needed to be a part of the larger movement of Fourierism, a model which seemed congruent with the community's social and organizational structure and present goals. Work should be done in organized groups rather than isolated labor and members would live together in one unitary dwelling called a "phalanstery." Although some in the community objected, it was renamed the "Brook Farm Phalanx," Fourier's term for a Utopian community, in January of 1844, a new constitution was drawn up to encompass Fourierist principles, and construction began on the phalanstery that spring.[4]

Since the farm's beginning it had continually suffered financial strain. The proceeds from the crops were simply not enough to support the costs. Ripley took out a third mortgage in 1843 and a fourth in 1845, making the total debt $17,445 in 1847.[5] In October of 1844, Secretary and Treasurer Charles A. Dana reported the first real profit of $1160.84, however it was swallowed up by the deficits of the previous years.[6] After the community's reorganization in 1845, Albert Brisbane and the Fourierists had also promised financial support but as late as the fall of 1846, nothing had been sent.[7] The greatest blow came on March 2, 1845, when the yet unfinished phalanstery caught fire and burned to the ground, causing a loss of over $7000. The community continued for some time amidst the financial troubles but finally disbanded in 1847.

The Historical Society holds the extant records of Brook Farm which include letters written primarily by Marianne Dwight and Anna Q. T. Parsons; the constitution and minutes (1843–1847); a ledger containing the daily purchases and sales for the community (1845–1847); and another ledger containing daily statements of profit and loss (November 1844–October 1846).

Although not the first Utopian community of its kind, Brook Farm was one of the most famous in the United States, due to its many well-known participants. It never achieved financial success, but it did fulfill Ripley's dreams for a social application of the Transcendentalist movement.

B.M.L.

1. Curtis 1961, p. 53.
2. Ibid., pp. 79–81.
3. Crowe 1967, pp. 151–157.

4. Ibid., pp. 172–182.

5. Rose 1981, p. 136.

6. Curtis 1961, p. 222.

7. Crowe 1967, p. 182.

138

Josiah Wolcott (ca. 1815–1885)

Brook Farm

1844

Oil on panel

14 in. (35 cm) x 19½ in. (49 cm)

Gift of Benjamin H. Codman, 1926

Josiah Wolcott's rendition of Brook Farm, the only contemporary view, captures the entrance to the community, along with the various buildings—the Hive, Shop, Eyrie, Cottage, and Pilgrim House—and the foundations for the new building, the phalanstery, which was begun in 1844 and burned to the ground in March 1846, prior to its completion. The setting for the community was bordered by a brook on one side and a pine forest on the other and was accessed by a private drive from the road. On the back of the painting panel is a pencil sketch detailing the specific buildings, primarily the Hive. The Hive, home of the previous owner Charles Ellis, was the center of Brook Farm from its inception, housing George Ripley's office, the dining room, kitchen, meeting rooms, and a number of sleeping quarters. Early in 1842, due to a housing shortage, the Eyrie was built to house the Ripleys and a number of new members and their families. When more accommodations were needed later that year, the Cottage and Pilgrim House were built, the latter also housing the laundry and the printing presses. Construction on the phalanstery began in 1844 upon the community's change in philosophy to Fourierism.[1]

The artist Josiah Wolcott was listed in the *Boston Directory* for many years as an "ornamental painter," and in 1837 he exhibited three landscapes at the Boston Athenaeum.[2] Wolcott later became better known as one of the illustrators for the *Carpet-Bag*, a weekly published in Boston in the early 1850s. The editors in their opening issue of March 29, 1851, wrote that Wolcott "has a peculiar genius for designing, and we expect many rich things from his pencil." In addition to individual drawings for the stories, Wolcott also designed the masthead for the *Carpet-Bag*.[3] His later work is unknown, but his occupation was still listed as artist at the time of his death.[4]

In January of 1837, Wolcott became a charter member of the Boston-based organization of the Religious Union of Associationists, one of several groups founded as followers to the theories of Fourierism. Other charter members included George and Sophia Ripley, the founders of Brook Farm, John S. Dwight, and Albert Brisbane, the leader of the Fourierist movement in America. Another member of the society was the former owner of the painting, John T. Codman, son of John Codman, a member of Brook Farm.[5]

B.M.L.

1. Crowe 1967, p. 182.

2. Groce 1957, p. 698; Athenaeum 1837.

3. Princeton 1968, 2:152.

4. MVR.

5. Religious Union of Associationists Records, MHS.

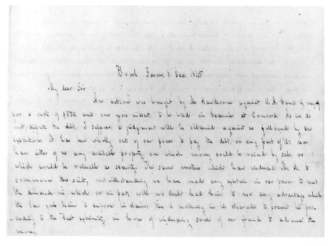

139

139

George Ripley (1802–1880)

Letter to Richard Henry Dana, Jr., Brook Farm,

December 8, 1845

Manuscript

3 p., 9¹¹⁄₁₆ in. (24.7 cm) x 7¹³⁄₁₆ in. (19.8 cm)

From the Richard Henry Dana Papers

140

Nathaniel Hawthorne (1804–1864)

The Blithedale Romance

Boston: Ticknor, Reed and Fields, 1852

228 p., 7⅛ in. (18 cm) x 4½ in. (10.4 cm)

Gift of Elizabeth H. Andrews, 1958

Nathaniel Hawthorne was invited to join the Brook Farm community by the Reverend George Ripley, whom he knew through occasionally attending meetings of a group called the Transcendental Club. Hawthorne became one of the original investors and spent six months of 1841 there. At first wildly enthusiastic, he soon found the novelty of the daily physical toil of carting wood, feeding cattle, milking, and shoveling manure wore off. Hawthorne discovered, not for the first time, that he needed to be alone in order to write, and the life of the commune offered no appropriate time or place to satisfy that need. Ripley's aspiration to create a community which would allow its members to find a balance and a union between manual and intellectual labors did not offer the solitude and leisure required by an artist of Hawthorne's habits and temperament.[1]

Hawthorne left the farm in August, but returned in September as a boarder, an arrangement which required no labor in the fields. Although he was now elected as a trustee, he still realized the communal activities were incompatible with his creative work. In a letter to his fiancée Sophia Peabody, dated September 3, 1841, he explained that the "real Me was never an associate of the community."[2] By the spring of 1842, he had left the farm completely, and, with money an ever-present concern, he wished to have his initial investment returned with interest.[3]

Hawthorne had purchased two shares of stock at $500 each in the hopes that Brook Farm would provide him the financial means to marry. On October 17, 1842, he wrote to Treasurer Charles A. Dana requesting the return of his investment. Ripley and Dana scraped together $475.95 and signed a note on November 7, 1842, promising to pay the remaining balance of $524.05. Hawthorne received subsequent payments of $32 on November 7, 1843 and $35 on November 23, 1844, however these were the last payments he would ever see. In September of 1845, Hawthorne finally sought legal action, suing for $800 by laying claim not only to his original investment but also for "other money . . . diverse Goods, Wares, and Merchandise . . . and for certain labor performed."[4] Suing for labor must have been the ultimate insult to Ripley as it directly clashed with his basic ideals of shared labor and profits in a communal setting.

Show here, Ripley's December 8, 1845 letter to attorney Richard Henry Dana, Jr., his wife's uncle, requested his advice in the matter. In the letter, Ripley disregarded Hawthorne's additional claims and worried solely about his claims for the remaining $530 for the debt plus interest. Ripley did not dispute the claim nor his guilt in the matter, but explained that he and Charles A. Dana had been "Wholly out of power to pay." Among other legal questions, Ripley requested advice on the Brook Farm Phalanx's responsibility in the matter, since neither he nor Dana had any money or property with which to pay the debt and since the Phalanx had assumed all debts of Brook Farm in its new incorporation, and inquired whether "going into Chancery" would protect them individually.

The case did not reach the courts until March 9, 1846, only a few days after the devastating fire in the Brook Farm phalanstery. The defendants did not appear, and the court awarded Hawthorne $585.90 for his claim against the debt in addition to court costs. Hawthorne never received his payment.

Despite the lawsuit, Hawthorne appears not to have had any bitterness about his stay there nor any personal animosity toward the group. His interlude at Brook Farm, which he described later "as being certainly the most romantic episode of his own life," did provide the material for his novel entitled *The Blithedale Romance*.

Hawthorne's two previous novels, *The Scarlet Letter* (1850) and *The House of the Seven Gables* (1851), remain today as his most popular works, but *The Blithedale Romance* is particularly interesting for the picture it presents of the failure of a communitarian enterprise. Hawthorne claimed that his story was to be read as fiction. Nevertheless, contemporary reviewers criticized him for using a fictional guise to distort the story of Brook Farm, while his characters were so realistic they were easily identifiable as known persons in the movement.[5] Whatever the author's intent, certainly the Brook Farm experiment provided the stuff from which a drama was created, a drama concerned with the roles of men and women in a self-governing society.

V.H.S., B.M.L.

1. Arvin 1929, pp. 95–106.
2. Lowance 1989, p. 72.
3. Curtis 1961, pp. 81–84.
4. Ibid., pp. 115, 147, 220, 262.
5. Lowance 1989, pp. 65, 91.

PREFACE.

In the "BLITHEDALE" of this volume many readers will, probably, suspect a faint and not very faithful shadowing of BROOK FARM, in Roxbury, which (now a little more than ten years ago) was occupied and cultivated by a company of socialists. The author does not wish to deny that he had this community in his mind, and that (having had the good fortune, for a time, to be personally connected with it) he has occasionally availed himself of his actual reminiscences, in the hope of giving a more life-like tint to the fancy-sketch in the following pages. He begs it to be understood, however, that he has considered the institution itself as not less fairly the subject of fictitious handling than the imaginary personages whom he has introduced there. His whole treatment of the affair is altogether incidental to the main purpose of the romance; nor does he put forward the slightest pretensions to illustrate a theory, or elicit a conclusion, favorable or otherwise, in respect to socialism.

In short, his present concern with the socialist

140

141
Samuel Sewall (1652–1730)
The Selling of Joseph
Boston: Printed by Bartholomew Green and John Allen, 1700
Pamphlet
3 pp., 10¹³⁄₁₆ in. (27.5 cm) x 7³⁄₁₆ in. (18.2 cm)
Gift of Robert C. Winthrop, 1863

This is the only extant copy of a remarkable pamphlet, written by Boston merchant and magistrate Samuel Sewall (see no. 26), and is the first anti-slavery tract to be published in New England.[1] In it Sewall set forth such proposals as "Liberty is in real value next unto life: None ought to part with it themselves or deprive others of it, but upon most mature Consideration"; "all Men, as they are the Sons of Adam, are Co-heirs; and have equal Right unto Liberty, and all other outward Comforts of Life"; "Originally, and Naturally, there is no such thing as Slavery"; and "There is no proportion between Twenty Pieces of Silver, and Liberty." This tract, so ahead of its time, has been characterized as "an acute, compact, powerful statement of the case against American slavery, leaving, indeed, nothing new to be said a century and a half afterward, when the sad thing came up for final adjustment."[2]

The pamphlet was possibly inspired by the case of Adam, the slave of John Saffin, a Boston merchant, land-

The Selling
OF
JOSEPH
A Memorial.

FORASMUCH *as Liberty is in real value next unto Life: None ought to part with it themselves, or deprive others of it, but upon most mature Consideration.*

The Numerousness of Slaves at this day in the Province, and the Uneasiness of them under their Slavery, hath put many upon thinking whether the Foundation of it be firmly and well laid; so as to sustain the Vast Weight that is built upon it. It is most certain that all Men, as they are the Sons of *Adam,* are Coheirs; and have equal Right unto Liberty, and all other outward Comforts of Life. *GOD hath given the Earth* [*with all its Commodities*] *unto the Sons of* Adam, *Psal* 115. 16. *And hath made of One Blood, all Nations of Men, for to dwell on all the face of the Earth, and hath determined the Times before appointed, and the bounds of their habitation : That they should seek the Lord. Forasmuch then as we are the Offspring of GOD &c. Act* 17.26,27,29. Now although the Title given by the last ADAM, doth infinitely better Mens Estates, respecting GOD and themselves; and grants them a most beneficial and inviolable Lease under the Broad Seal of Heaven, who were before only Tenants at Will : Yet through the Indulgence of GOD to our First Parents after the Fall, the outward Estate of all and every of their Children, remains the same, as to one another. So that Originally, and Naturally, there is no such thing as Slavery. *Joseph* was rightfully no more a Slave to his Brethren, than they were to him : and they had no more Authority to *Sell* him, than they had to *Slay* him. And if *they* had nothing to do to Sell him ; the *Ishmaelites* bargaining with them, and paying down Twenty pieces of Silver, could not make a Title. Neither could *Potiphar* have any better Interest in him than the *Ishmaelites* had. *Gen.* 37. 20, 27, 28. For he that shall in this case plead *Alteration of Property,* seems to have forfeited a great part of his own claim to Humanity. There is no proportion between Twenty Pieces of Silver, and LIBERTY. The Commodity it self is the Claimer. If *Arabian* Gold be imported in any quantities, most are afraid to meddle with it, though they might have it at easy rates ; lest it it should have been wrongfully taken from the Owners, it should kindle a fire to the Consumption of their whole Estate. 'Tis pity there should be more Caution used in buying a Horse, or a little lifeless dust ; than there is in purchasing Men and Women : Whenas they are the Offspring of GOD, and their Liberty is,
——————— *Auro pretiosior Omni.*

And seeing GOD hath said, *He that Stealeth a Man and Selleth him, or if he be found in his hand, he shall surely be put to Death.* Exod. 21. 16. This Law being of Everlasting Equity, wherein Man Stealing is ranked amongst the most atrocious of Capital Crimes : What louder Cry can there be made of that Celebrated Warning,

Caveat Emptor !

And

owner, slave-trader, deputy, Speaker of the House, councilor, and judge. Saffin hired out Adam for a term of seven years and promised him ensuing freedom upon his good behavior. Adam was apparently not at all docile, and Saffin decided to deny his freedom. After several trials over a few years, Adam eventually won his freedom in November 1703, with the help of Samuel Sewall. During the proceedings in 1701, Saffin attacked Sewall in print with *A Brief and Candid Answer to a late Printed Sheet Entitled the Selling of Joseph*, in which he defended slavery and his personal actions in Adam's case as if Sewall's tract had been directed against him personally.[3]

After Adam won his freedom, Sewall continued his mission as a defender of personal liberty. In late 1705 Sewall reprinted a "question-and-answer" from a London magazine, the *Athenian Oracle*, as a four-page sheet, which argued that slavery was unlawful and contrary to the laws of Christianity. While probably written by an Englishman, this pamphlet became the second anti-slavery tract printed in New England because of Sewall. He published this pamphlet as ammunition against a bill that had been introduced in the General Court against fornication or marriage of whites with Blacks or Native Americans. While Sewall succeeded in getting Native Americans excluded from the bill, the "Act for the Better Preventing of a Spurious and Mixt Issue" was passed to the detriment of Blacks. During the remainder of his life, Sewall's anti-slavery efforts were mostly limited to sending out copies of *The Selling of Joseph* and *The Athenian Oracle* to inquiring correspondents. This in itself was the act of a brave man who would feel adverse social repercussions as a result.[4]

K.H.G.

1. Kaplan in Sewall 1969, p. 28.
2. Tyler 1878, p. 100.
3. Kaplan in Sewall 1969, pp. 35–44
4. Ibid., pp. 46–51.

142

Phillis Wheatley (1754–1784)
Poems on Various Subjects, Religious and Moral
London: Printed for Archibald Bell, Bookseller, Aldgate; and sold by Edward Cox and Edward Berry, King-Street, Boston, 1773
124 p., 6 7/8 in. (17.4 cm) x 4 5/8 in. (11.7 cm)
Bequest of Robert Cassie Waterston, 1899

Phillis Wheatley, the author of this first book of poetry by a Black American, was born in West Africa. Between the ages of seven and eight, she was kidnapped and brought to America on the slave ship *Phillis*. After her arrival on July 11, 1761, the frail child was put up for auction by Boston slave dealer John Avery and purchased by Susanna Wheatley, wife of prominent Boston merchant John Wheatley.[1]

The Wheatleys provided Phillis a life and education far superior to that of the average Boston woman. She was tutored by the Wheatleys' daughter, Mary, and is said to have mastered English in sixteen months. Her status as a slave is somewhat misleading, as she was treated almost as a member of the family, serving as Mrs.

Wheatley's companion, doing very little menial labor, and often eating with the family. Her position in the household also allowed her to meet with many prominent Boston citizens of the day and her literary pursuits were encouraged when she began to write poetry, about the age of twelve.[2]

Her first poem to be published was "On Messrs Hussey and Coffin" in the Newport (Rhode Island) *Mercury* for December 1767.[3] In 1772, after having several poems individually published, Phillis attempted to publish a volume of her collected works. Her proposal to raise subscriptions listed twenty-eight titles and was printed in the *Boston Censor* in early 1772. However the advertisement did not generate enough response, and she then attempted a British publication.[4] Susanna Wheatley became involved in the proposed publication by writing to the Countess of Huntingdon and promoting her slave's work.[5]

In 1773 Phillis was advised to get some sea air because of her frail health, and she decided to accompany the Wheatley's son Nathaniel on a trip to London aboard the family-owned ship, the *London Packet*. Phillis was well-received in England but was unable to meet the Countess of Huntingdon, to whom the book was dedicated, who was in Wales at the time. Phillis felt obliged to return to Boston in July when she was informed of her mistress's ill health.[6]

Poems on Various Subjects, Religious and Moral contains thirty-nine poems, one-third more than were listed in her 1772 proposal. Due to growing political tensions, several poems were changed to better suit the British audience, and at least one poem, "A Farewell to America" was added after Phillis's arrival in London. The volume was published in London in September of 1773 through London subscriptions and the combined efforts of the Wheatleys and the Countess of Huntington. During that fall, Phillis was legally freed by her master.[7]

Upon her return to America, the advantages previously enjoyed by Phillis began to wane. Mary Wheatley had left the family home in 1771 to marry the Reverend John Lothrop, pastor of the Second Church in Boston, and Susanna Wheatley died in 1774, but Phillis was allowed to remain with the family until the death of her former master in 1778. In April of 1778, she married John Peters, a free black man, and they had three children, only one of whom survived. The marriage encountered disillusionment and financial difficulties, forcing Phillis to earn her living working in a boarding house. She lived the remainder of her life in poverty and misery, and her lifetime of poor health came to an end on December 5, 1784. She was buried with her last remaining child in an unmarked grave.[8]

Phillis's *Poems on Various Subjects* was her only published collection. She published two proposals for a second volume, in 1779 and 1784, however wartime shortages doomed the project to failure.[9] The first American edition was published in Philadelphia in 1786. It has been reprinted numerous times and widely anthologized. The volume shown here is at least a second printing, as it contains the dedication to the Countess of Huntingdon, a preface by the poet, a brief biographical sketch of her by John Wheatley, and an attestation signed by eighteen prominent Bostonians certifying the credibility of Wheatley's poems; none of these were present in the first printing. The frontispiece of both editions contains an engrav-

Publiſhed according to Act of Parliament, Sept.ˢ 1, 1773 by Archᵈ Bell.

Bookſeller Nº 8 near the Saracens Head Aldgate.

POEMS

ON

VARIOUS SUBJECTS,

RELIGIOUS AND MORAL.

BY

PHILLIS WHEATLEY,

NEGRO SERVANT to Mr. JOHN WHEATLEY,
of BOSTON, in NEW ENGLAND.

LONDON:

Printed for A. BELL, Bookſeller, Aldgate; and ſold by
Meſſrs. COX and BERRY, King-Street, BOSTON.

M DCC LXXIII.

ing of Wheatley, done by Scipio Moorhead, the slave of Rev. John Moorhead, pastor of the First Church of Presbyterian Strangers. At the insistence of the Countess of Huntingdon, Moorhead traveled to London to do the engraving specifically for the frontispiece. Wheatley's poetic tribute to him, "To S.M. [Scipio Moorhead]. A Young African Painter, On Seeing His Works," is published in her collective volume.[10] This edition was probably the "blue paperback sewn edition" rebound into an early-nineteenth-century hardcover binding.[11]

The Massachusetts Historical Society holds several of Wheatley's manuscript poems, some variations of those published in her 1773 collection, first published in the Society's *Proceedings*, as well as her letters to her friend Obour Tanner.[12]

B.M.L.

1. Wheatley 1989, pp. 2–3.
2. Ibid., pp. 4–5.
3. Robinson 1975, p. 14.
4. Wheatley 1989, pp. 186n–188n.
5. Robinson 1975, p. 14; Wheatley 1989, pp. 186n–188n,193n–194n.
6. Ibid., pp. 6, 8.
7. Ibid., p. 8.
8. Ibid., p. 10.
9. Ibid.
10. Kaplan 1973, pp. 157–158.
11. Robinson 1981, pp. 14–15.
12. MHS *Proceedings* 7(1863–1864):165–167, 267–279.

Elizabeth "Mumbet" Freeman (ca. 1742–1829)

Elizabeth Freeman, generally known as "Mumbet," was the first slave to be freed in Massachusetts as a result of the Bill of Rights to the 1780 state constitution. She and her younger sister Lizzie grew up as slave children and first lived in Claverack, Columbia County, New York, about twenty miles south of Albany.[1] John Ashley of Sheffield, Berkshire County, Massachusetts, acquired the girls from their owner, a Dutchman named Pieter Hogeboom, upon his marriage to Hogeboom's daughter, Annetje. The event, according to folklore, which prompted Mumbet to sue for her freedom occurred when the mistress of the house, Mrs. Ashley, attempted to strike Mumbet's sister with a heated kitchen shovel. Mumbet blocked the blow, but her arm was injured and she never regained its full use. According to novelist Catharine Maria Sedgwick, Mumbet was prompted to seek freedom after hearing the Declaration of Independence spoken, and according to historian Arthur Zilversmit the people of Berkshire County then adopted Mumbet's cause to test the constitutionality of slavery following the passage of the new state constitution.[2]

Whatever the reason, Elizabeth Freeman sought the help of Theodore Sedgwick (1746–1813) of Sheffield, prominent attorney and newly appointed member of the General Court. He was only at the beginning of an illustrious legal career, serving at various times in the state legislature, as a Senator from Massachusetts, and as a justice of the Mass. Supreme Judicial Court. Sedgwick accepted the case, in spite of the fact that the defendant, John Ashley, was a relative, a close friend, and a man of considerable political importance in the western part of the state.[3] Mumbet and another black slave, Brom, were the plaintiffs in the case *Brom & Bett v. J. Ashley Esq.*, and Sedgwick and Tapping Reeve served as their counsel. Ashley was also represented by two prominent attorneys, David Noble and John Canfield. A writ of replevin was filed by Sedgwick on behalf of the slaves to regain possession of their personal chattels, arguing that the slaves were not the legitimate property of Mr. Ashley. Ashley refused to release them, however, and was ordered to appear in the Court of Common Pleas in Great Barrington on August 21, 1781. Sedgwick argued that under the new Bill of Rights which read, "all men are born free and equal, and have certain natural, essential, and inalienable rights," among them the right to be free citizens of the Commonwealth, Mumbet and Brom were not legally slaves. The jury was persuaded and argued in favor of the plaintiffs, ordering Ashley to pay thirty shillings in damages and the cost of the suit. Ashley appealed the decision but later dropped the appeal, probably because the case of *Caldwell v. Jennison*, which ruled that slavery was unconstitutional in Massachusetts, had been decided in the intervening months.[4]

Following the decision, Mumbet became the paid domestic servant of Theodore and Pamela Sedgwick and their children. She served the family loyally, and protected the Sedgwick home alone against an attack in the winter of 1787 by followers of Shays's Rebellion while Theodore Sedgwick was working to end the insurrection.[5] Mumbet was greatly loved and respected by the Sedgwick family, and through her work in the household she was also able to achieve a certain level of financial independence. Before her death on December 28, 1829, she managed to purchase a small home of her own.

Elizabeth Freeman is buried next to Catharine Maria Sedgwick in the Sedgwick family plot in Stockbridge, Massachusetts, where the family moved from Sheffield in 1785. She is the only non-Sedgwick to be buried in the "Sedgwick Pie," a series of concentric circles of family headstones with Theodore and Pamela Sedgwick in the center. Her epitaph, written by Charles Sedgwick, son of Theodore, reads:

> ELIZABETH FREEMAN, known by the name of MUMBET died Dec. 28 1829. Her supposed age was 85 years. She was born a slave and remained a slave for nearly thirty years. She could neither read nor write, yet in her own sphere she had no superior nor equal. She neither wasted time, nor property. She never violated a trust, nor failed to perform a duty. In every situation of domestic trial, she was the most efficient helper, and the tenderest friend. Good mother fare well.

B.M.L.

1. Swan 1990, p. 51.
2. Zilversmit 1968, p. 619.
3. Foster 1974, p. 29.
4. Swan 1990, p. 54.
5. Ibid., p. 55.

143

143

Catharine Maria Sedgwick (1789–1867)
Mumbett, 1853
Manuscript
36 pp., 9 ¾ in. (24.7 cm) x 7 ⅞ in. (20.1 cm)
From the estate of Katherine Minot Channing, 1963

This manuscript story of the life of Mumbet was written by author Catharine Maria Sedgwick, and published as "Slavery in New England" in *Bentley's Miscellany* in 1853. The youngest daughter of Judge Theodore Sedgwick and Pamela Dwight Sedgwick, Catharine was born and educated in Stockbridge, Massachusetts. As a young adult, she divided her time between Stockbridge, Albany, where she lived with her brother Theodore, and New York with her sister. After the death of their father in 1813, she returned to Stockbridge to preside over the family home.

As an author, Sedgwick is considered responsible for the beginnings of the American domestic novel and by 1835, she was the most famous female author in the country. In 1822, she anonymously published her first novel, *A New England Tale*, and in 1824 she published *Redwood*. In addition to her novels, many of which were set in the Berkshire Hills of Massachusetts, she also published biographical sketches and books designed to help less fortunate individuals. She was active in the work of the Unitarian church and spent some years helping the Women's Prison Association.

Sedgwick's novels portray the American domestic scene and are often laced with a moral purpose. Her other works include *Hope Leslie* (1827), *The Linwoods: or "Sixty Years Since" in America* (1835), *The Poor Rich Man, and the Rich Poor Man* (1835), *Married or Single?* (1857), and *Letters from Abroad to Kindred at Home* (1841) written after a fifteen-month trip abroad in 1839–1840.[1]

Sedgwick was very close to her nurse, Elizabeth "Mumbet" Freeman, and this manuscript reflects her love and respect for the former slave. In it, Sedgwick describes Mumbet helping a poor black child who appealed to Mumbet's master, John Ashley, for assistance; her request to Judge Sedgwick and her fight for freedom; and her subsequent lifelong service to the Sedgwick family, including her loyal defense of the Sedgwick home during Shays's Rebellion in 1787.

In addition to three collections of Catharine Maria Sedgwick papers, the Society also holds several collections of Sedgwick family papers, including those of Judge Theodore Sedgwick, Pamela Dwight Sedgwick, and other Sedgwick children.

B.M.L.

1. DAB.

144 (see also color plate IX)

144

Susan Anne Livingston Ridley Sedgwick (1789–1867)
Elizabeth "Mumbet" Freeman (ca. 1742–1829)
1811
Watercolor on ivory
3 in. (7.5 cm) x 2 ⅛ in. (5.5 cm)
Gift of Maria Banyer Sedgwick, 1884

The artist of this miniature was Susan Anne Livingston Ridley Sedgwick, a granddaughter of Governor William Ridley of New Jersey and the wife of Theodore Sedgwick, Jr. Her husband, son of Judge Sedgwick, was well known in his own right as a lawyer, member of the Massachusetts state legislature in 1824, 1825, and 1827, and as the author of *Public and Private Economy*, published in 1836–1839. Due to ill health, Theodore was forced to retire from his law practice in Albany in 1821 and then moved to Stockbridge, Massachusetts, with the rest of the family. It was at that time that Susan began to write her didactic works for children. Although not a professional, her painting and writing made her a "welcome addition to the cultivated society which centered about the Sedgwicks."[1] Among her works were *The Morals of Pleasure* (1829), *Children's Week* (1829), and *The Young Emigrants: A Tale Designed for Young People* (1830).

The miniature of Mumbet is presented in a half-length format, with the sitter close to the picture plane and turned slightly. The face and body were probably added over the stippled gray background. Mumbet's face is realistic, although her body perspective is slightly skewed. She is wearing a blue dress typical of the

Federalist period, with drawstrings at the neck and waist, a white fichu tucked into her dress, a white cap, and gold beads (see no. 145). With the exception of the accomplished stippled background, the style is that of an amateur. The watercolors used are darker and more opaque than those generally used by contemporary professional miniaturists, and Sedgwick may have followed more closely the style of earlier artists.

B.M.L.

1. DAB.

145

Bracelet
Late eighteenth century
Double strand of gold beads made into a bracelet with etched clasp
L. 5 ¾ in. (14.6 cm), W. in. (1.3 cm)
Engraved, inside clasp: *Mumbet*
Gift of William Minot, 1884

These gold beads were worn by Elizabeth "Mumbet" Freeman as a necklace as shown in Susan Ridley Sedgwick's 1811 miniature portrait of her (no. 144). Prior to her death in 1829, Freeman gave the beads to Catharine Maria Sedgwick, daughter of Judge Theodore Sedgwick. Some of the beads were apparently lost over the years, and Catharine had the remainder remade into a double strand bracelet with gold separators between beads to replace those lost. The clasp with its rococo-revival engraving probably dates from this time, approximately 1840.[1]

Catharine Maria Sedgwick in turn gave the bracelet to her favorite niece, Katharine Sedgwick Minot (1820–1880). Her husband, William Minot, donated the beads to the Society in 1884.

B.M.L.

1. MHS *Proceedings*, 2nd ser., 1(1884):2–4.

145

146

146

Albert Sands Southworth (1811–1894) and Josiah Johnson
Hawes (1808–1908)
The Branded Hand
Boston, ca. 1845
Daguerreotype
3 in. (7.7 cm) x 3½ in. (8.9 cm)
Gift of Nathaniel Bowditch, 1930

The letters "S.S.," for slave stealer, were branded on the
hand of Captain Jonathan W. Walker, an ardent abolitionist, as shown in this dramatic photograph. Walker
was born in Harwich on Cape Cod in 1799 and spent
his early years between the shipyard and the sea. His lifelong interest in the abolition of slavery probably began in 1835 when he went on an expedition to Mexico to
assist in the colonization of escaped American Black
slaves, and he was also one of the conductors along the
underground railroad.[1]

By 1844, Walker moved to Florida where his efforts
for the abolitionist cause met with adversity. In that year,
he attempted to assist seven escaped slaves to freedom by
sailing them from Florida to the West Indies. During the
voyage, he became ill. His crew was untrained in sailing
and navigational procedures and, as a result, they were
"rescued" by a proslavery wrecking sloop and returned to
Florida. The slaves were returned to their masters, and
Walker was arrested. He was convicted and sentenced in
a federal court, spent one year in solitary confinement,
and was fined $600. It was at this time that his right palm
was branded with the letters "S.S."[2]

The event did not deter Walker from spreading the
abolitionist word. His fine was paid by Northern abolitionists, and between 1845 and 1849 he lectured throughout the country on antislavery subjects.[3] He settled in
Muskegon County, Michigan, where he died in 1878; a
monument to him was unveiled there in the same year.[4]
John Greenleaf Whittier, the poet and abolitionist, paid
tribute to Walker in his poem "The Branded Hand"
which first appeared in a book of abolitionist poetry entitled *Voices of Freedom* in 1846 and included the passage:

Then lift that manly right-hand, bold ploughman of the
wave!
Its branded palm shall prophesy, "SALVATION TO THE
SLAVE!"

The photograph of Walker's hand was commissioned
by Henry Ingersoll Bowditch (1808–1892), a Boston
abolitionist, while Walker was in that city, probably in
1845.[5] It was taken at the daguerreotype studio of Southworth and Hawes, a prominent partnership famous for
its daguerreotypes of renowned individuals, groups, and
views of Boston, and it has been called "one of the earliest conceptual portraits in that a body part can stand
for the total personality."[6] Due to the reverse image con-
sistent with the daguerreotype process, the image appears
to be the left hand, but is in fact the right.

Josiah Johnson Hawes and Albert Sands Southworth
opened their daguerreotype studio in 1843, inspired by an
1840 lecture by François Gouraud, Louis Daguerre's
American agent. Hawes, born in East Sudbury, Massachusetts, worked as an itinerant portrait painter from
1829, but in 1841 he began to pursue the commercial prospects of this new permanent photographic process.
Southworth was born in West Fairlee, Vermont, and,
after hearing Gouraud's lecture, opened a daguerreotype
studio with an old Phillips Academy classmate, Joseph
Pernell, in Cabotville. After this business was ruined by
Southworth's experiments, he joined forces with Hawes
in 1843. The partnership ended temporarily in 1849
when Southworth left for California in search of gold. His
health failed, however, and he returned to Boston in 1851
to resume his partnership with Hawes. Southworth and
Hawes received a patent for their invention, the "Grand
Parlor Stereoscope," in 1854. The partnership was dissolved
in 1861–1862 but not before the partners created some of
the most famous daguerreotypes produced in the United
States, some of which are now held by the Museum of
Fine Arts, Boston; the Metropolitan Museum of Art, New
York; and the International Museum of Photography
at George Eastman House, Rochester, New York.[7]

B.M.L.

1. Kittredge 1899, p. 12.
2. Sobieszek 1976, p. 23.
3. Appleton 1889, p. 378.
4. Kittredge 1899, pp. 21–23.
5. Bowditch Memorial Catalogue, MHS, p. LXXIV, no. 109.
6. Sobieszek 1976, p. 23.
7. Auer 1985.

Washington, Monday 29. March 1841. Five

29. IV:30. Monday
Munroe E

Rain the greater part of the last night, and of this day, with a chilling east wind requiring a small fire in my chamber, just enough to be kept burning. Mr. Munroe was a stranger from Boston, who brought a parcel for Elizabeth. I completed the assortment and filing of my Letters received since the beginning of this year, and find myself with a task before me perfectly appalling — I am yet to revise for publication my argument in the case of the Amistad Africans, and in merely glancing over the Parliamentary Slave-trade papers lent me by Mr. Fox, I find impulses of duty upon my own conscience which I cannot resist, while on the other hand, the magnitude, the danger, the insurmountable burden of labour to be encountered in the undertaking to touch upon the Slave-trade — No one else will undertake it — No one but a spirit unconquerable by Man Woman or Fiend, can undertake it, but with the heart of Martyrdom — The world, the flesh, and all the devils in hell are arrayed against any man, who now, in this North-American Union shall dare to join the standard of Almighty God, to put down the African Slave-trade — and what can I, upon the verge of my Seventy-fourth birthday, with a shaking hand, a darkening eye, a drowsy brain, and with all my faculties dropping from me, one by one, as the teeth are dropping from my head, one by one, what can I do for the cause of God and Man? for the progress of human emancipation? for the suppression of the African Slave-trade? — Yet my conscience presses me on — Let me but die upon the breach —— I walked about half an hour for exercise before dinner, and called at the house of Mr. S. H. Fox the British Minister to have some conversation with him — It was 2. O'Clock P.M. The Servant at the door told me that he was not up, and that he was unwell. I enquired at what time he was usually visible — he said between 3. and 4. I had heard that his usual hour of rising was 3. In my second walk after dinner I met Mr. Jesse D. Miller, first Auditor of the Treasury; from which Office it is said he is to retire at the close of the present month and quarter — This evening I answered an old and repeated invitation to deliver a Lecture at Richmond Virginia; and postponed answering the Letters received last Evening from the Amistad Committee, and from Lewis Tappan. I read judge Betts's opinion upon the 14th Section of the Tariff Act of July 1832, and the reversal of his decision by judge Thompson. And I made several minutes from the Parliamentary Slave trade papers Class A. 1839-40, shewing the enormous extent to which that trade was in those and the two preceding years, carried on in American vessels under the patronage of N. P. Trist.

147
John Quincy Adams (1767–1848)
Diary, December 5, 1836–January 4, 1837,
July 29, 1840–December 31, 1841
Manuscript
584 pp., 8⅞ in. (22.7 cm) x 7 in. (17.8 cm)
Gift of the Adams Manuscript Trust, 1956

The world, the flesh, and all the devils in hell are arrayed against any man, who now, in this North-American Union, shall dare to join the standard of Almighty God, to put down the African Slave-trade.[1]

This entry, written in 1841 by John Quincy Adams in his diary, had its origins in an event that occurred two years earlier. In 1839 a group of about fifty Africans who had been illegally kidnapped from their homeland, transported to Cuba, and sold as slaves, revolted against their captors and seized their ship, the *Amistad*. They intended to sail home but were deceived by the Spanish slave trader crew who covertly steered the ship towards the coast of the United States. The Africans were apprehended by the United States coastal survey ship *Washington* off Montauk, N.Y., and taken into custody in Connecticut. Two issues were at stake: whether the African captives could be considered "property" and if so, whose claim to "ownership" was valid, that of the *Washington's* captain or that of the Spanish traders (with the support of the Spanish government). The complicated diplomatic case of the *Amistad* captives moved from the district court to the Supreme Court and attracted the attention of abolition and antislavery forces along the way.[2]

To bolster their cause, abolitionists Ellis Gray Loring of Boston, and Lewis Tappan of New York, personally appealed to former President and current United States Representative John Quincy Adams to assist the defense counsel before the Supreme Court. Adams was reluctant to undertake a courtroom role in the case after a thirty-year absence from the law, but he freely offered to advise the chief counsel, Roger S. Baldwin. Loring and Tappan were not satisfied, however, and Adams finally yielded to their entreaties in this critical case.[3] It was not a decision that he made easily; though he was in favor of an end to slavery through constitutional amendment, he was often at odds with the actions and rhetoric of the abolitionists. It was their appeal to his conscience and his belief in the principle of habeas corpus that gave him the determination to fight.[4]

On February 24, 1841 John Quincy Adams appeared before the United States Supreme Court to argue the defense of the *Amistad* captives. Though he approached his appearance with "increasing agitation of mind . . . little short of agony," his distress vanished as he began to speak—for eight and one half hours over the course of two days.[5] Justice Joseph Story called Adams's argument "extraordinary . . . for its power, for its bitter sarcasm, and its dealing with topics far beyond the record and points of interest."[6] Adams "waited upon tenterhooks" when the court returned with a decision one week later; Justice Story delivered the opinion that the *Amistad* captives were free and directed their release from custody. The court refused to consider the Africans as "property," and also reversed the decision of a lower court placing them in the custody of the President of the United States to be returned to Africa.[7] Adams was elated. With great joy he informed Tappan, "The Captives are free! . . . thanks—thanks! in the name of humanity and of Justice to *you*."[8] For the seven years remaining in Adams's life, the congressman continued to resist any expansion of slavery and persevered in the search for a peaceful end to its horrors. He confided to his diary:

> what can I, upon the verge of my seventy-fourth birthday, with a shaking hand, a darkening eye, a drowsy brain, and with all my faculties, dropping from me, one by one, as the teeth are dropping from my head, what can I do for the cause of God and Man? for the progress of human emancipation? for the suppression of the African Slave-trade? Yet my conscience presses me on— let me but die upon the breach.[9]

John Quincy Adams kept his diary for sixty-eight years, from November 1779, when he was twelve, to December 1847, just a few months before he died. It consists of fifty manuscript volumes of various sizes, and although it contains gaps and the length of some of the entries is no more than a line, there is a twenty-five year period of full entries with no interruption—an extraordinary feat. Adams reveals his diplomatic and political pursuits along with his personal and family life in this manuscript, which is currently being published in full by the Historical Society and Harvard University Press.

C.W.

1. John Quincy Adams, Diary, March 19, 1841, Adams Papers, MHS.
2. Bemis 1956, p. 384–393.
3. J. Q. Adams, Diary, October 27, 1840, Adams Papers, MHS.
4. J. Q. Adams to C. F. Adams, April 14, 1841, Adams Papers, MHS.
5. J. Q. Adams, Diary, February 23, 24, March 1, 1841, Adams Papers, MHS.
6. Story 1851, 2:348.
7. J. Q. Adams, Diary, March 9, 1841, Adams Papers, MHS.
8. J. Q. Adams to Lewis Tappan, March 9, 1841, Adams Papers, MHS.
9. J. Q. Adams, Diary, March 19, 1841, Adams Papers, MHS.

148

Abraham Lincoln (1809–1865)
The Emancipation Proclamation
Washington: Government Printing Office,
ca. January 5, 1863
Broadside
13 1/16 in. (33.2 cm) x 8 5/8 in. (21.3 cm)
Gift of Helen Wood, 1944

There were two emancipation proclamations. The first, drafted by Abraham Lincoln at a time of great military crisis in July 1862, was withheld from public circulation until the North turned back Robert E. Lee's invasion of Maryland at the Battle of Antietam on September 17, 1862. Even then, in the preliminary proclamation, the Confederacy was given one hundred days to end the rebellion or slavery would be abolished in the secessionist states. On January 1, 1863, a second proclamation put the threatened emancipation into effect.[1]

The Emancipation Proclamation served moral and practical purposes by clarifying and rallying support for the antislavery cause, and also as an instrument for the prosecution of the war. The Proclamation launched the recruitment of Black soldiers, many of whom were former slaves, for the war effort. Massachusetts led the way in this policy (see nos. 155–161).[2]

While the Emancipation Proclamation lacks the eloquence of the Declaration of Independence or the simple grandeur of Lincoln's Gettysburg Address, it remains an extraordinary historical document and an important step in the extension of the idea of equality for all Americans.[3]

Charles Sumner (1811–1874), then serving in the United States Senate from Massachusetts, sent the document displayed here, the "official copy of the Proclamation from the Department of State," to a Mr. Wood of Milford on April 6, 1863. Only four copies of this early State Department circular copy have been located. The

BY THE PRESIDENT OF THE UNITED STATES OF AMERICA.

A PROCLAMATION.

WHEREAS, on the twenty-second day of September, in the year of our Lord one thousand eight hundred and sixty-two, a proclamation was issued by the President of the United States, containing, among other things, the following, to wit:

"That on the first day of January, in the year of our Lord one thousand eight hundred and sixty-three, all persons held as slaves within any State or designated part of a State, the people whereof shall then be in rebellion against the United States, shall be then, thenceforward, and forever, free; and the Executive government of the United States, including the military and naval authority thereof, will recognize and maintain the freedom of such persons, and will do no act or acts to repress such persons, or any of them, in any efforts they may make for their actual freedom.

"That the Executive will, on the first day of January aforesaid, by proclamation, designate the States and parts of States, if any, in which the people thereof, respectively, shall then be in rebellion against the United States; and the fact that any State, or the people thereof, shall on that day be in good faith represented in the Congress of the United States, by members chosen thereto at elections wherein a majority of the qualified voters of such States shall have participated, shall, in the absence of strong countervailing testimony, be deemed conclusive evidence that such State, and the people thereof, are not then in rebellion against the United States."

Now, therefore, I, ABRAHAM LINCOLN, President of the United States, by virtue of the power in me vested as commander-in-chief of the army and navy of the United States, in time of actual armed rebellion against the authority and government of the United States, and as a fit and necessary war measure for suppressing said rebellion, do, on this first day of January, in the year of our Lord one thousand eight hundred and sixty-three, and in accordance with my purpose so to do, publicly proclaimed for the full period of one hundred days from the day first above mentioned, order and designate as the States and parts of States wherein the people thereof, respectively, are this day in rebellion against the United States, the following, to wit:

Arkansas, Texas, Louisiana, (except the parishes of St. Bernard, Plaquemines, Jefferson, St. John, St. Charles, St. James, Ascension, Assumption, Terre Bonne, Lafourche, St. Mary, St. Martin, and Orleans, including the city of New Orleans,) Mississippi, Alabama, Florida, Georgia, South Carolina, North Carolina, and Virginia, (except the forty-eight counties designated as West Virginia, and also the counties of Berkeley, Accomac, Northampton, Elizabeth City, York, Princess Ann, and Norfolk, including the cities of Norfolk and Portsmouth,) and which excepted parts are for the present left precisely as if this proclamation were not issued.

And by virtue of the power and for the purpose aforesaid, I do order and declare that all persons held as slaves within said designated States and parts of States are and henceforward shall be free; and that the Executive government of the United States, including the military and naval authorities thereof, will recognize and maintain the freedom of said persons.

And I hereby enjoin upon the people so declared to be free to abstain from all violence, unless in necessary self-defence; and I recommend to them that, in all cases when allowed, they labor faithfully for reasonable wages.

And I further declare and make known that such persons, of suitable condition, will be received into the armed service of the United States to garrison forts, positions, stations, and other places, and to man vessels of all sorts in said service.

And upon this act, sincerely believed to be an act of justice warranted by the Constitution upon military necessity, I invoke the considerate judgment of mankind and the gracious favor of Almighty God.

In witness whereof I have hereunto set my hand and caused the seal of the United States to be affixed.

Done at the city of Washington this first day of January, in the year of our Lord one [L. s.] thousand eight hundred and sixty-three, and of the Independence of the United States of America the eighty-seventh.

ABRAHAM LINCOLN.

By the President:
  WILLIAM H. SEWARD, *Secretary of State.*

148

date of publication is provided by another surviving copy received by Charles Francis Adams at the American Embassy in London.[4]

Sumner had been a lifelong outspoken opponent of slavery. He was one of the most vehement supporters of emancipation and as early as July 4, 1862, had urged Lincoln to "reconsecrate" the anniversary of independence "by a decree of emancipation." Impatient with the speed of Lincoln's efforts, Sumner rejoiced when the final Proclamation was announced on New Year's Day 1863. Here in Boston, the "Day of Days" for African-Americans and their abolitionist supporters was celebrated at two great public meetings.[5]

The presence at the Historical Society of a large collection of Sumner Papers, including hundreds of his letters and manuscripts, reflects a happy reconciliation. A bitter, thirty-year political and personal feud between Sumner and the president of the Historical Society, Robert C. Winthrop, kept Sumner from membership in the Society until the last year of his life, when the two lifelong political opponents finally made peace. When Sumner died in 1874, all Boston stopped to mourn, and Winthrop served as one of his pallbearers.[6]

P.D.

1. Eberstadt 1950, pp. 5–22.
2. Franklin 1963, pp. 149–154.
3. Ibid., p. 153.
4. Eberstadt 1950, p. 18.
5. Donald 1970, p. 60; Franklin 1963, pp. 109–11.
6. Donald 1970, p. 537.

149

Daniel Chester French (1850–1931)
Abraham Lincoln (1809–1865)
Bronze
New York, 1927
H. 33 in. (83.8 cm), W. 24 7/8 in. (63.2 cm),
D. 26 7/8 in. (68.0)
Inscribed, at bottom left: *D. C. French, March 1916*; at rear of base: *Roman Bronze Works NY*
From the estate of Henry Saltonstall Howe, 1931

Congress established the Lincoln Memorial Commission in 1911 for the purpose of erecting a national monument to the sixteenth president in Washington. A site on the westward extension of the Mall was chosen, and the commission invited the architect Henry Bacon (1866–1924) to prepare a design. Early in 1913 Bacon's plan for a Doric temple was accepted. His plans included a statue of Lincoln in the interior, for which he recommended Daniel Chester French, then the country's most respected sculptor. The Lincoln Commission selected French in December 1914.

French had received his early training in sculpture from his neighbor, Abigail May Alcott, who had studied art in Paris, and in drawing from William Morris Hunt at the Massachusetts Institute of Technology. He spent a month in the New York studio of John Quincy Adams Ward and studied art anatomy with William Rimmer before his first major commission, the *Minute Man* (1875) for his hometown of Concord. Following further training in Italy under Thomas Ball, French turned to creating a

149

variety of sculptures, including groups for public buildings in Philadelphia, Boston, and St. Louis, the 1884 seated figure of John Harvard for Harvard College, and portrait busts of Bronson Alcott and Ralph Waldo Emerson. He combined realism with allegory in all his works and proved his versatility through a wide range of subjects from the seventy-five foot sculpture of *The Republic* for the World's Columbian Exposition (1893) to the bronze doors of the Boston Public Library (1904).[1]

By mid-June 1915 French had completed his design work for a seated figure of President Lincoln with a sketch model. He chose a seated pose and sought to portray "the mental and physical strength of the great President and his confidence in his ability to carry the thing [the Civil War] through to a successful finish." For the face and hands the sculptor relied heavily upon commercially obtained copies of the Volk life casts (see no. 151). The next step in creating the statue was to complete a working model in clay in March 1916. At this stage French changed the position of the hands and feet, the treatment of the chair was changed, and draped an American flag over the chair. As he explained to a friend, French felt that the success of the result was "probably as much due to the whole pose of the figure and particularly to the action of the hands as to the expression of the face."[2] Indeed, the resulting monument has become not only French's most famous sculpture but also the most celebrated image of President Lincoln.

A seven-foot model was completed by French at his home and studio Chesterwood in the summer of 1916, and the carving of the enlarged final version was turned over to the Piccirilli family of New York with French himself executing some of the final carving. By 1920 the sculpture was completed and assembled on site in the new Lincoln Memorial, which was officially dedicated on May 30, 1922.[3]

This cast was sold to Henry S. Howe by the sculptor in October 1927 for the "special price" of $1000, as opposed to the usual $2000.[4] It is one of perhaps nine bronze castings of the Lincoln sculpture made during the artist's lifetime, while others were cast in the 1950s. Two of the other early examples are in the Fogg Art Museum, Harvard University, and the Heckscher Museum, Huntington, New York.[5]

E.W.H.

1. Adams 1932, esp. ch. 1.
2. Daniel Chester French to Charles Moore, May 13, 1922, quoted in Richman 1976, p. 184.
3. Ibid., pp. 171–184.
4. Daniel Chester French, Account book, pp. 55, 57, Chesterwood, Stockbridge, Mass.
5. Richman 1976, p. 186.

150

Imposing Stone for The Liberator
Pine, iron
H. 39 ⅝ in. (100.7 cm), W. 29¼ in. (74.5 cm), D. 39¼ in. (99.7 cm)
Gift of Francis J. Garrison, 1911

The imposing stone on which William Lloyd Garrison composed type for his abolitionist newspaper, The *Liberator*, has been symbolically linked at the Massachusetts Historical Society with Daniel Chester French's bronze of the Liberator, Abraham Lincoln (no. 149), since the 1930s.

One of the first American abolitionists to demand immediate and complete emancipation of slaves, Garrison gave full voice to his radically abolitionist ideas in his newspaper, *The Liberator*. Each issue bore the motto "Our Country is the World, our Countrymen are all Mankind," and the very first issue on Jan. 1, 1831 concluded its lead story with Garrison's promise, "I am in earnest—I will not equivocate—I will not excuse— I will not retreat a single inch—and *I will be heard*." Intractable in his convictions, Garrison was subjected to threats and indignities and was literally tarred and feathered by a Boston mob in 1835. His reaction was predictable. "It seems to me that we ought to resolve that the Liberator, despite all opposition, shall continue to be printed—and printed, too, in Boston."[1] For thirty-five years the newspaper did carry its message of liberation until it closed in 1865 after the conclusion of the Civil War.

This imposing stone, actually a thick sheet of iron encased in a pine stand, was used by William Lloyd Garrison for at least twenty years (1845–1865), and of it he wrote, "How many days and nights have I wearily bent over it in getting ready the paper for prompt publication! What a 'stone of stumbling' and a 'rock of offense' it was to all the enemies of emancipation!"[2] After the *Liberator* closed, Garrison sold the stone to George W. Stacy of Milford, Massachusetts, a fellow printer and abolitionist, who likewise used it for twenty years (1866–1885), after which it reverted to the Garrison family.

E.W.H.

1. Garrison 1971, 1:541.
2. MHS *Proceedings*, 44(1910–1911):659.

150

151

Leonard Wells Volk (1828–1895) and Truman Howe Bartlett (1835–1923)
Life Mask and Hands of Abraham Lincoln (1809–1865)
Bronze
Paris, ca. 1875
Mask: W., 7¾ in. (19.6 cm), L. 8¾ in. (22.1 cm), D. 5⅝ in. (14.3 cm); left hand: L. 6⅝ in. (16.8 cm), W. 4⅜ in. (11.1 cm), D. 2½ in. (6.3 cm); right hand: L. 6⅝ in. (16.8 cm), W. 5⅛ in. (13 cm), D. 3⅝ in. (9.2. cm)
Gift of Mary Orne Bowditch, 1948

The sculptor Leonard Wells Volk was raised in New York state and western Massachusetts, where he began carving marble in his father's shop. After practicing his craft in New York, he moved to St. Louis, where he began to teach himself modeling and drawing and attempted his first sculptures. In 1852 he married a cousin of Senator Stephen A. Douglas, who became interested in Volk's career and provided the funds for Volk to spend two years in Rome and Florence studying art. Upon settling in Chicago in 1857, Volk became a leader in the art circles there, where he was a founder of the Academy of Design and for eight years its president.[1] The Lincoln-Douglas debates of 1858 provided the opportunity for a statue of Douglas and a promise from Lincoln to sit for a bust. Two years later Volk reminded Lincoln of his promise, and Lincoln sat for this life mask in Chicago while representing a court case in April 1860. Describing the process of removing the mask, Volk wrote:

> Being all in one piece with both ears perfectly taken, it clung pretty hard, as the cheek bones were higher than the jaws at the lobe of the ear. He bent his head low and took hold of the mould and worked it off himself without break or injury; it hurt a little, as a few straggling hairs about the

tender temples pulled out with the plaster and made his eyes water.[2]

The bust which was based on this mask pleased Mr. Lincoln for when asked for some good likenesses of himself, he replied via a third party: "If your friend could procure one of the 'heads' 'busts' or whatever you call it, by Volk at Chicago, I should think it the thing for him."[3] The original bust was exhibited in Paris in 1867 and returned to the Chicago Historical Society, but was destroyed by the great fire of 1871.[4]

In May 1860, on the day after Lincoln's nomination for the presidency, Volk was in Springfield to make casts of his hands for use in a full-size statue.

> I wished him to hold something in his right hand, and he looked for a piece of pasteboard, but could find none. I told him a round stick would do as well as anything. Thereupon he went to the woodshed, and I heard the saw go, and he soon returned to the dining room whittling off the end of a piece of broom handle. I remarked to him that he need not whittle off the edges. 'Oh, well,' said he, 'I thought I would like to have it nice.'[5]

The right hand was still swollen from excessive handshaking the day before, and the left thumb bore a scar from his railsplitting days. This old injury clearly shows in the original cast and in this bronze casting, but not in later casts, as it was thought to be a defect.

Volk sent the first plaster copy of the original plaster cast of the mask to the French painter Jean-Léon Gérôme (1824–1904), who was the teacher of his son Douglas in Paris. Gérôme later gave the copy to the American sculptor Truman H. Bartlett, who had this bronze life mask cast from it in Paris about 1875, and gave the bronze

to Alfred Bowditch, father of Mary Orne Bowditch, who gave it to the Historical Society.[6]

Douglas Volk later gave the original plaster casts of the mask and hands to a fellow art student Wyatt Eaton. In 1886 Richard Watson Gilder, editor of the *Century Magazine*, formed a committee to raise money through subscription to purchase the casts from Eaton for presentation to the National Museum (Smithsonian Institution). Each of the thirty-three subscribers, who included Augustus Saint-Gaudens, the Boston Athenaeum, and the Irish author Bram Stoker, received a casting from the original. Five or six of the subscription sets were done in bronze and the balance in plaster. Other sets were later produced commercially (see no. 149), but the Historical Society's bronzes are a unique set based on the earliest version of the casts.

E.W.H.

1. Bullard 1952, p. 91.
2. Volk 1922, p. 22.
3. Abraham Lincoln to James F. Babcock, Springfield, Ill., Sept. 13 1860, in Lincoln 1953, 4:114.
4. *DAB*.
5. Volk 1922, p. 24.
6. *Boston Evening Transcript*, March 12, 1917; MHS *Proceedings* 69(1947–1948):458–459.

151

152

Edward Everett (1794–1865)
Letter to Abraham Lincoln, Washington, November 20, 1863
Manuscript copy
1 p., 9 15/16 in. (26.3 cm) x 7 9/16 in. (19 cm)
Gift of Charlotte Everett Wise on behalf of the heirs of Edward Everett, 1930

153

Abraham Lincoln (1809–1865)
Letter to Edward Everett, Washington, November 20, 1863
Manuscript
1 p., 9 7/8 in. (25 cm) x 8 in. (20.5 cm)
Gift of Charlotte Everett Wise on behalf of the heirs of Edward Everett, 1930

Edward Everett, the most renowned American orator of his generation (see no. 112), was a highly popular speaker for the Union cause during the Civil War, and for many years before had aligned himself against every movement that threatened disruption of the Federal Union. So widespread was his fame that Everett was the logical choice to deliver the address at the consecration of the Soldiers' National Cemetery at Gettysburg, Pennsylvania, on November 19, 1863. His two-hour oration, excruciatingly long by present-day standards, was considered the appropriate length for a patriotic speech in that era. It is ironic that Abraham Lincoln's eloquent remarks, barely two minutes in length, have completely eclipsed the crowning occasion of Everett's career. Indeed, in his diary account of what occurred at Gettysburg that day,

152

153

Everett discussed his own speech but took no notice of Lincoln's address. The next day, however, he wrote to the President praising his speech: "I should be glad, if I could flatter myself, that I came as near to the central idea of the occasion in two hours, as you did in two minutes." The same day Lincoln replied, "In our respective parts yesterday, you could not have been excused to make a short address, nor I a long one. I am pleased to know that, in your judgment, the little I did say was not entirely a failure."

These letters are part of a much larger collection of Edward Everett papers at the Historical Society which include the correspondence, letterbooks, and diaries of Edward Everett.

K.H.G.

154

Thomas Ridgeway Gould (1818–1881)
John Albion Andrew (1818–1867)
1864
Marble
H. 23 1/8 in. (58.7 cm), w. 17 5/8 in. (45 cm),
D. 8 3/4 in. (22.4 cm)
Inscribed, on back: *T. R. Gould Sc: 1864*
Bequest of Edith Andrew, 1923

The great Civil War governor of Massachusetts, John Albion Andrew came to Boston from his native Maine in 1837 to study law in the office of Henry Fuller, who was an uncle of Margaret Fuller. An early and ardent abolitionist, Andrew opposed the Fugitive Slave Law in 1850 and in 1854 represented the defendants indicted at Boston for rescuing the fugitive slave Anthony Burns. He became a leader of the movement when elected to the Massachusetts legislature in 1857, and when John Brown was imprisoned for his raid at Harper's Ferry, Andrew took a leading part in raising funds for Brown's defense. Elected governor of Massachusetts in 1860, he is best remembered for providing the first troops to answer Lincoln's call to arms and for organizing the first Black regiment in the north, the 54th Massachusetts Regiment (see nos. 155–161).[1]

Governor Andrew was elected to membership in the Historical Society in 1866, and his personal and official papers were donated to the Society by his children. The collection includes a gruesome assortment of slave artifacts—slave whips, part of a slave auction block, and a punishment collar—sent to Andrew by the Massachusetts troops as a reminder of the grim reality of bondage.[2] The Society also has a study portrait of Andrew by William Morris Hunt (1867), painted in preparation for the full-size painting at Faneuil Hall.

The sculptor Thomas Ridgeway Gould was a Boston native and began his career as the local representative of a family-run mercantile business based in New Orleans, while during his spare moments he studied sculpting in the studio of Seth Cheney. When the Civil War ruined the family business, Gould turned his amateur interest in sculpting to professional benefit and opened a small studio in Boston. His earliest surviving work is a bust of Ralph Waldo Emerson (1861, Harvard Portrait Collection). This bust of the governor was another of Gould's early works and shows Andrew in a characteristic attitude, without his trademark spectacles but wearing a cape tightly drawn with tassels around his shirt collar. This conservative pose suited Andrew's personality better than a bare-chested or toga-draped representation would. Gould later also created the full-length sculpture of Governor Andrew for his funerary monument in Hingham, Massachusetts. Among his other portrait busts, Gould carved Junius Brutus Booth, the actor and stage manager then living in Boston, and the artist became so interested in his subject that he later wrote a book on Booth's career. Gould moved to Italy in 1868 and, apart from two

154

brief visits home, spent the rest of his life abroad. He is perhaps best known for his nine foot bronze sculpture of King Kamehameha I, the original of which is near the king's birthplace on the island of Hawaii, while the more famous copy stands in front of the old Judiciary Building in Honolulu.[3]

E.W.H.

1. MHS *Proceedings* 18(1880–1881):41–64.
2. MHS *Proceedings* 54(1920–1921):82–83.
3. Craven 1968, pp. 204–205.

Fifty-Fourth Regiment Massachusetts Volunteer Infantry

The Massachusetts 54th Regiment was the first military unit consisting of Black soldiers to be raised in the North during the Civil War. Prior to 1863, no concerted effort was made to recruit Black troops as Union soldiers. At the beginning of the war, Black men offered to serve as soldiers for the Union cause, however these offers were rejected by the military establishment and the country as a whole. A few makeshift regiments were raised—including the First South Carolina Regiment with whom the 54th Regiment would serve at Fort Wagner—however most were raised in the South and consisted primarily of escaped and abandoned slaves.[1] The passage of the Emancipation Proclamation in December of 1862 provided the impetus for the use of free Black men as soldiers and, at a time when state governors were responsible for the raising of regiments for federal service, Massachusetts

was the first to respond with the formation of the 54th Regiment.[2]

Massachusetts Governor John A. Andrew had long been in favor of using Black soldiers for the Union cause. An outspoken abolitionist, Andrew had taken the lead to raise money for John Brown's defense in 1859. When the door finally opened in 1863, Andrew was one of the first to pursue the idea. On January 26, 1863, Secretary of War Edwin M. Stanton authorized Andrew to begin recruiting and enlisting Black soldiers for his new regiment.[3]

As one of his first orders of business, Governor Andrew chose Robert Gould Shaw as commander of the regiment. Shaw was born in Boston on October 10, 1837, the son of Francis G. and Sarah (Sturgis) Shaw. The Shaws were a prominent Boston family, involved in the China Trade, and were sympathetic to the abolitionist cause. Robert had studied in Europe and entered Harvard College in 1856, his course of study abandoned in his third year. Prior to his appointment to the 54th, Shaw had served in the 7th Regiment of the New York National Guard and had seen action as a captain with the Second Massachusetts Infantry Regiment.[4] Governor Andrew wrote directly to Robert's father on February 2, 1863 to request that the young, only twenty-five years of age, captain take the position. Robert refused the position at first, but changed his mind the following day.[5] Captain Norwood P. Hallowell of the 20th Massachusetts Infantry was commissioned lieutenant.

Twenty-seven Black volunteers assembled at Camp Meigs, Readville, on February 21, 1863. By the end of the first week of enlistments, seventy-two recruits were present and by May 11 more had arrived than were needed. The overflow would become the nucleus of the 55th Massachusetts Infantry Regiment.[6]

The formation of the regiment was a matter of controversy and public attention from its inception. Questions were raised as to the Black man's ability to fight in the "white man's war." Although Andrew believed that Black men were capable of leadership, it was felt that commissioning Blacks as officers was simply too controversial; Andrew needed all the support he could get. The commissioned officers, then, were white and the enlisted men Black. Any Black officers up to the rank of lieutenant were non-commissioned and reached their positions by moving up through the ranks. The national publicity and attention received by the unit continued. On May 28, 1863, upon the presentation of the unit's colors by the governor and a parade through the streets of Boston, spectators lined the streets with the hopes of viewing this experimental unit. The regiment then departed Boston on the transport *De Molay* for the coast of South Carolina.

The regiment reported to General David Hunter at Hilton Head, South Carolina, on June 3rd and were quickly transported to Beaufort. During June, the unit visited New Frederica, St. Simon's Island, and St. Helena Island. On July 8, it became part of General Terry's expedition to James Island. Serving as a diversion for the intended attack on Morris Island, Colonel Shaw's regiment saw its first action on James Island on July 16, losing forty-five men. On July 18, after several days with little sleep, food, or water, the regiment was instructed to lead the attack against Fort Wagner on Morris Island. In the disastrous assault led by Colonel Shaw, the 54th suffered very heavy losses, most notably the loss of their command-

155

er, and nearly half of the men present were among the killed, wounded and missing. Despite this, the unit showed exceptional bravery and honor, never retreating as they waited for the reinforcements which would never arrive. At the loss of the unit's color bearer, Sergeant William H. Carney took hold of the flag and never let it touch the ground; he eventually received the Congressional Medal of Honor for his actions in 1900, the first Black man to be so recognized. The unit was taken over by Colonel M. S. Littlefield of the 4th South Carolina. Colonel Edward N. Hallowell, brother of Norwood P. Hallowell, the leader of the 55th Regiment, later assumed command until the unit was disbanded.[7]

Following the unsuccessful assault on Fort Wagner, the regiment saw further action in Olustee, Florida, Honey Hill, Savannah, and Boykin's Mills near Georgetown. The unit was mustered out on August 20, 1865, reached Boston on August 27 and 28, and was paid off and disbanded, following a parade in Boston, on September 1 and 2.[8]

While the 54th suffered heavy losses at Fort Wagner, there is no evidence that the unit was chosen because they were thought of simply as cannon fodder.[9] When the news of the attack reached home, the news was very well received. The unit which had received so much attention, publicity, and skepticism had finally earned the respect as good fighting men that they deserved. Despite the defeat at Fort Wagner, the use of Black soldiers in the 54th was viewed as a success and opened the way for numerous other Black units as Union troops for the remainder of the war.[10]

The Society holds manuscripts and photographs related to the Massachusetts 54th Regiment. Among these are the Nathaniel Bowditch photograph albums containing portraits and scenes of Fort Wagner; papers of Governor John A. Andrew related to the recruitment and enlistment of the regiment; the personal papers of Norwood P. Hallowell of the 54th and 55th regiments; and a small collection of letters from Robert Gould Shaw to his friend Charles F. Morse, which were written from Boston, Readville, and South Carolina prior to the assault on Fort Wagner. Among the Society's related papers of the 54th are the records of the other Black Massachusetts regiments, the 55th Infantry, including the Association of Officers records and the personal papers of Colonel Charles B. Fox, whose diary was used for the regimental history; and the 5th Massachusetts Cavalry. Among the library's other manuscript, photographic, and printed materials are a large number of collections related to other Massachusetts regiments and all facets of the Civil War.

B.M.L.

1. Burchard 1965, p. xi.
2. Hargrove 1988, p. ix.
3. Ibid., p. 77.
4. Emilio 1894, p. 5.
5. Burchard 1965, pp. 2, 76.
6. Ibid., pp. 19–24.
7. Hargrove 1988, pp. 153–156.
8. Mass. 1931, 4:657.
9. Burchard 1965, p. 149.
10. Hargrove 1988, pp. 157–159.

155–158
54th Massachusetts Regiment Photographs
Gift of Mary Silsbee Emilio, 1920

These four photographs are part of the Luis Fenollosa Emilio (1844–1918) Collection on the Massachusetts 54th Regiment. In addition to photographs of white officers and Black enlisted men, the Emilio Collection consists of material gathered for his regimental history, *A Brave Black Regiment: A History of the Fifty-fourth Regiment of Massachusetts Volunteer Infantry, 1863–1865* (1891), and includes excerpts from diaries, government records, and newspapers, and Emilio's own papers pertaining to the regiment in which he served as a captain.

155
Private Charles H. Arnum, Company E,
54th Mass. Regiment
Photographer unknown
Morris Island, S.C., 1864
Tintype
3 7/8 in. (9.8 cm) x 2 5/8 in. (6.5 cm)

Listed as a teamster and a resident of Springfield, Massachusetts, the twenty-one year old Arnum enlisted at Littleton and was mustered in as a private into Company E on November 4, 1863. He served with the regiment until it was disbanded on August 20, 1865. He received $325 as a state bounty, and his last known address was North Adams, Massachusetts.[1]

This full-length study of Arnum shows him in uniform with his hand resting upon the American flag, which is draped over a table in the foreground. Behind him is a painted backdrop representing a seashore military camp.

B.M.L.

1. Emilio 1894, p. 359; Mass. 1931, 4:680.

156
Private John Goosberry, Company E, 54th Mass. Regiment
Photographer unknown
ca. 1865
Tintype
4 1/2 in. (10.7 cm) x 3 1/4 in. (8.2 cm)

One of the twenty-one Black recruits from Canada, twenty-five-year-old Goosberry, a sailor of St. Catharines, Ontario, was mustered into Company E on July 16, 1863, just two days before the fateful assault on Fort Wagner.[1] He was mustered out of service on August 20, 1865, at the disbanding of the regiment.

Goosberry appears in this full-length photograph wearing his uniform as a company musician, holding a fife and standing before a plain backdrop. The buttons and buckle of the uniform have been hand colored, and there is an impression remaining on the tintype from an earlier oval frame.

B.M.L.

1. Kaplan 1989, p. 30; Mass. 1931, 4:682.

156

Private Richard Gomar, Co. H, 54th Mass. Regiment
Photographer unknown
After 1880
Tintype
3½ in. (8.9 cm) x 2½ in. (6.3 cm)

Richard Gomar[1] enlisted in Company H on April 17, 1863 at the age of seventeen and was mustered in on May 13. He was a laborer from Battle Creek, Michigan. He was mustered out after the regiment's return to Boston on August 20, 1865. He received a state bounty of $50, and his last known address was Cedar Rapids, Iowa.[2]

Portrayed here in a half-length study, Gomar is in civilian clothes and on his waistcoat is wearing a membership badge of the Grand Army of the Republic, the Union veterans' organization. This version of the badge was adopted in 1880.[3] According to regulation, Gomar wears the badge on the left breast of his waistcoat, but the tintype process has reversed the image.

B.M.L.

1. Listed as Richard Gomes in Emilio 1894, p. 374; as Richard Gomar in Mass. 1931, 4:696, and according to his muster record (MMA).
2. Mass. 1931, 4:696; Emilio 1894, p. 374.
3. Beath 1889, p. 656.

157

158

159

158

Sergeant Henry Steward, Company E, 54th Mass. Regiment
Photographer unknown
1863
Ambrotype
4¼ in. (10.7 cm) x 3 in. (7.7 cm)

A twenty-three year old farmer from Adrian, Michigan, Henry Steward[1] enlisted on April 4, 1863 and was mustered in on April 23. As a non-commissioned officer, as were all Black officers, Steward was actively engaged in the recruiting of soldiers for the regiment. He died of disease at the regimental hospital on Morris Island, South Carolina, on September 27, 1863, and his estate was paid a $50 state bounty.[2]

Standing at attention with his sword drawn in this full-length study, Steward is posed in front of a plain backdrop, but a portable column has been wheeled in to add detail on the left. Hand-colored trousers and buttons highlight the uniform in this ambrotype of Sergeant Steward.

B.M.L.

1. 1894, p. 131, lists him as Henry Stewart, however his roster of enlisted men, p. 362, as well as Mass. 1931, 4:684, spells the surname Steward.
2. Emilio 1894, pp. 131, 362.

159

James H. Smith and William J. Miller
Shaw Memorial Dedication, Boston, May 31, 1897
Boston, 1897
Albumen print
6¼ in. (15.7 cm) x 9¼ in. (24.3 cm)
Gift of Mary Silsbee Emilio, 1920

The dedication of the monumental bronze relief of Colonel Robert Gould Shaw and the Black soldiers of the Massachusetts 54th Regiment, as sculpted by Augustus Saint-Gaudens (1848–1907), took place on Decoration Day 1897, thirty-two years after a committee for the erection of a memorial had been appointed by Governor John A. Andrew.

The first attempt to commemorate the assault on Fort Wagner was made by the veterans of the 54th and the 1st South Carolina Infantry and the Black community of Beaufort, South Carolina. Poor ground conditions and the hostility of the local whites prevented the memorial from being erected on the site of the assault, and the money raised for the purpose was channeled into the first free school for Blacks in Charleston, South Carolina, named for Shaw.[1]

Soon after the close of the war, in the fall of 1865, Governor Andrew made another attempt by appointing a committee to procure an equestrian sculpture of Shaw and to raise the necessary funds. By 1876, the fund stood at $7000, and then Edward Atkinson, the treasurer of the project, appointed John Murray Forbes, Henry Lee, and Martin P. Kennard as an executive committee with full authority over the project, with Atkinson continuing as treasurer and secretary.[2]

In 1883 when the subscriptions reached $16,656, the committee set out to find a sculptor. The architect for the project, Henry H. Richardson, recommended a young sculptor, Augustus Saint-Gaudens. Saint-Gaudens contracted in February of 1884 to complete the sculpture in two years for $15,000.[3]

Saint-Gaudens, the son of French and Irish immigrants, studied and worked in France, Rome, and New York. He has become famous for his interpretations of Americans and, in particular, Civil War figures. Along with the Shaw Memorial, these works include sculptural portraits of Admiral David G. Farragut, Abraham Lincoln, and General William T. Sherman.[4]

By 1891, with the Shaw Memorial work still not completed and the executive committee becoming very impatient, Edward Atkinson inquired of Saint-Gaudens as to its status; the sculptor replied that the modeling would be done in nine months. In 1893, the committee threatened to commission a new sculptor, Daniel Chester French (see no. 149), to do the work. Finally, in 1897, after a battle between John Murray Forbes and Henry Lee regarding the choice of inscription, the monument was completed and Saint-Gaudens was paid $22,000, almost all of the money in the account to date.[5]

At the unveiling and dedication of the memorial, which stands between two elm trees on Boston Common facing the Massachusetts State House, Henry Lee presented the monument to the City of Boston on May 31, 1897. The dedication ceremony which took place at Boston's old Music Hall included addresses by Lee, Massachusetts Governor Roger Wolcott, Boston Mayor Josiah Quincy, William James, and Booker T. Washington. At the head of the procession, shown in this photograph, were the remaining officers and soldiers of the Mass. 54th including, as flagbearer, Sergeant William H. Carney of the 54th, who would be the first Black man to receive the Congressional Medal of Honor three years later.[6]

The photograph was taken for use in the *Boston Journal* on the following day. In addition to printed accounts of the dedication ceremony, the Society holds Henry Lee's records of the executive committee in the Lee Family Papers.

B.M.L.

1. Whitfield 1987, pp. 7–8.
2. Riley 1963, p. 30.
3. Ibid.
4. Kaplan 1989, pp. 20–24.
5. Riley 1963, pp. 32–36.
6. Shaw 1897.

160

Dress Sword, Scabbard, and Sash
W. Clauberg
Solingen, Germany, ca. 1864.
Steel, silver, brass wire and gilt
Blade: L. 30 ⅞ in. (78.4 cm), w. (at hilt) 1 1/16 in. (2.7 cm); overall: L. 36 ¾ in. (93.3 cm)
Gift of Vida Woley, 1968

Frederick Hedge Webster, the son of John Gerrish and Mary (Moulton) Webster of Boston, was born on August 2, 1843.[1] An unmarried clerk before the war, he was commissioned a second lieutenant in Company G of the 54th

160

Massachusetts Infantry Regiment on May 4, 1864. He reported for duty and was mustered in on July 16, 1864, following the regiment's return to Morris Island from James Island, South Carolina.[2] On January 25, 1865, news came to the regiment that Lieutenant Webster had died of fever at the General Hospital at Beaufort, South Carolina, the only officer of the 54th lost to disease.[3] Upon the regiment's return and parade in Boston on September 2, 1865, a window on Tremont Street displayed a portrait of Webster, draped in mourning.[4]

Along with the sword, scabbard, and crimson sash, Vida Woley also donated a portrait of Lieutenant Webster by Benjamin Curtis Porter, and a carte-de-visite photograph by Marshall and Company of Tremont and Bromfield streets, Boston, showing Webster in his full-dress uniform, including this sword and sash. The scabbard shown in the photograph is a plain leather one with brass fittings, rather than the dress scabbard which survives. This dress scabbard is woodlined, chrome-plated steel with brass asymmetrical drag, bands with carrying rings, and throat. All the mounts are decorated *en suite* with the hilt. It is inscribed, "Lieut. Fred. H. Webster / 54th Reg't Mass. Vol."

The sword has a chrome-plated steel blade, of triangular section and is hollow-ground. At above mid-length, both faces are etched with lobated cartouches whose foliated tendril terminals frame a device. On the obverse are the Arms of the Republic, and on the reverse the upper-case block letters "US" rendered in a cornucopia manner. The reverse of the ricasso bears the stamped trademark of the Clauberg firm. The ornate, demi-basket hilt is brass-gilt, with a pair of stout bars forming the counterguard, and united with a curved, ribbed knuckle-guard. The pommel cap is of the Phrygian helmet form, bordered below in a carved row of overlapping oak leaves. The grip is of silver, wrapped with a tightly coiled brass wire.

Many Clauberg swords and blades were imported during the Civil War. These were handled by military outfitters such as Horstmann & Company (Philadelphia) and Schuyler, Hartley & Graham (New York). A number of Clauberg swords of this type are preserved in the National Museum of American History, Washington.[5]

B.M.L.

1. *NEHGR* 40(1886):416; Emilio 1894, p. 338.
2. Mass. 1931, 4:694; Emilio 1894, pp. 233, 338.
3. Emilio 1894, pp. 272–273.
4. Ibid., p. 318.
5. Belote 1932.

161

To Colored Men. 54th Regiment! Massachusetts Volunteers, Of African Descent
Boston: J. E. Farwell & Co., 1863
Broadside
43¼ in. (109.9 cm) x 29⅝ in. (75.2 cm)
Provenance unknown

161

Soon after Governor John A. Andrew was allowed to begin recruiting Black men for his newly formed 54th Regiment, Andrew realized the financial costs involved in such an undertaking and set out to raise money. He appointed George L. Stearns as the leader of the recruiting process, and also appointed the so-called "Black Committee" of prominent and influential citizens. The committee and those providing encouragement included Frederick Douglass, Amos A. Lawrence, William Lloyd Garrison, and Wendell Phillips, and $5000 was quickly raised for the cause. Newly appointed officers in the regiment also played an active part in the recruiting process.[1]

An advertisement was placed in the *Boston Journal* for February 16, 1863 addressed "To Colored Men" recruiting "Good men of African descent." It, like the recruiting posters, offered a "$100 bounty at the expiration of the term of service, pay $13 per month, and State aid for families"; it was signed by Lieutenant William J. Appleton of the 54th.[2] Twenty-five men enlisted quickly, however the arrival of men at the recruiting stations and at Camp Meigs, Readville, soon slowed down. Stearns soon became aware that Massachusetts did not have enough eligible Black men to fill a regiment and recruiters were sent to states throughout the North and South, and into Canada.

Pennsylvania proved to be a fertile source for recruits, with a major part of Company B coming from Philadelphia, despite recent race riots there. New Bedford and Springfield, Massachusetts, Blacks made up the majority of Company C, while approximately seventy men recruited from western Massachusetts and Connecti-

cut formed much of Company D.[3] Stearns's line of recruiting stations from Buffalo to St. Louis produced volunteers from New York, Illinois, Indiana, Ohio, Pennsylvania, and Canada. Few of the men were former slaves; most were freemen working as seamen, farmers, laborers, or carpenters. By May 14, 1863, the regiment was full with 1000 enlisted men and a full complement of white officers. The remaining recruits became the nucleus of the 55th Massachusetts Regiment, commanded by Norwood P. Hallowell, who, for a short time, had served as second-in-command to Robert Gould Shaw of the 54th.[4]

The question of pay to the volunteers became an important issue, even before the regiment's departure from Boston on May 18. When Governor Andrew first proposed the idea to Edwin M. Stanton, Secretary of War, Andrew was assured that the men would be paid, clothed, and treated in the same way as white troops. As the recruiting posters and newspaper advertisements stated, this included a state bounty and a monthly pay of $13. In July of 1863, an order was issued in Washington fixing the compensation of Black soldiers at the laborers' rate of $10 per month. This amount was offered on several occasions to the men of the 54th, but was continually refused. Governor Andrew and the Massachusetts legislature, feeling responsible for the $3 discrepancy in pay promised to the troops, passed an act in November of 1863 providing the difference from state funds. The men refused to accept this resolution, however, demanding that they receive full soldier pay from the federal government. It was not until September of 1864 that the men of the 54th received any compensation for their valiant efforts, finally receiving their full pay since the time of enlistment, totalling $170,000.[5] Each soldier was paid a $50 bounty before leaving Camp Meigs and this is the extent of the bounty that many received. By a later law, $325 was paid to some men, however most families received no State aid.[6]

Although the Massachusetts 54th Regiment was the first to enlist Black men as soldiers in the North, it was only the beginning for Blacks as Union soldiers. By the end of the war, a total of 167 units, including other state regiments and the United States Colored Troops, were raised, totaling 186,097 men of African descent recruited into federal service.[7]

B.M.L.

1. Hargrove 1988, pp. 77–78.
2. Emilio 1894, pp. 8–9.
3. Ibid., pp. 9–10.
4. Burchard 1965, pp. 83–90.
5. Mass. 1931, 4:657.
6. Emilio 1894, pp. 327–328.
7. Hargrove 1988, p. 2.

Selected Bibliography

MANUSCRIPT REPOSITORIES

AAA-SI
Archives of American Art-Smithsonian Institution

BPL
Boston Public Library

CSM
Chesterwood, Stockbridge, Mass.

MFA
Museum of Fine Arts, Boston

MHS
Massachusetts Historical Society, Boston

MMA
Massachusetts Department of Military Archives, Natick, Mass.

MVR
Massachusetts Vital Records, Massachusetts State Archives, Boston

SCP
Suffolk County Probate Records, Massachusetts State Archives, Boston

SECONDARY SOURCES

Abernathy 1967
Abernathy, Thomas J. "American Artillery Regiments in the Revolutionary War: Volume I, Col. Richard Gridley's Regiment, 1775." Massachusetts Historical Society. Typescript.

Adams 1895
Adams, Charles Francis. *Richard Henry Dana: A Biography.* 4th ed. Boston, 1895.

Adams 1928
Adams, Henry, II. "The Adams Mansion: The Home of Presidents John Adams and John Quincy Adams." *Old-Time New England* 19 (1928), pp. 3–17.

Adams 1932
Adams, Adeline. *Daniel Chester French, Sculptor.* Boston, 1932.

Adams 1961
Diary and Autobiography of John Adams. L. H. Butterfield et al., eds. 4 vols. Cambridge, Mass., 1961.

Adams 1963
Adams Family Correspondence. L. H. Butterfield et al., eds. 4 vols. Cambridge, Mass., 1963–1973.

Adams 1965
Adams, Thomas R. *American Independence: The Growth of an Idea.* Providence, R.I., 1965.

Adams 1977
Papers of John Adams. Robert J. Taylor et al., eds. 8 vols. Cambridge, Mass., 1977–1989.

Adams Papers 1965
Legal Papers of John Adams. L. Kinvin Wroth and Hiller B. Zobel, eds. 3 vols. Cambridge, Mass., 1965.

Alden 1954
Alden, John Richard. *The American Revolution, 1775–1783.* New York, 1954.

Alexander 1976
Alexander, Michael, ed. *Discovering the New World: Based on the Works of Theodore De Bry.* London, 1976.

Allison 1947
Allison, Anne. "Peter Pelham—Engraver in Mezzotinto." *The Magazine Antiques* 52 (1947), pp. 441–443.

Ambler 1975
Ambler, Louise Todd. *Benjamin Franklin: A Perspective.* Exhibition catalogue, Fogg Art Museum, Harvard University. Cambridge, Mass., 1975.

Amory 1859
Amory, Thomas C. *Life of James Sullivan with Selections from His Writings.* 2 vols. Boston, 1859.

Amory 1989
Amory, Hugh. *First Impressions: Printing in Cambridge, 1639–1989.* Cambridge, Mass., 1989.

Anderson 1980
Anderson, Patricia A. *Promoted to Glory: The Apotheosis of George Washington.* Exhibition catalogue, Smith College Museum of Art. Northampton, 1980.

Appleton 1889
Appleton's Cyclopedia of American Biography. James Grant Wilson and John Fiske, eds. New York, 1889.

Arvin 1929
Arvin, Newton. *Hawthorne.* Boston, 1929.

Athenaeum 1837
Catalogue of the Eleventh Exhibition of Paintings in the Athenæum Gallery. Boston, 1837.

Auer 1985
Auer, Michèle, and Michel Auer. *Encyclopédie Internationale des Photographes de 1839 à nos Jours.* 2 vols. Hermance, Switz., 1985.

Baigell 1969
Baigell, Matthew. "James Hoban and the First Bank of the United States." *Journal of the Society of Architectural Historians* 28 (1969), pp. 135–136.

Bail 1949
Bail, Hamilton Vaughan. *Views of Harvard: A Pictorial Record to 1860.* Cambridge, Mass., 1949.

Baillie 1947
Baillie, G. H. *Watchmakers and Clockmakers of the World.* 2d ed. London, 1947.

Barber 1982
Barber, James, and Frederick Voss. *The Godlike Black Dan.* Exhibition catalogue, National Portrait Gallery. Washington, 1982.

Beath 1889
Beath, Robert B. *History of the Grand Army of the Republic.* New York, 1889.

Belknap 1959
Belknap, Waldron Phoenix, Jr. *American Colonial Painting: Materials for a History.* Cambridge, Mass., 1959.

Belote 1932
Belote, Theodore T. *American and European Swords in the Historical Collection of the United States National Museum.* Washington, 1932.

Bemis 1956
Bemis, Samuel Flagg. *John Quincy Adams and the Union.* New York, 1956.

Bentley 1905
Bentley, William. *The Diary of William Bentley, D.D. Pastor of the East Church, Salem, Massachusetts.* 4 vols. Salem, 1905–1914.

Bernier 1983
Bernier, Olivier. *Lafayette, Hero of Two Worlds.* New York, 1983.

Billias 1976
Billias, George A. *Elbridge Gerry: Founding Father and Republican Statesman.* New York, 1976.

Bingham 1927
Bingham, Robert W. "George Washington in Liverpool Ware." *The Magazine Antiques* 12 (1927), pp. 32–35.

Bishop 1981
Bishop, Robert, and Patricia Coblentz. *A Gallery of American Weathervanes and Whirligigs.* New York, 1981.

Blair 1968
Blair, Claude. *Pistols of the World.* London, 1968.

Blair 1983
Blair, Claude, ed. *Pollard's History of Firearms.* Feltham, England, 1983.

Bolton 1921
Bolton, Ethel Stanwood, and Eva Johnston Coe. *American Samplers.* Boston, 1921.

Bolton 1927
Bolton, Charles Knowles. *Bolton's American Armory.* Boston, 1927.

Bolton 1927 (2)
Bolton, Theodore. "A Biographical Dictionary of the Artists." In *American Miniatures, 1730–1850.* Harry Wehle, ed. Garden City, N.Y., 1927.

Bolton 1951
Bolton, Theodore. "The Book Illustrations of Felix Octavius Darley." *Proceedings of the American Antiquarian Society* 61 (1951), pp. 137–182.

Bolton-Smith 1984
Bolton-Smith, Robin. *Portrait Miniatures in the National Museum of American Art.* Chicago, 1984.

Bolus 1973
Bolus, Malvina. "The Four Kings Came to Dinner with Their Honours." *The Beaver* (1973), pp. 4–11.

Boston 1842
Boston Artists' Association. *Catalogue of Paintings of The First Exhibition of the Boston Artists' Association,* Harding's Gallery. Boston, 1842.

Bostonian Society 1908
"Historic Processions in Boston, 1789–1824." *The Bostonian Society Publications* 5 (1908), pp. 65–119.

Boyd 1943
Boyd, Julian. *The Declaration of Independence: The Evolution of the Text as Shown in Facsimiles of Various Drafts by its Author.* Washington, 1945.

Boyer 1974
Boyer, Paul, and Stephen Nissenbaum. *Salem Possessed.* Cambridge, Mass., 1974.

Bradford 1958
Bradford, Gershom. "Captain Gamaliel Bradford, Soldier and Privateersman." *Old-Time New England* 49 (1958), pp. 29–40.

Breen 1988
Breen, Walter. *Walter Breen's Complete Encyclopedia of U.S. and Colonial Coins.* New York, 1988.

Brigham 1954
Brigham, Clarence S. *Paul Revere's Engravings.* Worcester, Mass., 1954.

Brissot 1964
Brissot de Warville, Jacques Pierre. *New Travels in the United States of America, 1788.* Cambridge, Mass., 1964.

British Library 1975
The American War of Independence, 1775–83. Exhibition catalogue, British Library. London, 1975.

Brown 1900
Brown, Abram English. *Faneuil Hall and Faneuil Hall Market or Peter Faneuil and His Gift.* Boston, 1900.

Brown 1919
Bibliotheca Americana: Catalogue of the John Carter Brown Library. 3 vols. Providence, 1919–1931.

Brown 1946
Brown, Frank C. "John Smibert, Artist, and the First Faneuil Hall." *Old Time New England* 36 (1946), pp. 61–63.

Brown 1980
Brown, M. L. *Firearms in Colonial America: The Impact on History and Technology, 1492–1792.* Washington, 1980.

Bryan 1989
Bryan, John M., ed. *Robert Mills, Architect.* Washington, 1989.

Buckingham 1853
Buckingham, Joseph T., comp. *Annals of the Massachusetts Charitable Mechanics' Association.* Boston, 1853.

Buhler 1956
Buhler, Kathryn C. *Colonial Silversmiths, Masters & Apprentices.* Exhibition Catalogue, Museum of Fine Arts, Boston. Boston, 1956.

Buhler 1972
Buhler, Kathryn C. *American Silver 1655–1825 in the Museum of Fine Arts.* 2 vols. Boston, 1972.

Bullard 1952
Bullard, F. Lauriston. *Lincoln in Marble and Bronze.* New Brunswick, N.J., 1952.

Burchard 1965
Burchard, Peter. *One Gallant Rush: Robert Gould Shaw and His Brave Black Regiment.* New York, 1965.

Butler 1976
Butler, Jeanne F. *Competition 1792: Designing a Nation's Capitol.* Capitol Studies Series, vol. 4. Washington, 1976.

Calef 1972
Calef, Robert. *More Wonders of the Invisible World, 1700 by Robert Calef.* Introduction by Chadwick Hansen. Facsimile reproduction. Bainbridge, N.Y., 1972.

Callahan 1958
Callahan, North. *Henry Knox: General Washington's General.* New York, 1958.

Callahan 1964
Callahan, North. "Henry Knox: American Artillerist." In *George Washington's Generals*, George Athan Billias, ed. New York, 1964.

Cannon 1850
Cannon, Richard. *History of the Twenty-third Regiment, or the Royal Welsh Fusiliers.* Historical Records of the British Army. London, 1850.

Carrick 1928
Carrick, Alice Van Leer. *Shades of Our Ancestors: American Profiles and Profilists.* Boston, 1928.

Carter 1967
Carter, John, and Percy Muir, comps. *Printing and the Mind of Man* London, 1967.

Chase 1982
Chase, Sara. "A Brief Survey of the Architectural History of the Old State House, Boston, Massachusetts." *Old-Time New England* 68 (1978), pp. 31–49.

Child 1881
Child, Elias. *Genealogy of the Child, Childs and Childe Families of the Past and Present in the United States and the Canadas from 1630 to 1881.* Utica, N.Y., 1881.

Church 1975
Church, Benjamin. *Diary of King Philip's War, 1675–76.* Chester, Conn., 1975.

Clarke 1932
Clarke, Hermann F. *John Coney, Silversmith, 1655–1722.* Boston, 1932.

Clarke 1940
Clarke, Hermann F. *John Hull: A Builder of the Bay Colony.* Portland, Me., 1940.

Clement 1880
Clement, Clara Erskine, and Laurence Hutton. *Artists of the Nineteenth Century and Their Works.* 2 vols. Boston, 1880.

Cohen 1941
Cohen, I. Bernard, ed. *Benjamin Franklin's Experiments: A New Edition of Franklin's Experiments and Observations on Electricity.* Cambridge, Mass., 1941.

Cohen 1982
Cohen, Sheldon S., "Harvard College on the Eve of the American Revolution," in *Publications of the Colonial Society of Massachusetts*, vol. 59 (1982), pp. 173–190.

Columbia-Rediviva 1966
Papers of the Ship Columbia-Rediviva, 1745–1848. Portland, Ore., 1966. Microfilm.

Cooper 1982
Cooper, Helen. *John Trumbull: The Hand and Spirit of a Painter.* New Haven, 1982.

Crafts 1893
Crafts, James M., and William F. Crafts. *The Crafts Family.* Northampton, Mass., 1893.

Crane 1972
Crane, Sylvia E. *White Silence: Greenough, Powers, and Crawford, American Sculptors in Nineteenth-Century Italy.* Coral Gables, Fla., 1972.

Craven 1968
Craven, Wayne. *Sculpture in America.* New York, 1968.

Craven 1986
Craven, Wayne. *Colonial American Portraiture: The Economic, Religious, Social, Cultural, Philosophical, Scientific and Aesthetic Foundations.* New York, 1986.

Crosby 1875
Crosby, Sylvester S. *The Early Coins of America, and the Laws Governing Their Issue.* Boston, 1875.

Crossman 1973
Crossman, Carl L., *The China Trade: Export Paintings, Furniture, Silver & Other Objects.* Princeton, 1972; 1973.

Crowe 1967
Crowe, Charles. *George Ripley: Transcendentalist and Utopian Socialist.* Athens, Ga., 1967.

Cummings 1973
Cummings, Abbott Lowell. "A Recently Discovered Engraving of the Old State House in Boston." *Boston Prints and Printmakers, 1670–1775. Publications of the Colonial Society of Massachusetts* 46 (1973), pp. 174–184.

Cunningham 1904
Cunningham, Henry W., *Christian Remick.* Boston, 1904.

Cunningham 1907
Cunningham, Edith Perkins. *Owl's Nest: A Tribute to Sarah Elliott Perkins.* Cambridge, Mass., 1907.

Curtis 1861
Curtis, John K. "To Numismatists in Particular!" In W. S. Appleton Scrapbook, 1854–1872, Appleton Papers. Massachusetts Historical Society.

Curtis 1961
Curtis, Edith Roelker. *A Season in Utopia: The Story of Brook Farm.* New York, 1961.

DAB
Dictionary of American Biography. Allen Johnson and Dumas Malone, eds. 20 vols. New York, 1928–1936.

Dana 1865
Dana, Richard Henry, Jr. *An Address Upon the Life and Services of Edward Everett.* Cambridge, Mass., 1865.

Dana 1911
Dana, Richard Henry, Jr. *Two Years before the Mast. A Personal Narrative.* Boston, 1911.

Danforth 1983
Danforth, Susan L. "The First Official Maps of Maine and Massachusetts." *Imago Mundi* 35 (1983), pp. 37–39.

Darley 1978
Darley, Felix O. Carr. ". . . illustrated by Darley": An Exhibition of Original Drawings by the American Book Illustrator Felix Octavius Carr Darley (1822–1888).* Exhibition catalogue, Delaware Art Museum. Wilmington, 1978.

Davis 1971
Davis, Andrew McFarland. *Colonial Currency Reprints, 1682–1751.* Boston, 1910–1911; New York, 1971.

Deák 1988
Deák, Gloria Gilda. *Picturing America, 1497–1899.* 2 vols. Princeton, 1988.

Dearborn 1983
Dearborn, Mona L. *Anson Dickinson, The Celebrated Miniature Painter, 1779–1852.* Hartford, 1983.

Deiss 1969
Deiss, Joseph Jay. *The Roman Years of Margaret Fuller.* New York, 1969.

Demos 1982
Demos, John Putnam. *Entertaining Satan.* New York, 1982.

Denker 1984
Denker, Ellen. *After the Chinese Taste: China's Influence in America, 1730–1930.* Exhibition catalogue, Essex Institute. Salem, Mass., 1984.

Detweiler 1982
Detweiler, Susan Gray. *George Washington's Chinaware.* New York, 1982.

Deutsch 1977
Deutsch, Davida Tenenbaum, "Washington Memorial Prints." *The Magazine Antiques* III (1977), pp. 324–331.

Dickeson 1859
Dickeson, Montroville W. *The American Numismatical Manual.* Philadelphia, 1859.

DLB
Dictionary of Literary Biography. 6 vols. Detroit, 1978–1984.

DNB
The Dictionary of National Biography. Leslie Stephens and Sidney Lee, eds. 22 vols. 1885–1901; London, 1959–1960.

Donald 1970
Donald, David. *Charles Sumner and the Rights of Man.* New York, 1970.

Dorment 1986
Dorment, Richard. *British Painting in the Philadelphia Museum of Art from the Seventeenth Through the Nineteenth Century.* Exhibition catalogue, Philadelphia Museum of Art. Philadelphia, 1986.

Doughty 1962
Doughty, Howard. *Francis Parkman.* New York, 1962.

Drake 1971
Drake, Samuel Adams. *Old Landmarks and Historic Personages of Boston.* rev. ed. Rutland, Vt., 1971.

Dresser 1966
Dresser, Louisa. "Portraits in Boston, 1630–1720." *Journal of the Archives of American Art* 6 (1966), pp. 1–34.

Dunlap 1918
Dunlap, William. *A History of the Rise and Progress of The Arts of Design in the United States.* 3 vols. Boston, 1918.

Dunlap 1969
Dunlap, William. *Diary of William Dunlap, 1766–1839: The Memoirs of a Dramatist, Theatrical Manager, Painter, Critic, Novelist, and Historian.* 1931; New York, 1969.

Dunn 1984
Dunn, Richard S. "John Winthrop Writes His Journal." *William and Mary Quarterly,* 3d ser., 41 (1984), pp. 185–212.

Eberstadt 1950
Eberstadt, Charles. *Lincoln's Emancipation Proclamation.* New York, 1950.

Edmonds 1915
Edmonds, John A. "The Burgis Views of New York and Boston." *Proceedings of the Bostonian Society* (1915), pp. 29–50.

Edwards 1808
Edwards, Edward. *Anecdotes of Painters Who Have Resided or Been Born in England.* London, 1808.

Eisen 1932
Eisen, Gustavus A. *Portraits of Washington.* 3 vols. New York, 1932.

Emilio 1894
Emilio, Luis F. *History of the Fifty-fourth Regiment of Massachusetts Volunteer Infantry, 1863–1865.* 2d ed. Boston, 1894.

Fairchild 1976
Fairchild, Byron. "Sir William Pepperrell: New England's Pre-Revolutionary Hero." *The New England Historical and Genealogical Register* 103 (1976), pp. 83–106.

Fales 1958
Fales, Martha Gandy. *American Silver in the Henry Francis DuPont Winterthur Museum.* Winterthur, 1958.

Fales 1970
Fales, Martha Gandy. *Early American Silver.* rev. and enl. New York, 1970.

Fales 1973
Fales, Martha Gandy. "Heraldic and Emblematic Engravers of Colonial Boston." *Boston Prints and Printmakers, 1670–1775. Publications of the Colonial Society of Massachusetts* 46 (1973), pp. 185–220.

Fales 1987
Fales, Martha Gandy. "Federal Bostonians and their London jeweler, Stephen Twycross." *The Magazine Antiques* 131 (1987), pp. 642–649.

Farrand 1937
Farrand, Max, ed. *The Records of the Federal Convention of 1787.* 4 vols. New Haven, 1937.

Federhen 1988
Federhen, Deborah A. "From Artisan to Entrepreneur: Paul Revere's Silver Shop Operation." *Paul Revere—Artisan, Businessman, and Patriot: The Man Behind the Myth.* Exhibition catalogue, The Paul Revere Memorial Association. Boston, 1988.

Fielding 1974
Fielding, Mantle. *Dictionary of American Painters, Sculptors and Engravers.* rev. ed. Philadelphia, 1974.

Flexner 1967
Flexner, James Thomas. *George Washington in the American Revolution.* Boston, 1967.

Flexner 1972
Flexner, James Thomas. *George Washington: Anguish and Farewell (1793–1799).* Boston, 1972.

Flynt 1968
Flynt, Henry N., and Martha Gandy Fales. *The Heritage Foundation Collection of Silver.* Deerfield, Mass., 1968.

Foote 1950
Foote, Henry Wilder. *John Smibert, Painter.* Cambridge, Mass., 1950.

Foote 1958
Foote, Henry Wilder. "Benjamin Blyth, of Salem: Eighteenth-Century Artist." *Proceedings of the Massachusetts Historical Society* 71 (1953–1957), pp. 64–107.

Forbes 1942
Forbes, Esther. *Paul Revere & the World He Lived In.* Boston, 1942.

Ford 1922
Ford, Worthington C., comp. *Broadsides, Ballads &c. Printed in Massachusetts 1639–1800. Collections of the Massachusetts Historical Society* 75 (1922).

Ford 1924
Ford, Worthington C. "Franklin's New England Courant." *Proceedings of the Massachusetts Historical Society* 57 (1923–1924), pp. 336–353.

Ford 1938
Ford, Worthington C. "Francis Russell Hart." *Proceedings of the Massachusetts Historical Society* 66 (1936–1941), pp. 427–433.

Forman 1971
Forman, Benno M., "The Osborne Family Chest Rediscovered." *Historical New Hampshire* 26 (1971), pp. 26–30.

Foster 1974
Foster, Edward Halsey. *Catharine Maria Sedgwick*. New York, 1974.

Fowler 1980
Fowler, William M., Jr. *The Baron of Beacon Hill: A Biography of John Hancock*. Boston, 1980.

Franklin 1956
The New-England Courant: A Selection of Certain Issues Containing Writings of Benjamin Franklin. Boston, 1956.

Franklin 1959
Labaree, Leonard W., and William B. Willcox, eds. *The Papers of Benjamin Franklin*. 27 vols. New Haven, 1959–1988.

Franklin 1963
Franklin, John Hope. *The Emancipation Proclamation*. Garden City, N.Y., 1963.

Franklin 1986
Lemay, J. A. Leo, and P. M. Zoll, eds. *Benjamin Franklin's Autobiography: An Authoritative Text*. New York, 1986.

Freeman 1952
Freeman, Douglass Southall. *George Washington: A Biography*. Volume 5: *Victory with the Help of France*. New York, 1952.

Freiberg 1969
Freiberg, Malcolm. "The Winthrops and Their Papers." *Proceedings of the Massachusetts Historical Society* 80 (1969), pp. 55–70.

French 1934
French, Allen. *The First Year of the American Revolution*. Boston, 1934.

Frothingham 1925
Frothingham, Paul Revere. *Edward Everett: Orator and Statesman*. Boston, 1925.

Fuess 1930
Fuess, Claude Moore. *Daniel Webster*. 2 vols. Boston, 1930.

Fuld 1988
Fuld, George J., and Barry D. Tayman. "The Montreal and Happy While United Indian Peace Medals." In *The Medal in America*. Alan M. Stahl, ed. New York, 1988.

Fuller 1983
Hudspeth, Robert N., ed. *The Letters of Margaret Fuller*. 5 vols. New York, 1983–1988.

Gardiner 1969
Gardiner, C. Harvey. *William Hickling Prescott: A Biography*. Austin, 1969.

Garrison 1971
The Letters of William Lloyd Garrison. Louis Ruchames, ed. 6 vols. Cambridge, Mass., 1971–1978.

Gilbert Stuart 1967
Gilbert Stuart: Portraitist of the Young Republic, 1755–1828. Exhibition catalogue, National Gallery of Art and Rhode Island School of Design Museum of Art. Washington and Providence, R.I., 1967.

Goff 1976
Goff, Frederick R. *The John Dunlap Broadside: The First Printing of the Declaration of Independence*. Washington, 1976.

Goodale 1900
Goodale, George Lincoln. "New England plants seen by the earliest colonists." *Transactions of the Colonial Society of Massachusetts* 3 (1895–1897), pp. 180–194.

Gordon 1987
Gordon, Elinor. "Chinese Export Porcelain." *The Magazine Antiques* 132 (1987), pp. 182–187.

Gourley 1963
Gourley, Hugh J. "A Miniature by Malbone." *Bulletin of the Rhode Island School of Design* 50 (1963).

Grancsay 1945
Grancsay, Stephen V. *American Engraved Powder Horns: A Study Based on the J. H. Grenville Gilbert Collection*. New York, 1945.

Great Britain 1775
Great Britain. War Office. *A List of the General and Field Officers, As they Rank in the Army; of the Officers of the Several Regiments . . . for the Year 1775*. London, 1775.

Green 1907
Green, Samuel Abbott. *Ten Fac-simile Reproductions relating to Old Boston and Neighborhood*. Boston, 1907.

Greene 1911
Greene, Francis Vinton. *The Revolutionary War and the Military Policy of the United States*. New York, 1911.

Greenwood 1827
Greenwood, F. W. P. *A Funeral Sermon on the Late Hon. Christopher Gore, Formerly Governor of Massachusetts*. Boston, 1827.

Griffin 1958
Griffin, Gillett. "John Foster's Woodcut of Richard Mather." *Printing & Graphic Arts* 6 (1958), pp. 1–19.

Groce 1957
Groce, George C., and David H. Wallace. *The New-York Historical Society's Dictionary of Artists in America, 1564–1860*. New Haven, 1957.

Gummere 1967
Gummere, Richard M. *Seven Wise Men of Colonial America*. Cambridge, Mass., 1967.

Hall 1979
Hall, James. *Dictionary of Subjects and Symbols in Art*. New York, 1979.

Hamlin 1944
Hamlin, Talbot. *Greek Revival Architecture in America*. New York, 1944.

Hammond 1982
Hammond, Charles A., and Stephen A. Wilbur, "Gay and Graceful Style": A Catalogue of Objects Associated with Christopher & Rebecca Gore*. Waltham, Mass., 1982.

Hanley 1969
Hanley, Hope. *Needlepoint in America*. New York, 1969.

Hansen 1969
Hansen, Chadwick. *Witchcraft at Salem*. New York, 1969.

Harding 1989
Harding, Jonathan P. "Edward Greene Malbone's Portraits of Colonel William and Catherine Scollay: Two Recently Found Miniatures." *American Art Journal* 21 (1989), pp. 13–17.

Hargrove 1988
Hargrove, Hondon B. *Black Union Soldiers in the Civil War.* Jefferson, N.C., 1988.

Harris 1982
Harris, John. *The Boston Globe Historic Walks in Old Boston,* Chester, Conn., 1982.

Hart 1897
Hart, Charles Henry. "Life Portraits of Daniel Webster". *McClure's Magazine* 9 (1897), pp. 619–630.

Hart 1905
Hart, Charles Henry. "Edward Savage, Painter and Engraver, and His Unfinished Copperplate of 'The Congress Voting Independence.'" *Proceedings of the Massachusetts Historical Society* 19 (1905), pp. 1–19.

Harvard 1906
Memorial of the Harvard College Class of 1856. Boston, 1906.

Hitchings 1975
Hitchings, Sinclair H. "Fine Art Lithography in Boston: Craftsmanship in Color, 1840–1900." In *Art & Commerce: American Prints of the Nineteenth Century.* Proceedings of a conference held in Boston, May 8–10, 1975, Museum of Fine Arts, Boston. Boston, 1978.

Hodge 1907
Hodge, Frederick Webb, ed. *Handbook of American Indians North of Mexico.* 2 parts. Washington, 1907.

Holman 1960
Holman, Richard B. "John Foster's Woodcut Map of New England." *Printing and Graphic Arts* 8 (1960), pp. 53–93.

Holman 1973
Holman, Richard B. "William Burgis." *Boston Prints and Printmakers, 1670–1775. Publications of the Colonial Society of Massachusetts* 46 (1973), pp. 57–81.

Holmes 1895
Holmes, Oliver Wendell. *The Complete Poetical Works of Oliver Wendell Holmes.* Cambridge, Mass., 1895.

Howay 1941
Howay, Frederic W., ed. *Voyages of the "Columbia" to the Northwest Coast, 1787–1790 and 1790–1793. Massachusetts Historical Society Collections* 79 (1974).

Howe 1946
Howe, M. A. DeWolfe. "The New England Scene, 1814–1821: Passages from a Journal of Eliza Susan Quincy." *The Atlantic Monthly* 178 (1946), pp. 94–100.

Howe 1946 (2)
Howe, M. A. DeWolfe. *Boston Landmarks.* New York, 1946.

Hull 1857
Hull, John. "The Diaries of John Hull, Mint-master and Treasurer of the Colony of Massachusetts Bay." *Transactions and Collections of the American Antiquarian Society* 3 (1857), pp. 109–316.

Hulton 1977
Hulton, P. H. *The Work of Jacques Le Moyne de Morgues: A Huguenot Artist in France, Florida, and England.* 2 vols. London, 1977.

Hunter 1943
Hunter, Dard. *Papermaking. The History and Technique of an Ancient Craft.* New York, 1943.

Jacobs 1977
Jacobs, Phoebe Lloyd. "John James Barralet and the Apotheosis of George Washington." *Winterthur Portfolio* 12 (1977), pp. 115–137.

Jefferson 1950
The Papers of Thomas Jefferson. Julian P. Boyd et al., eds. 23 vols. Princeton, 1950–1990.

Jefferson 1955
Jefferson, Thomas. *Notes on the State of Virginia.* William Peden, ed. Chapel Hill, 1955.

Jefferson 1976
Jefferson and the Arts: An Extended View. William Howard Adams, ed. Exhibition catalogue, National Gallery of Art. Washington, 1976.

Johnson 1976
Johnson, Christopher S. "Henry Knox and his "noble train of artillery." *Harvard Magazine* 78 (1976), pp. 26–33, 56.

Jones 1930
Jones, E. Alfred. *The Loyalists of Massachusetts: Their Memorials, Petitions and Claims.* London, 1930.

Josselyn 1672
Josselyn, John. *New-Englands Rarities Discovered.* London, 1672.

Josselyn 1988
Josselyn, John. *John Josselyn, Colonial Traveler.* Paul J. Lindholdt, ed. Hanover, N.H., 1988.

Julian 1977
Julian, R. W. *Medals of the United States Mint: The First Century, 1792–1892.* N. Neil Harris, ed. El Cajon, Calif., 1977.

Kane 1976
Kane, Patricia E. "Furniture owned by the Massachusetts Historical Society." *The Magazine Antiques* 109 (1976), pp. 960–969.

Kane 1987
Kane, Patricia E. "John Hull and Robert Sanderson: First Masters of New England Silver." Ph.D. diss., Yale University, 1987.

Kaplan 1973
Kaplan, Sidney. *The Black Presence in the Era of the American Revolution, 1770–1800.* Washington, 1973

Kaplan 1989
Kaplan, Sidney. "The Sculptural World of Augustus Saint-Gaudens." *Massachusetts Review* 30 (1989), pp. 17–64.

Kaye 1974
Kaye, Myrna. "Eighteenth-century Boston Furniture Craftsmen." In *Boston Furniture of the Eighteenth Century. Publications of the Colonial Society of Massachusetts* 48 (1974), pp. 267–302.

Kershaw 1976
Kershaw, Gordon E. *James Bowdoin: Patriot and Man of the Enlightenment.* Exhibition catalogue, Bowdoin College Museum of Art. Brunswick, Me., 1976.

Kimball 1916
Kimball, Fiske. *Thomas Jefferson, Architect.* Cambridge, Mass., 1916; reprint, New York, 1968.

Kirker 1964
Kirker, Harold. and James Kirker. *Bulfinch's Boston, 1787–1817.* New York, 1964.

Kirker 1969
Kirker, Harold. *The Architecture of Charles Bulfinch.* Cambridge, Mass., 1969.

Kittredge 1899
Kittredge, Frank Edward. *The Man with the Branded Hand: An Authentic Sketch of the Life and Services of Capt. Jonathan Walker.* Rochester, N.Y., 1899.

Klamkin 1973
Klamkin, Marian. *American Patriotic and Political China.* New York, 1973.

Knox 1933
"Major General Henry Knox." *The Bulletin of the Fort Ticonderoga Museum* 3 (1933), pp. 62–69.

Korshak 1988
Korshak, Yvonne. "The Winds of Libertas: Augustin Dupré's *Libertas Americana.*" In *The Medal in America.* Alan M. Stahl, ed. New York, 1988.

Krueger 1978
Krueger, Glee. *New England Samplers to 1840.* Sturbridge, Mass., 1978.

Lane 1914
Lane, William Coolidge. "Early Harvard Broadsides." *Proceedings of the American Antiquarian Society,* n.s. 24 (1914), pp. 264–304.

Latourette 1964
Latourette, Kenneth Scott. *The History of Early Relations between the United States and China, 1784–1844.* New Haven, 1917; New York, 1964.

Lawrence 1888
Lawrence, William. *Life of Amos A. Lawrence.* Boston, 1888.

Leach 1958
Leach, Douglas E. *Flintlock and Tomahawk: New England in King Philip's War.* New York, 1958.

Leach 1977
Leach, Douglas E. "Brothers in Arms? Anglo-American Friction at Louisbourg, 1745–1746." *Massachusetts Historical Society Proceedings* 89 (1977), pp. 36–54.

Leehey 1988
Leehey, Patrick M. "Reconstructing Paul Revere: An Overview of His Ancestry, Life, and Work." *Paul Revere—Artisan, Businessman, and Patriot: The Man Behind the Myth.* Exhibition catalogue, The Paul Revere Memorial Association. Boston, 1988.

Lefevre 1939
Lefevre, Edwin. "Washington Historical Kerchiefs." *The Magazine Antiques* 36 (1939), pp. 14–17.

Lemay 1964
Lemay, J. A. Leo. "Franklin's Dr. Spence." *Maryland Historical Magazine* 59 (1964), pp. 199–216.

Levin 1978
Levin, David. *Cotton Mather: The Young Life of the Lord's Remembrancer, 1663–1703.* Cambridge, Mass., 1978.

Lincoln 1953
Basler, Roy P., ed., *The Collected Works of Abraham Lincoln.* New Brunswick, N.J., 1953.

Linzee 1917
Linzee, John William. *The Linzee Family.* 2 vols. Boston, 1917.

Lipton 1981
Lipton, Leah. "William Dunlap, Samuel F. B. Morse, John Wesley Jarvis, and Chester Harding: Their Careers as Itinerant Portrait Painters." *American Art Journal* 13 (1981), pp. 34–50.

Lipton 1985
Lipton, Leah. *A Truthful Likeness, Chester Harding and his Portraits.* Washington, 1985.

Little 1972
Little, Nina Fletcher, "The Blyths of Salem: Benjamin, Limner in Crayons and Oil, and Samuel, Painter and Cabinetmaker." *Essex Institute Historical Collections* 108 (1972), pp. 49–57.

Littlefield 1907
Littlefield, George E. *The Early Massachusetts Press, 1638–1711.* 2 vols. Boston, 1907.

Lloyd 1927
Papers of the Lloyd Family of the Manor of Queens Village, Lloyd's Neck, Long Island, New York, 1654–1826. Collections of the New-York Historical Society 60 (1927).

Loehr 1954
Loehr, George R., "A. E. van Braam Houckgeest: The First American at the Court of China." *The Princeton University Library Chronicle* 15 (1954), pp. 179–193.

Longfellow 1956
Longfellow, Fanny Appleton. *Mrs. Longfellow: Selected Letters and Journals of Fanny Appleton Longfellow (1817–1861).* Edward Wagenknecht, ed. New York, 1956.

Loring 1852
Loring, James Spear. *The Hundred Boston Orators Appointed by the Municipal Authorities and Other Public Bodies from 1770 to 1852.* Boston, 1852.

Loubat 1878
Loubat, Joseph F. *The Medallic History of the United States of America, 1776–1876.* 2 vols. New York, 1878.

Loveland 1971
Loveland, Anne C. *Emblem of Liberty, The Image of Lafayette in the American Mind.* Baton Rouge, 1971.

Lowance 1989
Lowance, Mason. "Hawthorne and Brook Farm: The Politics of *The Blithedale Romance.*" *Essex Institute Historical Collections* 125 (1989), pp. 65–91.

Marshall 1976
Marshall, Douglas W., and Howard H. Peckham. *Campaigns of the American Revolution: An Atlas of Manuscript Maps.* Ann Arbor, 1976.

Mason 1879
Mason, George C. *The Life and Works of Gilbert Stuart.* New York, 1879.

Mass. 1854
Records of the Governor and the Company of the Massachusetts Bay in New England. Nathaniel B. Shurtleff, ed. 5 vols. Boston, 1853–1854.

Mass. 1869
The Acts and Resolves, Public and Private, of the Province of the Massachusetts Bay. 21 vols. Boston, 1869–1922.

Mass. 1931
Massachusetts Soldiers, Sailors, and Marines in the Civil War. 8 vols. Norwood, Mass., 1931–1934; Brookline, Mass., 1935.

Mather 1911
Mather, Cotton. *Diary of Cotton Mather, 1681–1724.* 2 vols. In *Collections of the Massachusetts Historical Society,* 7th ser., vols. 7–8 (1911–1912).

Mather 1971
[Mather, Cotton]. "Some Considerations on the Bills of Credit now passing in New-England." In *Colonial Currency Reprints 1682–1751,* 1 (1910), pp. 189–196. Boston, 1910–1911; New York, 1971.

Mayo 1948
Mayo, Lawrence Shaw. *The Winthrop Family in America.* Boston, 1948.

McCaughey 1974
McCaughey, Robert A. *Josiah Quincy, 1772–1864: The Last Federalist.* Harvard Historical Studies Series, vol. 90. Cambridge, Mass., 1974.

McCusker 1978
McCusker, John J. *Money and Exchange in Europe and America, 1600–1775: A Handbook.* Chapel Hill, 1978.

McKechnie 1978
McKechnie, Sue. *British Silhouette Artists and Their Work, 1760–1860.* London, 1978.

McKey 1962
McKey, Richard H., Jr. "Elias Hasket Derby and the Founding of the Eastern Trade (Part II)." *Essex Institute Historical Collections* 92 (1962), pp. 65–83.

MFA 1982
Fairbanks, Jonathan L., and Robert F. Trent. *New England Begins: The Seventeenth Century.* 3 vols. Boston, 1982.

MHS 1967
Massachusetts Historical Society. *Here We Have Lived: The Houses of the Massachusetts Historical Society.* Boston, 1967.

MHS 1969
Collecting for Clio: An Exhibition of Representative Materials from the Holdings of the Massachusetts Historical Society. Boston, 1969.

MHS Collections
Collections of the Massachusetts Historical Society. 83 vols. Boston, 1792–1981.

MHS Proceedings
Proceedings of the Massachusetts Historical Society. 101 vols. Boston, 1791–1990.

Miller 1936
Miller, John C. *Sam Adams: Pioneer in Propaganda.* Stanford, 1936.

Miller 1974
Miller, Nathan. *Sea of Glory: The Continental Navy Fights for Independence, 1775–1783.* New York, 1974.

Miller 1989
Miller, Marc H. "The Farewell Tour and American Art." In *Lafayette, Hero of Two Worlds.* Exhibition catalogue, Queens Museum. Flushing, N.Y., 1989.

Mongan 1975
Mongan, Agnes. *Harvard Honors Lafayette.* Exhibition catalogue, Fogg Art Museum, Harvard University. Cambridge, Mass., 1975.

Morgan 1939
Morgan, John Hill. *Gilbert Stuart and His Pupils.* New York, 1939.

Morgan 1958
Morgan, Edmund S. *The Puritan Dilemma: The Story of John Winthrop.* Boston, 1958.

Morison 1921
Morison, Samuel Eliot. *The Maritime History of Massachusetts, 1783–1860.* Boston, 1921.

Morison 1930
Morison, Samuel Eliot. *Builders of the Bay Colony.* Boston, 1930.

Morison 1933
Morison, Samuel Eliot. "Needlework Picture Representing a Colonial College Building." *Old-Time New England* 24 (1933), pp. 67–72.

Morison 1935
Morison, Samuel Eliot. *The Founding of Harvard College.* Cambridge, Mass., 1935.

Morison 1936
Morison, Samuel Eliot. *Harvard College in the Seventeenth Century.* 2 parts. Cambridge, Mass., 1936.

Morison 1955
Morison, Samuel Eliot, ed. *The Parkman Reader.* Boston, 1955.

Morison 1959
Morison, Samuel Eliot. *John Paul Jones: A Sailor's Biography.* Boston, 1959.

Morris 1926
Morris, Frances. *Notes on Laces of the American Colonists.* New York, 1926.

Mossiker 1976
Mossiker, Frances. *Pocahontas.* New York, 1976.

Mount 1964
Mount, Charles Merrill. *Gilbert Stuart: A Biography.* New York, 1964.

Mudge 1981
Mudge, Jean McClure. *Chinese Export Porcelain for the American Trade, 1785–1835.* 2d ed. Newark, Del., 1981.

NEHGR
New England Historical and Genealogical Register. 154 vols. Boston, 1847–1990.

Newman 1990
Newman, Eric P. *The Early Paper Money of America.* 3d ed. Iola, Wisc., 1990.

Nichols 1961
Nichols, Frederick Doveton. *Thomas Jefferson's Architectural Drawings.* Boston, Mass., and Charlottesville, Va., 1961.

Oakes-Jones 1922
Oakes-Jones, H. "The Evolution of the Gorget." *Journal of the Society of Army Historical Research* 1 (1922), pp. 115–118, 170–176, 246–255; 2 (1923), pp. 22–31.

Oedel 1981
Oedel, William Townsend. "John Vanderlyn: French Neo-classicism and the Search for an American Art." Ph.D. diss., University of Delaware, 1981.

Oliver 1967
Oliver, Andrew. *Portraits of John and Abigail Adams.* Cambridge, Mass., 1967.

Oliver 1973
Oliver, Andrew. "Peter Pelham (c. 1697–1751), Sometime Printmaker of Boston." In *Boston Prints and Printmakers 1670–1775. Publications of the Colonial Society of Massachusetts* 46 (1973), pp. 133–173.

Oliver 1988
Oliver, Andrew, Ann Millspaugh Huff, and Edward W. Hanson. *Portraits in the Massachusetts Historical Society.* Boston, 1988.

Park 1917
Park, Laurence. "An Account of Joseph Badger and a Descriptive List of His Work." *Proceedings of the Massachusetts Historical Society* 51 (1917), pp. 158–201.

Parker 1938
Parker, Barbara N., and Anne B. Wheeler. *John Singleton Copley: American Portraits in Oil, Pastel, and Miniature, with Biographical Sketches.* Boston, 1938.

Parker 1979
Parker, Peter J., and Stefanie Munsing Winkelbauer. "Embellishments for Practical Repositories: Eighteenth-Century American Magazine Illustration." In *Eighteenth-Century Prints in Colonial America: To Educate and Decorate*. Joan D. Dolmetsch, ed., pp. 71–97. Williamsburg, 1979.

Parkman 1947
Parkman, Francis. *The Journals of Francis Parkman*. Mason Wade, ed. 2 vols. New York, 1947.

Parry 1974
Parry, Ellwood. *The Image of the Indian and the Black Man in American Art, 1500–1900*. New York, 1974.

Peabody 1912
Peabody, Robert E. *Merchant Venturers of Old Salem*. Boston, 1912.

Pell 1937
Pell, Stephen H. P. "The Gorget—As a Defense, As a Symbol, and as an Ornament." *The Bulletin of The Fort Ticonderoga Museum* 4 (1937), pp. 126–141.

Pennington 1982
Pennington, Richard. *A Descriptive Catalogue of the Etched Work of Wenceslaus Hollar, 1607–1677*. New York, 1982.

Peterson 1987
Peterson, Merrill D. *The Great Triumvirate: Webster, Clay, and Calhoun*. New York, 1987.

Phillips 1924
Phillips, P. Lee. *Notes on the Life and Works of Bernard Romans*. *Publications of the Florida Historical Society*, no. 2. Deland, Fla., 1924.

Phillips 1947
Phillips, James Duncan. *Salem and the Indies: The Story of the Great Commercial Era of a City*. Boston, 1947.

Phillips 1955
Phillips, John Marshall, Barbara N. Parker, and Kathryn C. Buhler, eds. *The Waldron Phoenix Belknap, Jr., Collection of Portraits and Silver*. Cambridge, Mass., 1955.

Pierce 1987
Pierce, Sally. *Whipple and Black: Commercial Photographers in Boston*. Boston, 1987.

Pierson 1976
Pierson, William H., Jr. *American Buildings and Their Architects: The Colonial and Neo classical Styles*. Garden City, N. Y., 1976.

Pilling 1891
Pilling, James Constantine. *Bibliography of Algonquian Languages*. Washington, 1891.

Pitre 1980
Pitre, David W. "Thomas and John Fleet." In *Boston Printers, Publishers and Booksellers: 1640–1800*. Benjamin Franklin, V, ed. Boston, 1980.

Pollard 1960
Pollard, Maurice J., comp. *The History of the Pollard Family in America*. Dover, N.H., 1960.

Poole 1886
Poole, William F. "Witchcraft in Boston." In *The Memorial History of Boston, including Suffolk County, Massachusetts*. Justin Winsor, ed. vol. 2, pp. 131–172. Boston, 1886.

Prescott 1838
Prescott, William Hickling. "Memoirs of Sir Walter Scott." *North American Review* 46 (1838), pp. 431–474.

Prescott 1925
The Correspondence of William Hickling Prescott, 1833–1847. Roger Wolcott, ed. Cambridge, Mass., 1925.

Princeton 1968
Early American Book Illustrators and Wood Engravers, 1670–1870. 2 vols. Princeton, N.J., 1968.

Prown 1966
Prown, Jules David. *John Singleton Copley*. 2 vols. Cambridge, Mass., 1966.

Prucha 1971
Prucha, Francis P. *Indian Peace Medals in American History*. Madison, 1971.

Quincy 1850
Quincy, Josiah. *Memoir of John Bromfield*. Cambridge, Mass., 1850.

Quincy 1884
Quincy, Eliza Susan. "Memoir of Edmund Quincy (1681–1738) of Braintree, Massachusetts Bay." *The New England Historical and Genealogical Register* 38 (1884), pp. 145–156.

Quinn 1977
Quinn, David B. *North America from Earliest Discovery to First Settlement*. New York, 1977.

Randall 1965
Randall, Richard H. *American Furniture in the Museum of Fine Arts, Boston*. Boston, 1965.

Rawlyk 1967
Rawlyk, G. A. *Yankees at Louisbourg*. University of Maine Studies, 2d ser. no. 85 (1967).

Reps 1973
Reps, John W. "Boston by Bostonians: The Printed Plans and Views of the Colonial City by its Artists, Cartographers, Engravers, and Publishers." *Boston Prints and Printmakers, 1670–1775*. *Publications of the Colonial Society of Massachusetts* 46 (1973), pp. 3–56.

Revere 1968
Paul Revere's Three Accounts of His Famous Ride. Introduction by Edmund S. Morgan. Boston, 1968.

Reynolds 1977
Reynolds, Donald Martin. *Hiram Powers and His Ideal Sculpture*. New York, 1977.

Ribaut 1927
Ribaut, Jean. *The Whole & True Discouerye of Terra Florida*. *Florida Historical Society Publications*, no. 7. Deland, Fla., 1927.

Richman 1976
Richman, Michael. *Daniel Chester French: An American Sculptor*. Exhibition catalogue, Metropolitan Museum of Art. New York, 1976.

Riley 1963
Riley, Stephen T. "A Monument to Colonel Robert Gould Shaw." *Proceedings of the Massachusetts Historical Society* 75 (1963), pp. 27–38.

Riley 1971
Riley, Stephen T. "John Smibert and the Business of Portrait Painting." In *American Painting to 1776: A Reappraisal*. Ian M. G. Quimby, ed. Charlottesville, 1971.

Ring 1975
Ring, Betty, *Needlework: An Historical Survey*. New York, 1975.

Ristow 1985
Ristow, Walter W. *American Maps and Mapmakers: Commercial Cartography in the Nineteenth Century*. Detroit, 1985.

Williams 1863
Williams, Samuel Wells. *The Chinese Commercial Guide*. 5th ed. Hong Kong, 1863.

Willoughby 1935
Willoughby, Charles C. *Antiquities of the New England Indians*. Cambridge, Mass., 1935.

Wills 1984
Wills, Garry. *Cincinnatus: George Washington and the Enlightenment*. Garden City, N.Y., 1984.

Winship 1945
Winship, George Parker. *The Cambridge Press, 1638–1692*. Philadelphia, 1945.

Winthrop 1826
Winthrop, John. *History of New England from 1630 to 1649*. James Savage, ed. 2 vols. Boston, 1825–1826.

Woodhouse 1935
Woodhouse, Samuel W., Jr. "Martha Washington's China and 'Mr. van Braam.'" *The Magazine Antiques* 27 (1935), pp. 186–188.

Woodward 1862
Woodward, W. Elliot. "A Priced Catalogue of the 'Finotti Sale' is now ready." In W. S. Appleton Scrapbook, 1854–1872, Appleton Papers. Massachusetts Historical Society.

Woodward 1933
Woodward, Arthur. "A Brief History of the Montreal Medal." *Bulletin of the Fort Ticonderoga Museum* (1933), pp. 15–28.

Woodward 1967
Woodward, D. "The Foster Woodcut Map Controversy: A Further Examination of the Evidence." *Imago Mundi* 21 (1967), pp. 52–61.

Wright 1986
Wright, Esmond. *Franklin of Philadelphia*. Cambridge, Mass., 1986.

Yanikoski 1987
Yanikoski, Richard Alan. "Edward Everett and the Advancement of Higher Education and Adult Learning in Antebellum Massachusetts." Ph.D. diss., University of Chicago, 1987.

Zilversmit 1968
Zilversmit, Arthur. "Quok Walker, Mumbet, and the Abolition of Slavery in Massachusetts." *William and Mary Quarterly*, 3d ser. 25 (1968), pp. 614–624.

Zobel 1970
Zobel, Hiller B. *The Boston Massacre*. New York, 1970.

Index to the Catalogue

Items from the collection of the Massachusetts Society are highlighted in *italics* in this index. Noted in **bold** are the exhibited pieces from "Witness to America's Past." These pieces are all discussed in detail and illustrated.